Indigenous Citizens

Indigenous Citizens

Local Liberalism in Early
National Oaxaca and Yucatán

KAREN D. CAPLAN

Stanford University Press
Stanford, California

Stanford University Press
Stanford, California

© 2010 by the Board of Trustees of the Leland Stanford Junior
University. All rights reserved.

This book has been published with the assistance of Rutgers
University.

Printed and bound by CPI Group (UK) Ltd, Croydon, CR0 4YY

Library of Congress Cataloging-in-Publication Data

Caplan, Karen Deborah, 1970–
    Indigenous citizens : local liberalism in early national Oaxaca and
Yucatán / Karen D. Caplan.
        p. cm.
    Includes bibliographical references and index.
    ISBN 978-0-8047-5764-5 (cloth : alk. paper)
    1. Indians of Mexico—Mexico—Oaxaca (State)—Government
relations.   2. Indians of Mexico—Mexico—Yucatán (State)—
Government relations.   3. Liberalism—Mexico—Oaxaca
(State)—History—19th century.   4. Liberalism—Mexico—Yucatán
(State)—History—19th century.   5. Local government—Mexico—
Oaxaca (State)—History—19th century.   6. Local government—
Mexico—Yucatán (State)—History—19th century.   I. Title.
F1219.1.O11C248 2009
323.1197'0727409034—dc22

                                                      2009022700

Typeset by Thompson Type in 10.5/12 Bembo

Contents

Acknowledgments

THIS BOOK WOULD have been impossible without the untiring and friendly aid of all those who work at the archives and libraries that I consulted in Mexico. Thank you in particular to, in Yucatán, Piedad Peniche Rivero, Candelaria Flota García, and Andrea Vergara Medina; and, in Oaxaca, Rosalba Montiel, Nemesio Martínez Galván, and Blanca Sofía Moreno Cruz. Carlos Sánchez Silva, who runs Oaxaca's municipal archives, was particularly helpful in orienting me to research possibilities in that city. In Mérida, Othón Baños Ramírez did the same. Many people made my time in Mexico enjoyable as well as productive—especially Sarah Buck, Cynthia Brock, Ray Craib, Todd and Kathline Hartch, Juliette Levy, Rick López, and Jolie Olcott. Jacques and Renate Levy opened their home in Mexico City to me and helped me to get settled. And special thanks go to Mara Villegas Pedraza and Diana Torres Canto, who were the best of companions, and to their generous and welcoming families.

A number of organizations provided the funds and support that allowed me to research and write this book. At Princeton, the Graduate School, the Department of History, the Council on Regional Studies, the Program in Latin American Studies, and the University Center for Human Values were particularly generous. Thank you especially to Rosalía Rivera, David Myrhe, David Figueroa-Ortiz, Kathy Baima, Melanie Bremer, Leah Kopscandy, and Audrey Mainzer. Thank you also to the members of the Princeton Center for Human Values graduate seminar, the Princeton Latin American History Workshop, the Princeton history department's Dissertation Writers' Group, and the New York City Latin American History Workshop. John Coatsworth, David Freund, Peter Guardino, Dirk Hartog, Jennie Purnell, Richard Turits, and Francie Chassen-López have all offered crucial readings and interventions. Peter in particular has been extremely generous with his own work on Oaxaca. Kenneth Mills has made an indelible mark on how I understand the people whom I write about and has provided inspiration in the creative and respectful way that he approaches both research and the profession itself. And I feel privileged to have worked with Jeremy Adelman, who has been an incredibly supportive adviser for this project from start to finish and whose suggestions are built into the fabric of this book. Thank you to all my colleagues at Rutgers University, especially Susan Carruthers, Prachi Deshpande, and Jan Lewis. Mark Hadzewycz provided able research assistance. To Christina Strasburger go profound thanks and respect for all the amazing things that she makes possible. My students over the years—at Princeton, Rutgers, and the University of Maryland—have contributed to this work in both tangible and intangible ways. Many thanks to the folks at Stanford University Press, especially Norris Pope, Sarah Crane Newman, and Emily Smith, and to Margaret Pinette, for her excellent and indispensible copyediting.

And finally, there are many people whose contributions to my work and life are inseparable. In the academic world, Susan Carruthers, Meri Clark, Anastasia Curwood, Katie Holt, Sarah Igo, Lisa Purcell, and Nicole Sackley have all helped me to keep things in perspective. Liz Cook, Jason Frank, Kate Gordon, Daniel Handler, Nora Howley, Diana Linger, Courtney McCarthy, Gerard McCarthy, Elizabeth Meister, Kim Roberts, and Margot Sharapova contributed to this book in a less direct but no less important manner. Lorelei, Amelia, Owen, Rosalind, Isaac, Phineas, Alex, and Daria are small but inspiring. My family—Arna, Martin, Bill, Rachel, Maggie, and Rosie Caplan and Elaine Freund—are awesome. Thank you to Amtrak, to the garden, and to yarn. And thank you, lastly, to The Boys—David, Jonah, and Benjamin, who are, simply, the best.

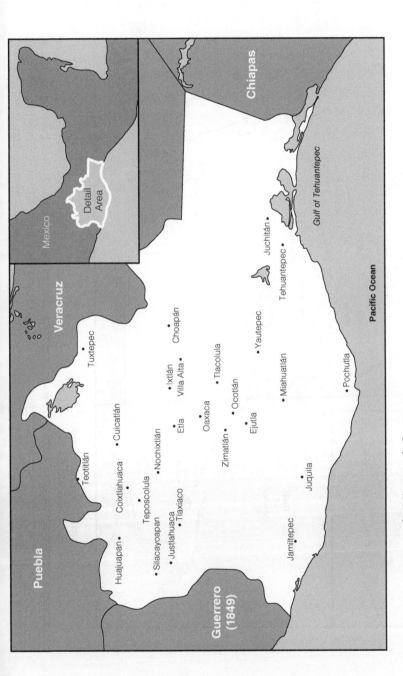

FIGURE 1.1 Oaxaca in the Nineteenth Century

The towns labeled here served as political and often economic centers. The vast majority of towns, however, cannot be represented here. At independence, Oaxaca counted approximately 913 towns, a number that varied over the course of the era discussed in this book, but remained high.

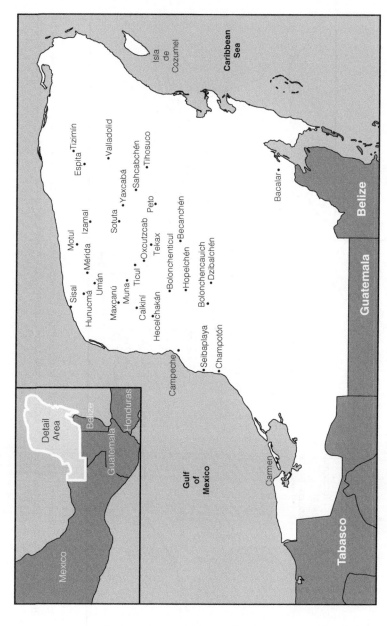

FIGURE 1.2 Yucatán in the Nineteenth Century

Yucatán, like Oaxaca, counted far more towns than can be represented here. It is difficult to know with precision how many recognized towns existed at any given point. Some idea can be derived from Robert Patch's compilations of towns in 1700 and 1716 (190) and between 1782 and 1791 (173, excluding the *partidos* of La Costa and Valladolid). See Robert W. Patch, *Maya and Spaniard in Yucatán, 1648–1812* (Stanford: Stanford University Press, 1993), 254–263.

Indigenous Citizens

CHAPTER 1

National Liberalism, Local Liberalisms

IN APRIL 1846, A YUCATECAN OFFICIAL traveled through his jurisdiction, Motul, to inspect the villages and report on their condition to the state government. The picture the *jefe político*, or political chief, painted in his report was not favorable. Most striking was the near-universal neglect of public buildings. In town after town he saw that the *casas consistoriales*, buildings intended to house the municipal authorities elected under new republican rules, were near ruin. Jails and military barracks were ill maintained and thus inadequate for the enforcement of republican law. Schools worried the jefe as well. Many villages lacked them entirely, and where they did exist it was often impossible to find a qualified teacher, someone prepared to teach villagers the fundamentals of republican government. The jefe suggested that village authorities levy taxes to address some of these problems, but he recognized that in most cases there were simply no resources to tax. The jefe's observations suggested that Mexico's new institutions were failing to transform the country's indigenous people from colonial subjects into liberal citizens. There was often little distinction in the villages between the older indigenous government bodies sanctioned by colonial Spain and the new republican town councils established for independent Mexico. Because traditional indigenous scribes were often the only literate villagers, the jefe observed, they often served as "perpetual mayors." Thirty-four years after the transition to liberalism, and twenty-five years after Mexico's separation from the Spanish monarchy and its establishment of a republican system, it appeared to officials across Mexico that in the villages little had changed.[1]

Was this perception correct? Certainly, by the time the Yucatecan jefe made his report, there had been significant transformations in Mexican political life. Beginning in 1812, nearly all adult male Mexicans could go to the polls to elect representative legislative bodies, and they did so in large numbers. On a local level, Mexicans now had the opportunity to elect and serve as members of newly established town councils that would oversee affairs in all but the smallest villages. And after Mexico gained its independence and established the republic in 1824, Mexicans acquired a government the ultimate authority of which was located not in far-off Spain, but in Mexico itself, and, practically speaking, in relatively nearby state capitals like Oaxaca City and Mérida. The population had gone in a few short years from being subjects to being citizens, a change that brought with it new ways of organizing administration and new bases for demands on the state.

And yet in some ways little had changed. The range of both candidates and issues on which new citizens could vote was nearly as limited as it had been under Spain, and indirect elections quickly filtered out the intentions of the majority of voters. Long-standing village hierarchies were reproduced in local councils, and thus the new bodies tended to replicate colonial arrangements. Colonial structures, both economic and political, often remained intact even where they had been officially abolished. In Oaxaca and Yucatán—the Mexican states that form the core of this study—most indigenous villagers were still poor, and their labor was still the primary source of income for the nonindigenous elite. And, like their colonial Spanish predecessors, new republican government officials struggled daily with their limited capacity to ensure the cooperation of new citizens. All that had changed, it seemed, were the words that government representatives and indigenous villagers used to describe the political and economic order, and the specific institutions that facilitated its perpetuation.

This book argues that this new language and these new institutions were significant. Evidence from the villages shows that new Mexican citizens, whether indigenous villagers, elites, or state officials, went through the motions that liberalism demanded: elections, representative governance, land reform, and the military draft. Because there was also continuity in the structures of authority, many scholars have seen their compliance with new institutional rules as inconsequential, little more than a veneer. Yet as they went through the motions of liberalism, Mexicans also engaged with the content of liberalism. Crucially, this occurred even where physical evidence of state presence was slight. The book traces the transition to liberalism in the states of Oaxaca and Yucatán, where more than three-quarters of the citizenry was indigenous and where these *indígenas*[2] composed the vast majority of those living outside of major cities. The Oaxacan and Yucatecan state governments—and certainly the federal government—had few resources to call on in controlling the everyday activities of this majority population, and the authority of the state was often in question. But changes in institutions nevertheless triggered intense negotiation between indigenous people and the state surrounding the meanings of liberal republican institutions, policies, and systems. The meanings that they could agree on became, for them, liberalism. Liberalism in nineteenth-century Mexico cannot be evaluated in reference to any liberal ideal. Rather, it was built in the context of politics on the ground.

Of course, there was not always consensus that this kind of liberalism was indeed liberal. The content of local agreements, forged in the context of local exigencies, often clashed with a developing "official" liberalism— the ideas, policies, and institutions articulated at the level of the national government. Thus, throughout the first half of the century, national leaders struggled to control the meaning of liberalism and to impose their often-changing vision of national politics. In 1857, when this study ends, Mexico's national state was beginning a concerted attempt to consolidate its control and regularize political practice across the country. It did not, however, do so in a vacuum. Liberalism, the guiding principle of Mexico's latter-century national reform, had by that time become entrenched in the regions. If national figures did not see local practices as liberal, local people—both villagers and officials—often did; and, to them, the national government's insistence on reform in the name of liberalism made little sense. A careful and locally grounded look at Mexico's *first* transition to liberalism between 1812 and 1857 helps explain both the appeal— and indeed often the success—of liberal politics in the regions both before and after the beginning of the Reform and the obstacles faced by the national government in consolidating and controlling liberal politics across the nation.

For much of Mexico in the nineteenth century, at the heart of the contradictions of liberalism was the political identity of indigenous people. Among the central goals of liberals at the national level was the elimination of ethnic distinctions believed to hamper the development of rational economic and political development. But, locally, these ethnic distinctions were crucial to the relationship between state and society; often they lay at the heart of the state's legitimacy among indigenous people. Any transition to new institutions had to take this into account. The indigenous question was, then, both at the center of the negotiation of local liberalisms and at the center of the contradictions between the local and the national. The relationships that developed in and around the dilapidated public buildings in villages like those in Motul were the foundation of the sometimes tenuous legitimacy of both state and national governments after independence. Precisely in the places where the Yucatecan inspector saw a severe disjuncture between liberal ideals and indigenous reality, it is possible to observe the negotiation of the terms of liberal citizenship and the roots of conflict over what those terms would be.

Why "Liberalism"?

It is necessary at the outset to explain my choice of the term *liberalism* to describe early nineteenth-century Mexican politics and government. The broad constellation of institutions and practices that characterized Mexico in these years could certainly be called by other names—*republicanism* or *constitutionalism* and perhaps even *democracy*. In a strict sense, these descriptors are more accurate; liberalism as an ideology does not imply a precise set of institutions or a particular way of structuring polities. Scholars have used other phrases such as *democratic revolution* or the *transition from the Old Regime* or even the *advent of modernity* to describe the broad global process of which the emergence of new Mexican institutions was a part. Yet *liberalism* best describes the political, ideological, and institutional changes of the early nineteenth century, in large part because it aptly describes what Mexicans *understood* to be shared by the numerous regimes that governed Mexico after independence.

To be sure, even if Mexicans could agree that the new system was liberal, there was little consensus about what, exactly, liberalism meant. Nineteenth-century ideological liberalism assumed, in Nils Jacobsen's words, a "bewildering array of guises," ranging from "a doctrine of emancipation to one of justifying a given status quo."[3] In the first half of the nineteenth century, those who actively espoused liberalism could agree, in general, that the state should be limited and that both its limitations and its duties were determined by the fundamental rights of citizens as detailed in constitutions.[4] Yet within this broad definition, numerous strands of thought emerged, coalesced, and evolved over the course of the first half of the century.[5]

Also significant is that this loose conglomeration of liberal ideas was not actively set against "conservatism." Liberalism and conservatism have often been treated as opposites, the differences between them forming the fundamental dividing line between nineteenth-century thinkers in Mexico reaching back to independence. But the tendency to project a liberal/conservative divide onto this early era is anachronistic. Scholars have shown that in early national Mexico, *all* elite political thought evolved from European liberalism. There were certainly those who were more "traditionalist" and others who were more "radical." But traditionalist and later centralist thought emerged out of the same body of influences—in particular, the ideas underlying the 1812 Spanish Constitution of Cádiz—

as did more radical or moderate thought. The word *conservative* was not used to describe political ideology until the later 1840s. Before that, it referred to conservative values, which were often as apparent in the words of moderate and radical liberals as in those of more traditionalist thinkers. The terms that politicians *did* use, especially *federalism* and *centralism*, are not analogous with liberalism and conservatism. Federalists and centralists were nearly all republicans, and federalists and centralists alike were reformers; they differed most clearly on the questions of how and how fast reform should occur. Even the group most often identified with an unrelenting conservatism, the church, participated in this general liberal consensus. At least until the 1850s, the church hierarchy defended itself not by assaulting liberalism but rather by claiming its own rights within it. The major coalitions that characterized postindependence Mexican politics developed as versions of the same basic beliefs that had not, before the 1850s, diverged to the point that any of them were no longer "liberal."[6]

This was reflected in the institutions that emerged in the first half of the nineteenth century. With one important exception, both the federalist and centralist governments established between the fall of the Spanish empire and 1857 were deeply influenced by liberal ideology writ large.[7] Practically speaking, this translated into a basic set of institutions, including most importantly elections for both local and supralocal offices that, although they varied in form, persisted throughout much of the period. In this sense, liberalism was not just an ideology but also a system of government. Certainly, it is possible to trace the origins of conservatism in these years and in these institutions, especially in the centralist regime of the late 1830s. But centralism was still deeply concerned with liberty; if it privileged liberty over equality, this does not make it antiliberal but rather, as Josefina Vásquez has argued, liberalism of a different kind.[8] Before the 1850s, *liberalism* remained a loose and expansive term, one that described not just a set of political beliefs but most importantly described the postcolonial system itself.

For most Mexicans in the early nineteenth century, it was liberalism as a system—as a set of institutions and practices—that mattered most. Mexicans, regardless of their social position and regardless of their particular political beliefs, understood that they now lived under a system that was fundamentally different from what had come before. This was not a monarchy; there was no longer an unquestioned source of authority that bound people to the state. What replaced the overarching notion of subjecthood, with its implication of subordination, was the idea of citizenship, backed up by the notion of liberty. Whatever precise institutions governed at any particular moment were understood to be informed by this fundamental change. As James Dunkerley has written, "imagination mattered throughout" the nineteenth century in Latin America; in the first half of that century, no matter what it actually looked like, "liberalism" was a central element of what Mexicans imagined they were doing, and Mexicans imagined they were doing something new. This book defines liberalism as the concept that best captures the political and ideological context that Mexicans believed that they shared.[9]

In proposing this definition, I make distinctions between liberalism as a proactive movement, liberalism as a system, and liberalism as a political culture. The first of these is least important here. In the first half of the nineteenth century there was no consolidated liberal "movement" in Mexico; there were certainly political activists who could be called "liberals," but their ideas and plans encompassed a broad spectrum of both ideas and institutions. More important is that in these years Mexico was consistently governed under a new set of institutions that could also be called liberal, including elections, a new tax structure, new definitions of land tenure, and new methods of allocating the military draft. As these were implemented, the people who participated in them—economic elites, political officials, urban plebeians, or indigenous villagers—had to abide by their basic terms. Finally, with this shared system came a shared sense of the transformation of local, regional, and national politics. The political culture of liberalism developed out of this shared sense, as Mexicans strove to incorporate new institutions and sought to make them meet their needs and conform to their beliefs.[10]

The incorporation of new institutions was made easier by the fact that those institutions were themselves notably hybrid, encompassing radical innovations but also constructed in ways that allowed for continuity with the Old Regime.[11] Even so, for many Mexicans, the process of implementation would raise contradictions. Colonial political cultures were deeply rooted in both the reciprocal obligations of monarchs and subjects and a fundamental distinction between Spanish and indigenous people. Liberal institutions, with their emphasis on individual citizenship and the erasure of ethnic differences, threatened many of the assumptions that had made colonial government function. These fundamental changes in political identity were not universally desired by either indigenous people or representatives of the state. The former, although they did gain certain advantages from their new juridical equality, were also reluctant to give up the privileges that the colonial system had offered. And the latter, although they saw ultimate advantages in a liberal transformation, worried that the elimination of colonial bonds and distinctions would make governance itself impossible. The challenge of Mexico's liberal experiment was to find ways to make liberalism's basic precepts compatible with those of deeply rooted political cultures. As they negotiated ways to make this happen, Mexicans created new political cultures, new sets of discourses and actions that gave liberal institutions and languages specific meaning and incorporated them into everyday political life.

In light of this process, it would not make sense to say that either government officials or indigenous people resisted liberalism, per se. Government officials were obligated to enforce the new national agenda, and they often agreed with the precepts that underlay it. When that agenda interfered with their ability to govern, they used their authority not to contradict new laws but to implement them in a way that was more acceptable but still recognizably "liberal." And indigenous people were not inherently unwilling to embrace the institutions of the new government, even though they threatened their ethnically defined political identity. Instead, they used them; as Antonio Annino puts it, they had an "extraordinary capacity . . . to use a liberal category like 'citizenship' to defend themselves from the liberal State."[12] Indigenous people and government officials, through their words and actions in response to institutional change, and through their negotiation with each other, pushed the boundaries of what liberalism as a system of government could mean. By doing so, they shifted that meaning often significantly. In majority indigenous Oaxaca and Yucatán, this would be the central process in the creation of unique liberal political cultures.

As such, that process was intensely local. In all of Mexico, the relationship between state and society had to be rebuilt around a new framework after independence, as colonial notions of state legitimacy met liberal ones. In each new state, however, local circumstances meant that the precise challenge that liberalism posed to existing relationships was also different, as were the responses of both the government and new citizens. The first Mexican federalism afforded state governments considerable latitude. Each state produced its own constitution, and these documents determined the basic structures of politics in each state's territory. As lawmakers in the states sought to accommodate and take advantage of new institutions in local contexts, they responded to the national liberal project by creating multiple systems that varied considerably on key points, including the structure of town government, the bases of the franchise, and taxation.[13] When put into practice by local officials and when negotiated by these officials and their constituencies, what began as a national project was immediately transformed into "local liberalisms," each with unique content and context.

The fact that what was understood to be liberalism could vary so widely is essential to our understanding of early-nineteenth-century Mexican politics. It is also crucial to our understanding of the latter half of the century. Indeed, the choice of "liberalism" to describe postindependence politics is a product of hindsight. Toward the end of the period that this book covers, liberalism coalesced as a proactive movement, as self-identified "liberals" began in earnest to organize themselves into a party that aimed to transform society, proposing a set of interlinked goals and aspirations in which the expansion of citizenship and property rights would ostensibly coincide with the freeing up of markets and capital, leading to prosperity and universal advancement. These latter-century "new liberals" were also nationalists; they hoped to consolidate the Mexican nation, in large part by removing the vestiges of competing associations and regularizing political practice throughout the territory. By 1857, these liberals were in power in Mexico City and had begun the conflictual process of transformation known as *La Reforma*, an attempt to achieve once and for all the kind of liberal society that they envisioned.[14]

This book's argument about the early nineteenth century suggests that liberals' task was made far more difficult by the fact that something called liberalism and understood to *be* liberalism was already established and familiar in the Mexico that they hoped to transform. Mexicans in countless local places had, over the course of the years since independence, incorporated new institutions into their political practice, new institutions they had learned to recognize as liberal. In the eyes of proactive liberals after 1857, these incorporations had been haphazard and incomplete at best. But to those who practiced daily politics on the ground, they *were* liberalism, and the distinctions between them and what the national liberals proposed were not nearly as clear as the latter might have hoped. Liberals' task was made even more difficult by the fact that liberalism, as understood by most Mexicans, was also multiple. After 1857, reformers had to convince Mexicans not only of the differences between their vision and the national liberalism that had come before but also of the differences between that vision and the many and deeply local liberalisms that had developed in the preceding years. The Reform arrived in a Mexico in which "liberalism" already had a long history and in which local people had given it meaning, content, and institutional force, a Mexico already liberal but in multiple and often contradictory ways.

Indigenous Citizens compares two Mexican states that shared certain characteristics but followed divergent paths as their governments and populations adapted to the changes in institutions and ideologies that followed independence—to the establishment and expansion of citizenship, to the encouragement of private property ownership, and to new fiscal and military duties to the state. While the comparison has much to tell us about what happened in these two places, it also clarifies what the simultaneous existence of a shared sense of liberalism and local differentiation meant for the development of Mexico as a nation. Oaxaca's and Yucatán's political systems and political cultures were not simply "variations" on a common liberal model. Nor were they "responses to" or even "engagements with" a clearly identifiable liberalism. Mexico's national liberalism appeared in local places not as a coherent guide to work from but rather as a set of basic assumptions represented by a set of baseline institutions that could be implemented in any number of ways. In the years after independence from Spain, Mexican liberalism was invented on the ground, producing multiple forms specific to local contexts. Reconstructing the content of each of Mexico's local liberalisms is crucial to understanding local politics. Yet what was and was not shared—and what was and was not *understood* to be shared—among all these local liberalisms is central to any characterization of liberalism in Mexico as a nation.

Popular Liberalism, Local Liberalisms, and the Comparative Project

In 1968, Charles Hale wrote that historiography on Mexican liberalism was dominated by two basic interpretations. One, advanced by liberals themselves, claimed that Mexican liberalism represented a struggle against deep-rooted colonial structures that had long oppressed the people of Mexico. These structures proved extremely difficult to displace and thus made the implementation of liberal reform exceedingly complicated. Proponents of the second interpretation countered that liberal policies had senselessly attacked forms of social life and power that had functioned quite well in colonial New Spain and that, by introducing inappropriate ideas into Mexico, liberalism had set in motion the cycles of disorder and instability that characterized the nation's nineteenth-century history.[15] Although these arguments are in many ways diametrically opposed, they share one important commonality. Both echo the worries of the Yucatecan inspector for Motul; both, in effect, are explanations of liberalism's failure to produce the results that were ostensibly intended.

Without doubt, postindependence governments did "fail" Mexico's and Latin America's majorities in many ways. Viewed both from the end of the nineteenth century and from the present day, nowhere is there universal prosperity; instead, social structures were and are characterized by deep inequalities. Accordingly, many scholars have attempted to explain why the liberal theory that informed nineteenth-century policy did not deliver on its promises. As they have done so, they have taken the two arguments described above in new but related directions. Some have argued that colonial economic structures continued to drive society through much of the nineteenth century and that, in the face of their strength, liberalism was relatively inconsequential; what is important to note is not the changes that liberalism brought but rather the "impressive continuity" of economic and political behaviors, attitudes, and mentalities through the colonial era and up to the present day.[16] Others have advanced a strictly culturalist argument, in which the persistence of Iberian political culture hindered and deformed the progress of the liberal transition to modernity.[17]

Still others have questioned the goals and methods of Latin America's liberal experiment. By the end of the nineteenth century, according to this argument, liberally inspired governments succeeded in their goal of reducing people's commitments to institutions or groups other than the state and of thus freeing up labor and capital markets to produce a more efficient and effective use of resources. This success, however, came at the expense of the people who would come to provide most of the labor and yet control few of the resources. Indigenous peoples, slaves and the descendents of slaves, and other groups ill-situated to take advantage of the new approach to national progress would come to form a disenfranchised underclass. The dismantling of colonial structures would result in a society in which liberal economic goals would overshadow related notions of political and economic equality. In the words of E. Bradford Burns, "the individual rights almost universally promised by the idealistic, if unrealistic constitutions proved meaningless to a repressed majority"; faced with the onslaught of "progress," he concludes, "folk society disintegrated."[18]

For Mexico and especially for Mexico's indigenous population, approaches to liberalism that posit its fundamental failure have contributed to a powerful narrative about the causes of the Mexican Revolution that began in 1910. According to this chronology, the gradual consolidation of liberalism through the first half of the nineteenth century culminated in the constitution of 1857, which affirmed the ascendancy of the liberal ideal. Most significant for indígenas and other rural agriculturalists, the accompanying *Ley Lerdo* declared that all land must be converted into private property, a decree that struck at the heart of indigenous communities where survival was based primarily on the use of communally held territory. Increasingly intense application of this law in the latter half of the century resulted in escalating unrest and finally in the explosion of popular violence in 1910. There is much of value in this narrative. Many Mexican peasants did lose their land over the course of the nineteenth century, and liberal state interventions certainly had something to do with it. In some cases at least, loss of land sparked popular participation in the Revolution. Despite revisionist attempts to reinterpret the Revolution as a movement of the Mexican bourgeoisie, most historians would concede that it also had deep popular roots and that, in many places, the expropriation of land was central to the equation.[19]

But an overwhelmingly negative interpretation of the effects of liberalism suffers from several related problems. First, it assumes that liberalism had a coherence that it lacked. Second, for much of the nineteenth century, the national government did not have either the institutional mandate or the practical power to enforce the uniform application of liberal principles in the states. At their inception, state systems were geared toward solving a variety of local problems and thus developed very different frameworks of governance. Finally—and most important—this approach to liberalism ignores the fact that elements of liberal policy and liberal ideology could in fact be made compatible with the interests of peasants, indígenas, and other local people, in varied and sometimes surprising ways. Most often, seeking out this compatibility was in the interest not only of local people themselves but also of regional elites and government officials.

Recent work on nineteenth-century Mexican politics addresses these problems with early interpretations. In 1991, Guy Thomson refuted the entrenched notion that the popularity of Mexican liberalism in the second half of the nineteenth century stemmed from a "favourable conjuncture" of events rather than from "deeper economic and social forces." In its place, he introduced the notion of "popular liberalism." The participation of a broad coalition of creoles, indigenous people, and mestizos in the wars of the 1850s and 1860s was, he suggested, the result of sustained and real engagement with liberal ideas and promises that proved attractive to a wide spectrum of communities and prompted them to support the national liberal movement.[20] Thomson was part of a group of historians who went on to revolutionize the study of politics among Mexico's popular classes. They have demonstrated convincingly that indigenous people and peasants were capable of political thought and capable of interpreting and acting on the ideologies at play in national politics. They have suggested that such people could change the meanings of those ideologies through their actions and words. And they have shown that those new, popular interpretations of national ideologies could affect the course of national events. Such interpretations were crucial for the midcentury rise of liberalism as a party and a movement and for its persistence in power. As Peter Guardino shows, the peasants of Guerrero helped fashion and then embraced a "popular federalism" that facilitated the cross-class alliances that brought the Liberals to power by 1856. Popular liberalism was also crucial in the later rise to power of Porfirio Díaz. In the long run, the incorporation by the state of popular versions of liberal and nationalist ideas was by no means complete; as Florencia Mallon suggests in her study of Morelos, the "alternative nationalist discourses" created during the wars of the 1850s and 1860s did not take center stage in late nineteenth-century state and nation building. But nevertheless, she argues, "popular creativity and political action put identifiable marks on the state being constructed in these years," and the popular political cultures they created "reemerged repeatedly" in the years thereafter.[21]

Much of this scholarship observes liberalism mostly in the context of overt conflict around nationally defined issues, first in the wars of independence and later in the wars of the Reform. Participation in national conflicts, scholars argue, played an important role in the development of local people's notions of citizenship, liberalism, and nation. The intense political engagement of war acted as a sort of preparation for citizenship, producing a populace with the vocabulary and skills to make coherent political demands on both a regional and a national level and the military experience to back up those demands. As Mallon puts it, it has been extremely fruitful to concentrate on "moments of national emergency" when "the richest, most varied and open possibilities for maneuver and discursive practice occurred." Conflicts such as the wars of independence, the Revolution of Ayutla, and the war against the French provided peasants and elites alike with the impetus to engage actively with the precepts of liberalism as they participated in movements the stated goals of which were far more than local, even when peasants' immediate goals were not. It is thus possible—and perhaps not surprising—to see these people explicitly articulating alternative versions of liberalism in the service of movements that demanded exactly that. "Popular federalisms," "popular liberalisms," and "popular nationalisms" were couched as demands for systemic change by people whose participation in national struggle made them well aware of the national government as a target, an audience, and a possible ally in their local struggles.[22]

Yet this book argues that for most Mexicans during the first half of the nineteenth century, liberalism was less a proactive motivating ideology than it was the set of ideas and institutions that governed quotidian contact with the state. It mattered to people not just in periods of sustained conflict but all of the time. And it mattered not just as an ideology that could promote and justify movements for change but also as the set of ideas that had to be reckoned with in the organization of daily life. These two kinds of liberalism often merged, to be sure, but it is impossible to understand the more self-conscious ideology without close attention to its everyday counterpart. And in some parts of Mexico the more everyday liberalism was far more formative. In both rural Oaxaca and rural Yucatán in the first half of the century, explicitly nationally oriented conflict had less immediate resonance than it did in many other parts of the country. In neither place could one expect the rapid evolution of political thought that scholars have demonstrated to occur in the context of war.[23]

Less overt conflict around national issues did not necessarily mean less intense engagement with liberalism. After independence, in parts of the country where there had been little war, the window of opportunity for institutional change was opened. The basic instruments through which the colonial state had engaged the population were officially discarded, and new institutions—a new kind of vote, new forms of local government, new structures of taxation, and new demands for service to the state—replaced them. Of particular importance here, the dual ethnic structure of government that governed the relationship between indigenous and nonindigenous people came under intense scrutiny and was rejected in favor of universal political participation and ethnic neutrality. This book shifts the locus of the study of liberalism from armed conflict to contention in everyday politics. In the regions of Mexico where war was not the central experience of the early nineteenth century, the engagement between peasants and elites hinged on quotidian negotiation over the nature of political institutions.

Still there were important similarities between the violent wars of the early nineteenth century and the (usually) less violent struggles over institutions in the same years. The same questions arise: Did elite and nonelite notions of political participation and government coincide at all? Did the transformation of the colonial political system into a liberal republican state change the manner in which peasants and in particular indigenous people understood their role, their relationship to government, and their political and ethnic identities? The engagement between elite and nonelite people over institutions was often as intense as the engagement between officially warring factions. As in war, there were vital differences between the goals and understandings of the various parties. As Eric Van Young has observed, there is much that was deeply unique and deeply local about peasant and indigenous aspirations, and local people and elites were not always legible to each other. And yet, that the practical goals and even understandings of peasants and nonpeasants were not always the same or even congruent does not preclude meaningful overlap. As peasants confronted sets of institutions whose bases were potentially deeply foreign to their notions of good government, their ability to find common ground with the elite in their discussion of those institutions was central to the stability of the state. That common ground also potentially provided an arena for real change, as all parties were forced to conduct their negotiations according to a new set of institutions and in a new language.[24]

Indigenous Citizens reconstructs the common ground of early nineteenth-century local politics. It identifies the points at which institutional change after independence most overtly affected indigenous people's lives—the workings of local government, taxation, the draft, and the ownership of land—and examines how those people negotiated the terms of that change with the state in each case. It also examines the way in which local people and representatives of the state communicated about those changes. In both Oaxaca and Yucatán, local people—indigenous villagers and representatives of the state—built local political cultures around ways of talking about the new system they lived within. They sought a common language that could enable everyday governance while meeting the requirements of the national political change. Without doubt, the point of coincidence between interpretations of the new system was a shifting one. As institutions themselves changed—and in early nineteenth-century Mexico they did so with some frequency—all participating parties had to readjust and relocate common ground. That ground could also easily evaporate entirely. If, in Oaxaca, political engagement and accommodation were usually (but not always) more peaceful, in Yucatán they were much more difficult to maintain, and they eventually collapsed. This book examines the way that a common language—a local liberalism—developed in both places, and, in the case of Yucatán, the way that it fell to pieces.

I also examine how the two local political cultures were different and argue that it is precisely in the multiplicity of local liberalisms that their national significance lies. In making this argument, I draw heavily on the rich literature of regional studies produced in the past thirty years. Regional historians have made it abundantly clear that local interpretations of national politics were contingent upon local circumstances, and that they could take any number of forms.[25] But the significance of this variation has not yet been made clear. A purely regional approach carries within it the danger of producing multiple and often contradictory narratives with little sense of the significance of processes that not only had a national element but were constitutive of a national experience. What is needed is an approach to studying national processes that recognizes the complexity of local places while keeping an eye on the national story.[26] The notion of "local liberalisms" is designed to address this need.

Two things about local liberalisms deserve comment. First, the political cultures that developed on the ground in Mexico after independence were not just local; they all shared the common framework of a national (and indeed international) liberalism and the common challenges that it posed. And second, liberalism was not *infinitely* local—local liberalisms were built primarily at the level of Mexico's states. While political culture may indeed have varied among the many subregions and even the towns and neighborhoods that comprised states like Oaxaca and Yucatán, the basic structures of local liberalisms were determined by shared institutions, and, because of the nature of Mexico's federalism, those institutions were established in state constitutions and state laws. I compare two of these state-level local liberalisms. I demonstrate how local particularities shaped the development of unique liberalisms, each one comprised of different notions of the role of the state and of distinctive political roles for its citizens, and argue that Mexican liberalism must be understood not as a monolithic set of institutions with predictable outcomes but rather as a set of local reactions to shared institutional and ideological challenges. In the process, I suggest that, for many Mexicans, the most salient experience of nineteenth-century politics was the process of rebuilding a relationship with the state after independence and of constructing a new legitimacy for that relationship out of a negotiated combination of colonial practices and liberal institutions.[27]

The book also argues that it is this experience that, for most Mexicans, constituted "liberalism." The first half of the nineteenth century has long been understudied, reflecting a tendency of historians of liberalism to dismiss it as a time of unmanageable conflict in which the promises of independence, nationhood, and Enlightenment were squandered by bickering ideologues, military dictators, and recalcitrant provincials.[28] The "real" history of liberalism, according to this notion, begins with its consolidation as a party and a movement, which did not occur until midcentury. Along with a growing scholarship on the first years after independence, this book argues, by contrast, that when looked at locally, the earlier years produced coherent if multiple ideological configurations. This conceptualization of Mexican liberalism as a collection of multiple yet linked political cultures has important implications for our understanding of Mexico's later struggles for national consolidation. These political cultures shared a name—*liberalism*—with the transformative movement that, in practice, later aimed to dismantle and replace them.[29] Those who sought, after 1857, to implement the Reform—which at its heart aimed for national consolidation—would confront, challenge, and be challenged by the multiplicity of local liberalisms as they worked to rebuild Mexico's national liberal republic.

The Case Studies: Oaxaca and Yucatán

In 1810, Oaxaca's population of nearly 600,000 was 90 percent indigenous. Between 1793 and 1860, this basic ratio did not change significantly.[30] Yucatán also had a majority indigenous population, approximately 70 percent of the state's total in 1806.* Because of their indigenous majorities, Oaxaca and Yucatán are among the most written about states in Mexico.

---

* See the maps of Oaxaca and Yucatán on pp. ix–x of the frontmatter.

For scholars, both states offer an opportunity to observe indigenous people in what has often been interpreted as relative isolation. There is extensive anthropological literature for both places, and ethnohistorians have carried the study of indigenous culture and society back to the colonial period and beyond. The notion that indigenous people in these places led isolated lives has been greatly complicated by this work, and it is now clear that their lives were closely linked to and affected by the wider politics and culture of New Spanish and later Mexican society. But both states' indigenousness remains an attraction to those interested in that interplay, and the study of each has become a field of its own.[31] Writing about liberalism in both Oaxaca and Yucatán after independence, then, means writing about indigenous people and their relationship to the liberal state, its ideologies, and its practices.

For Oaxaca, some have argued that political and economic modernization after independence had disastrous effects on indigenous communities, a process Marcello Carmagnani calls a "new conquest." More often, though, historians have focused on the persistence of indigenous communities and the seemingly unchanging nature of their customs. Oaxaca, as Francie Chassen-López observes, has often been seen as "backward" and "impenetrable by modernity," and in movements of national importance, "passive" and "reactionary." This perception of Oaxaca can have negative connotations, for those who are seeking a history of "modernization" and who place inherent value on the progressive development of nation and nationalism; or positive, for those who seek a history of peasant or indigenous "resistance" to foreign impositions on their way of life.[32] Yucatán, on the other hand, has long been seen mostly in the context of the violent clash of indigenous communities with the modernizing liberal state and of the rise of an extraordinarily exploitative economic and social system in its wake. The Caste War—the massive indigenous rebellion that began in 1847—can also be seen in both a negative light, as evidence of the liberal state's failure to incorporate the indigenous majority, and a positive one, as evidence, once again, of indigenous people's tenacious resistance to modernization.[33] Many interpretations of both states depict indigenous people as essentially traditional, antimodern, and resistant to change, whether those qualities are seen as shortsightedly backward or heroically strong.

Recent scholarship on both places has challenged the image of indigenous people as fundamentally traditional. For Oaxaca, scholars have shown how in the years before the Reform indigenous villagers engaged actively with new political ideologies and made them work according to their goals. Even Reform-era policies, in particular the assault on communal property holding, had limited effects in Oaxaca not because they were ignored but because indigenous people engaged them so effectively.

Some indigenous Oaxacans participated intensely in the wars of the Reform, and their experience resonated in their participation in Porfirian-era politics. In the latter half of the nineteenth century, liberal innovations provoked, in Chassen-López's words, "energetic responses" from indigenous villagers who negotiated a "hybrid modernity." Recent work thus demonstrates that Oaxacan indígenas were not inherently backward looking; they were deeply attached to their customs and traditions, to be sure, but also willing to engage innovations and thus to engage the state. In addition, as Carlos Sánchez-Silva has shown, the continuity between colonial and postindependence Oaxaca owes as much to the strategies and goals of the local nonindigenous elite as it does to the tenacity of the indígenas. The representatives of the "liberal modernizing state" depended on custom and tradition—both for preserving their economic ascendancy and protecting their political control—and they often proved as willing as their indigenous constituencies to engage innovations with an eye to preserving older ways of doing economics and politics.[34]

Yucatán's historiography for the nineteenth century has been slower to change. The state's nineteenth-century experience has been seen as the example par excellence of the negative effects of the modernizing liberal state on indigenous communities in the nineteenth century. Yucatán's Maya had had considerable success resisting the changes brought by the colonial regime, and their encounter with liberal institutional change was thus dramatic. It is here that the notion of a "second conquest" originated, in Nancy Farris's groundbreaking ethnohistory. And there is little doubt that in the nineteenth century indigenous communities here were explicitly targeted by the liberal state and that this resulted in devastating losses of both autonomy and land. Recent scholarship has shown, however, that this is not the entire story. Terry Rugeley's work on the origins of the Caste War confirms the importance of land to the rebellion but places its loss in the context of the integration of indigenous elites into nonindigenous society and their subsequent declining status.[35] Still, work that examines indigenous people's engagement with either political institutions or political ideology in early nineteenth-century Yucatán is rare, and there is a persistent assumption that the particulars of indigenous autonomy and political culture kept them separate from the ideas emanating from Mexico City and the state capital.

Indigenous Citizens seeks to expand upon the work being done for Oaxaca and to help develop the study of liberalism and the indigenous population in Yucatán. It is not a comprehensive study of either state in these years. Rather, it asks what a direct comparison of the two can tell us about liberalism. The comparison of Oaxaca and Yucatán is, in the first instance, a comparison of similarity, because both states have large indigenous majorities.

It is also, however, a comparison of difference because the Caste War of Yucatán has no statewide parallel in Oaxaca. Recent scholarship explains Oaxaca's relative quiescence by documenting indigenous people's engagement with liberalism, but there is no analogous historiography explaining Yucatán's rebellion in those terms.

Central to this book's argument is that different outcomes in these outwardly similar places cannot be explained by a scenario in which two sets of indigenous people engaged with liberal institutions to different degrees. Oaxacan indígenas were not inherently more willing to accept specific liberal innovations. And they were not, crucially, inherently more willing to accept liberalism in general. Rather, the book argues first that the liberalism they had to engage was at the outset somewhat different from that found in Yucatán. And second, from these different starting points, Oaxacans and Yucatecans—indigenous and nonindigenous alike—built different notions of liberal political culture and made different kinds of accommodations to the new liberal order. In the specific circumstances of each state, these local liberalisms were central to whether any kind of liberal order could be sustained among the indigenous population in the first half of the nineteenth century.

The Politics of Autonomy: Colonial Oaxaca and Yucatán

There is much that Oaxaca and Yucatán shared in the colonial era. The indigenous population far outnumbered the nonindigenous in both places. And, in both, the indigenous population dominated the countryside, whereas the nonindigenous population was clustered in a few urban places. Indigenous villages were often remote, linked to Spanish and mestizo centers only by ill-maintained roads. Thus, everyday colonial government was mostly a matter of a nonindigenous state administering a collection of largely self-governing towns and villages. Yet in both places, despite the sharp segregation of the population and the often daunting physical distance that divided it, the nonindigenous population—and through it the colonial government—was ultimately able to administer, govern, and reap resources from the far-flung indigenous majority.

Both systems of governance relied heavily on the maintenance of indigenous autonomy, of distinct limits to the state's control over indigenous communities. The notion of indigenous autonomy developed out of the Spanish juridical construct of *dos repúblicas*, or two republics. According to Spanish law, America's indígenas related directly to the Crown as members of the Republic of Indians, which theoretically stood alongside—rather than under—the Republic of Spaniards that encompassed all nonindigenous people. Each was governed by its own set of laws. Still, indígenas were not treated as equals. Members of the indigenous republic were understood to be in need of tutelage from the Spanish colonial state and were treated as minors in matters legal, political, and religious. Meanwhile, natives were to be isolated and protected in indigenous towns from the corrupting influences and abuses of Spanish and especially mestizo individuals.[36]

Whether or not such isolation fulfilled its protective goal, the political separateness of indigenous villages served an important practical purpose for Spanish colonial government. In Mexico as a whole and in Oaxaca and Yucatán in particular, it was often difficult for the state to gain access to the large and physically isolated indigenous population, and most duties of day-to-day administration were left to local indigenous delegates. The Spanish government relied on indigenous *gobernadores* (governors) and on locally chosen indigenous councils known as *repúblicas* or *cabildos de indígenas*,[37] an arrangement that provided the state with mediating bodies through which to implement policies and exert control in indigenous communities. Rooted in both precolonial practices and Spanish institutions, repúblicas provided the basic institutional framework for Spanish administration of indigenous people in the Americas. The members of the councils were responsible for the collection of royal tribute and had an important role in the distribution of labor drafts. As such, they were also essential to the extraction of resources from the indigenous population.[38]

The maintenance of indigenous self-government could, however, be a double-edged sword for the colonial state, for while it provided an entrée into the indigenous communities it also bolstered indigenous autonomy. Repúblicas buffered communities from the direct exploitation of Spanish officials and other nonindigenous people, and they made it difficult for Spaniards to interfere in village affairs. Yet these limitations, too, were constitutive of the Spanish ability to govern. Tristan Platt, in his study of indigenous villages in Bolivia, identified what he called a "pact of reciprocity," a tacit agreement in which indígenas in the colonial Andes agreed to pay tribute in exchange for access to land.[39] In Oaxaca and Yucatán, a broader definition of this colonial pact would substitute "autonomy" for "land." Autonomy meant freedom not just to own land but also to choose how that land would be distributed and used. It meant latitude in methods of choosing local officials. It meant that the state would not interfere unduly with social hierarchy and social control within the villages. And it meant freedom not just from Spanish interference but also from interference from other indigenous villages and villagers. In exchange, indigenous people agreed not just to pay tribute but to recognize the authority of the state. Indigenous people and representatives of the government did not always concur about the precise terms of the reciprocal pact.

But the relationship between state and society was profoundly shaped by this arrangement, which determined to what extent the state could make demands on indígenas and to what extent indígenas could make demands on the state.[40] Meanwhile, the precise nature of the demands varied significantly by region. And in Oaxaca and Yucatán, these variations resulted in very different notions of what it meant to indígenas to be autonomous.

OAXACA

At the beginning of the nineteenth century, Oaxaca was very much an indigenous place. The small, nonindigenous population was quite concentrated, and only in Antequera (Oaxaca City) did the nonindigenous population outnumber the indigenous. Outside of the capital city, by contrast, there were 35,272 nonindigenous people and 358,056 indígenas, with the nonindígenas clustered in larger towns such as Huajuapan, Teposcolula, Tehuantepec, and Juxtlahuaca. In 1777 in the Valley of Oaxaca, only forty-two of eighty-eight towns surveyed had any nonindígenas at all; in the Mixteca Alta in 1746, at most nine of sixty-five towns had nonindigenous residents; and in the Sierra Zapoteca, almost the entire nonindigenous population (only 179 people) made its home in the town of Villa Alta.[41]

Beyond the nonindigenous centers, then, were hundreds of indigenous villages. Even before the Spanish arrived, those villages had considerable autonomy from each other. Much of precolonial Oaxaca had long been dominated by two cultural groups, the Zapotec and Mixtec, each of them divided into numerous *cacicazgos* under the control of multiple noble lineages. By the fifteenth century, the Mexica (Aztec) empire had established some control over much of the area. Imperial relationships with subject communities were, however, based largely on tribute; most aspects of day-to-day life, including the structures of political authority, were determined locally. Those structures were as diverse as the indigenous population itself. According to Oaxacan governor José María Murguía y Galardi, writing in 1826, the people of Oaxaca spoke a total of twenty-one languages.[42] The various groups that made up the indigenous population had neither a shared political structure nor a shared ethnic identity.

Before the Spanish arrival, there were nevertheless crucial linkages between and among ethnic groups, and between and among towns and villages within those groups, including overlapping jurisdictions and crisscrossing lines of nobility. After the Spanish established control, contact between villages remained the norm. But, in terms of political administration, local structures and identities remained predominant and were even reinforced by colonial changes. Spanish law attempted to delineate clearly the existence of separate towns, each with its own structures of authority modeled after Spanish town councils. It limited the power of individual lords and their families to defined territories and reduced the number of nobles who could hold positions of power. The nobility remained intact, with nobles often holding the Spanish-defined office of gobernador and serving in the repúblicas. Indeed, precolonial lineage groups commonly manipulated Spanish structures to remain in positions of authority. Yet, increasingly, their power was subject to the approval of Spanish officials, and the Spanish engaged in a concerted effort to limit the privileges of their offices. Over time, the extent of the hereditary power of native lords declined and with it political linkages between villages. Spanish policies increasingly circumscribed local power, limiting it to smaller geographic spaces and forcing local authorities to seek recognition from the colonial state.[43]

Spanish policy also enhanced the fragmentation of indigenous villagers by other means. The *cabecera/sujeto* system common throughout New Spain, whereby certain "head towns" were granted limited jurisdiction over their neighbors, was unevenly applied in Oaxaca (Villa Alta, in particular, never instituted this system). And where it was applied, it was often resisted, leading to demands for autonomy from the subject communities. As Kevin Terraciano has shown for the Mixteca, the colonial era saw a movement toward greater and greater local autonomy, with the last twenty-five years of the eighteenth century constituting a "watershed" for sujeto campaigns to be separated from their cabeceras. In concert with the increasingly circumscribed power of the nobility, the process of pueblo fragmentation had, in the long run, the effect of multiplying the number of identifiable and autonomous Oaxacan towns. Although it is difficult to determine the exact number with precision, by 1793, Oaxaca counted over 900 pueblos.[44] In Oaxaca, then, one crucial meaning of autonomy was autonomy of each village from the other.

Of course, autonomy also meant autonomy from the state. The fragmentation of Oaxacan villages reflected the far-reaching effects of Spanish colonial rule on the organization of municipal authority. But at the same time, Spanish law did little to introduce direct Spanish control into the villages themselves. For the most part, late colonial Oaxaca consisted of numerous indigenous towns that, in their structures of governance, had been deeply affected by Spanish institutions but nevertheless retained a striking measure of independence from them.

This situation was in many ways the result of the particulars of Oaxaca's economy. Although far from a center of Spanish settlement, Oaxaca was important economically because of its near monopoly over the production of the red dye cochineal, after precious metals the most important product that New Spain exported. Oaxaca's other major product was cotton cloth for the internal New Spanish market. These two commodities provided the majority of the income of many of those Spanish and Creole people—merchants, government officials, their agents, and their creditors—who made their home, temporarily or permanently, in colonial Oaxaca.[45] Yet the goods that made Oaxaca so central to the colonial economy were not produced under the direct control of the nonindigenous people who benefited most from their sale. Rather, they were products of autonomous indigenous labor inside of indigenous villages. Despite some attempts to produce cochineal on Spanish-owned and Spanish-run haciendas, by the late eighteenth century, the vast majority was still cultivated in indigenous villages, where costs proved to be lower.[46] Similarly, during the colonial period, although cotton fiber itself could be grown either inside or outside of indigenous villages, the production of the finished woven products was largely done within them.[47]

In short, Oaxaca's colonial system was one of indirect exploitation. The Spanish population lived largely off products for export, but they neither produced those products themselves nor directly controlled indigenous labor. Instead, they depended on a system of incentives to keep indígenas producing. At the start of the colonial era, the Spanish obtained indigenous goods both through trade and through tribute. Over time, however, Spanish interventions in the market blurred the distinction between the two, as Spanish collection of tribute in the form of actual products gave way to insistence on tribute in money rather than in kind. Initially, indigenous marketers utilized long-standing trade networks to acquire the necessary cash. But, as the Spanish consolidated political control, they also consolidated control over the market, funneling more and more of the profit to themselves. In Oaxaca as elsewhere, nonindígenas used the *repartimiento* to do this. In Oaxaca, a nonindigenous individual, either the *alcalde mayor* (the government appointee in charge of indigenous affairs), his agent, or a merchant or trader, would offer prepayment to indigenous communities or individuals in exchange for the obligation to provide a designated amount of goods in the future. Spanish individuals replaced indigenous traders as intermediaries between indigenous producers and the market. The repartimiento ensured that indígenas would continue to produce their valuable products, while cutting indígenas off from direct participation in market activity. By the eighteenth century, Terraciano writes of the Mixteca Alta, "commerce was dominated by Spaniards in all but the most local venues of exchange."[48]

While the repartimiento pushed many indígenas into debt and doubtless left them open to abuses at the hands of government officials and

merchants, it also provided them with credit and allowed them to participate, if indirectly, in markets to which colonial law and circumstance limited their access. For this reason, the nonindígenas needed relatively little
direct force to keep the economic system functioning. Above all, Oaxaca's
colonial economic system engendered relatively little overt resistance because it retained crucial elements of indigenous autonomy by keeping the
process of production local. If it severely limited the ways in which most
indigenous people could live and make a living, it nevertheless allowed
them to continue to do so under community control rather than through
either forced or wage labor.[49]

The Spanish state was crucial to this arrangement. First, it worked to
dampen potential conflict between villagers and local indigenous authorities. Villagers disagreed with their local leaders frequently over the limits
of their power, issues of land tenure, and claims on villagers' services. The
traditional nobility competed with nonindigenous individuals over access
to the labor of *macehuales*, or commoners, prompting many complaints.
Sometimes these disagreements became violent. Court records from the
late eighteenth-century Mixteca Alta reveal that one-quarter of all armed
assaults involved village officials, who were attacked in response to al-
legations of rape, physical abuse, embezzlement, and forcing villagers to
work illegally.[50] Villagers could, though, also take advantage of the Spanish framework of judicial appeal, in which the very same complaints could
be addressed. Villagers initiated litigation against the nobility and/or municipal leadership over the limits of authority, issues of land tenure, and
claims on villagers' services; in the process, the Spanish state became a
crucial resource for maintaining local peace.

Second, the state mediated disputes between indigenous villages, usually over the delineation of borders and control over land. The growing
fragmentation of the population into numerous small settlements combined with population growth in the late seventeenth and eighteenth centuries to prompt constant jockeying for control over limited amounts of
arable territory.[51] Such disputes could be violent, involving pitched battles,
kidnappings, and armed invasions. Yet, as often, villages relied on the state
for mediation. In the Valley of Oaxaca, indigenous villagers turned to the
courts to resolve land disputes at least fifty-two times in the eighteenth
century; thirty-seven of those disputes were between indigenous towns.[52]

Of course, indigenous villagers often had good reason to complain not
just about other indígenas but also about nonindigenous people. Quite
often, the target of their anger was the alcalde mayor. Spanish individuals
used this position to enrich themselves; because of the cochineal trade,
an alcaldía mayor in Oaxaca was one of the most desirable posts in New

Spain. It was usually alcaldes mayores who extended repartimiento loans to indigenous communities. Not surprisingly, when indígenas encountered problems, it was often alcaldes mayores whom they blamed. But alcaldes mayores nevertheless commanded a good deal of respect and obedience, in large part because they also provided crucial services to the indigenous communities. Technically, they were responsible for the protection of indígenas. As such, they provided one crucial avenue for legal redress through their role as *justicias*, or justices, in which they acted as the court of first instance in cases involving indígenas. Most importantly, they also had the power to authorize boundaries and to officiate in boundary disputes. This could make them the target of indígenas' wrath. Spanish officials were routinely threatened with rocks and sticks when carrying out border surveys and ceremonies of land possession. Without doubt, they were often hated figures, "devil-dogs" with "thieving cronies," as one set of rioting villagers put it. But at the same time, their power made them vital figures in relations of power between villages. Where disputes either between indigenous communities and indigenous authorities or between indigenous villages were the most common kinds of daily conflict, villages looked to the Spanish state and its representatives to mediate. In the process, the state gained moral authority, as officials were cast as the arbiters of justice, fairness, and protection.[53]

Oaxacan indigenous autonomy was, then, intimately tied to the Spanish state. Indigenous people expected to control their own labor, to choose their own leaders, and to police their own borders. But autonomy did not necessarily mean either unity or unanimity—Oaxacan villages were often rife with conflict—and when unity broke down in ways that could not easily be solved within and among the villages, the Spanish state became particularly valuable. The flip side of autonomy in Oaxaca was the importance of the state in its maintenance. For the nonindigenous population, this translated into a relatively stable environment in which indigenous communities continued to provide the raw materials for nonindigenous wealth, as long as the balance of force and accommodation could be maintained.

In 1786, that balance was suddenly threatened when the Bourbon monarchs of Spain reorganized and centralized authority in the empire. New officials called *intendentes* were created to represent the Spanish state in large districts—there were nine in New Spain—and the alcaldes mayores were replaced by *subdelegados* directly responsible to the intendents. For the first time, Oaxaca became a political unit of its own when an intendent was installed in Antequera in 1787. The Crown also abolished the repartimiento. For nonindigenous Oaxacans, this spelled potential disaster. Under the new laws, prepayment for goods was prohibited, and indígenas were now allowed to trade with any merchant on whatever terms could be negotiated. The prohibition of the repartimiento was a part of the Spanish Crown's larger attempt to increase tax revenue, professionalize the bureaucracy, and promote the freer circulation of goods; it was also presented as an effort to mitigate the abuse of indígenas. But for the nonindigenous people who depended on the cochineal and cotton trades, it threatened to undermine the structures that allowed them to profit from indigenous production. Even the subdelegados, the officials who were supposed to represent the end of the abuses perpetuated by the alcaldes mayores, found it difficult to operate without the repartimiento and often tried to circumvent its prohibition. The official end of the repartimiento thus touched off a long debate in which economic profitability for Oaxacan merchants and officials was measured against economic efficiency in the empire as a whole and against the well-being of the indigenous population.[54]

It was in this atmosphere that news of the fall of the Spanish monarchy to Napoleon in 1808 arrived in Oaxaca. In August of that year, a group of Oaxacan merchants met to sign an oath of loyalty to Ferdinand VII and then proceeded to accuse regional royal authorities of treason for having opposed the oath. Behind these actions was the desire of merchants and other members of the provincial elite to restore the pre-1786 system and in particular to restore the repartimiento. Prompted into action by the crisis in Spain, Oaxaca's nonindigenous elite demanded confirmation that government authorities would support the interests of nonindigenous merchants before they would expand rights for indigenous communities.[55]

Most notable is what Oaxaca's nonindigenous elites did *not* do. They did not call for either the destruction or the undermining of autonomous indigenous communities. The call for the restoration of the old system in Oaxaca did not imply greater direct government control over the indígenas. On the contrary, it reaffirmed the integrity of autonomous indigenous towns, hearkening back to the pre-Bourbon colonial era, when the state watched over the economic exploitation of autonomous indigenous communities. This seemingly backward-looking local reaction to the crisis of the Spanish monarchy makes sense in light of the longer history of the relationship among indigenous communities, the nonindigenous population, and the Spanish state in Oaxaca. The region's nonindígenas depended on indigenous communities to produce both the subsistence goods that made life possible and the export products that made for nonindigenous wealth. The relationships and accommodations that this situation necessitated would go far to shape the possibilities for liberalism in Oaxaca and thus the potential for change after independence. Nonindígenas would be prepared to do whatever they could to see that new laws did not upset their relationship with the indigenous communities. As it turned out, this would not be difficult, as village autonomy was one area in which Oaxacan indígenas and nonindígenas could agree—even if they disagreed on the reasons for maintaining it.

YUCATAN

For much of the colonial era, the relationship between indígenas and nonindígenas in Yucatán was similar to that in Oaxaca. According to one estimate, in 1639, Yucatán's indígenas, exclusively Maya, outnumbered Spaniards forty-seven to one. The majority of Yucatán's nonindigenous population lived in cities, while the indígenas lived largely in towns in the countryside.[56] And the survival of Yucatán's nonindigenous population depended on exploiting the surplus production and labor of autonomous indigenous villages. Yet there were crucial differences in the way the states' indigenous populations were integrated into the Spanish system. For most of its colonial existence, Yucatán was, in Nancy Farriss's words, the "periphery of a periphery," with no precious metals, a poor climate, and land ill suited to the production of most European crops. Whereas cochineal drove the state's relationship to Oaxaca's indígenas, Yucatán's Maya produced nothing in great demand outside of the peninsula. Before the eighteenth century, most landed estates owned by nonindígenas were engaged in ranching, not agriculture, and thus did not demand large amounts of indigenous labor. What's more, the decline of the indigenous population after contact with the Spanish meant that there was land available for these estates and that indígenas produced a surplus that nonindígenas could exploit. The indigenous population was nonetheless crucial to the nonindigenous population because it produced most basic foodstuffs. The repartimiento was less effective in Yucatán—there was no one commodity to demand from indigenous communities—so Spaniards used other methods of extracting resources from the indigenous population. They required indigenous communities to contribute regularly to central grain repositories to guard against famine among the Spanish population. And they relied on the *encomienda*, which granted individual Spaniards the right to collect tribute and demand labor from the indigenous population. The encomienda in Yucatán lasted well into the eighteenth century, far after it had been virtually abolished in most of New Spain, including Oaxaca.[57]

The Spanish dependence on indígenas in Yucatán, although profound, did not require the same kind of constant and consistent regulation of the towns that Oaxacan cochineal production demanded. Instead, for much of the colonial era, Yucatán's indigenous towns were left to run their local affairs largely on their own. Yucatán's administrative structure reflected this in that there were no alcaldes mayores. A variety of officials with different names—*capitanes a guerra, jueces de milpas,* and *jueces de granas*—had contact with indígenas, especially in the collection of taxes, but they had no real administrative authority over indigenous communities and were thus unlikely to develop the close ties of reciprocity that alcaldes mayores relied on in Oaxaca.[58]

As elsewhere in New Spain, the colonial state imposed a system of indigenous self-governance and assigned local leaders and councils administrative duties. Across New Spain, the duties of the repúblicas replicated precolonial structures to some extent. But in Yucatán, the indigenous councils retained striking continuities with their precolonial predecessors. The precolonial Maya community, known as the cah, was an indivisible entity, unlike Oaxacan communities where the indigenous nobility maintained complicated overlapping jurisdictions. Each *cah* was governed by a *batab* chosen from an "eligibility group" of local notables. Under the Spanish, the batab quickly became nearly synonymous with the colonial gobernador (eventually referred to as the *cacique*). And whereas the gobernador was intended to be elected annually, in practice batabs could stay in power for up to twenty years without interference. Batabs could continue to function under the new institutions without significant transformation of their role. Although Maya communities faithfully used the terms of Spanish municipal governance, they retained substantial control over the real content of daily administration.[59]

Two other important differences from Oaxaca stand out. First, unlike Oaxacan towns, Yucatecan villages were not permanent settlements that could be easily controlled and monitored by the Spanish administration. In the mid-sixteenth century, the church in New Spain had attempted to concentrate scattered indigenous settlements into fewer and larger towns where indígenas could be supervised by church and state alike. In Oaxaca, as in much of New Spain, these larger towns tended to fragment but eventually settled into relatively stable territorial units. In Yucatán, the policy's failure was farther reaching. Yucatecan land was arid and fragile, requiring constant rotation of crops, and the land that was understood to belong to a community could be widely dispersed. Not all members of Maya communities resided in or worked on land in a contiguous area, and the physical concentration of communities made little sense to villagers. Not only did many of the newly imposed units fragment, but the settlements that they separated into continued to fluctuate. Indigenous villagers moved from town to town, started new towns on the outskirts of existing ones, or, when they felt it necessary, fled beyond the borders of Spanish influence. The last of these was possible because the Spanish did not exercise firm control over the entire territory inhabited by the Maya.

But even within the territory that was controlled, the indigenous population was particularly ill disposed to stay put. Spanish control was always in question; it was hard to make demands on a population of which state administrators could not always keep track.[60]

Second, the need for indigenous villages to cede some autonomy to the government in exchange for certain services was less pressing in Yucatán than it was in Oaxaca. For much of the colonial era, the Yucatecan indigenous population did not put excessive pressure on the land, both because it was slow to recover from its initial decline after the arrival of the Spanish and because large parts of the peninsula remained sparsely populated. Combined with nonindígenas' relative disinterest in the countryside, the lesser intensity of the everyday struggle with other villages over the control of land meant that the state was less salient in many Yucatecan indígenas' daily lives than it was in Oaxaca.[61]

Certainly, to say that Yucatán's indigenous villagers lived lives isolated from the Spanish colonial state would be an exaggeration. Yucatán was without doubt a colonial society. Batabs maintained relationships, both economic and social, with Spanish society and acted as brokers between it and the villagers. And indigenous villagers had regular contact with Spanish authority in the form of parish priests, many of whom were also landowners. The demands of the state circumscribed many aspects of indígenas' existence, limiting returns on labor and exposing them to abuses in the collection of products and tribute. Indígenas also participated voluntarily in the nonindigenous economy, especially the market for grain, in which they acted not only as producers but also as transporters. Still, in comparison to Oaxaca, the day-to-day presence of the government and of nonindígenas was less intense.[62] The smaller presence of the government in Yucatecan indígenas' lives may have been as much a result of the weakness of the state as it was of the strength of the indígenas. Whatever its source, Yucatecan indígenas' notion of autonomy, far more than Oaxacans', meant being left alone.

When incursions on that autonomy came, then, the results were dramatic in Yucatán. Over the course of the eighteenth century, those incursions became increasingly common. The indigenous population was rising in the early eighteenth century, and nonindígenas could not rely on its surplus production for survival. In response, nonindígenas increasingly turned to direct production, and ranching estancias grew and were slowly transformed into agricultural haciendas, a process Matthew Restall calls "conquest by purchase."[63] Indigenous land came under increasing pressure, and the increase in nonindigenous agricultural production produced a need for labor, which could only come from the indigenous villages. By 1800, substantial numbers of indígenas were living on landed estates; in the areas of most intense agricultural production, the numbers could be as high as 50 percent. Still more indígenas engaged in tenancy relationships in which they exchanged a limited amount of labor for the use of a plot of land.[64]

Still, at the time of independence, most haciendas were quite small and were concentrated in the areas around Yucatán's major cities. Estate indígenas often retained ties to their home communities, performing both labor on the estancia or hacienda and services in the community to which they still belonged.[65] But there is little doubt that even in the eighteenth century many of the Maya towns of Yucatán were under assault from the nonindigenous population. This was also an assault on the unique autonomy of Yucatecan pueblos. Estancia and hacienda expansion interrupted structures of authority that had remained strong through most of the colonial era and curtailed indigenous mobility. Indeed, the constant demand for labor and land put the very existence of autonomous villages into question.

The changes of the eighteenth century arguably produced at least one concerted indigenous rebellion, led by Jacinto Canek in the town of Quisteil in 1761.[66] But what are most striking about this rebellion are not the actions of the indígenas but the responses of the Spanish. Farriss reports that the Canek uprising, although limited, threw the "entire Spanish community" into panic. This panic highlights the overriding sense in late colonial Yucatán that, despite increasingly large numbers of nonindígenas in most parts of the peninsula, indígenas still dominated and were still perceived to be just out of the control of the Spanish. Restall refers to the Spanish attitude toward the indigenous population as a "siege-mentality collective psychosis."[67] But the Spanish response is also indicative of the contradictions of Yucatán in the late eighteenth century. Yucatán now contained both areas in which indígenas were deeply integrated into nonindigenous life and economy and regions where Spanish control of the indígenas was still extremely tenuous. But the disjuncture went beyond geography. Yucatán's indigenous communities were in the process of moving from a relatively expansive autonomy to a severely curtailed one, and the potential consequences of this were apparent to nonindígenas. Despite practical changes, indígenas still thought of themselves as autonomous in a uniquely Yucatecan way and as deserving of that unique autonomy. Nonindigenous Yucatecans had to take this into account.

Despite their ever-present fear of indigenous uprising, in the final years before independence, nonindígenas had increasingly ambitious plans for their peninsula. As Howard Cline writes, by the beginning of the nineteenth century in Yucatán there was "a climate of opinion saturated by the spirit of enterprise." Not only did nonindigenous Yucatecans want to increase their direct control over goods for the internal market, they also wished to develop some of their products for export. What Rugeley calls "economic quickening" created increased tension in the villages and prompted competition among the various parties interested in village affairs, including priests, landowners, batabs, and the new Spanish subdelegados.[68] For the nonindigenous population of Yucatán, the events that began in 1808 offered a host of related opportunities, ranging from increased integration of indigenous communities to lessened restrictions on trade. As they worked toward these changes, however, they were constantly forced to consider the realities and limitations of their relationship with the indigenous population.

Oaxacan and Yucatecan indigenous communities both based their relationship with the state on a notion of autonomy. But "autonomy" held different meanings to each. Oaxacan communities expected to be allowed to run their own local affairs. They accepted, however, significant supervision on the part of the Spanish state and entered into extensive economic networks with nonindigenous individuals, often themselves representatives of the government. Indeed, the government's presence was in many ways *constitutive* of indigenous autonomy. Autonomy, in Oaxaca, meant autonomy not just from the state but also from other villages, something the state worked actively to maintain. By comparison, Yucatán's Maya sought to have, in the words of Pedro Bracamonte y Sosa, the "least harmful" relationship possible with the colonial state, at times by entering into agreements with it but primarily by avoiding it whenever possible. Restall writes that the Maya cah "exhibited a remarkable ability to expose itself to Spanish influence with the least amount of cultural compromise."[69] For nonindígenas in Oaxaca, indigenous autonomy was constitutive of the system that allowed for their economic success, whereas in Yucatán it was an obstacle to nonindigenous economic goals. It would be easy to overstate these disparities. But in the nineteenth century the differences would come to the fore for all parties, as they sought to accommodate new ideas, new institutions, and new structures of government.

From Colonial to Liberal:
Indígenas and the State after Independence

Among the changes that came with independence was the end of any official distinctions between indigenous and nonindigenous Mexicans. For Oaxacans and Yucatecans, the legitimacy of the state had long been built on models of justice and moral economy based explicitly on notions of what the state owed indigenous people and of what indigenous people owed the state. Autonomy, the notion that underlay that legitimacy, was intimately linked to being indigenous. The advent of a liberal system that did not recognize that identity as politically relevant had the potential to cause significant disruption in the relationship between state and indigenous society.

But what exactly did *indigenous* mean? What determined the boundaries of that group, and how did both indígenas and nonindígenas understand those boundaries? At the time of independence, *indigenous* had two fundamental implications. First, it denoted a specific group of people. The boundaries of this group were not always entirely clear, nor were they always the most important factor in how groups saw themselves or others. But most members of society operated on the assumption that those boundaries existed and that there was an identifiable indigenous population in Mexico. At the same time, *indigenous* was also a political and legal descriptor. Indigenous people paid tribute to the Crown. They lived in indigenous villages, and they addressed their grievances in special courts. *Indigenous*, in this sense, denoted not a group of people but the relationship that those people had with others in the empire and especially with the colonial state. Before the arrival of the Spanish, no common identifier for all peoples living in the Americas had existed. When the colonial state legally defined the term, it created a group and a political identity.[70] To be sure, previously existing identities that distinguished among groups of indigenous people remained extremely significant to many local relationships. Yet over the course of the colonial era, "indigenousness" acquired practical significance. It took on cultural, social, and racial meanings that were used to varying extents by indigenous and nonindigenous people alike. And it had real political power; both populations explicitly used it to justify political behavior toward each other and demands on each other's resources, and the assumptions that underlay it were codified in law.[71]

With independence, the meaning of *indigenous* was suddenly up for grabs. Legal distinctions among ethnic groups were antithetical to liberalism, which would ideally eradicate this kind of differentiation. But indigenousness had played such a central role in the practice of colonial politics that this change was unlikely to occur easily. Indigenous people and nonindigenous officials alike had long used the notion of ethnic difference to further their aims. As they sought to meet the requirements of the new institutions, both groups tried to retain the advantages that such differentiation had brought. Despite the official erasure of the notion of indigenousness, its practical meaning became an often explicit arena of negotiation, and it remained a basis for claims made by all parties. In the process, indigenousness became a central tool in the arsenal of those who sought to give new institutions practical content.

The strategies that indigenous people and the state government used to strike a balance between old and new did not prove the same in the two places, and the outcomes would be markedly different. In Oaxaca, the state was a largely willing participant in the process of rebuilding old relationships under new names. Entrenched political and economic structures, especially the relative autonomy with which indigenous people produced cochineal, meant that the elimination of explicitly ethnic distinction would not fundamentally threaten either ethnic privilege or ethnically specific exploitation. In Yucatán, the nonindigenous population was far more disposed to take steps to gain better access to the indigenous population. The Yucatecan state made concessions to indígenas grudgingly and only partially as it tried to accommodate a growing nonindigenous landowning class. The meanings of indigenousness in each place reflected these situations. In Oaxaca, ethnicity was largely unspoken both in the law and in the context of village politics. The division among groups was implicit; political and economic structures reflected but did not name ethnic differentiation. In Yucatán, on the other hand, the elimination of ethnic privilege was both explicit and incomplete, and both indigenous and nonindigenous people openly defended the relevance of indigenousness to further their goals. In the end, in Oaxaca, shared assumptions about justice and legitimacy were adapted to liberal institutions relatively peacefully; in Yucatán, the introduction of new institutions altered such assumptions, eventually provoking a violent rupture between state and society.

The character of liberalism in Mexico's regions derives not only from the actions of the indigenous population but also from those of government officials. Nonindigenous figures deserve more attention from scholars than they have often received. Local liberalisms were forged in the relationship between the villagers and agents of the state and in the various points at which their interests and aspirations intersected or conflicted. This book approaches representatives of the state not as "liberals"—they did not necessarily share a set of political beliefs—but rather as administrators trying to govern according to a set of liberal laws and institutions. Indigenous villagers and government officials had to confront two powerful realities as they sought to solve problems of governance and order in the early nineteenth century: The majority of the population was "indigenous"—a status that had long had legal and political meaning—and new liberal institutions were designed to erase indigenousness. The ways in which these two parties negotiated those two realities, and how they sought to find a common language that could incorporate both, is central to the formation of local political cultures.

Indigenous Citizens approaches these common languages not as constituting the whole "truth" of what either of the participating parties actually thought but rather as expedient vehicles for negotiation and political strategy. The historian's capacity to discern what "subaltern" individuals and populations believed has been the subject of much theoretical debate, and most scholars would admit that such capacity is limited. And, despite more readily available documentation, the same is, to a large extent, true of the government officials with whom indigenous villagers communicated. This book is explicitly concerned with what James Scott calls the "public transcript"; it analyzes the official communication between indigenous villagers and officials. The questions it asks are not primarily about the local motivations that may have underlain the positions of either party, motivations that I assume were often different from those presented in official communication. Rather, the book seeks explicitly to reconstruct the discursive ground that made negotiation between villagers and the state possible. How villagers and government officials presented themselves to each other, it argues, and the extent to which they could reach an agreement about the workings of their relationship through those presentations, is a crucial element of the construction, reconstruction, and sometimes the collapse of the legitimacy of the state and of its ability to govern.[72]

Summary of the Study

As this introductory chapter demonstrates, unique economic and political relationships between the Spanish colonial government and indígenas produced different kinds of expectations for self-administration among the indigenous populations of Oaxaca and Yucatán. And by the end of the eighteenth century, the goals of the nonindigenous populations of the two regions had diverged significantly. In many ways, Oaxaca's indigenous population, though fiercely protective of village autonomy, was more integrated into the state and into nonindigenous society than was Yucatán's; at the same time, Yucatán's nonindigenous population was more intent on changing the way it extracted resources from the indigenous population than was Oaxaca's. These crucial differences set the stage for the way that Oaxacans and Yucatecans would approach the rapid changes that began in 1808 with the collapse of the Spanish monarchy.

Those two approaches are detailed in Chapter 2. Both Oaxaca and Yucatán faced a challenge to local notions of autonomy when the government in Spain issued a liberal constitution in 1812. This constitution retooled not only the structures of municipal administration but also the legal status of indígenas, proclaiming them equal citizens of the new constitutional monarchy and eliminating the distinctions between indígenas and nonindígenas that had pervaded Spanish colonial government and society. Using local records of the establishment of new municipal bodies, Chapter 2 compares the experience of the creation of those bodies in the two regions. It demonstrates how, in Oaxaca, new institutional forms could be made to replicate old ones in many ways, as Oaxacan indígenas retained their ability to elect and participate in local government under new names. In Yucatán, the growing numbers of nonindígenas living in indigenous towns complicated the situation, as the new administrative bodies often fell into the hands of nonindígenas without entirely eliminating the influence of older indigenous authorities. Taken together, Chapters 1 and 2 demonstrate that local political relationships that had developed over the long colonial era strongly influenced the way that Spanish liberalism was received in New Spain's regions.

Chapters 3 and 4 address the period from independence until 1847, years that saw a cycle of changes in government, from a federalist to a centralist and finally back to a federalist administration. The state constitutions produced just after independence provided the legal framework for the implementation of liberal republicanism. Drawing on constitutional laws, legislative developments, and most importantly the extensive correspondence between indigenous village authorities and officials, these two chapters discuss how indígenas and state officials, accustomed to operating according to colonial assumptions about state legitimacy, adapted to new institutions after independence, developing new understandings of the responsibilities of the government and the rights of new indigenous citizens. In other words, these chapters detail the creation of Oaxaca's and Yucatán's local liberalisms.

Chapter 3 demonstrates that, in Oaxaca, the state and indigenous villages developed a relationship of mutual flexibility. Despite the swings between federalist and centralist political systems, the state and indigenous citizens, in most cases, maintained a stable association based on constant negotiation over issues important to both—taxes, the draft, village government, and the use of village lands. In many ways, the Oaxacan government exercised only tenuous control over the internal affairs of indigenous villages. To ensure a minimum of cooperation from indígenas, it had to remain responsive to villagers' needs. Indigenous villagers, for their part, accepted sometimes exorbitant taxes and demands upon their labor in exchange for flexibility, a measure of autonomy, and the state's protection. And significantly, under federalist and centralist regimes alike, both indígenas and the state government made adjustments that kept this relationship in balance, by reworking changing institutions to accommodate both of their needs. In short, the legitimacy of the Oaxacan state depended on the continued willingness of both state officials and citizens to make concessions, not on specific federalist or centralist institutions.

By contrast, indigenous Yucatecans came to associate good government with particular institutions, a process that is detailed in Chapter 4. Here, where pressure on indigenous land and autonomy was greater, indigenous villagers had less power to shape the form that liberalism took. Federalism, with its built-in assumptions about local power, proved more suited to the protection of indigenous interests than did centralism. During the first federalist era, Yucatecans too developed a shared local liberalism. But the agreements that underlay it were always tenuous, and they came under obvious strain under centralism. On federalism's return in the 1840s, however, the state became increasingly intrusive, attempting to wrest control of land from indigenous villages and making more and more tax demands. As a result, indígenas came to believe that the government was unlikely to fulfill its promises under either system. By late 1847, faith in the shared political culture of federalism had been destroyed, the government had lost its tenuous legitimacy among many indígenas, and the state was on the brink of war.

Chapters 3 and 4 demonstrate that the ideas and institutions of liberal republicanism could be made both to strengthen and to erode the bases of stability in local places. In both states, the state and indígenas initially forged local political cultures that drew on both liberal and colonial languages and institutions. But differing exigencies of governance and economics meant that the various parties who participated in local politics were not equally committed to the maintenance of shared local liberalisms. By 1847, Oaxacan indígenas and nonindígenas had adapted a preexisting relationship to accommodate liberalism, and they agreed on many of the basic terms of that relationship. Yucatecan nonindigenous elites, despite gestures toward that older relationship, used aspects of liberal ideology to sanction activities that made that relationship seem increasingly unworkable to the indigenous population.

Chapters 5 and 6 discuss the attempts of the two governments to transform the structure of administration in their states after 1847. In Mexico as a whole, this year marked the beginning of the consolidation of a national liberal movement that hoped to realize, finally, the transformations that Mexican liberalism had been supposed to bring about. It also marked the beginning of proactive conservative politics. Both sides of the debate would propose changes to the way that the government dealt with the indigenous population. But like the local liberalisms that had developed in Mexico's states after independence, reform would also be a local affair. The changes that the Oaxacan and Yucatecan governments attempted were contingent on the relationships that the governments had developed with indígenas in the preceding years. Accordingly, the governments' success or failure would also be affected by the exigencies of those earlier relationships. Even as they drew on ideas and proposals produced at the national level, Oaxacan and Yucatecan administrators and indígenas continued together to make the national local.

Chapter 5 addresses the years between 1847 and 1857 in Oaxaca. For much of this time, Oaxaca's governor was the liberal activist and reformer Benito Juárez. The Juárez administration focused on improvement of the administration of town finances and of education, both of which would theoretically prompt indígenas to behave in a manner more befitting the liberal citizen. One of the central features of that liberal citizen would be the disappearance of his distinct ethnic identity; citizens, liberalism posited, should not be indigenous or nonindigenous but simply Oaxacan. But state-sponsored reforms came up against a political culture dependent on ethnic distinctions and a body of practices that were identified as "indigenous custom." Oaxacan officials had to make concessions to custom because they understood that it made governance of indigenous villages possible. In the eyes of indigenous people, among the most important customs was that of communal landholding. This came under attack nationally in 1856 when the Ley Lerdo decreed the privatization of village lands. When they worked together to implement the law in its first few years, Oaxacan government officials and indígenas drew not only on custom, and not only on the tenets of liberal reformism, but also on their long-standing agreement that one of the government's most important roles was the protection of village autonomy and thus of village land. In Oaxaca, liberal reforms could only go forward if all parties were willing to make compromises, which they proved remarkably willing to do.

In this same period in Yucatán, by contrast, the government believed that compromise was no longer possible and that the adoption of universal male citizenship had been a mistake. Chapter 6 discusses the reaction of the Yucatecan state to the massive indigenous uprising that would come to be known as the Caste War. When the war began in 1847, the Yucatecan government revoked the equal citizenship of indígenas, a declaration that the government controlled the way that indígenas could exercise their political rights. Noncombatant indígenas had to choose between accepting their new status or joining the rebels; yet, as the government began to gain the upper hand, the latter option seemed less and less viable. Although it would never entirely disappear, the old relationship of duty and obligation between state and indigenous society thus crumbled in the years after the start of the Caste War. The closing of spaces for negotiation, intended by the state government to facilitate its administration of the indigenous population, also facilitated an economic transformation. As the war came to an end, nonindigenous encroachment on indigenous land—which had contributed to the Caste War in the first place—accelerated. Now, however, the indígenas could not draw on their older understandings of the state but rather had to scramble to negotiate a new political culture that offered them little protection. In Oaxaca, where the government embraced liberal reform, daily politics impeded the "liberal" transformation of land tenure. In Yucatán, where the government rejected political liberalism but embraced economic liberalism, private ownership of land would become the norm, at the expense of indigenous villagers.

Together, the chapters of *Indigenous Citizens* draw on both national and local stories and consider the ways that those stories intersect. The common experience of this period was the negotiation of new relationships between state and society after the collapse of colonial institutions. In Oaxaca and Yucatán, that negotiation began with the 1812 Spanish constitution, which altered the terms of local autonomy. It continued in the twenty years after independence, as indigenous villagers and the nonindigenous state reconstructed the terms of the governments' legitimacy. And it reached a turning point in the late 1840s and 1850s, when both state and national governments embarked on programs of reform. Autonomy, legitimacy, and reform were crucial arenas of political negotiation and conflict in this era. Liberalism, both as a set of institutions and as a proactive movement, had something to say about all three. But, in practice, what it had to say would be tempered and shaped by local politics and by the aspirations of local people, both indigenous and not. Liberalism did not lack its own character; rather it forced people across Mexico to consider a similar set of issues. But because those issues had different implications in different contexts, early Mexican liberalism was refracted, malleable, and local. This book reconstructs the peculiar relationship between a national ideology and the local political cultures that shared its name.

CHAPTER 2

The Institutional Revolution in Town Politics

OAXACA AND YUCATAN, 1812–1821

IN MAY 1813, ONE YEAR AFTER the passage of a new, liberal Spanish constitution, Ceferino Domínguez, the newly elected alcalde (mayor) of the
Yucatecan town of Nohcacab, reported a sudden burst of disorder among
the indigenous population. A group of *"Yndios revoltosos"* had incited the residents of a small settlement outside of town to live "as if independent from
justice," refusing to hear mass, confess, or pay their church fees. Things
were not much better inside the town, where, he explained, the *cacique*, the
town's highest indigenous official, was constantly drunk and mistreated
the Indians under his charge. Yet despite his behavior and despite the new
authority represented by Domínguez, the cacique still commanded respect
and obedience among the indígenas. Every day, Domínguez wrote, one
could see "mobs of Indians that this cacique calls to the town hall without
a known reason." The alcalde was quite certain about the source of all this
disorder. It began, he said, with the decree of the Spanish Cortes issued on
November 9, 1812, which had declared Indians free of the tax and service
burdens of the colonial era and proclaimed their equality with Spaniards.
Since this decree, Domínguez opined, all Indians were living "without God,
without Law, without Religion."[1]

There is little doubt that the impetus for the villagers' actions was, as
Domínguez claimed, the implementation of the new system. But to what
precisely were indigenous people reacting? On the one hand, their actions
seem to be a rejection of the colonial order and an embrace of the liberal.
The trappings of colonial control of which Domínguez lamented the demise were all inextricably linked to the juridical inequality of indígenas:
the religious structures that labeled indigenous people as permanent minors under the close observation of the clergy, the notion that Spaniards

should have some control over the administration of towns inhabited entirely or mostly by indígenas, and the tax structure based on a fundamental distinction between *indios* and *españoles*. In abandoning those things, indígenas, arguably, were merely exercising their new rights. On the other hand, the villagers' actions also made a clear statement about their attachment to the *colonial* order by expressing loyalty to the cacique. Caciques had no legal standing in the new order and indeed represented the very distinctions between indigenous and nonindigenous people that liberalism aimed to displace. Continued faith in the cacique, then, suggests that indígenas did not embrace liberalism unequivocally. Indígenas may indeed have taken the radical idea of equality very seriously in the case of their colonial obligations, but they maintained a deep attachment to self-rule in the villages and thus to a structure of authority rooted in juridical distinctions between indígenas and nonindígenas. Indigenous Yucatecans thus actively embraced some aspects of the new order while ignoring others.

Officials also proved ambivalent about liberalism. Central to Domínguez's complaint was that the indigenous villagers would not recognize his authority as alcalde. That position was created by the liberal 1812 constitution and represented the shift to universal suffrage and individual citizenship. But Domínguez's conclusions about the consequences of the change reveal his own attachment to colonial notions and forms. As he saw it, by not recognizing his authority indigenous people had proven themselves incapable of comprehending the new liberal order. To him, the decree of November 9 had been fundamentally misguided. The Yucatecan countryside could not accommodate liberal equality, as it could lead only to disorder. Things, Domínguez seemed to suggest, should go back to the way they used to be.

The incidents in Nohcacab occurred in the midst of tremendous changes in New Spain. In the seventeen years between 1808 and 1824, residents experienced the collapse of Spanish monarchical authority, its modification in a liberal Spanish constitution, its reinstitution as an absolutist system, and finally the independence of the republic of Mexico. Uncertainty over the location of authority led them to articulate competing visions of their place in the Spanish empire and eventually to consider and realize the possibility of severing ties with the metropole. These experiences forced residents of New Spain to contemplate the implications of new political and ideological systems and in particular to confront the introduction of liberalism. The process began in Spain, when Napoleon's toppling of the Spanish monarchs triggered the organization of a *Junta Central*, or central committee, claiming that in the absence of the true king sovereignty devolved on the representatives of the people. After a power struggle between rival offshoot bodies, the liberal junta in Cádiz gained control of the opposition and convened the legislative sessions known as the Cortes of Cádiz. With the participation of both Spanish and American deputies, the Cortes produced a framework for a constitutional monarchy, rejecting both the relatively decentralized Habsburg oversight that had characterized the sixteenth and seventeenth centuries and the more recent Bourbon absolutism of the eighteenth. In 1812, the Cortes approved a new constitution for Spain. And by 1813, a host of new laws, including the one Domínguez complained about, institutionalized the notions of popular sovereignty and individual citizenship.[2]

The Cádiz constitution was promulgated in Mexico City in September 1812 and soon after in the provinces, but it remained in effect for only two years. In 1814, the Spanish opposition regained control over Spain, and Ferdinand VII resumed his throne. The king, however, refused to abide by the new constitution and attempted to reestablish himself as an absolute monarch on the Bourbon model. But six years later a rebellion in Spain called for the reinstatement of the constitution, and Ferdinand eventually agreed to sign it back into law. There were, then, two periods of Spanish constitutional government in New Spain, between 1812 and 1814 and again from 1820 until 1821, when, after an uprising led by Agustín Iturbide, Mexico declared its independence. Not all parts of New Spain were equally affected by the constitution, which was unevenly implemented in the war-torn colony. Oaxaca did not put the constitution into practice in 1812; instead, the insurgent army of José María Morelos entered the capital city of Antequera that year and set up a rebel government that lasted until 1814. But relatively speaking neither Oaxaca nor Yucatán was a center of rebel activity. In Yucatán during both constitutional periods, and in Oaxaca during the second, Spanish reforms were implemented in a context of relative stability. In these two regions, the overriding experience of the years from 1808 to 1821 was not war, as it was for much of New Spain. Instead, both regions grappled with constitutional, ideological, and political change.

The events that took place between Napoleon's invasion of Spain in 1808 and the passage of the Constitution of 1812 did not constitute a revolution against Spanish rule in the Americas. Yet, as the incident from Yucatán demonstrates, they struck at the core of the agreements and understandings that underpinned the Crown's legitimacy. First, by raising questions about the king's authority in the American colonies, these events opened the door for Creoles—people of Spanish descent who were born in and resided in America—to articulate and often act on their desire for autonomy within the empire. And second, by introducing liberal reforms into Spanish law, the 1812 constitution prompted a complete reconsideration of the nature of political personhood. For the first time, Spanish subjects were also to be "citizens," both exercising a range of political rights and participating in a system based in theory on popular sovereignty. And also for the first time, indigenous and nonindigenous people would participate in the Spanish system not as members of separate ethnically defined polities but as undistinguished individuals within one single res publica.

These two movements—for Creole autonomy and for universal citizenship—were in crucial ways at variance with each other. For if Creoles were to be autonomous, they wished also to be in charge, and the liberal impulses emanating from Spain did not unequivocally support that desire. Creoles had benefited from the ethnic hierarchy maintained by the colonial system; they saw themselves as rightfully exercising authority over indigenous labor and resources. Spanish liberalism—in particular its insistence on juridical equality—was bound to upset this assumption. Unlike its colonial predecessor, the new system assumed that indígenas had no distinctive legal personality and thus that no formal ethnically specific mechanism of control could exist. The extinction of institutions that had supported colonial ethnic differentiation was a foregone conclusion.

For Creoles, the potential results of this change were ambiguous. They would now have a chance to assert direct authority in indigenous communities where their influence had long been limited by colonial rules of self-government. But they might no longer be able to depend on indigenous authorities as mediators and facilitators of Spanish policy. For indígenas, too, the implications of the changes of 1812 were ambiguous. The foundations of indigenous autonomy, long the central characteristic of Mexican indígenas' relationship with the state, suddenly shifted under their feet. One indigenous response to the changes would be retrenchment; indígenas in both Oaxaca and Yucatán sought to retain their ethnically defined autonomy even in the new context of liberal equality. At the same time, local circumstances would determine to what extent indigenous people could and would also seek to benefit from constitutional changes.

It was during Spanish constitutional rule that villagers and the state first engaged in negotiation over liberal institutional change. Each element of liberal law displaced and altered some element of colonial law, and these changes were keenly felt among indigenous and nonindigenous people alike. Despite its many failings, colonial law had made sense to both groups in crucial ways. A certain logic had governed the colonial status quo, and agreements about the meanings and the limits of Spanish power had allowed for a relatively quiescent relationship between Spanish authorities and indigenous subjects. Conflict was rife in colonial New Spain, but it had to do as often or even more so with violations of that logic and those agreements than it did with disagreement with their fundamental bases.[3] When put into practice, liberal laws tore that logic and those agreements apart, and rural Mexicans were faced with the task of building new concepts of state legitimacy that were compatible with liberalism yet not destructive of contracts and distinctions that both indigenous villagers and nonindigenous officials continued to see as crucial.

In some ways, this process of reconciling the old and new would be relatively smooth. Recent scholarship has shown how the nature of the Cádiz reforms facilitated the process. François-Xavier Guerra has examined the notion of "citizenship," showing how Cádiz-era thinking cast it as simultaneously modern and traditional, not as the introduction of entirely new rights but rather as the recuperation of rights that had been unjustly usurped by the monarchy. Even elections, which were ostensibly designed to reflect the will of individuals, reflected the continued importance of corporate identities in both their form and their understood purpose. Guerra reveals that hybridity was built into the Cádiz reforms, both because the laws themselves proved ambiguous and because those who put them into practice did so in the context of the survival of a "traditional imaginary" in which the "registers" of tradition and modernity were not irreconcilable.[4] At the outset, then, the traditional and the modern were in constant dialogue in New Spain, and the new institutions were open to interpretation.

Yet the actual process of interpretation would occur not just at the level of lawmaking but also on the ground when new institutions were put into practice. In the indigenous villages of places like Oaxaca and Yucatán, the need to interpret was immediate, as villagers responded to a sudden change in structures of local governance that served as instruments not only of administration but of identity, social control, and even survival. The dialogue between indigenous villagers and the state over the meanings of liberalism began early and with relatively little disruption in Oaxaca and Yucatán. Thus, when independence came to these two states, it was in crucial ways the culmination of a process of transition to liberalism rather than a beginning. By the time of the passage of the first Mexican national constitution in 1824, and by 1825, when local constitutions were passed in the states, both indigenous and nonindigenous Oaxacans and Yucatecans were already aware of the kinds of changes and accommodations that liberalism required and were well on the way to making them.

Political Participation in Constitutional New Spain, Oaxaca, and Yucatán

Among the most important changes that Spanish liberalism required was the significant expansion of political participation. The 1812 constitution introduced three major innovations. The first was to declare that, with important exceptions, all men who traced their lineage to the Spanish possessions in either hemisphere and resided in a town within those possessions were "citizens" as well as subjects of the Spanish empire. The second was to allow these new citizens to vote in elections for deputies to the Cortes in Spain. And the third was to allow all of those citizens (rather than just a select few) to elect the town councils known as *ayuntamientos*.[5] Together, these activities were understood by the deputies at the Spanish Cortes to constitute citizens' exercise of popular sovereignty.

But *sovereignty* had different meanings for the state than it did for many citizens, especially indigenous and rural ones. In theory, in participating in elections for the Cortes, citizens were choosing the men who would represent them. But the Cortes elections were extremely indirect. Voters met at the parish level to select electors, who then traveled to the seats of their districts to choose another set of electors, who then met in the district capital to select the deputies who, finally, traveled to Spain.[6] Guerra argues that the indirect form of the elections recapitulated traditional forms of representation in that the electors and deputies represented an abstract "will of the people" rather than a concrete set of aspirations. There were no candidates and no campaigns; potential electors and deputies were not supposed to have different opinions or different plans but were chosen instead because they were recognized as the most apt because, as Jaime Rodríguez O. puts its, villagers "trusted them and because they believed that these individuals possessed the education and the experience necessary to defend local interests." If debate occurred, it was over the qualities of the potential elector or deputy, not over his opinions. In any given community, it was usually clear who the best candidate according to these criteria would be; the majority of electors were chosen from among local functionaries and the clergy.[7]

Thus, novel as elections for deputies were, their indirect nature, along with traditional assumptions about the electoral process, meant that they had far less immediate significance to most rural people than did elections for local office. In the latter, one knew precisely for whom one voted, what his duties would be, and how those duties might affect one's affairs. For the state, then, sovereignty was composed of a combination of political participation through the vote for deputies and local self-administration through the vote for town councils. But, locally, most new citizens would see the election of ayuntamientos as the central act of sovercignty, and it would have much farther-reaching effects than would elections for deputies on the way that most newly minted citizens understood the importance of the Spanish liberal system.[8]

This disjuncture between intention and practice was particularly apparent in America. The colonies had not been the primary target of the new municipal laws; rather, the democratization of ayuntamientos had its origin in uniquely Spanish concerns. The peninsular liberal project had as one of its central aims the dismantling of the seigniorial system that reigned in the Spanish countryside and the elimination of the power of the nobility. A crucial tool in accomplishing this change was to be the elected local government. In America, where virtually no nobility had been allowed to develop, such concerns about the power of hereditary fiefdoms did not exist. Rather, American deputies at the Cortes supported the formation of ayuntamientos because they believed that they would strengthen Creole autonomy and increase the weight of American representation within the Spanish system. In colonial New Spain, ayuntamientos had existed only in large towns, where they were often the bastion of the Creole elite in the absence of access to other forms of power and in the presence of powerful appointed peninsular officials; these ayuntamientos were relatively few and far between. When they argued for more ayuntamientos, then, the American deputies were hoping for more Creole institutions in towns with large Creole populations. But the overriding preponderance of Spanish deputies at the Cortes meant that, when the new provisions were codified, the privilege of electing a town council would be open to almost everyone. Inevitably, in the American colonies, this included the indigenous population. The legislators in Cádiz ruled that where it was "convenient," towns would elect ayuntamientos; all towns that had at least 1,000 inhabitants must have ayuntamientos, but towns that were smaller *could* have them as well.[9] This opened the door to a new form of local administration in a wide variety of places, including indigenous towns in New Spain.[10] It was thus primarily through the ayuntamientos that citizenship would be extended to New Spain's indigenous population.

In Oaxaca and Yucatán, these changes presented both potential advantages and potential problems not only for indigenous communities but also for provincial governments. In the eyes of the framers of the constitution, the new councils would bring an expansion of local sovereignty. But indigenous people in New Spain already had an institution that facilitated something like local sovereignty: the república de indígenas. After 1812, in indigenous towns, the ayuntamiento technically replaced the república. But the ayuntamiento was not precisely the same as its predecessor. The new ayuntamientos were not intended to serve a representative but merely an administrative function, and they were intended to reflect the desires of individual citizens, not of the commons. Most importantly, whereas the república was elected only by the indigenous population, the new municipal councils were to be elected by the population of each town as a whole.

Thus, for indigenous people, the ayuntamientos represented a new and possibly disruptive way of designating authority within villages, especially in that they raised the possibility of sharing power with—or losing power to—local nonindígenas. For provincial governments as well, the value of the new system was ambiguous. The ayuntamientos eliminated the legal requirement of recognizing traditional indigenous authorities but at the same time threatened to loosen the legal and traditional bonds that governed the state's relationship with the indigenous population. Officials worried whether the state would be able to retain access to the products, labor, and taxes that it had long extracted from the villages. Thus, who exactly would gain and lose from the change was not immediately clear.

In this context of ambiguity, the transition to the new institutions would work out differently in different places. Between Oaxaca and Yucatán, differences hinged on the divergent nature of the two regions' economies and the political assumptions that undergirded them. In Oaxaca, the nonindigenous elite depended on the autonomous production of indigenous villages to maintain their often considerable wealth. They thus faced a contradiction between new structures of village administration that stressed universal citizenship and older needs that called for a continued distinction between indigenous production and nonindigenous commerce. In Yucatán, by contrast, elites saw indigenous villages as the untapped resource that could facilitate the launching of a new market-oriented boom in what had long been an extreme periphery of the Spanish American economy. They embraced the notion of universal citizenship because it offered them access to previously inaccessible indigenous resources and labor. And yet their more tenuous control over indigenous villages at the outset made the implementation of that ideal both difficult and dangerous. In the end, the two states emerged from the Spanish constitutional experience with political assumptions altered by the introduction of liberalism in peculiarly local ways.

THE POLITICS OF LOCAL ADMINISTRATION IN OAXACA

The wars of independence arrived in Oaxaca in 1812 when the rebel leader José María Morelos triumphantly entered Antequera in November. There was considerable violent conflict in that city and in the nearby Mixteca, which constituted an important passage between the viceregal capital and the province of Puebla, but the fighting itself never reached great proportions in other parts of the Oaxacan countryside.[11] A rebel administration governed the province until 1814, when royalist troops entered the city. Thus, rebel forces were in control throughout the first period of Spanish constitutionalism. But the rebel government did not have much chance to put its often radical ideas about social organization into effect and certainly not beyond the confines of the capital city. There is little clear evidence of how much control the rebels exercised in the countryside, but it seems that, both under the rebels and the royalists, the colonial system of town government remained the norm.[12] Repúblicas de indígenas continued to be elected regularly throughout these years, but there is no record of any ayuntamientos elected in the villages.[13] Thus, when the liberal Spanish government reissued the decree calling for ayuntamientos in 1820, the councils had to be elected from scratch. In 1820 and 1821, then, the government scrambled to oversee the creation of new town councils throughout the province.

In his study of this process of "municipalization," Rodolfo Pastor argues that the formation of ayuntamientos represented "the violent plundering of [indigenous] political prerogatives and the abolition of racial segregation," resulting in a drastic loss of autonomy for indigenous pueblos and the ascendance of a white and mestizo elite. "In the future," he wrote, "the Indians would not have an exclusive political space in which to express themselves, nor an organ that would represent their particular interests." Certainly, the laws threw village government in Oaxaca into disorder, as both new institutional requirements and new political concepts were confronted and absorbed. However, the disruption caused by this initial phase of the transition to liberalism did not fundamentally alter either the state's relationship with the pueblos or indígenas' ability to govern themselves.[14] Because indígenas dominated the Oaxacan countryside, new ayuntamientos were dominated by indígenas, and there was little threat of nonindigenous incursions on local authority. To be sure, the new laws demanded that indígenas reconceptualize local political power both within the villages and between them. In practice, however, the new institutions did not disrupt the central notion that indígenas should govern themselves with a significant degree of autonomy from the regional government. For Oaxacan political elites, for whom this system had long worked in a relatively stable and productive fashion, there was little impetus to change. Indeed, they proved willing to negotiate solutions to any problems that arose, particularly when those problems threatened the stability of the relationship between the government and the villages.

In October 1820, authorities in Teposcolula began the process of ayuntamiento elections. Writing to the royalist official in the cabecera of Tlaxiaco, Manuel Megía sent along a copy of the constitutional laws regarding elections and recommended that the local priest explain the constitution to his parishioners, "in order that the people be instructed in the great purposes that our wise government proposes on establishing order and method in these elections."[15] From then until mid-1821, Spanish officials struggled with the complicated process of determining which of the numerous small indigenous pueblos under their jurisdiction should elect ayuntamientos. In Oaxaca, Spanish officials such as Megía exercised a great deal of control over the process of the creation of the new councils, deciding which villages could have ayuntamientos, overseeing the elections, and helping villagers negotiate the change. The state had long supervised the election and functioning of the repúblicas; it would do the same for the ayuntamientos that replaced them.

The change from one form of administration to another was not, however, entirely seamless. Government officials observed a considerable amount of disruption and confusion. In particular, they found that it was impossible to maintain a one-to-one correspondence between repúblicas and ayuntamientos. According to the new laws, only pueblos that had at least 1,000 residents had the automatic privilege of electing town councils. But in Oaxaca, with its extremely fragmented population, very few villages fulfilled this requirement. In Teposcolula, for instance, most towns could claim only several hundred community members. Although some such towns did apply to elect their own ayuntamientos, the Oaxacan government generally demanded the aggregation of small towns into electoral units that would then elect a single council. In March 1821, for instance, the towns of San Vicente Ferrer, Santa María Nduayaco, Santo Domingo Ticú, and San José de Gracia, the combined population of which came to more than 1,010 people, agreed to join together to create one ayuntamiento after government officials rejected their requests to elect separate councils.[16] In cases like this, the pueblos were to agree upon some method of power sharing. In one aggregation of three villages, for instance, leadership of the council would rotate according to the following arrangement:

Each year . . . the job of Alcalde revolves, first on some individual of the Pueblo of San Juan: in the next year on one of San Pedro Mártir and in the third of San Andres de la Laguna: . . . [T]he *Regidor* who results or *síndico* of their respective Pueblos, should oversee public order, and if there is no obedience, he should be aided according to the case that occurs, by the Alcalde or by the entire Ayuntamiento, and the annual election should be celebrated in the Pueblo of the Alcalde [whose term] has ended. . .[17]

According to this arrangement, clusters of villages would work together in some things but not in others, each village retaining autonomy under the authority of one of the councilmen unless there was conflict that required intervention from the shared alcalde.

Many villagers met this attempt to unite previously autonomous towns with distrust. Subjection to another village in some matters was not in and of itself the problem; in much of Oaxaca, villages had long been arranged according to the cabecera/sujeto system, whereby several villages were subordinate to a central town.[18] Instead, the conflicts were often specific to the particular villages included in the aggregation. The town of San Antonio Monteverde, for example, had previously been subject to the cabecera of Chilapilla. Under the new system, however, its population was united with that of the town of San Marcos. In April 1821, the regidor (councilman) and *principales* (elders, or prominent men) of San Antonio complained that under the new arrangement, "we have experienced a disturbance of government." The present alcalde was from San Marcos, and "said Alcalde wants with too much authority to insult us and impose on us taxes . . . for anything [he wishes]." To solve this problem, the villagers wanted not to be released entirely from outside control but rather to be returned to the authority of "our cabecera Chilapilla."[19]

Objections to aggregation could also be reactions to the prospect of uniting with a pueblo already perceived to be an enemy. San Francisco Nuzaña, for example, did not wish to unite with the town of Magdalena because the two villages were involved in pending litigation, and "the sons of the one view with total rivalry the sons of the other."[20] In another case, representatives of six Mixteca pueblos—Santa Catarina Tlasila, San Bartolomé Satola, Santa Marta Yolotepec, San Juan Talistlahuaca, Santiago Camotlán, and Santiago Ystalhua—noted that even their combined population amounted to an aggregation of only 719 villagers, making it "almost impossible to complete the number suggested by the wise constitution" to establish an ayuntamiento. State authorities had proposed that they should thus add their population to that of other pueblos that were located at some distance from theirs, a measure they thought was unacceptable, both because of the difficulty of travel and because it would require them to "mix ourselves with others of diverse customs." They thus requested permission to elect an ayuntamiento among themselves despite the shortfall in population, a privilege that the local Spanish official granted.[21] The same official reacted similarly to a case involving the towns of San Martín Huamelupan, Santa Cruz Tayata, San Pedro Mártir Yucuxaco, and Santa María del Rosario. Here, the pueblo representatives complained that they were all to be attached to the large town of Tlaxiaco, that this aggregation was made against their will, and that the great distance to the seat of the ayuntamiento would be prohibitive to good town government.[22]

The confusion over what to do in cases like these delayed the creation of many ayuntamientos indefinitely. In fact, the process was so taxing to the official in charge that in March 1821 he asked to be able to turn the job over to someone else, arguing that to continue would mean the near abandonment of all his other duties.[23] But if delay was problematic for government officials, it was often more so inside the villages. While provincial authorities deliberated on what to do (or perhaps simply failed to resolve the issue), towns were experiencing crises of authority. In many villages, the old repúblicas had remained in power pending the transition to the new system. But república posts were supposed to be only one-year tours of duty. By March and April 1821, many individuals had been serving in these posts for upwards of fifteen months. For these men, the danger was not of losing power but rather of keeping it. República posts could be expensive, as officials were expected to devote time and often money to village administration. The officials in the town of Yucunama, for example, foresaw disaster if they were not allowed to step down soon:

It is constant that the individuals that make up the body of the república in particular are significantly harmed, because in order to attend to our obligations, we forget our families, houses, duties, and what's more our crops which facilitate our annual sustenance, and it is clear that we perish from hunger for this cause, and we fear what will happen to us in this year if we remain in the duty (*cargo*) that we have suffered for fifteen months.

Not only were the officers of Yucunama in financial trouble, they were also losing control of the village, where "the *vecinos* (inhabitants) no longer respect us, nor obey us. And aside from our being extremely sensitive to this scorn in particular . . . it all redounds on harm to peace and public tranquility."[24]

Indeed, all over the district of Teposcolula, outgoing indigenous officials complained that they were unable to retain authority over their indigenous constituencies. Now that the regime transition had held up the process of turnover in the town governments, villages were experiencing a new kind of crisis, as the authority of local officials in office for too long was questioned. For many pueblos, the creation of an ayuntamiento became an imperative not just because it was legally mandated but because it meant the end of this interim during which there was no recognized authority in the village. The imperative held for both the outgoing officials, who were unable to maintain control over a recalcitrant populace, and the rest of the townspeople, who were forced to endure the rule of officers they saw as illegitimate. Most pleas for intervention from the government came in the form of requests for a *cambio de varas* (change of staffs), the term for the ceremony in which the staff of office was passed from incoming to outgoing officers under the supervision of a Spanish official. Until this ceremony occurred, the old república was still in power. What most pueblos wanted from the government was official recognition of the council that they had elected or were to elect; whether the council would be called ayuntamiento or república was of secondary importance.

At the same time, conflict over the new councils could also reflect knowledge of the innovations that the ayuntamiento system introduced. The authorities of San Pedro Tidaá, for instance, wrote that the lack of obedience on the part of their fellow villagers, prompted by the illegitimacy of the república after its term of duty had expired, was aggravated by the fact that "the system that governs is a different one than that of the present one of the constitution."[25] The authorities of San Francisco Nuzaña were even more explicit:

[T]he sons [of the pueblo] do not obey because . . . there should be an Ayuntamiento, and the Gobernador and other officials do not conform to the present system whereby an Alcalde has more authority than a Gobernador, and that in the Pueblo we lack that privilege, to which they add that the present república expired at the end of last year.[26]

Outgoing village authorities often paired these two explanations for crisis together. The república was considered invalid because it had overstayed its official term of office and also because it was not an ayuntamiento. Such cases most likely resulted from power struggles within the villages touched off by the new laws. The laws governing the election of the ayuntamientos represented a drastic broadening of the franchise within villages and introduced new sectors of the population into the practice of politics. This change had the potential to throw traditional forms of local government into disorder.

And yet, in the eyes of Spanish officials, the shallowness of the change was discouraging. When one official asked his superiors for advice on the many difficulties he was encountering, he complained that the villagers of San Bartolomé Soyaltepec had taken it upon themselves to elect a new council made up of "Gobernador and other officials of the República, created in the old system, and this is contrary to what is required in the constitution." This was a problem in the whole of his district: "Most of the pueblos of this partido are applying to solicit the cambio de varas in the old system, or that of illegitimately elected Ayuntamientos."[27] Thus, while some villages seemed to be taking advantage of new laws to effect real change in how authority functioned, others used them to perpetuate an older system of local power.

All in all, continuity in local administration outweighed change. By 1821, many if not most indigenous villages had their ayuntamientos; according to one estimate there were 232 established municipalities in the state by 1822.[28] Some were probably much like their predecessors, while others may have reflected the villagers' embrace of new liberal forms of allocating authority. But all were locally elected, and all, crucially, reflected the continued autonomy of the pueblos and, in particular, of indigenous people.

Continuity in assumptions about indigenous self-governance is clear even in cases from towns where Oaxaca's minority nonindigenous population clustered. Here, villagers had, in the past, worked out methods of allowing self-government for each group. As Oaxaca's intendent Francisco Rendón put it,

The old political institutions wisely established in [these towns] two repúblicas, one of Indians, and the other of Pardos, and so it is that, although united in residence, they are governed economically by Alcaldes and Regidores of their particular nature, and they maintain order and tranquility without resentment of being judged one by the other.[29]

The advent of the ayuntamiento system, which demanded only one shared council, had the potential to upset such arrangements. The new ayuntamiento could, in these cases, pose the very kind of threat to the indigenous community that Rodolfo Pastor observed, in that new mestizo councils could replace the old indigenous repúblicas. In some places, especially larger political cabeceras, this did happen.[30]

In smaller towns, though, the situation would prove more complicated. Here, too, the ayuntamiento posed a threat, not to the indígenas but to minority nonindigenous communities who feared an end of legal separation would mean an end to their own autonomous governance within the indigenous milieu they inhabited. In particular, they were concerned that in a universal election, the indigenous majority would easily gain control of the government and the indigenous officials "in no case will know how . . . to govern the others, neither will those accommodate themselves to it." These were the words of José Joaquín Péres, a representative of the southern coastal town of Huazolotitlán, which had 470 *casta*, or mixed-race, families. Convinced that the indígenas of his town were sure to win any general election, Péres proposed that the castas should continue to have their own separate ayuntamiento. For many such towns, political amalgamation under the indígenas was similarly unthinkable. An official in the region of Tehuantepec asked what should happen in the town of Juchitán, which was composed of both indígenas and a smaller population of mulattos. Should these two "repúblicas" be governed by one "Ayuntamiento de Yndios," or should they elect two ayuntamientos, "one of each class"? In the case of the town of Yxtaltepec, where the numbers were reversed, the same official wondered "of which of the two classes should [the ayuntamiento] be composed?" And Rendón, the intendent, complained that after the ayuntamiento elections in the regions of Tehuantepec and neighboring Jamiltepec, in towns that originally had "diverse repúblicas," the nonindígenas "will inevitably remain subject to the Indians," a sure recipe for resentment and disaster.[31]

There is no evidence of how these multiethnic towns eventually resolved their constitutional crises. But outside of major towns, all parties seemed to assume that indígenas should continue to govern themselves. At no point during the Spanish constitutional interim did either local nonindigenous people or regional officials suggest explicitly that indígenas should not have control over their local affairs, and at no point did their actions suggest that they were eager to supplant the indígenas and control the towns as a whole. Even where nonindígenas had a significant local presence, they did not take advantage of the situation to diminish indigenous autonomy. In short, the early implementation of the liberal municipal system did not prompt any significant questioning of whether indigenous self-governance was a desirable thing. The transition introduced some problems for the state and for indígenas, to be sure, but neither threatened the fundamental basis of indigenous autonomy nor fundamentally altered the balance of power in the countryside.

THE POLITICS OF LOCAL ADMINISTRATION IN YUCATAN

In Yucatán as in Oaxaca, institutional innovations during the Spanish constitutional period transformed local structures of power. Yucatán's experience, however, was far more conflictual and, in the long run, far more transformative. Before the eighteenth century, Yucatán's elite had also depended on the indirect exploitation of production in indigenous communities. But by 1812, the Yucatecan economy was based increasingly on direct production by nonindígenas and on the paid labor of indigenous individuals who would have to be drawn away from their towns. Thus, whereas Oaxaca's nonindigenous population was largely content to maintain village autonomy even after the new constitution offered the possibility of change, many of Yucatán's nonindígenas wished to assert more control over village affairs.

By the turn of the nineteenth century, the transformation of Yucatán's economy had progressed significantly. The towns had an increasing number of nonindigenous residents well-positioned to take control of the new constitutional ayuntamientos. So, in some ways, the laws of 1812 seemed perfectly suited to facilitate the changes nonindigenous people desired. But indigenous autonomy would not prove to be an easy target. In the early nineteenth century, Yucatán was considered to be—and in many ways was—an overwhelmingly indigenous place, a near frontier of European settlement. In large parts of the region, state control over the indigenous population was tenuous at best. And even where control was clearly established, indigenous communities retained a good deal of autonomy. This was a different sort of autonomy than that of Oaxacan indígenas, whose status was always defined closely in relation to both their concessions to and their demands on the state. Yucatán's communities had long proven resistant to state attempts to curtail their independence.

Between 1812 and 1821, the Yucatecan state would try to accommodate both this entrenched indigenous autonomy and the desires of nonindígenas to lessen it. The creation of ayuntamientos seemed well suited to fulfilling the latter goal. But it also brought conflict in the countryside as indígenas and nonindígenas jockeyed for control. Indígenas frequently rejected new nonindigenous authorities, sometimes withdrawing their support for Spanish government as a whole. Terry Rugeley calls the upheaval of these years "the Caste War's first rehearsal," in that it provided the indigenous peasantry with an experience of organized dissent and revealed the possibilities of agrarian revolt.[32] This may well have been the case. But of more immediate significance, the disorder revealed the limits of Spanish access to indigenous communities. As in Oaxaca, the events that followed 1812 forced both the state and indigenous villagers to define and redefine their relationship and cleared the way for a unique local conception of the place of indigenous villagers in the republican polity. But in contrast to the Oaxacan experience, in Yucatán the Spanish liberal experiment also revealed the contradictions between the interests of the state's various constituencies, as the government found itself caught between the demands of the nonindigenous population and the exigencies of governing indígenas.

Before 1812, the nonindigenous individuals living among Yucatán's indigenous population, mostly small-scale commercial agriculturalists, had formed something of a community apart. They were not officially under the jurisdiction of the colonial repúblicas, nor did they technically have a role in either the election or the administration of those local councils. Yet they were certainly affected by república administration, especially regarding the use of resources such as water and land. They thus led an anomalous and sometimes insecure life, and the institutional rearrangement laid out in the 1812 constitution offered them the possibility of real change. In Yucatán, the shift to a system of universal participation in local government would have a particularly profound effect on the nature of local administration, as a growing sector of the population that until now had been unable to exercise control over its immediate environment was suddenly given the chance to vote and serve on local councils. While in

Oaxaca nearly everyone agreed that the new constitutional ayuntamiento would be a largely indigenous institution, in Yucatán it provided an opportunity for the growing rural population of nonindigenous people to make incursions on de facto indigenous control in the countryside.[33]

Rugeley and Marco Bellingeri have both examined Yucatecan *planes de arbitrios*, the plans drawn up by town representatives in 1813 and 1814 to demonstrate the towns' ability to function as constitutional municipalities. These documents show that indigenous people often did participate in the formation of the new town councils but also that their participation was neither universal nor evenly distributed. Some ayuntamientos were entirely indigenous, while others had no members with Maya surnames. In most cases, there were one or two indigenous participants.[34] It is quite likely that the indigenous political elite was expected to take part in some way in the formation of the ayuntamientos; indigenous officials were, after all, usually the only administrators that a town had had, and their participation was essential to local legitimacy. This was true even in towns where indígenas were not the vast majority. Thus, in the western towns of Chicbul and Sahcabchén, with relatively high percentages of nonindigenous residents—approximately 40.2 and 30.7—the ayuntamientos had some members with Maya surnames as regidors and, in the latter case, as the town's legal representative. Even in Buctzotz, where in the 1780s above 80 percent of the residents were nonindigenous, indígenas were involved in the request for an ayuntamiento.[35]

Given the long history of indigenous self-government, however, what is striking is not indigenous participation in the ayuntamientos but rather the relative lack thereof. There is little doubt that, for the most part, the newly elected councils were staffed by nonindígenas. In the town of Tahdzibichén, for instance, which had a small 16.7 percent nonindigenous community, only half the members of the new ayuntamiento had Maya surnames.[36] Relatively complete records exist for the election of the ayuntamiento in the town of Ucú, near Mérida. Ucú's elections took place on February 6, 1814. The residents of Ucú elected sixteen electors; and of these men, half had Maya surnames. On the six-member ayuntamiento they selected, however, only one man, Juan Santos Chan, was likely to have been indigenous.[37] The election process winnowed the majority of indigenous candidates out, producing a mostly nonindigenous council.

These new, largely nonindigenous ayuntamientos assumed the institutional role formerly held by the indigenous councils. In land disputes from the early 1820s, the ayuntamiento was consistently the major player. Ayuntamientos were expected to turn in plans for local spending to be approved by the *Diputación Provincial* and to collect taxes, as one official in the Costa district emphasized in 1820. They were also responsible for local education and for the building and repair of schools. Clearly ayuntamientos had become a real force in village life, and clearly most ayuntamientos were controlled by nonindígenas.[38]

This did not mean that explicitly indigenous interests would no longer figure in local politics. Even where the ayuntamiento was controlled by nonindígenas, it often recognized and sometimes even advocated the unique interests of its town's indigenous community. For instance, when the ayuntamiento of Hampolol, a town located in what is now Campeche state and having more than 80 percent nonindigenous residents, became involved in a land dispute with neighboring *hacendados* in 1823, it cited the provisions of the Laws of the Indies dealing with communal land for indígenas.[39] Most towns, unlike Hampolol, still had indigenous majorities; these majorities were too important to the functioning of any town to be ignored, and traditional rights were deeply engrained.

In addition, although the ayuntamiento theoretically replaced the república, in practice the repúblicas themselves would not simply disappear. The tacit abolition of the repúblicas by the distant Spanish Cortes had limited effect, as repúblicas were largely self-perpetuating and the state made no move to force them to stop functioning. For the most part, indigenous people would continue to elect repúblicas and to see the older councils as their legitimate representatives. As Antonio Escobar Ohmstede has observed elsewhere in Mexico, the introduction of alternative and nonindigenous administrations "did not prevent indigenous pueblos from carrying out their own forms of self control (government, economic and religious administration, customary law, etc.)."[40] The repúblicas remained. And so, after the election of ayuntamientos, many Yucatecan villages found themselves with two local councils.

But the relationship between the two was not necessarily one of competition. Villagers were quick to recognize the importance of the ayuntamientos, and there was substantial indigenous interest in participation in both the new councils and in the old repúblicas. Meanwhile, nonindigenous council members recognized the authority of the repúblicas in crucial instances. Regular government activities such as census taking necessarily involved the traditional indigenous officials because, in practice, nonindigenous ayuntamiento members often could not keep track of the indigenous population. The indigenous hierarchy also had a hand in land transactions, such as the arrangement in Tiholop in 1823, which involved both the ayuntamiento, as the deciding party, and the cacique, who certified the claims made by the individual concerned.[41]

Still, the advent of the new councils did place an intervening party between the indigenous communities and the state, and the new universally elected town councils forced indígenas to share local power with nonindígenas for the first time.[42] In 1813, for instance, in Champotón, a town on the west coast of the peninsula that was approximately two-thirds nonindigenous, the newly elected ayuntamiento wrote to the Diputación Provincial to report on a request received from the "principal Indians of this pueblo in the name of their *común.*" Apparently, these principales had requested the division of village lands, but the ayuntamiento was convinced that they had none, "not even with the name of Community."[43] In this town, the ayuntamiento was clearly not a replacement for the older indigenous council, as the indigenous community still called on traditional, ethnically specific leaders to represent itself. But the ayuntamiento had taken on the role of representing the indigenous population to higher authorities, with unfavorable results for the indígenas. The insertion of the ayuntamiento into towns' communications with the provincial government had the potential to and would soon become contentious.

Indeed, it was soon clear to nonindígenas that gaining control of local government did not automatically mean gaining control over the people to be governed and over the resources they represented. The implementation of the new constitutional system prompted many of Yucatán's indígenas to assert their own autonomy and retreat from imposed village structures. Indigenous villagers took advantage of the crisis of authority on the peninsula to express their dissatisfaction, abandoning their duties to local landowners, agents of the state, and the church. They deserted haciendas, refused to pay taxes, and failed to attend schools and masses. And they often cited the constitution, which ended personal service and abolished religious taxation, as their justification.[44] In the end, conflict in rural Yucatán after 1812 would center around the issue of governability and the question of how, quite literally, to keep the indígenas in their place.

The church was a direct target of the indigenous reaction. Priests responded to events with alarm, claiming by 1814 that indigenous villagers were abandoning their duties en masse. Both parish priests and their superiors interpreted this retreat as a direct response to the 1812 proclamations, in particular the abolition of Yucatán's religious taxes, known as *obvenciones.* High church authorities complained that the loss of these taxes would eliminate a major source of church income and destroy the fabric of authority that held local parishes together. After 1812, Yucatán's priests claimed to be seeing the evidence of this disaster unfolding before their eyes. In the town of Uayma, for instance, near the eastern city of Valladolid, Fray Pedro Guzmán complained in May 1813 that since the publication of the new constitution, he had lost control of his parish. The Indians were, he claimed, misinterpreting the constitution to mean that they were released from the "obligations of a Christian" and that the churches should be closed and abandoned. He could not convince his parishioners to provide the services they owed to the church, not even by offering them double pay. "Every day," he wrote, "the insubordination increases, until it is almost an insurrection."[45]

In late 1813 or early 1814, higher church authorities took the initiative in investigating such incidents by sending a questionnaire to priests stationed in indigenous villages, asking them if they had observed any signs of rebellion among their parishioners.[46] In response, a number of priests reported failings similar to those of the villagers of Uayma, claiming that their charges were not participating properly in the religious life of their towns. Several priests made an explicit connection between the insubordination they were observing and the new institutional context, just as had Guzmán. As Don Juan Pío Albarado y Domínguez, the *cura* of Tixcacaltuyú, wrote in 1814, "the lack of obedience, subordination and respect that appears in the Indians may be in part the effect of the influence of certain seducers; but the principal cause is that they now consider themselves exempt from all punishment, the only thing that they have feared."[47]

In interpreting this seemingly universal indigenous retreat from the villages, however, Yucatán's priests may have overestimated the particular significance of the church as the target of indigenous anger. Yucatecan indígenas were quick to take advantage of their legal liberation by refusing to pay both religious *and* secular taxes, abandoning churches and schools, and generally failing to submit to Spanish authority. As Rugeley has noted, the indigenous reaction in 1812 was often confused and unfocused and consisted of indígenas taking advantage of the situation to try to right a variety of wrongs, both sacred and secular.[48] Such wrongs were highly local in nature and thus called for specific local responses. Not all villagers reacted similarly to the lifting of colonial burdens; in Espita, although the children were not coming to school, the local priests had heard no news of either a retreat from the town or an abandonment of the haciendas. One priest reported from Ichmul that no news at all of Indian retreat had come to his notice.[49] Disorder in the years after 1812 was generalized but not consistent, and its causes were difficult to pin down.

It is clear from the reaction of government officials that they saw the problem as extending far beyond the church. Even where indigenous actions were clearly aimed at religious authorities, the state, too, responded with alarm. The government was highly dependent on the church, which in colonial Yucatán often provided the closest approximation to representatives of the Spanish state in the villages. Because parish priests facilitated taxation and labor drafts, the state counted on priests' ability to influence the actions of indigenous communities. But the decrease in church authority after 1812 alerted the state to the woeful inadequacy of this situation. By the 1820s, representatives of the state were fast realizing that their control over what happened in the villages was far too tenuous. They did not, however, agree with the church that the solution was to return to colonial structures. Instead of seeking to shore up the church, they increasingly sought a secular solution. In the midst of the chaos, state officials thus saw an opportunity to assert their own control. The new constitutional ayuntamientos seemed to offer the perfect tool to do so; increasingly, regional representatives of the state would turn to these new councils as a way of both reestablishing order and of wresting control of the indigenous population from the church.

The problem was that the establishment of ayuntamientos had itself exacerbated the disorder by threatening indigenous autonomy. Villagers in towns where ayuntamientos pressed their authority could react to this new and often unwelcome imposition just as they did to their sudden "freedom." In 1814, for example, the first act of the new ayuntamiento of Ucú was to select auxiliary alcaldes for three neighboring *ranchos*, San Antonio Papacab, San Antonio Huch, and San Antonio Telchac. Of these three men, only the new alcalde of Telchac had a Maya name. By May 1814, the other two men were in trouble and asked for the Ucú ayuntamiento's help in containing the locals' disobedience. If the population did not begin to obey, the alcaldes would have to penalize them, "severely applying enough punishment to contain the abuses and insurrections that have occurred against order and the common good, seeing that obedience is the principal base on which the honest administration of justice is supported."[50] These nonindigenous officials observed in their new constituencies the same kind of behavior that priests were seeing; they saw it, however, as a threat to *secular* authority.

Administrators nevertheless expressed great hopes for the ayuntamientos; if they could be strengthened, they believed, the councils could provide a solid presence for the state in the indigenous villages. To varying degrees, administrators hoped that the new town councils would foster democracy in the villages, eliminate obstacles to the administration of indigenous communities, and, once and for all, consolidate Yucatán's towns into something approaching the ideal the Spanish had been promoting since the earliest years of the empire. Secular administrators were just as concerned with the dispersion of the indígenas as were their ecclesiastical counterparts. Their reasons, however, were not entirely the same, nor were their proposed solutions. While the church argued that a liberal system that failed to support its religious base was morally bankrupt, the members of the Diputación Provincial were convinced that the answer to the problem of control over the indígenas lay in the new structures proposed by liberal Spain.

As early as 1814, the Diputación made a clear statement of its priorities when its deputies exhorted the priests to take advantage of the power of the councils. Thus, in response to Father Guzmán in Uayma, the Deputy for Valladolid suggested the following:

[Father Guzmán] should turn to the Political Chief of the district . . . and to the respective Constitutional Alcaldes, and they will help him in pastoral care, compelling and obligating those who lack plots of land (*milpas*), occupations, or known modes of subsistence to work and serve with preference to the Parishes for prudent pay [so] that they punctually attend to all their Christian duties, punishing those who are stubborn and rebellious.

The Diputación suggested that nonindigenous power in the villages—in particular, power over the villages—was no longer to be the sole preserve of the priests. Religion, it conceded, was vitally important, but it would be the ayuntamientos who made it possible for the priests to function. The deputy hinted at further secular action to stem the tide of withdrawal: "Very soon, this Diputación will circulate a Plan of general and economic government . . . in all the inferior Pueblos of this Province, which will end as much as possible these maladies."[51]

Such assertions indicated a profound ideological shift. Just as they pushed for secular control over the villages, the deputies also projected a new and more secular characterization of the villages themselves and promoted a definitively civic rather than religious ideal. Deputy José María Ruz responded to the disgruntled mayor of Nohcacab, Ceferino Domínguez, with this suggestion:

If generally it has been necessary that men live in society, under the order and immediate watch of their respective authorities, because failing this, ignoring the law, people will lack education, enlightenment, and Religion, and far from being useful to the state they will be [unreadable] to their Patrias; with greater reason we should avoid this pernicious abuse in the class of the Natives, who unfortunately . . . have been regularly abandoned to their passions. . . . I feel that you should circulate decisive and clear dispositions to the Ayuntamientos, so that they . . . avoid these arbitrary settlements and destroy those already established, effecting a reunion of the individuals of which they are composed and locating them in the nearby Pueblos that are most convenient.[52]

Ruz envisioned the new councils as a tool to enforce the final congregation of the indígenas into towns and to integrate them into the larger polity as educated citizens and sovereign political beings. Since the earliest years of colonization, the indígenas had been resistant to Spanish attempts to get them to live consistently in towns. But the major Spanish player in such attempts, in the past, had been the church. Now, in the hands of the Diputación Provincial, the town ideal had a new liberal and democratic face, and the vehicle of its dissemination was clearly to be the ayuntamiento.

The new institution of local secular administration, the ayuntamiento, thus became a central component of a new state project. Unlike its Oaxacan counterpart, the Yucatecan ayuntamiento was a decidedly nonindigenous institution, one that was intended to and indeed did disrupt the very structures that the Oaxacan councils helped to maintain. It is worth noting, however, that the interests of the state were not precisely the same as the interests of the non-indígenas who staffed those councils. State officials were concerned with taxation, political control, and a civic ideal; they believed that the ayuntamientos could help facilitate these needs. Nonindigenous town residents—and the nonindigenous population of Yucatán as a whole—were concerned with control over indigenous resources. While state officials certainly also desired such control, they were well aware of the potential disruption and resistance from indígenas that pushing that agenda would cause; the disorder of the implementation of the laws of 1812 had made that potential painfully clear. Thus, whereas in Oaxaca the state, villagers, and the nonindigenous population could agree on the importance of the autonomy of the villages, in Yucatán, rifts between the interests of the three parties were already becoming clear.

Antonio Annino has argued that the establishment of ayuntamientos in small villages in the Spanish constitutional period and beyond opened a breach in the colonial system of social and political control, providing an opportunity for communities to deepen their autonomy from the central state. Citing the large numbers of ayuntamientos established, especially in highly indigenous areas, Annino asserts that the villagers' interpretation of the role of the new councils led to "the disintegration of the Viceregal political space" and to a shift of the locus of power from the cities to the countryside. As Annino suggests, the establishment of ayuntamientos did not have precisely the same effect everywhere, and the key to regional differentiation lay in the ayuntamientos' relationship with their predecessors, the repúblicas. This relationship varied widely over the territory of New Spain, depending both on the density of the indigenous population and on the persistence of indigenous forms of government. Ayuntamientos and repúblicas were ideologically at variance, the first based on liberal assumptions about equality and universal citizenship and the latter on colonial ethnic distinctions. But, in practice, both government officials and indigenous people sought ways of making the new bodies serve at least some of the same functions as the old, especially that of mediation between the indigenous population and the state. Such mediation was vital, especially in both Oaxaca and Yucatán, where almost the entire nonindigenous economy revolved around the capacity of nonindígenas to exploit the capacity of the indigenous population. Depending on who controlled it, the ayuntamiento could either provide a tool to enhance that capacity, or it could potentially undermine it.[53]

In comparing Oaxaca and Yucatán, it becomes clear that what happened after 1812 hinged on two factors. To what extent could the new councils be made to replicate the older ones in practice? And to what degree did the local and regional nonindigenous elite desire that replication? In many ways, these two factors worked in opposite ways in Oaxaca and Yucatán. From early in the colonial period, indigenous autonomy had been composed of different elements in the two regions, and this would prove vital to the way that the transition to liberalism affected the relations between indigenous villages and regional governments. The differences between the two were accentuated by a process of economic change in Yucatán that had begun in the eighteenth century, one that had no significant parallel in Oaxaca. Whereas Oaxacan indígenas and the Oaxacan state continued to maintain a mutually acceptable balance of demand, obligation, and independence, Yucatecan indígenas were facing a determined assault on what had been an even deeper autonomy.

Oaxaca after 1812, then, more closely resembled Annino's model, as villagers elected ayuntamientos in indigenous towns where few if any nonindigenous individuals resided. While it was often disruptive within and among villages, however, the process of implementing this system did not fundamentally alter the relations of power between villagers and the state. Instead, it was an affirmation of a kind of autonomy for indígenas that had been carefully constructed during the colonial era. Because they were not fundamentally interested in—or perhaps simply had little hope of—altering a successful system of economic exploitation, most Oaxacan nonindígenas had little motivation to reverse this situation, and few stepped in to try to extend their control. In Yucatán, by contrast, the ayuntamiento seemed to offer nonindigenous elites a way to diminish indigenous autonomy within the towns and thus to advance their own economic aspirations. Here, the most notable effect of the establishment of ayuntamientos was the granting of political rights to nonindigenous newcomers; these individuals quickly moved to take advantage of the new institutions and, just as quickly, to displace indigenous authorities. This rapid shift to nonindigenous town government threw the Yucatecan countryside into disorder, as indigenous people reacted to what they saw as a violation of long-standing arrangements of fair and just government and as the tenuous hold the Yuctecan state had on indigenous communities came to the fore. This opened up a gap between the interests of the

Yucatecan state and the Yucatecan elite, as the state sought to avoid the widespread disorder that change might bring. In Oaxaca, on the other hand, the state enjoyed a firmer hold over the population, as local Spanish officials and indigenous villagers were already integrated into a mutually agreeable system that allowed for both village autonomy and state oversight. As for local nonindígenas, they were few and far between. With some hitches, the Spanish liberal experiment in Oaxaca allowed for a replication of the system that both townspeople and the state had participated in for years.

To be sure, the implementation of new institutions during the Spanish constitutional era was often piecemeal and, without doubt, too rapid and chaotic to change fundamentally the way that the state and its new citizens understood each other. And yet, in the events of the chaotic years of 1812–1814 and 1820–1821, it is possible to see the beginnings of the construction of new relationships between state and society, relationships that accommodated the trappings and sometimes the intentions of liberalism while adapting them both to local circumstances. In both Oaxaca and Yucatán, the town council would come to stand at the center of those relationships. It would do so in a way that reflected not only preexisting colonial structures but also the aspirations of both villagers and the state. In the years between the implementation of the Spanish Constitution of 1812 and the independence of Mexico, indígenas and nonindígenas took active part in a learning process, one that they would build and expand on in the years to come, as they collectively determined what, precisely, liberal citizenship in independent Mexico would mean.

CHAPTER 3

Reluctant Taxpayers, Unwilling Soldiers, but "Submissive Sons"

OAXACAN VILLAGES AND THE STATE, 1824-1848

IN 1825, OAXACA'S STATE GOVERNMENT attempted to grant a monopoly on salt production on the isthmus of Tehuantepec to one nonindigenous individual. Resistance quickly surfaced among the indígenas who had previously used the salt beds, especially in the town of Juchitán. Ten years later, the Juchitecos again resisted incursions on their rights to the salt, now in response to the Oaxacan state's claim on income from the beds and changes in tax law. Their rebellion, carried out with the aid of a local landowner named José Gregorio Meléndez, was put down. But soon enough, other pressures on the villages developed. In 1836, the state allowed the private purchase of the lands that had been the seigneurial possessions of the family of Hernán Cortés, and the new owners began to make claims on land long held by Zapotec indígenas. In 1843, the Oaxacan government sold the salt beds. Although the purchaser never consolidated his control and Juchitecans retained much of their access, in 1847 Meléndez once again led an army of isthmus villagers in rebellion, this time sparking a conflict that would last until the early 1850s. Among other demands, this rebellion called for the restoration of lost village lands.[1]

If one focuses on this chain of events, liberalism appears to have been a disruptive and destructive force for indigenous people in Oaxaca in the years after independence, one that provoked a sustained and violent response.[2] Yet, in Oaxaca as a whole, the Isthmian rebellions were an exception. As Chassen-López points out, there were only two "true regional rebellions" in Oaxaca in the first half of the century. Although there was constant low-level conflict on the village level throughout the state, for the most part Oaxaca did not witness the sort of large-scale violent uprisings that characterized much of Mexico. Historians of Mexico's transition to liberalism have tended to concentrate heavily on such large-scale violence.[3] Yet, like the upheavals, the more peaceful state of affairs in most of Oaxaca most of the time demands explanation.

This chapter makes two central claims. First, Oaxaca's relative quiescence was not the result of the absence of liberalism. Oaxacan villagers after independence did not, as one scholar puts it, "retrench . . . into an isolated world characterized by near self-sufficiency" but rather engaged in constant negotiation over the implementation of liberal laws.[4] In the first two decades after independence, those laws and the institutions they established became deeply engrained in Oaxacan ways of doing politics. And second, as they engaged those laws and institutions, Oaxacans forged a local liberalism, a system understood to be liberal—and following the most basic dictates of the new regime—but at the same time meeting the needs of the population and the state.

This striking ability to absorb new institutions without fundamental disruption reflected a unique stalemate between the two parties. The primary aim of the Oaxacan government in the years after independence was to ensure that the residents of the villages pay the taxes and provide the labor that would make the new state of Oaxaca function. For the villages, the primary goals were survival and the preservation of autonomy. Each party was uniquely suited to fulfill the other's needs. In the game of Oaxacan politics, neither indigenous villagers nor the state government entirely held the upper hand; for either party to push harder on the other was always risky. Liberalism, in both its federalist and centralist incarnations, might have offered the government the tools to break this stalemate by destroying the notion of indigenous privileges. And, indeed, Oaxacan officials were not inherently unwilling to use liberal ideas in this manner, as they did in Tehuantepec. Alternatively, the weakness of the state might have offered indigenous villagers the opportunity to push their own interpretations of liberalism through concerted violence. Again, they were not inherently unwilling to do so, as they did on the isthmus. Yet few Oaxacans, overall, wished to endanger the benefits that all parties reaped from the system as it stood.

This stalemate translated into a durable state legitimacy that withstood frequent institutional change. Between 1824 and 1848, the governing system at the national level shifted frequently. The year 1824 brought the final establishment of the Mexican federal republic; in 1836, a centralist government supplanted the federal system; and in 1846, the nation returned to federalism. In these years, Oaxacan villagers paid taxes to and provided soldiers for federalist state authorities, centralist state administrators, the national centralist state, and the national federalist government. Under all of these regimes, they sought and often found every opportunity to avoid burdens they could ill afford. That this situation did not produce more conflict stemmed in part from the inability of the Oaxacan and Mexican states to enforce their demands. But at the same time, Oaxacan villagers rarely questioned the right of the state to make those demands in the first place. They accepted a fundamental assumption behind their ties to the government: that in exchange for certain advantages villagers remained obligated to the state.

Behind this agreement was a paradoxical economic reality. On the one hand, in the words of Sánchez Silva, Oaxaca's indígenas were "the possessors of the wealth." The products that drove the Oaxacan economy—especially cochineal and cotton cloth—were primarily indigenous products, produced autonomously in indigenous villages. This made the nonindigenous population deeply dependent on those villages. Individually, however, most indígenas did not derive much material benefit from this situation. The wealth, such as it was, was spread thinly over the indigenous population. In addition, after independence, the price of cochineal dropped consistently, so that even greater production could not produce great profits, and the cotton trade contracted significantly.[5] And so, Oaxaca's villagers were generally very poor. Government officials knew this; in the words of an early governor, "not producing with their personal labor anything other than a small day's wage, [they] scarcely acquire what is necessary for their sustenance."[6] Nonindigenous officials, then, faced a quandary. Their own livelihood and security depended on pressing the indigenous villages for the maximum possible production, the maximum possible payment of taxes, and the maximum possible number of draftees. But, at the same time, everyone in Oaxaca was well aware that the indigenous population was unable to provide all that nonindígenas wanted and needed.

That government officials acknowledged their constituents' poverty was central to the political culture created in Oaxaca in this era. To be sure, government officials complained constantly about indígenas. But they also consistently expressed a sense of responsibility. The colonial notion of protection of indigenous people continued to permeate politics in independent Oaxaca. Indígenas insisted that because they were poor they were in need of flexibility, sympathy, and aid from the state. More often than not, officials responded by providing such protection. This implicit contract served as the ideological underpinning of the stalemate between state and indigenous communities, combining with economic and political realities to make Oaxaca's state–indigenous relationship strikingly impervious to change.

Understanding this political culture helps to explain why the swings between federalist and centralist institutions caused, relatively, so little disorder in Oaxaca. Federalist institutions were more obviously suited to the state, in that they allowed for wide variation in state administrative systems and for the maintenance of village autonomy. But centralist institutions, despite their implication of more direct state control over village affairs, did not, in Oaxaca, result in fundamental disruption. After 1836, indígenas and representatives of the state government continued, as they had since 1812, to negotiate mutually acceptable ways of using new institutions. In the end, the introduction of centralism solidified rather than threatened the legitimacy of the Oaxacan government by reinscribing the parameters of the relationship between state and citizens. Institutional change was a major feature of the Oaxacan political experience in these years. And, yet, the fundamental bases of the relationship between state and society remained much the same. Local circumstances gave Oaxacans a remarkable ability to turn change into continuity.

By 1847, something crucial had nevertheless occurred, as liberalism became a central element of the language of the Oaxacan state and of the language that the state and villagers used to communicate with each other. It was not, by any means, the only element. But each time villagers and officials had to confront and negotiate the meaning of a new institution, a new law, or a new concept, they introduced liberalism into their political world. Oaxacans did not, generally speaking, reject liberalism. Most embraced it. They did so by turning it into what they wished it to be. And as long as they could make liberalism work for them, they would think of themselves as having a system that was fundamentally liberal and that adhered fundamentally to the requirements of the national state. This does not indicate the irrelevance of liberal ideology in Oaxaca, nor does it reveal an essential ignorance or confusion about that ideology on the part of either indigenous Oaxacan villagers or Oaxacan state administrators. Rather, it reveals that ideology was subject to local interpretations and, crucially, that those interpretations could subvert the intentions of liberal laws, institutions, and concepts without explicitly rejecting the laws, institutions, and concepts themselves.

Oaxaca's New "República de Indios"

Oaxaca began to break from Spain in June 1821, when Antonio de León, a Creole army captain who had fought against the insurgency, declared independence in response to the Plan de Iguala and marched on the city of Oaxaca. After the fall of Iturbide, in 1823, Oaxaca was among the first of the new states to install its own sovereign legislature in an attempt to force the national congress to adopt a federal system. By November, Oaxaca had confirmed its place in the new Mexican republic and convened the sessions of a state constitutional congress. That congress issued a *"Ley Orgánica"* for the internal government of the state in May 1824, followed by the constitution itself in January 1825. The Mexican constitution of 1824 explicitly left the interior government of the towns to the states, and most states used the Spanish laws of 1812 as a model. The Oaxacan congress felt no immediate need to make major reforms to the Spanish municipal system. The Ley Orgánica expressed without reservation the need to maintain the Spanish constitutional status quo: "The alcaldes and ayuntamientos of the pueblos of the state will continue, as they have until now, in the use and exercise of the functions that the laws presently in force on the matter designate for them."[7]

In the writing of the constitution, however, legislators would make several key changes. The Spanish system of 1812 had allowed towns of 1,000 or more inhabitants to elect their own ayuntamientos. This provision had caused difficulty in Oaxaca, where many towns had far fewer than 1,000 residents and where smaller villages were often unwilling to combine and share a single council. In part to address this problem, the state constitution instituted two kinds of council in place of the Spanish constitution's one. Oaxacan towns that had at least 3,000 inhabitants would elect ayuntamientos, and in villages of fewer than 3,000 townspeople the new citizens would elect smaller municipal councils called repúblicas.[8]

This change was more than just an attempt to solve an administrative problem. For why not simply allow each town, regardless of size, to elect its own ayuntamiento? Why was the addition of the república necessary? The two kinds of council were responsible for a similar range of duties, including the establishment and running of primary schools, the management of resources, the administration of common funds, and, of course, the collection of state taxes. Formally, the major difference between the two bodies was simply one of size, both of the town and of the council itself. Ayuntamientos would consist of at least two alcaldes, five regidores, and one síndico (legal representative), while repúblicas could be as small as one alcalde and two regidores. But it was also legally possible for the two councils to be the same size. The law on local governments established a sliding scale for the size of the councils, based on a settlement's population. According to this scale, the smallest of the ayuntamientos would elect a council made up of two alcaldes and five regidores, exactly the same as that elected for the largest of the repúblicas.[9]

The vital distinction between the two councils lay in something beyond numbers: namely, ethnicity. Ayuntamientos were clearly intended to be the governing institutions in towns that had substantial nonindigenous communities, as these towns were most likely to meet the population requirements. Tellingly, some nonindigenous towns that did not have the sufficient numbers had a chance to elect ayuntamientos as well. In a law published in 1825 to regulate the town councils, Congress stipulated that if a town with fewer than 3,000 inhabitants could establish that its "enlightenment or industry" were sufficient, it could be considered for an ayuntamiento. Although literacy was not a requirement for either voting for or serving on ayuntamientos and repúblicas, it was an important factor in whether a town could gain an ayuntamiento in this manner. Congress was to make the final decision based on the following criterion: "The enlightenment of the towns is measured principally according to the number of their vecinos who can read and write."[10] Implicit in this statement is that they would be able to read and write in Spanish, a requirement that eliminated the large majority of new indigenous citizens. Meanwhile, the constitutional república, as its very name suggested, was assumed to be an institution of indigenous self-governance. In the most obvious ways, the new república replicated its colonial predecessor.

In effect, this system created a new constitutional República de Indios; like the colonial government, the Oaxacan state system divided the population into indígenas and nonindígenas and suggested that this division was significant for people's relationship with the state. For Oaxaca's legislators, ethnic distinction continued to play an important role in politics; it allowed them to assert the basic authority of the government while avoiding threats to social peace by reaffirming the fundamental right of indígenas to govern themselves in a relatively autonomous manner. This was neither an oversight on the part of officials who misunderstood the liberal laws that they were implementing nor a deliberate attempt to subvert liberalism. The retention of the repúblicas was, as Chassen-López puts it, "conciliation" rather than "confusion."[11] It was also expediency; Oaxacan legislators had deftly rewritten both colonial and liberal forms into state law without fundamentally threatening an arrangement that had resulted in relative order and prosperity throughout the colonial era.

This compromise between liberal law and traditional practice made for a unique political landscape in Oaxaca. While in most of Mexico new state constitutions reduced the numbers of municipalities in comparison to the Spanish constitutional era, in Oaxaca the numbers increased nearly fourfold. Because indígenas predominated, the municipal organization set out in the 1825 constitution meant that there were very few ayuntamientos and many repúblicas in federalist Oaxaca. In 1837, at the end of the first federalist era, the department of Tehuantepec, for instance, had only three ayuntamientos (in Tehuantepec, Juchitán, and Guichicovi), while reporting ninety-seven repúblicas. In Teotitlán del Camino, out of seventy-eight municipalities, only the cabecera elected an ayuntamiento. This imbalance reflected both the ethnic distribution of the population and the extreme fragmentation of Oaxaca's population into separate municipal entities. Shortly after independence, the government issued a seemingly exhaustive list of towns that gave the names of 913 municipalities. Many were very small. Out of seventeen villages in the district of Teposcolula, for example, all but three reported fewer than 1,000 inhabitants, and nine turned in numbers under five hundred; the smallest village in this group was San Pablo de Chiniega, which counted thirty-seven villagers. Too small to meet the numerical requirements for ayuntamientos and too indigenous to be granted the right to elect them by special dispensation, the vast majority of Oaxaca's towns would proceed to elect repúblicas in the years after 1825.[12]

To be sure, not all repúblicas were indigenous. Villages with repúblicas were not recognized officially as indigenous entities, and there was no official requirement that the councils consist of indígenas. And indeed there were exceptions to that general rule. Some smaller Oaxacan villages had been settled by nonindigenous families, and these towns, if unsuccessful at gaining an ayuntamiento, would then elect a república. Even political cabeceras might elect repúblicas rather than ayuntamientos, as did the mestizo town of Villa Alta in 1829, which had fewer than the requisite 3,000 people.[13] But the vast majority of repúblicas were indigenous institutions elected in indigenous towns. Conversely, not all indigenous Oaxacans elected repúblicas; many indigenous people lived in larger towns where local officers were usually nonindigenous. But over the breadth of the territory of the new state, most indigenous citizens were governed locally by indígenas. The new constitutional república system served not only the needs of the state and the nonindigenous elite but also the expectation of indigenous villagers that they would retain their colonial autonomy.

The transition from colonial to constitutional república was nevertheless not entirely smooth. The route to colonial office had been complicated; in the colonial cargo system, an ascending ladder of village duties culminated in the higher república offices. Once one reached the top of the ladder, one became part of an elite group (the principales) who could in turn choose those who served. The new constitutional laws allowed for the continuation of the cargo system as such. But at the same time, they relaxed the complicated colonial rules for ascension up the ladder by making nearly all officeholding subject to the vote. Officially, every male villager over the age of twenty-one (or eighteen if married, which was common) could now participate in elections. Furthermore, any of these villagers could now serve on the councils as alcaldes or regidores. This change could throw village politics into confusion. Guardino demonstrates that, after 1825 in the district of Villa Alta, men were elected to village office without having participated in the cargo system according to colonial rules; such men—"individuals whom indigenous culture considered to be mere boys"—often faced serious problems of legitimacy. This could cause disorder within the villages as factionalism that had remained muted under colonial rules came to the fore. In some places, it resulted in a veritable "youth movement" in which the authority of the principales came under critical scrutiny.[14]

Such conflict was common but not universal. Several circumstances made it possible to avoid dissension. First, the republican electoral system was indirect, calling for a vote for electors who would then meet to choose the members of the new council. The final choice, then, lay with a small group, a situation that could be made to reproduce some of the colonial exclusivity.[15] Second, by the late eighteenth century, stratification within many Oaxacan villages had already begun to break down, and the hereditary distinction between principales and macehuales (commoners) that had characterized the earlier colonial cargo system was losing its hold, a process that continued into the independence era.[16] Finally, and perhaps most importantly, without close government supervision or significant government interest in maintaining strictly democratic electoral procedures, villagers were likely to do more or less as they pleased; this could mean adhering to older methods of allotting authority within towns, or it could mean experimenting with new ones.

Electoral records and disputes clearly reveal the persistence of older methods of choosing local authorities that did not quite adhere to the republican ideal. Guardino suggests that many villages most likely reached agreements giving the local traditional elite a crucial advisory role in election. As late as 1833, the alcalde of Santa María Roaló, for instance, could describe the proper procedure for elections as follows: "All the *patricios* in enjoyment of their rights" would meet to elect village authorities. And in Chilapa in 1830, José Bruno Reyes complained that instead of allowing an open election, the previous year's alcalde had suggested the nine electors himself, standing before the gathered crowd and asking, "What do you say, Sirs, would you like it if citizen Juan Felipe Ortiz is the first Elector?" Despite Reyes's objection, the investigation that followed reveals most villagers' acceptance of this method. Witnesses' descriptions of the electoral proceedings show the process to have been quite irregular, yet none of the witnesses saw the irregularities as a problem. Everything, claimed Gil Manuel, had been done in the customary manner, "in the same terms in which it is always done," by "acclamation of the Pueblo, because the junta proposed each one and the president proposed them to the Pueblo who unanimously answered out loud with their consent and will."[17] Remnants of the older system remained not only in the electoral process but also in modes of governance. In the new democratic Oaxaca, repúblicas, as groups of elected officials with a popular mandate to govern, should theoretically have acted alone. But in practice they usually did not. In much of their communication with government officials, they identified themselves as acting either in concert with, for, or certified by the "*ancianos* and principales." Important decisions were thus made in conjunction with this group of notables, who may or may not have coincided with the república itself.[18] Much as the colonial república had overlain precolonial modes of local governance, the constitutional república became the public face of a complex system of town authority, the trappings of which did not have official names or roles in the republican world.

None of these adaptations were universal; they were the effect of very local power relationships, as all sides sought to use old and new institutions to protect their interests. They did so without significant interference from the state. Whether villagers wholeheartedly embraced the new laws and found themselves embroiled in a power struggle, whether they melded liberal and colonial forms, or whether they continued on as they always had, they chose for themselves the way they would incorporate the new forms now available to them. Although villages had to produce records of elections proving that they held them, in the first federalist era no one representing the government was likely to enter a Oaxacan town and insist on strict adherence to either the letter or the spirit of the law except in cases of overt conflict. In practice, then, Oaxacan villages had significant autonomy in determining how they would or would not adapt to new electoral institutions.

The state was nonetheless important because villagers often saw it as a crucial ally in the maintenance of autonomy. In the eyes of the villagers, harm was most likely to come not from the government but from other towns, which constantly threatened to encroach on village lands and other resources. The government was an important resource in settling intervillage disputes through mediation or through the courts. Of all land conflicts decided in Oaxacan courts, the vast majority were disputes between pueblos, cases that could drag on for years.[19] For instance, Magdalena Jicotlán's disagreement with three neighboring towns over boundaries in 1825 began at least as far back as 1807. Similarly, the town of Santiago Plumas, one of the accused in the Jicotlán case, was also involved in a land dispute with another town, La Concepción Buenavista, which lasted at least until 1844.[20] At any given time, regional courts were busy with several such disputes, as in the case of Teposcolula, where the courts adjudicated numerous land cases between 1823 and 1836.[21] Villagers did not always respect the courts' decisions. Cases that had been decided officially often resurfaced later as conflict over the same pieces of land flared up. After carrying out a "restitution" and boundary recognition between the Hacienda Rosario and the town of San Antonio de la Cal, one judge expressed his certainty that the government could expect "some disorder" from the town in the future.[22]

The Oaxacan state's protection of village autonomy was not limited to cases of disagreement over land. Villagers were also concerned about their administrative autonomy, and they worried about the possibility of having to answer to authorities in other villages or to depend on them for certain services. Federalism seemed to protect this kind of independence. Because Oaxaca's new laws established no minimum population requirements for having a república, it was possible for the aggregate towns created under Spanish liberalism to fragment into their constituent parts, each one electing its own república. So it was, for example, that the town of Santos Reyes Tepejillo, which had been attached to Tlacotepec during the "first installation of Ayuntamientos" in 1821, reemerged as an independent pueblo after independence, elected its own constitutional república, and took over the management of its common funds.[23] Federalism drew indigenous villagers into a binding pact with the state, one in which the state's continued protection of autonomy was an inextricable part of what it meant for indígenas to be members of the Oaxacan polity.

While state legislatures and officials continued to recognize and even encourage the maintenance of indigenous autonomy, and while Oaxaca's rural townspeople continued to be firmly tied to and part of the Oaxacan state, it is clear that villagers knew that something had nonetheless changed. This change made some townspeople question the methods of self-governance they observed in their towns. In the incident from Chilapa, where most villagers did not question the irregular form that local elections took, at least one was concerned; the complainant, Reyes, worried that this procedure had "deprived the citizens of their liberty to elect individuals freely." More typical, however, was the ability of villagers to overlook the contradictions between liberal law and customary practice. In Santa María Roaló, where the "patricians" had chosen the council, the alcalde insisted that this was the system followed "especially [by] those well-known as liberals and addicts of the public cause." To this town official, then, customary practices were not merely customary; they were *also* liberal. As long as no one questioned this assertion, it would, in effect, continue to be true. Over the course of the first half of the nineteenth century, villagers would be asked to accommodate a number of changes. They did so not by ignoring those changes, some of which would be much more potentially disruptive than the initial shift in the forms of town government. Instead, they found ways of talking about those changes that made them compatible with their requirements for survival and good government. In the process, villagers began to see themselves as part of a liberal order and as good citizens of a liberal state.

Liberal Citizenship in the "Shadow of Misery": Taxation and the Draft, 1825–1848

In 1827, the highest judicial official in Teotitlán complained that the villages under his jurisdiction owed considerable back taxes to the government. None of the alcaldes in the region of Huautla had answered the letters that he had sent, and he worried that "in very little time we will find total insubordination to the laws and the authorities." Similarly, after the villagers of Lachixila refused to participate in the construction of a jail that same year, one government authority proclaimed of the villagers that "not only are my . . . orders illusory, but . . . in haughtiness [the villagers] live, proceed and operate."[24] These officials painted a picture of an early independent Oaxaca in which the state had little hold over the loyalties of its largely indigenous citizens. But seen from the perspective of the villagers, the failure to obey the state looks slightly different. When San Martín Lacatepec and its annexes failed to pay taxes in 1834, town authorities blamed it on a cholera epidemic and urged that the government not interpret their refusal as "uncultivated resistance, or disobedience to the sacred Laws, erected with such zeal by such noble legislators, who represent the Majesty of the Oaxacan people." They went on: "No, Sir, You should see this only as a favor, or grace, that as most immediate Father you should accede to the supplication of your Submissive sons, who implore confidently to your just audience." In concluding, these village leaders signed their letter as "your humble sons, who lie in the shadow of ignorance and misery."[25] They refused to obey but simultaneously insisted on the fundamental right of the Oaxacan state to make demands. Those demands could be onerous, backbreaking, and sometimes disastrous. But for villagers who depended on the state for some of their most important privileges, the decision about how to respond was not always clear cut.

In early nineteenth-century Oaxaca, there was nothing novel about resistance to the payment of taxes. In making their excuses, Oaxacan villagers could draw on discourses that had proven efficacious for hundreds of years. But after independence, villagers also had to contend with a new demand: the military draft. Here, authorities consistently met refusal, as in Tlacolula in 1831, where according to town officials "the vecinos of this municipality are totally opposed to being soldiers; they scarcely perceive that we are discussing a list when there is a certain disquiet in the population."[26] And yet, ultimately, many indígenas served in Oaxaca's military, just as most Oaxacans paid at least some of their taxes. Villagers knew that they had to accommodate the state or risk losing very real advantages and privileges. They also knew, though, that they held an important card: Oaxacan government officials could not force villagers to comply with their demands in full without risking violence and even rebellion. And so, when Oaxacan villagers declined to pay taxes or to provide men for military service, they did so in large part knowing that it would not bring the wrath of the state squarely down on their heads.

As Oaxacans negotiated this situation, they participated in a conversation about indigenous citizenship in which indígenas themselves set many of the terms. As they talked about the way they would and would not comply with the state's demands, villagers articulated their own definition of good citizenship. This was a definition that drew heavily on colonial notions of state responsibility but that inserted those notions into a liberal framework. Good citizenship in Oaxaca, as villagers came to define it, was both ethnically specific and morally laden. But this definition also depended on the participation of the state in its creation and maintenance. State officials had to implement new laws. In Oaxaca, they ultimately found a way to do so that conformed with and helped cement this ethos. The nature of citizenship here was inherent not in the state's laws but rather in the manner in which the state chose—or was forced—to implement them.

RELUCTANT TAXPAYERS

In 1824, when he introduced a new tax code for the state of Oaxaca, Governor Murguía y Galardi acknowledged that many of Oaxaca's new citizens were ill able to afford any taxes at all. In fact, Murguía claimed, Congress would exonerate such people from the payment of the personal contribution if the state's financial circumstances had not made the legislature "unable for now to fulfill its ideas of beneficence." Without the aggregated taxes of the very poor, the income of the Oaxacan government would be greatly reduced and insufficient for the effective work of the state. The greater good, Murguía stressed, would thus be served through these small sacrifices.[27] Relatively speaking, the sacrifices were indeed quite small. The new tax code established a sliding scale of rates, with a bottom level low enough to bring nearly everyone into the taxpaying community. Oaxacan men from the ages of sixteen to seventy who "enjoyed or could acquire a salary, wage, or use from one to four reales daily" or who owned property worth between 100 and 1,000 pesos would pay one real each month. This tax would be called the *contribución personal*, or personal contribution.

Villagers clearly understood their obligation to pay this tax as part of an explicit bargain struck with the state. Above all, the state protected the autonomy of the villages, but it provided more tangible services as well, and taxes constituted the indigenous side of the contract. Villagers depended on the government to step in to mitigate the effects of crisis situations such as epidemics, grain shortages, and famine.[28] Payment of taxes also enabled villages to justify other kinds of demands on the state, such as requesting grants of land when the town had none or at least not enough "to subsidize their necessities."[29] And it was not uncommon for villagers to use their past record of prompt payment to demand particular aid, as did those of Yalalag in 1840, who wanted better vigilance against banditry on the roads that they traveled on the way to market.[30]

Still, for the majority of Oaxaca's indigenous villagers, even one real was often too much to ask.[31] Collection proved ineffective. In May 1830, the governor of Teotitlán del Camino reported that the seventy-seven villages outside of the cabecera owed a total of 6,602 pesos on the personal contribution. By 1835, the total debt in Ejutla came to 33,000 pesos, and the debt in Tehuantepec was close to 18,000.[32] Villagers devised a myriad of ways to avoid payment. And so, the government struggled with the fact of its dependence on a tax that villagers had both great difficulty providing and substantial ability to circumvent.

The ability to avoid taxation was rooted in the law. Under federalism, elected municipal officials not only collected the taxes, they also had a good deal of power in determining who should pay. The república provided a range of general information about the town, dividing its population into classes of taxpayers and updating previous lists to reflect those villagers who had come of age, those too old to pay, and those who had died; it was then expected to submit an amount that reflected this information.[33] To expect any returns whatsoever, then, Oaxacan authorities relied on the probity, loyalty, and authority of the elected alcaldes and repúblicas in the villages. In practice, such cooperation was not always forthcoming. Municipal officials often took liberties with the tax collection process in an attempt to lessen the burden on their villages. Some pueblos, such as many of those in Teotitlán, failed to produce the reports determining who should pay; in 1827, the departmental governor complained that only ten pueblos—"the least stupid"—had followed the proper procedure and that he had had to send the representatives of the other towns home with their taxes unpaid.[34] But even when town officials turned in their reports, they still had considerable room for manipulation. It was not difficult for village governments to engage in subterfuge, using the system to create uncertainty about how much they owed. Town officials were sometimes accused of outright falsification. José Mantecón, the governor of Tehuantepec in 1832, noted that during his personal visits to some of the towns in his department he had located seventy-five more contributors than the repúblicas had enumerated only two years before. Because there was often no one to contradict them, alcaldes could justify tax shortfalls by misrepresenting the ages and living arrangements of the villagers. As José María Pando wrote from Villa Alta in 1840, because of the contribution "the young men do not want to pass fifteen years, and those that scarcely have arrived at fifty wish to appear as old men." Technically, subprefects had a supervisory role in the taxation process, and departmental governors were ultimately responsible for the funds. But their dependence on village authorities made their power largely ceremonial.[35]

Officials did have some recourse. They could use force, as did the departmental governor of Teotitlán del Camino in 1829 when he sent a military officer to the towns under his jurisdiction to collect back taxes. That year, the governor of Tehuantepec requested state military help with collection as well.[36] Appointed officials could also confiscate the goods of alcaldes who failed to pay. Thus, after the towns of Tamasulapán and Teotongo defaulted on their debts in 1836, one local official seized the belongings of the offending alcaldes and sold them at auction.[37] Departmental governors had some discretionary power to suspend local elected officials who had committed some error in their collection of taxes or even to remove those who had significant debts. In Ayuquila in 1826, Manuel José Norutia removed alcalde Mariano Gómez for "bad conduct" in the tax-collection process and replaced him with the "most able regidor." And Ramón Ramírez, the governor of the Centro, suspended the alcalde of San Antonio de la Cal in 1829 for a debt of three months' taxes.[38] But such punitive actions were not the norm. As long as the government had no direct supervisory power over the pueblos—or capacity to enforce it—neither military intervention nor punishing alcaldes was likely to stem the tide of tax resistance.

And yet, despite the failure of the state to secure consistent material commitment from its citizens, relations between the state and the villages did not break down. Instead, villagers and government officials developed a language with which to talk about taxes that could explain and justify the failures of both within the context of the legitimacy of the Oaxacan state. Rather than eroding that legitimacy, the refusal of indigenous villagers to comply with tax demands to their full extent in some ways actually strengthened it by prompting the development of a shared vocabulary about justice and obligation. When villagers spoke about taxes, they used a language that had deep roots in the colonial state's protective and justificatory project. State officials, well aware of the difficulties villagers faced, shared a key element of that language in recognizing the fact that many indigenous people simply could not afford to pay. Despite constant day-to-day conflict over taxation, villagers ultimately found a receptive audience in Oaxacan officials, even at the highest levels of the Oaxacan government.

At the center of this shared language about taxes was poverty. Indigenous villagers consistently cast themselves as the poorest of the poor. In 1825 and 1826, when the state government asked the repúblicas to report on the condition of their commonly administered funds (*fondos del común*), the villages responded nearly unanimously that they lived in great destitution. The funds were supposed to derive from a subset of common village land. In some cases, pueblos claimed to lack such land entirely or to rent it out for only a meager income.[39] And in almost all cases, the lack of common funds was linked more broadly to the villagers' individual and collective poverty. The alcalde of Santos Reyes Michiapa, for instance, wrote: "I make it known that this pueblo does not enjoy any community goods nor is there or has there been any common fund, the case of which is attributed to the misery of the inhabitants." In Santiago Cuicoyán the alcalde argued that the lack of funds was due to both "the sterility of the land [and] the misfortune of the inhabitants." Santiago Yucuyache had had funds in the past, but they were annihilated during the independence wars; now the townspeople were in a state of beggary. And from San Miguel Peras, a town of only thirteen married couples, alcalde Andrés Miguel reported that "all of life . . . we have been poor . . . , this is the answer of all the old people and the past alcaldes."[40]

Protestations of poverty served as a sort of catchall excuse for the pueblos. The alcalde of Huautla, as he refused to take responsibility for the forced distribution of tobacco in his town in 1829, argued that he would not do so simply because "it is extremely burdensome to us." In 1827, Manuel González, the alcalde of Santa María Ecatepec, requested that tax payment be suspended for two years after a hurricane had destroyed much of his village. He asked that the departmental governor favor "his most humble unlucky subjects."[41] In the years after 1836, when national policies, civil conflicts, and the war with the United States conspired to increase the tax pressure on Mexican villages, townspeople continued to plead destitution. The municipal authorities of Santo Domingo Tonaltepec blamed their failure to pay on a famine, the alcalde of Huilotepec cited his village's recent loss of land, and, after the state government issued a three-day ultimatum in 1848, the authorities in Tuxtepec wrote that the new demands had "filled us with terror because it is humanly impossible."[42]

Most of these villagers were almost certainly telling the truth. They were indeed poor and ill able to withstand the pressures of taxation. But, for the most part, villagers excused themselves only in extraordinary circumstances, and they did not claim that poor villagers should be exempt from taxes in general. Rather, they often expressed their regrets, as did the villagers of San Martín Lacatepec, who refused to pay taxes in the wake of an epidemic just as they stressed their continued adherence to the government as "submissive sons." In response to an 1848 decree calling for a new kind of personal contribution, seven alcaldes in the towns around Nisaviquiti lamented "with much feeling and pain that they cannot comply with the new contribution of four months because of the extreme necessity in which they live." They conceded that the tax was "extremely efficacious for some Populations that are supplied with the necessary utensils," but there was simply no way that *their* pueblos could pay, given their circumstances.[43] Taxation in general was just, but in the particular it often was not.

This position could be extremely useful for village authorities caught between state demands and local exigencies. For poor pueblos, the requirement of paying more money than they could possibly spare was an injustice on the part of the government, and if village authorities were to comply with state demands, they argued, they would be complicit in a great crime. The *juez de paz* (justice of the peace) of San Pedro Mártir, after making an enormous effort to collect taxes, believed that the people of the town should be excused, as they barely had enough to subsist. Similarly, in the town of Tepelmeme in 1839, after a famine had depopulated much of the region, one local official wrote of the municipal body that "we cannot achieve the collection of contributions and we have taken the steps of a true collection and only found closed houses and those that have remained have no resources not even for any sustenance." When the municipal officers tried to collect the personal contribution, the townspeople complained bitterly. According to the juez de paz, this was only just: "We cannot obligate them or punish them for compliance in the area of Contributions because we find them very afflicted and if we punish them we would lack faith and charity and would incur mortal sin."[44]

Most of the time, state officials were engaged in the difficult process of trying to get indigenous villagers to pay up. But because of the difficulty and often the impossibility of their task and their lack of sufficient power to enforce collection, appointed regional officials often acted as patrons of the pueblos. They frequently found themselves having to explain tax shortfalls to higher authorities, and in doing so they consistently used a language similar to that of the villages, claiming that the government had an obligation to take the situation of the pueblos into account before demanding taxes that villagers might not be able to provide. In 1831, José María Pando reported a drought in Zoochila; the price of grain rose so high that indígenas could not afford to buy it and certainly could not afford to pay taxes. He thus explained the meager amounts he had been able to collect and asked that the state governor "extend [his] paternal protection toward these indígenas, providing their necessities in that part that [he] can." In 1836, he insisted that the villagers deserved a dispensation in the face of a major crop failure because they had always paid their taxes promptly in the past. José María Parada, the governor of Jamiltepec in 1835, noted that many villagers were taking away from their subsistence production to pay their taxes, a situation he described as "unjust." And, during the famine of 1839, the subprefect of Tlaxiaco expressed his regret that he could not provide the taxes demanded as he knew that the treasury was desperately short of funds; more important, however, was that the pueblos "in general tell me, that every day their necessities abound to the extreme of not finding corn expensive or cheap," and that there was scant hope of a better harvest in the months to come.[45] Like the villagers, these officials balanced legitimization of the tax laws themselves with the importance of making exceptions.

At times, the state's central government also took on this role. In 1840, when the pueblos had accumulated huge debts of back taxes after a devastating famine, the departmental junta moved to exonerate them from payment until January of the next year. Similarly, it declared the town of Lachixola to be in a state of insolvency in 1841 and excused it from payment of the contribution. And in the village of Tonalá in 1834, when the villagers asked to be let out of paying the personal contribution for a period of four months, the state congress responded with regrets, insisting that there were not enough public funds to allow compliance with the multitude of such requests it had received. Nevertheless, in a gesture of support, the legislature ruled that members of Congress should take up a collection, ceding from their stipends the fifty pesos that the town owed on its personal contribution.[46]

The state government was also quick to plead the poverty of its villagers to the national government. After the advent of Santa Anna's centralist regime in 1836, taxation became a national issue. The centralist state was chronically short of funds, and new legislation allowed it to impose a wide variety of direct taxes, a privilege previously held only by the states. In late 1838, in addition to levying a tax on both urban and rural property, the federal government imposed a *capitación* (head tax) on all Mexican families. Most poor families, and thus most of Oaxaca's villagers, were exempt from this tax, as its payment required an income of at least twelve reales a day. But in 1841 and 1842, the government extended the reach of the capitación, until every male Mexican over the age of eighteen was required to pay 1.5 pesos to the treasury each year. This tax would replace state personal taxes such as that of Oaxaca.[47] For most Oaxacan villagers, the amount of actual taxes demanded changed very little; they would have already been paying about this much to the state government as personal contribution under Oaxaca's laws. But the new national tax policy *was* a problem for the Oaxacan government. Given the inefficiency of tax collection, the state would have difficulty submitting the required amounts to the central government. According to the law, departmental governments could keep as much of the income from this tax as they needed for their local expenses. But even when this provision was honored, Oaxacan officials worried that they would still have to provide a substantial amount to the federal government and that this could mean a major drop in income for the region.[48]

The new tax codes as they were published in Mexico City made certain concessions to the particularities of the departments (as the states were now called). Especially important to Oaxaca was the provision, in the 1841 law, that in departments that were already charging personal contributions similar to the new national tax, the methods of collection might be allowed to remain the same. Despite this exception, some Oaxacan officials were confused about what was required and concerned that the new system would throw tax collection into turmoil. According to the governor of Villa Alta in 1841, "the law that has made the Personal Contribution extensive to the entire Republic" would be difficult to implement in Oaxaca. Many of the articles of the new law that determined how Oaxacan authorities would establish tax rates for each village were simply impracticable among Oaxaca's indígenas because many of them knew little Spanish. The governor for one had been unable to find individuals who could manage the complicated procedures. But he also argued that the poverty of Oaxaca's people made the new law inapplicable there: "The indígenas in general are nothing but day laborers or farmers whose [income] does not extend beyond what is necessary to eat."[49]

The language of protection, justice, and poverty was thus used at all levels of Oaxacan society, from the villages to the highest levels of Oaxacan government. Without doubt, this language did not have entirely the same meaning for government officials as it did when used by indigenous villagers. First, officials had a practical reason to adopt this discourse. Departmental governors, who were ultimately responsible for tax collection, had to make their own excuses to the state treasury. When returns were less than census information predicted, or when alcaldes failed to provide needed information, governors often validated the excuses of the pueblos to avoid having to pick up the tab themselves or face the wrath of higher authorities, hoping for dispensation from the state government. The same could be said for the relationship between state governments and national authorities.

In addition, when invoked by nonindigenous officials, the use of the language of poverty was consistently paired with a general denigration of the capacities of indigenous Oaxacans and especially of their municipal authorities. Officials expended a good deal of energy blaming the "delinquency and rusticity of the Alcaldes of the Pueblos" for their own inability to collect as much tax revenue as the laws said that they should. In facing the national government, such excuses were particularly important, as they allowed Oaxacan officials to argue that the new laws of the 1840s were "incompatible with the ignorance of indigenous collectors." State officials were constantly faced with villagers who, in the words of the governor of Tehuantepec in 1848, "say that they won't give a *tlaco* more than they have each month."[50] But fear of indigenous wrath, incapacity to contradict the villagers, and doubts about indigenous capacities were not necessarily incompatible with the sincere use of the language of poverty. In May 1848, for example, the governor of Villa Alta combined all of these justifications when he asked that some of the pueblos in his department be let out of an extraordinary tax passed that year:

Scarcely had I published the decree than the indígenas already prepared not to obey, such it is [that] if Your Excellency wished to conserve the order in this partido it is necessary to consider that the unfortunate Indians . . . do not earn two reales daily and have to cover the capitación monthly from which the pueblos owe me a tremendous amount (*un platal*).[51]

When it came to taxes, the Oaxacan system was remarkably flexible. It was also remarkably legitimate in the eyes of what could easily have cast itself as an oppressed population. Oaxaca's indigenous villagers had the autonomy and thus the power necessary to retract their monetary support of the government when they felt it to be justified. Government officials, in part because they were forced by circumstances and in part because they inherited a colonial ideology that mandated a kind of protection for *indígenas*, acknowledged and often accepted indigenous excuses. Villagers, for their part, accepted the state's fundamental right to tax as long as government officials legitimized, sometimes tacitly and sometimes explicitly, the basis of villagers' refusal to comply in full.

UNWILLING SOLDIERS

If indigenous people saw taxation as unjust only when the villagers were in dire straits, drafting Oaxaca's "submissive sons" into military service was unjust all of the time. Indeed, trying to force Oaxacan villagers to comply with the draft could be dangerous. After the villagers of Mitla informed him that "in no way do they want to enlist," alcalde Juan Martín reported that "I cannot make the list [of recruits] without the consent of the común" and that, if he tried, the townspeople would likely try to kill him. Similarly, the alcalde of San Juan del Río lamented that "there are no men useful for service, and . . . I will not risk my life naming one because they will rise against me alone."[52]

Nonetheless indigenous villagers adapted to the new and near-constant demand for military personnel and remained committed to the Oaxacan state. They could do so because of their autonomy and because they found ways to use the draft to serve their purposes. As with taxation, the autonomy of the villages helped mitigate the effects of forced military recruitment. In many cases, villagers could simply ignore it. As with taxation, the government had only limited resources to enforce its attempts to recruit soldiers, contributing to a sense that the draft was less onerous than it could have been. In addition, many local authorities were not averse to using the draft to solve problems within their towns. The draft could be a potent weapon against troublemakers or those individuals whom village authorities saw as outside of their immediate community. This worked to mitigate the effects of the draft in two ways. First, it made pueblos reliant on a state mechanism for solving internal problems, increasing their dependence on the state. And, second, it contributed to villagers' explicit portrayal of themselves as good citizens, by singling out those who they claimed were *not* for the "punishment" of military service. If taxation was a theoretically legitimate demand with which villagers nevertheless did not always comply, the draft was a burden that towns sometimes took on despite their claim of its fundamental illegitimacy.

There were several ways that Oaxacan villagers could end up as part of military units. The Mexican national army consisted of two types of forces, the *permanentes*—the standing army—and the *activos*, a larger reserve force called on in times of national emergency. For the manning of both forces, the federal government assigned quotas to the state governments, which made use of the *leva*, or forced recruitment from the villages, to meet their obligation. In 1824, for example, Oaxaca pledged to provide one young man to serve in Mexico's regional forces for every fifty families that each village contained.[53] Both the permanentes and the activos remained in existence throughout the period in question, although the method of recruitment changed to that of *sorteo*, or lottery, in 1839. Villagers served in local units as well. In 1827, in an attempt to curb the independence of the national army, the Mexican congress instituted the civic militia, also in the hands of the states. Oaxaca passed regulations for its civic militia in 1828. As with the national army, all male Oaxacans from the age of eighteen to fifty were eligible to be drafted into the militias, where they were obligated to serve for eight years. Service in the permanent army could and sometimes did mean participation in military actions far from home, as these units were the Mexican government's main weapon in the internal and external conflicts that rocked the country between 1824 and 1848. But, precisely because of this constant turmoil, both the activos and the civic militias could easily become embroiled in conflict as well; by the mid-1840s, the activos were in a state of nearly constant service and were barely distinguishable from the regular army.[54]

There was no dispensation for indígenas. The laws regulating the draft expressed the total number of men recruited in any given year in terms of villages; for the civic militia, for instance, each village would provide one man for every hundred townspeople. Only very small villages—with populations of fewer than seventy—were exempt.[55] Indigenous villages were thus the primary source of soldiers. But most such towns could ill spare even a man or two. For small indigenous settlements, the absence of several productive male townspeople could be damaging to the well-being of the town and to the families that lived there. And, for the individuals who served, participation in the military could mean not only actual physical danger but also, as Guardino puts it, "social death . . . when the man was taken from the community and thus could not marry or begin climbing the cargo ladder."[56] Oaxacan villagers resisted the draft fiercely and without discrimination between service in the different bodies. If in some parts of Mexico the civic militias became an important site of national pride, in Oaxaca, like other forms of military service, they were, in the early part of the century at least, a hardship that villagers avoided at all costs.[57]

In theory, the process for recruitment went as follows: Each alcalde prepared a list of the eligible individuals in his pueblo, indicating the numbers of married, widowed, and single men between the ages of sixteen and forty.[58] From these lists, the departmental government determined how many men each pueblo should contribute to the military, and the alcalde then proposed a set of names. Armed soldiers brought these men to the cabecera or the capital city, where officers determined their suitability for military service. The state government had little direct power of enforcement. Not only was it the duty of the alcaldes to provide recruits, they were also responsible for the safe conduct of new soldiers through the villages on the way to the cabeceras and capital cities and for hindering the escape of recruits in transit. With so much of the responsibility for the smooth functioning of the draft in their hands, alcaldes could use many of the same methods they had used to avoid taxation to frustrate the draft. They often provided faulty information, claimed legal exemptions, or simply refused to comply.

Accordingly, providing recruits for the army caused appointed officials as much as if not more difficulty than did collecting taxes. In 1829, the governor of Huajuapan reported that he was not able to recruit enough people to fill his quota, citing "the difficult job that the Repúblicas of the Pueblos of this Department give me" in convincing them to turn the men in. And in 1835, José María Pando complained that many of the pueblos in Zoochila had not turned in their recruits, for which he believed that they should be fined. Four years later, Pando complained that many alcaldes under his jurisdiction in Villa Alta were leaving able men off their lists. He had already punished the alcaldes of Betaza, Yazona, and Solaga but could not prove his case anywhere else. Similarly, one official in Tlacolula claimed that the local authorities manipulated their lists to eliminate the most able-bodied men: "[They] always seek the weakest so as not to harm the truly free." Some authorities noted particularly strenuous attempts at draft avoidance; one official suggested that some people were getting married simply to avoid service, and another claimed that "since the indígenas have become aware that the lack of knowledge of the Castilian language is an exception in order to liberate their sons from service at arms; they now . . . prohibit that they learn [this] language, which in their opinion will harm them."[59]

Whether because of alcaldes' manipulation or not, many of the recruits who actually arrived at their posts were not suitable for military service according to the government's own rules. Of particular importance was the preference for potential soldiers who were conversant in the Spanish language. The laws themselves acknowledged that this could be a problem, stipulating that "in those pueblos where no one speaks Castilian, one should look in recruits for those with the most quickness and comprehension possible, always preferring those who do speak it." In practice, if on arrival at their units individuals proved unable to communicate, they would often be sent back to their villages, and a new search would begin. It was not uncommon for men who did not speak Spanish to arrive at their assignments. In 1830, the commander of the Fourth Batallion in Oaxaca City reported that he had recently received two men, Miguel Jacinto and José María, as replacements for two deserters. Their arrival was a mixed blessing, however; the men were "useful for their age and robustness but they do not possess Castilian, they speak only Mixteco being from the Alta." The wide variety of languages that Oaxacan villagers spoke exacerbated the problem; the 129 recruits in Teotitlán in 1839 required "a multitude of Interpreters."[60]

In 1826, Mariano Conde wrote from Tehuantepec about his constant difficulties in providing men for the battalions. Many of the men proposed for military service, he complained, were justifiably exempt: "[O]ut of twenty-five scarcely four remain due to just reasons of law." Similarly, in 1838, Tomás Gallangos reported that out of twenty-eight men from the village of Tututepec, only seven met the requirements.[61] The Spanish language requirement was just one of several ways in which a Oaxacan villager could claim exemption. "Just reasons of law" also included minimum height and weight, and, most importantly, the familial responsibilities of the individuals proposed for service. Technically, single men with no dependents were the primary candidates to become soldiers. Only in desperate circumstances would the army demand that married men with children or individuals with dependent parents enlist. But men without close family relations were a relative rarity in a small Oaxacan village.

Oaxacan government officials sought ways to explain their failure to fill their quotas, just as they had their failure to collect taxes. By their accounts, indígenas were particularly reluctant to serve. One official, reporting on his inability to find soldiers for the national militias as ordered by Mexico City, noted that the problem was twofold: Most villages were too small to provide men to the army without harming their productive capacities, and the villages were composed of "an *indiada* dedicated to the labors of the field, and who therefore lack civilization, for which motive they see with horror service to the Nation."[62] But just as they derided the indígenas' behavior, they offered suggestions as to how to improve the situation. More often than not, these suggestions were drawn from villagers' requests. Among the most common of village petitions was the request to contribute money or goods in lieu of persons. The alcalde of Nochistlán assured the government in 1833 that things would be much better if, for each man a village was short in fulfillment of its quota, it were allowed to donate the value of six sets of tack. In 1838 and 1839, the jueces de paz of Santa María Chachiapa, San Baltasar Chuicapam, Amatlán, and San Andrés Chicahualco suggested similar arrangements. At least some government officials thought this might not be a bad idea. One, while noting that "there is certainly no service that the Pueblos view with more horror than that of contributing people for service at arms," suggested a contribution of money rather than men. Government officials understood that lenience could work in the government's favor. In 1835, departmental governor José María Pando was visited by a soldier named Manuel Mariano, who claimed that he had recently been wounded and wished to return home.

Pando was not certain that this injury had actually occurred in the course of any campaign, but he nevertheless suggested that it would be a good idea to release him and provide him with assistance:

I do not know whether in accordance with the ordinances of the army, he is or is not deserving of some monthly aid; but the luck of this unfortunate for the rest of his life could strongly influence the other pueblos to turn in with more willingness the recruits that we demand.[63]

Despite these limits on the draft, however, many Oaxacan villagers, even those with families, found themselves forced to leave home to serve. Miguel Gerónimo was forced to abandon his widowed mother in 1830; Juan Rey, who had a wife and two children, was drafted the same year; and authorities removed Pablo Sánchez from his farm in 1835, leaving behind his wife, son, mother, and four younger brothers. Innumerable others or their families sent petitions to government officials in attempts to avoid the draft or gain discharges.[64] Such individuals often received the aid of their villages, as did Dionisio Favián; the "alcalde Diego Pérez," the regidores, and the "Indians and natives of this Pueblo" all claimed that he had paid his contributions and had two children in a letter they sent to the government in 1841.[65]

As such unfortunate individuals saw it, there was no excuse for a government demand that not only put them in danger but also had the potential to plunge their wives, children, and elderly parents into destitution. Their claims to exemption were based on the same assumption that prompted villagers to refrain from paying their taxes in times of need: The government did not have the right to make demands on its citizens that endangered their ability to sustain themselves. Thus villagers were grudgingly willing to turn in people without dependents. Antonio García, from the town of Huazolotitlan, was chosen because he had no mother or father to support, and Agustín Turivio's mother in Tlacamama was married and thus did not depend on him for sustenance. One alcalde, in filling his quota, wrote that "the indígena Juan de la Cruz . . . does not suffer any defect, he simply has no one who will miss him."[66] Yet villagers usually considered family responsibilities to be an incontrovertible justification for refusing. In making his excuses in 1836, the alcalde of Teutila noted that "although it is true that there are men, . . . these are all married and of the single men some are sick and others are the sons of widows and widowers, already of advanced age, [and] fed with their sweat." For the government to expect such people to serve was tantamount to forcing their relatives to beg in the street to survive.[67]

In resisting the draft, village authorities also drew on laws regarding vagrancy to make their claims. Although official rhetoric made it clear that serving in the army and defending the nation were the patriotic duties of Mexican and Oaxacan citizens, the laws also stipulated that the military could be used to isolate those with no steady employment and to put them to good use; towns were expected to provide, in the first instance, "those vagrants (*vagos*) and misbehavers whom the law has marked for the exercise of arms."[68] And so village authorities consistently insisted that potential recruits not only had families but were also employed. In 1833, the alcalde of Nochistlán claimed that among the seventy-eight single men in his town, all were "hardworking men with interests, and only children of widowed mothers." The juez de paz of San Baltasar Chuicapam in 1838 wrote of the villagers that "I have not found a single individual who is not hard-working, honorable and well engaged," and suggested "the drafting of another class of men in whom are found better qualities for military service."[69]

The vagrancy statutes also played another important role in both mitigating the effects of the draft and bolstering the importance of the state to the villages. In specific circumstances, villagers saw the draft as an opportunity to winnow troublemakers—"misbehavers," as the laws put it—out of their towns. Victoriano Martín, for instance, became a recruit in 1830 after local arbitration failed to resolve complaints about his wife, who was living with another man. When Juan Sárate complained that the alcalde of Santa María Ejutla had sent him to the army illegally, the alcalde claimed that Sárate was a notorious problem, as he failed to support his wife and routinely found other men to take care of her. When attempts to punish him failed to change his behavior, the alcalde included him on the list of recruits. After an investigation of some questionable recruits in Oaxaca City, one official found that "the Alcalde of the town to which they belong, not being able to tolerate the repeated demands between them due to their abundant vices," had ordered them sent away to the army. And in turning in one Justo Osorio, the juez de paz of San Pablo Coatlán wrote that he was doing it "for the sake of the peace and tranquility that is my responsibility . . . as this individual is proper for the troops because he respects no authority, is very haughty, and insults everyone."[70] Even the despised draft could help maintain village harmony, tying Oaxacan villagers yet closer to the state.

But perhaps most importantly, the vagrancy laws solidified state legitimacy by helping to clarify indígenas' definition of citizenship. One of the primary identifying features of a vago was that he did not pay his taxes. For instance, Miguel Domínguez, a twenty-two-year-old man who came from Cortijos in 1829, was described as follows: "His occupation is vagrancy both for the contribution and for any service, [he is] robust and healthy and suffers from no illness."[71] Men such as Domínguez, villagers argued, were proper material for military service; those who did fulfill their obligations to the state simply were not. Consistent taxpayers, villagers believed, met all the requirements for good citizenship. As a municipal authority in Testitlán four years later wrote, "we have understood that vagrant and ill-behaved men . . . are those who should be remitted; there are none of these, only pure *hombres de bien* with responsibility for their families, and taxpayers giving service to the pueblo and their duties."[72]

Notably, villagers often juxtaposed their objections to the draft with their commitment to paying taxes. In 1831, the república of the town of San Pablo Guila'a received an order from Oaxaca City to provide recruits. They refused, insisting that "we are obedient to Your Supreme Order but it happens that all of us in the pueblo do not want the militias to go out," and they explained their indignation at the government's draft demands by claiming that "we are already paying the contribution monthly." Similarly, when alcalde Alverto Gutiérrez sought to put together information about his town, the people of Santa María Guelace told him that "to ask for the list was in vain for the reason that the money of the contributions was given in complete." And when José Vernardo, the alcalde of San Sebastián Teitipac, submitted his request for a list of eligible men to the "ancianos and principales" of the pueblo, they failed to submit it "because they and all are contributors."[73] Even as they resisted government demands, villagers reiterated their commitment to the state and articulated their own definition of what it meant to be a Oaxacan citizen. They were willing to be taxpayers, but not soldiers.

In effect, indigenous authorities were quick to take advantage of the state. But just as they did so, they adopted a language of good citizenship that in and of itself invalidated the state's military claims. This strategy had the double effect of justifying draft resistance and tightening the ties between the state and the villages. It was this combination of commitment to, autonomy from, and dependence on the state that made Oaxacan villagers such "submissive sons." Precisely because they were to a large extent able to define what citizenship would mean in their daily lives, Oaxacan villagers remained committed Oaxacan citizens.

"The Public Good and the Good of our Barrio": Oaxacan Town Government after 1836

The combination of commitment and selective noncompliance that characterized Oaxacan villagers' relationship to the state was possible only as long as the villages retained their autonomy in government and administrative action. This autonomy faced a major challenge in 1836, when a national centralist administration took over the government in Mexico City. How villagers and officials approached this challenge reveals not just the strength of their commitment to each other but also the importance of villagers' commitment to what they understood to be liberalism.

In December 1836, the new centralist government under Santa Anna published its constitution. The new national code called for the replacement of elected municipal officers with appointed officials. Under the centralist regime, nationwide, the only towns that would continue to elect their own local governments would be the state capitals, other towns with at least 8,000 inhabitants, and port towns with at least 4,000. In all other places, jueces de paz (justices of the peace) would govern, "proposed by the subprefect, named by the prefect, and approved by the governor."[74] Even before the official publication of the new laws, Oaxaca began to rearrange its internal administration to comply with the centralist regime. In early December, the government ordered the suspension of elections for ayuntamientos and repúblicas, clearing the way for the appointment of jueces de paz in the villages. In mid-1837, after the national government insisted that the jueces be in place within a month, regional officials began the process of choosing the men who would serve in these positions.[75]

Jueces de paz were not simply ayuntamientos and repúblicas by a different name. Under the new policies, Oaxacan villagers forfeited important privileges that they had held under federalism. First and foremost, they lost the power to choose their own local officials, ending a government sanction of municipal elections that stretched back into the colonial era. Villages also lost much of their official autonomy, with each small town becoming part of a larger municipality represented by an ayuntamiento. State officials exercised tighter control over village finances, insisting on regulating village fees and taxes and requiring government permission to use common funds for unusual projects. In towns with populations smaller than 1,000—many of Oaxaca's villages—the jueces de paz had somewhat limited powers, making them dependent in certain legal matters on the closest larger town.[76] In short, centralist municipal policies worked to counteract village autonomy on a number of fronts. In the words of one town official, writing in 1841, "since the Constitution of 1836 was promulgated the pueblo has lost its rights."[77]

And yet, all in all, Oaxacan villagers confronted this potentially drastic change with relative equanimity. They used their practical leverage with the state to manipulate the system to their advantage and thus force continuity in the actual practices of town government. Even if the method of choosing municipal authorities was new, the nature of their duties was similar. Jueces de paz, according to national law, would exercise "the same faculties detailed for the alcaldes and those designated for the ayuntamientos." Their responsibilities were almost exactly the same as those of the now defunct repúblicas, encompassing, in most cases, close to the full range of both administrative and judicial functions that the alcaldes and regidores had served.[78] What's more, the Oaxacan government allowed for the continuation of the cargo system for offices below that of the juez.[79] But the obstacles to continuity that the abolition of elections represented were considerable. Centralist policies struck at the heart of villagers' understanding of their rights to self-government. For the system to continue to meet pueblo expectations, state officials and villagers would have to reach some kind of agreement that would mitigate the effects of centralist law.

Municipal records after 1836 do reveal the survival of older forms. Where they had once referred to the "alcalde and república," villagers now invoked the "juez and república," referring by name to an institution that in law no longer existed. Pedro Santiago, for example, the juez's designated substitute in the town of San Juan Copala, referred to himself as the "substitute of this República in the charge of the Juez de Paz."[80] As under the federalist system, towns continued to rely on the opinions and authority of a larger group of notables whose power was not codified by law. The juez of San Juan Tosula in 1838 claimed to act in concert with a group of "principales" and "the others of the body of this municipality." In Huautla in 1837, an official reported the words of Antonio Nicolás describing a meeting he had attended during a land dispute: "It being in his pueblo the custom to call together those known as ancianos and principales when there is business pertinent to the común . . . he was called about two months ago."[81] For these villagers, then, the juez de paz was essentially the titular head of the república, which was still a council advised and aided by the principales as a whole. Even centralist-appointed government officials used older words with frequency, as did the subprefect of Teposcolula in 1839, referring to the town government of San Pedro Tidaa as its "república."[82]

But such continuity was not a foregone conclusion; jueces de paz were still appointed rather than elected. Theoretically, appointing the highest town official would allow state administrators to choose men who met their own rather than the town's criteria. Ideally, the juez de paz would be literate, hold some property, and have at least some education, a complex of qualities that made him an "hombre de bien."[83] But in most of Oaxaca's indigenous towns, such men were difficult to find. In one town near Justlahuaca in 1837, for instance, when he had to replace a juez he believed to be supporting bandits, the subprefect appointed a man known as Antonino, whom he described as "the only hombre de bien in this area."[84] Indeed, the attempt to produce acceptable candidates for the position of juez de paz sometimes produced lamentable results. Subprefects occasionally appointed men who did not actually reside in the town in question, making them unacceptable to the villagers. These appointees found themselves in difficult situations; Miguel María Callejas, the juez of the town of Yxcatlán, complained that he was unable to do his job "because the pueblo is of pure indígenas whose language is entirely unknown to me."[85] In Jamiltepec, the prefect lamented "the lack of suitable subjects of some proportions . . . so that they can discharge [their] duties" and noted that he had been forced in one instance to appoint

two unlucky artisans who in order to subsist are tied to their workshops, [and who] with notable harm to the subsistence of their families have to leave them . . . for the Administration . . . ; when they have to instruct in the first diligences in some case of death or wounding they find it necessary . . . to pay someone who has experience in these matters, or they have to neglect it because there is no scribe or subject who can use the pen.[86]

Of course, there were many men in any given village who, despite not being "hombres de bien," had governing experience, having served in repúblicas during the federalist era. And apart from some failed attempts to bypass such men in the search for a juez de paz, Oaxacan government in the centralist era generally reflected this situation; and, in practice, the majority of jueces were, in the words of the prefect of Teotitlán, "unfortunate indígenas."[87] Without intimate knowledge of the villagers, subprefects relied on local knowledge to provide them with acceptable candidates for office, and they regularly solicited names from the outgoing officers in the towns themselves. In some cases, the subprefect contradicted the requests. After the municipal corporation of San José Chicahuastla "elected" Balentín José in 1839, one subprefect claimed to be alarmed by the man's daily drunkenness and scandalous behavior and replaced him with another villager named Ysidro Martín.[88] But most often, if state officials failed to heed the suggestions of the outgoing officers, they faced the towns' refusal to accept the alternative candidate. In Santiago Plumas in 1838, the outgoing local administration objected to the appointment of Juan Santiago and Mariano Hernández, neither of whom had been on their list of proposed officers. Juan Santiago was a particularly offensive choice. He did not live in the pueblo despite having been born there and was widely known as a vago "because he does not pay the contribution nor is he written in the catalog or list of the Municipality." Some villagers considered him a traitor, as he had fomented discord between Plumas and the town of Jicotlán by illicitly selling some of Plumas's common land to the other village. Once again, the officers sent in their own list of proposals of men more suited to administer the affairs of the town.[89] In Villa

Alta, as Guardino demonstrates, officials often named men younger and less experienced than many villagers may have desired, and responses to them may indicate real disagreement within the villages about who should hold power.[90] But in general, if the juez de paz appointed by the government proved unacceptable, substantial numbers of villagers might simply not obey him at all. The net effect of the villagers' insistence, then, was to force subprefects to name the people the villages requested.

Dependence on villagers' consent also forced subprefects to respond when villagers decided that their juez no longer suited their purposes. Like the alcaldes before them, jueces sometimes lost the confidence of villagers while in office. In June 1838, villagers in both Chiquiquitlán and San Andrés violently deposed their jueces de paz, taking their staffs of office and giving them to others. In this case, the representatives that the villagers sent to Oaxaca City to report the new officers were pursued as criminals.[91] But most state officials were loath to force unwanted jueces on the villages. In San Pedro Tidaa in 1839, after an unspecified dispute, the principales threw their juez out of office. The subprefect responded by putting the previous year's "república" back into place rather than attempting to impose the individuals that he had named.[92]

Because jueces were appointed rather than elected, the Oaxacan state had more leeway in removing them if they became a problem than it had had with the alcaldes and repúblicas. Jueces were often removed for "bad conduct," including violation of draft laws, theft of contribution funds, disobedience to higher authorities, and unspecified "excesses and ineptitude."[93] But in many cases, it is difficult to ascertain if the townspeople or a state official initiated the proceedings against the juez. A number of jueces were removed for constant drunkenness, a stock accusation, certainly, but also a problem that could cause no end of trouble for a village. When one subprefect visited the town of Talpan in 1840, he found the juez, Felipe Santiago, on a drunken binge and suspended him for several months. After he returned to office, some villagers complained of the juez's continued inebriation, which they claimed was interfering with his administration of justice; this time, the subprefect removed him permanently.[94] Dionisio de la Cruz lost his position after a village woman complained that he was denying her access to town water because she did not have enough money to bribe him.[95] And when another official investigated the juez of Atatlanca on a charge of adultery, he found that the juez did not actually live in the town and that the villagers despised him. This juez, too, lost his job.[96]

While replacement of the repúblicas with jueces de paz presented some difficulties, it was in the long run a surmountable obstacle for villages. Villagers could expect the state to respond to their complaints about jueces who did not meet expectations. Oaxacan townspeople thus quickly

learned how to counteract the potentially intrusive effects of the imposition of an entirely new system, using their leverage with the state to mold
the new institutions into a form more congenial to their ideas of good town
government.

Indeed, many townspeople actually managed to use the provisions of
centralism to improve their situation. By the end of the centralist period,
having a juez de paz became a sought-after privilege in and of itself. Under
the legislation passed in 1837, all towns that did not have ayuntamientos
were to have jueces de paz, a provision that made for a smooth transition,
with towns that had previously had repúblicas replacing them with the
new officials. But small settlements that had not previously had repúblicas
saw the new laws as a chance to legitimate their autonomous existence.
Most of these "pueblos" were officially designated as barrios of recognized
towns, and in practice were often dependent settlements that had long
wished to escape from the jurisdiction of their legitimate neighbors. After
1837, residents of such settlements saw the reorganization of village administration as an opportunity to gain the autonomy they believed themselves to deserve.

Such was the case in San Francisco Yucucundo, which was officially a
barrio of the town of Santa María Huistepec. In 1837, after an investigation of the relationship of the two villages, Oaxacan officials assigned
the former settlement its own officers, claiming that the town "had before
an equivalent corporation with diverse title" and thus essentially recognizing Yucucundo's existence as a town. After the juez was named, the
villagers proclaimed that "they consider themselves free and independent
of the pueblo of Huistepec," especially in the matter of village fees and
taxes. In 1838, Huistepec fought back, claiming that Yucucundo had none
of the prerequisites for being a pueblo, "as although they do have a certain
number of vecinos, they do not have lands, water, sacred silver, Church
ornaments, [and] they have only a wooden chapel, and this has such a
limited license that one can only celebrate three masses a year." The conflict lasted until late 1840, when the departmental junta finally ruled in
Yucucundo's favor. The junta asserted that this would not constitute the
creation of a new pueblo but rather a return to the village's former state.[97]
Other small villages were not so successful in their search for autonomy.
In 1841, the departmental junta considered and rejected a request by the
barrio of San Pedro to be detached from Zaachila and given a juez de
paz.[98] In the same year, the junta revoked the pueblo status of the hacienda of Yutacuini, removing its juez and making it subject to the town of
Atoyaquillo.[99] Having a juez de paz was clearly a mark of autonomy in the
eyes of the pueblos, one that had, for some, become available only under
the centralist administration.

The settlements that sought jueces de paz under the 1837 legislation were mostly dependent settlements for whom the new system presented a distinct advantage in comparison to the first federalist regime. In 1844, in the wake of the national reform movement codified in the *Bases Orgánicas* of the previous year, Oaxaca passed new legislation that made the jueces de paz even more important by requiring that only cabeceras would have them. Smaller pueblos would now have appointed officials known as jefes or *agentes de policía* (police chiefs or police agents), officials with comparatively limited powers; they were subject to the authority of the nearest cabecera and unable to carry out most judicial functions. This legislation was intended to address the perceived lack of "suitable" administrators in many small towns, a response to the assumption that judicial functions could not be exercised by people with no education. But the new laws were a blow for pueblos that had long placed their confidence in people whose skills at governing were not dependent on literacy. By limiting the judicial powers of the local administrator, the laws would force pueblos to depend on larger towns for the settlement of local disputes, thus significantly reducing villages' autonomy.[100]

Right away, the pueblos asserted their independence. Towns had the right to appeal, and if they could prove that they had the prerequisites to have a juez, the prefect could make the appointment. Appeals were common. In late 1844 and early 1845, pueblos requested jueces de paz by citing the distance from their cabecera, the difficulty posed by travel to that town to resolve judicial matters, their capacity to govern themselves, and their history of doing so. The results were mixed. San Gerónimo Ystepec was once a cabecera and was far from the new one in Juchitán; the subprefect granted its request. An official in Teposcolula made a similar concession for the town of Santiago Yosondua. The town of Capulalpan had had a juez de paz in the past, and the villagers believed that they thus deserved one now. As they wrote, "using the privilege granted to us by the . . . law, we find ourselves in necessity of applying to Your Excellency . . . [for] the right to institute a Juez de Paz in our Pueblo, or better said to continue having one." Capulalpan claimed that "its vecinos are not purely indígenas, but rather those called vulgarly *Ladinos* or *de razón*," people who could read and write. The prefect, Francisco Franco, granted their request. He failed, however, to recommend jueces de paz for twelve other pueblos in his region, claiming that there was simply no one in the towns who could do the job.[101]

A closer look at two of the cases that arose after 1844 reveals the complexity of the local politics that state and regional officials were now forced to navigate. In northwestern Oaxaca, for example, officials found themselves embroiled in long-standing village rivalries enflamed by the new policies. In October 1844, the governor and departmental assembly granted the request of the town of Concepción Buena Vista for a juez de paz. Four settlements were to be subject to Buena Vista's jurisdiction: Santiago Plumas, Santo Domingo Tepelmeme, San Miguel Astatla, and Rancho de las Naranjas. It was soon clear, however, that this arrangement was not acceptable to most of the villagers involved. In late November, the departmental government received a letter from Vicente Rodríguez, the jefe de policía of Plumas, in which he insisted that Plumas was far more deserving of a juez de paz than was its neighbor Buena Vista. Plumas had a larger population and a more central location, it was the residence of the local priest, and, he claimed, "the civilization of Plumas is well-known and greater than that of Buena Vista and therefore there are a larger number of people able to carry out the position of Juez de Paz." He explicitly noted that the vecinos of Plumas had no interest in taking away Buena Vista's new authority; they simply did not want to be subject to it themselves. The problem was that the two towns were rivals, the result of a long-standing dispute over land. The people of Plumas, wrote Rodríguez,

have not been able to view with a good eye and indifference that they be submitted to the jurisdiction of their rivals or opponents, having to beg from them that they administer justice, not having the appropriate partiality . . . ; above all, I know that the people of Plumas deplore with much feeling and see with suspicion a Juzgado de Paz in Buena Vista, [that town] being lesser in every way with respect to Plumas where we were born."[102]

Soon thereafter, Tepelmeme also asked to be free of Buena Vista's subjection and to have its own juez de paz. By November 29, the word had gotten out that the government was considering this request, and the común of Astatla wrote to ask that the village's judicial authority be shifted from Buena Vista to Tepelmeme. In 1837, the officials wrote, there had been a violent confrontation between Astatla and Buena Vista, resulting in the death of one vecino of Astatla and the wounding of many others. As in Plumas, the villagers of Astatla were worried that the juez in Buena Vista would not have the necessary impartiality to do his job properly.[103] In the end, the government proved amenable to all these requests, and the prefect wrote to the departmental assembly recommending the changes. Plumas, Buena Vista, and Tepelmeme all had jueces de paz in the following year.[104] Given the ability of pueblos to turn jueces de paz into stand-ins for more representative institutions, this chain of events had essentially subverted the intentions of centralist law, while still operating within its terms.

The way this could occur is apparent in a second example, this one from the village of San Francisco Telistlahuac. In February 1845, this town's inhabitants received word that they were to be subjected to the judicial authority of the juez de paz of neighboring San Pablo Hizo. Manuel José Pérez, the new appointed local administrative official for the town, wrote to the regional government to complain:

I am far from censuring a decree that without doubt is the result of meditation and serious and educated discussions; but as the law can never foresee all things . . . , it happens many times that a disposition beneficial in itself or considered in general, applied in the particular, produces effects harmful and perhaps contrary to the thought of the legislator and it is necessary to dispense with its fulfillment and concede an exception.

What the government did not know in this particular case was that the people of Telistlahuac were locked in a dispute with those of San Pablo Hizo: "Not only [is there] discord between the vecinos of both pueblos, but also between the juez of San Pablo and the private individuals of Telistlahuac." New laws that subjugated one pueblo to another were not a general problem, Pérez was quick to note, but were rather a problem in this particular case. After consideration, the subprefect and prefect agreed and granted the town of 1,200 inhabitants its own juez by the end of the year.[105]

Oaxacan villagers believed that the most important aspect of the Oaxacan state was its obligation to protect pueblo autonomy. As long as the government was amenable to this notion, new laws and institutions that challenged that autonomy could be reshaped and reinterpreted. Most often, the government did indeed prove amenable. Villagers'—and thus most Oaxacan citizens'—commitment to the state depended on precisely the privileges that centralism denied, and the Oaxacan departmental government was thus willing to make concessions that would lessen the detrimental effects of the new regime. Villagers quickly learned the avenues by which they could gain such concessions, and in the process they even discovered advantages that the centralist order might present. Despite the fact that centralism by its very nature attacked the autonomy of the pueblos, villages and officials together made the new system into a tool for protecting and even enhancing that autonomy. By 1846, when the central government fell, its institutions in Oaxaca were both centralist and not centralist, as villagers and state officials had bent them to their needs.

So effectively did the state and indígenas accommodate each other under centralism, the return to national federalism in 1846 actually caused problems. In September of that year, after the 1824 constitution was reinstated, the Oaxacan government decreed that the pueblos should once again hold municipal elections. In December, Oaxaca's towns elected new repúblicas according to the rules that had been abandoned in 1836.[106]

The nature of federalism suggested that such a reinstatement should have been a boon for the pueblos. And indeed, the document that the villagers of Yxtlán signed in support of the old system's return expressed this potential:

In [this plan] are consigned the most healthy principles that indicate to the pueblos the remedy to the evils they have suffered until now. . . . [A]chieving this object will see established the popular system that the majority of the Nation has defended in diverse ways, believing it to be most analogous to its prosperity; . . . establishing this system, the pueblos will not be attacked in their sovereignty . . . [107]

Yet because of what had transpired in the years since 1836, in some cases towns now actually lost privileges that they had gained under centralism. The barrio of Guelatová, for example, claimed that the government had granted it a "república" under centralism and that they thus deserved one now. The reestablished congress, however, wrote that Gregorio Toribio, the teniente de policía who had made the request,

is wrong to assert that a república was conceded to the said barrio in the central regime, which is very distinct from the jueces de paz which in that era they established even in haciendas and ranchos that had the necessary population signaled by the law without this giving a guarantee that they would be converted into pueblos.[108]

Guelatová thus lost its "república" because the reestablishment of federalism limited the privilege of elected government to towns of a certain size. Of course, according to centralist law, Guelatová had never had a república at all. But in taking advantage of centralist law, the villagers had turned their jueces de paz into an institution that was essentially equivalent.

Despite Guelatová's failure, the reinstated federalist laws proved in many cases to be as flexible in the face of pueblo discontent as had been their predecessors. In December 1848, one authority in San Antonio Abad wrote that "all the vecinos have presented me with their disgust that this population does not enjoy adequate Authority as in all the other pueblos, for the Administration of Justice." The república had been suspended in 1847 because the town had only 193 inhabitants, and it now had only a regidor. For the villagers, this meant unacceptable and unprecedented reliance on another pueblo. They claimed to have all the prerequisites for their own complete government, including lands, funds, public buildings, a church, and religious articles. But most of all, they deserved a república because they had always had one, "this Pueblo being one of the oldest and always considered between all the others as Pueblo although its population is small." In this case, the prefect agreed to restore the república that the pueblo felt to be its due.[109] Similarly, in the barrio of Guadalupe Morelos, the villagers met in "popular junta" and decided to ask for an alcalde and regidores, so they would not have to travel to Nuchita to conduct judicial affairs. In 1847, their request, too, was granted.[110] Under the new federalism as under centralism, when the pueblos asked, they could often expect to receive.

It is crucial to note, however, that neither villagers nor officials were unaware of the ideological differences between the two systems, nor did they ignore those differences. Indeed, through Oaxacans' experiences in these years, the terms *federalism* and *centralism* carried specific meanings inextricable from the process of institutional adaptation that Oaxacans devised. In Oaxaca, federalism and centralism were recognizable in both their institutional and ideological forms but were deployed in a uniquely Oaxacan manner. In practice as well as theory, the lines between the two systems became blurred.

One final example from the transition back to federalism illustrates the way that Oaxacan officials and villagers navigated both the different institutional demands of federalism and centralism and their different ideological implications. In December 1846, Fernando de León and the principal citizens of the barrio of La Ciénaga wrote to the governor of their department to make a request. For the past ten or twelve years, they wrote, they had had their own town government, "in virtue of the laws in force that ruled that it be so." Yet the subprefect of Zimatlán was insisting that La Ciénaga should be governed from Zimatlán itself, a ruling that the villagers were certain was incorrect:

Presently because of the change in system it has been believed quite wrongly that those laws no longer reign; this error has given place to [a belief that] we wish to return to the old system and to subject ourselves to the municipality of Zimatlán, which would cause us a thousand harms and problems and would extort the good management of our neighborhood with detriment to the best public service.

Under the reestablished federalist statutes, La Ciénaga was not considered a pueblo and thus would not have the privilege of electing its own alcalde and república. But the villagers were quite sure that they deserved this privilege, "as is the custom, as thus it will conform to justice and the public good and [the good] of our Barrio." Moreover, they argued that in granting that right the government would in fact be doing something fundamentally *federalist*. In the villagers' effort to escape what they considered to be an oppressive dependency on Zimatlán, they revealed their understanding of the federalist ideology of administration: "This is not opposed to the system of the established government . . . it is very much in conformity with that in which *each numerous population distant from another has its independent and free government without being subjugated to another.*"[111]

La Ciénaga's actual experience did not conform to the ideal forms of either federalism or centralism. Local autonomy was associated with federalism. Theoretically, the change to a centralist regime should have stifled the village's local government, subjecting it to outside control and taking away its right to elect its own municipal officers. But according to La Ciénaga's representatives, the townspeople had in fact spent the ten years of centralist rule choosing one of their own to administer the town's affairs. Now a federalist government threatened to take away that privilege. Thus, while revealing a precise understanding of the benefits that federalism ought to bring to the indigenous towns of Oaxaca, the townspeople were arguing for a privilege that they had in fact only gained under centralism, after the fall of the federalist government that had prevailed from 1824 until 1836.

Government officials proved receptive to La Ciénaga's arguments. According to the departmental governor, the official who had taken away the barrio's privilege of self-government had clearly misunderstood the situation. Under federalism, self-governance was a given: "In every free Government and principally in the Federal the Citizens have the right to be governed by themselves, so that they can attend their interests, which does not happen when they are governed by outside authorities, as frequently happens in populations of indígenas." In January of the following year, the federalist Oaxacan state government granted La Ciénaga the right to elect its own authorities.[112] Under both centralism and reestablished federalism, political systems grounded in diametrically opposed ideas about local autonomy, the villagers of this small town of 800 citizens went about the business of choosing the men who would serve as their municipal officers.

In the first two decades after Mexican independence, Oaxacan government officials and indigenous villagers were often working at cross purposes. Government officials wished to extract as much tax money and as many soldiers as possible out of the villages, and villagers wished to provide as little of both as they could get away with. To some extent, villagers avoided these obligations by taking advantage of the weaknesses of the state. But the state also had a more positive role, one that villagers both expected and, again, exploited. In addition to providing concrete aid in times of crisis, the state functioned as a tool for pueblos to work out problems internal to their villages and between towns. The dependencies in early independent Oaxaca worked both ways. If the state could not function without its reluctant taxpayers and unwilling soldiers, the villages had come to bank on the state's limited participation in their local affairs.

Despite the contrary motives with which indígenas and state officials approached the issues of taxation, recruitment, and village autonomy, their actions were in consonance often enough to allow the villagers to believe that they possessed a good deal of leverage with the state and that they could influence its actions if they had to. This belief was not unfounded. If the power imbalance between indígenas and the state was skewed in nearly every way, when it came to battles over the concerns that made daily life bearable, indígenas knew that in their contest with the government they had reason to expect at least some success in achieving their goals.

Oaxacan villagers understood "citizenship" in terms of the obligation of the state to provide protection, justice, and autonomy for its pueblos. This definition, which had its roots in colonial New Spain, was broad enough to encompass a variety of institutional arrangements. Federalism, centralism, and reestablished federalism all presented Oaxacan pueblos with different sets of institutions for governing the towns. But the long-term effect of the townspeople's insistence on autonomy and independent government made each form of government look in many ways the same on the ground. The flexibility of the Oaxacan government in the face of that insistence meant that most Oaxacans did not consistently identify a particular system as the best one, nor did they tie their commitment to the state to particular institutions. Oaxacans' commitment to their government depended instead on that flexibility itself, which was based in the structures of production and marketing that characterized the state. As long as the government remained flexible and responsive at key moments, rural villagers would count themselves good citizens of Oaxaca.

And yet, despite the malleability of institutions, systems, and ideologies, Oaxacans were nevertheless aware of institutional and ideological change. They developed attachments to particular concepts, such as "federalism" or "centralism," because they found them, in particular circumstances, to be useful tools for furthering their interests. Because Oaxacan villagers were so successful in bending each set of institutions to their will, systems of governance in and of themselves enjoyed a great deal of legitimacy. That legitimacy, though, was contingent on villagers' continued ability to work with the state government to reinterpret and reorient the elements of those systems. Literal enforcement of institutions and laws was rarely an option. By 1848, when liberal ideologues in Mexico City and the states began to formulate plans to turn liberal ideas and theories into more faithful practice throughout the nation, Oaxacans already had a great deal of experience with subverting the intentions of institutional change. Seen from one angle, very little actually happened in Oaxaca between 1825 and 1848; there were almost no large-scale uprisings, no fundamental structural changes, and no real change in the relationship between state and society. But the unique way in which Oaxacans had avoided such changes would prove crucial to their response to concerted liberal reform in the years to come.

One final observation about Oaxaca is noteworthy. Largely missing from the villagers' discourse about their relationship with the state was a consistent and explicit claim to "indigenousness." In part, this is a result of there being no one predominant ethnic group in Oaxaca. But indigenous Oaxacans, in their correspondence with the state, were no more likely to call themselves "Zapotecs" or "Mixtecs" than they were to call themselves "indígenas." Instead, they most consistently identified themselves by referring to their villages of origin.[113] By contrast, for the state, the structure of politics was based explicitly on a distinction between indigenous and nonindigenous Oaxacans. State officials were much more likely than villagers to use the word *indigenous* to describe their constituents, and that word conveyed assumptions about both the specific obligations of the state to indigenous people and the perceived shortcomings of indigenous people as a race. But because almost all "villagers" were also "indigenous," it is difficult to separate the two identities. Villagers may, in the eyes of officials, have been poor in large part because they were indigenous, but in the day-to-day practice of politics, it was the poverty, not the indigenousness, that mattered most. The basic political relationship in Oaxaca was between the state and *villagers*. Circumstances in Oaxaca produced a fundamental compromise about village autonomy, and so neither villagers nor state officials saw the need to use ethnicity as a central justification in making claims on each other. This situation contrasted sharply with that in Yucatán, where indigenousness would play a crucial role in the relationship between state and indigenous society, and indeed in the process of the building and then the deterioration of the legitimacy of the liberal state.

CHAPTER 4

The Disintegration of a Divided Polity

YUCATAN, 1825-1847

BETWEEN THE MID-1750S and the early 1800s, Yucatán was transformed by the steady movement of nonindigenous agricultural entrepreneurs into the countryside and by their efforts to gain control over both the land and the labor of indigenous villagers.[1] Such nonindígenas argued that indigenous production was woefully inefficient and that only by breaking down indigenous control over the countryside would Yucatán be able to progress. Their words and actions constituted a gradual but constant assault on the indigenous villages, not unlike the classic narrative of liberalism in nineteenth-century Mexico. And also as in that classic narrative, their actions would result in violent rebellion. Yet the story of liberalism in early nineteenth-century Yucatán is neither straightforward nor archetypal but rather rooted in the complexities of local political culture and economy. Despite profoundly different outcomes in Oaxaca and Yucatán, for much of the period in question the two governments' dealings with indigenous people were more similar than they were different. As in Oaxaca, the legitimacy of the Yucatecan government among indígenas was built on an implicit contractual relationship whereby the state promised to protect village autonomy in exchange for the payment of taxes. And Yucatán's unique municipal system seemed similarly designed to favor the autonomy of indigenous people because it retained the república de indígenas. As in Oaxaca, the Yucatecan state found itself forced by the limits of its own reach to allow for explicitly indigenous self-government.

But Yucatán was different in two crucial interrelated ways. First, in contrast to Oaxaca, Yucatecan villages regularly housed both indigenous and nonindigenous people, and the term *villager* was thus increasingly not synonymous with *indigenous*. Second, the political culture of the protection of indígenas clashed with Yucatán's developing political economy. For the government, this produced a quandary. The state had to find a way to balance the demands of nonindígenas, who promised to transform the state's economy, with those of indigenous people, the majority of the population. The Yucatecan government attempted to achieve this balance by placing ethnicity at the center of the political relationship between state and society. State officials were wary of the potential power of nonindigenous entrepreneurs and yet cognizant of the danger inherent in losing indígenas' support. And so they tried to accommodate both indigenous and nonindigenous constituents by building a separate relationship with each. By identifying indigenous people as fundamentally unique in political personality, the state hoped to simultaneously protect and isolate them.

As late as the mid-1840s, this strategy seemed to be working fairly well. In 1845, the secretary general of Yucatán reported confidently to the departmental assembly that all was well in the state's towns and villages. "It cannot be denied," he proclaimed, "that in the pueblos of the department interior order is conserved, and that policing has not been unattended, contributing principally to the presentation of this pleasing result, the morality of those same pueblos."[2] For much of the early independence era, Yucatán's indigenous and nonindigenous populations coexisted fairly peacefully, if uneasily and certainly unequally. But in the two decades following passage of Yucatán's first state constitution, that relationship gradually became more unstable. For indígenas, a strong ethnic identification was a mixed blessing. On the one hand, it gave them a powerful language in which to couch their demands, and they embraced it as such. In the face of the encroaching threat from nonindigenous people, the colonial claim that the state was obligated to protect indígenas *because* they were indigenous was a potent weapon. But on the other hand, the liberal claim that indígenas were an obstacle to economic growth left them vulnerable, as pressures on the villages for land, labor, and political control increased.

Institutional change also contributed to conflict. Yucatán's state government, like Oaxaca's, alternated between federalism and centralism in response to national developments. As in Oaxaca, indigenous citizens learned about the possibilities and limits of various forms of government and about how to act on what they had learned. Yet unlike Oaxaca's indígenas, who used their leverage with the state to negate much of the difference between the ruling systems, Yucatecan indígenas, because of competing claims from the nonindigenous community, had divergent experiences under federalism and centralism. Their expectations of the state became tied not only to ethnicity but also to the state's continuing adherence to particular institutions: those associated with federalism, which tended to protect local autonomy. Where in Oaxaca institutional change only strengthened the ties between the government and indigenous citizens, the frequent shifts in Yucatán's administrative system undermined the indigenous population's trust in the state.

By late 1847, the uneasy peace between the indigenous and nonindigenous populations in Yucatán had come almost entirely undone. Despite its careful balancing act, the Yucatecan state had not foreseen that its institutional forms would ultimately accentuate, reinforce, and exacerbate the divide between indígenas and nonindígenas. Just three years after the Yucatecan secretary general issued his glowing report on village morality, the nonindigenous population of Yucatán was in danger of having to flee the peninsula under the threat of the rebellious inhabitants of those very villages, who were on the verge of capturing the state's capital. Official reports now sounded different; in the words of the governor,

There is no longer in Yucatán any industry, commerce, or business of any kind; private fortunes have disappeared; revenues, taxes, and other resources of the Government have been exhausted completely: and what's more half the pueblos are in the power of the Indians, who imprint their mark of desolation and extermination.[3]

From 1847 until the mid-1850s the Yucatecan state faced a widespread, violent, and nearly successful indigenous rebellion. This conflict, known as the Caste War, would depopulate much of the Yucatecan countryside and forever alter political relationships on the peninsula.[4] There is little doubt that Yucatecan indígenas rebelled violently, a circumstance that has led to the characterization of the conflict as a race war. But if it was a race war, "race" must be understood as the product of distinctions made on an institutional level, distinctions that had their roots in Spanish legal procedures, reiterated and retooled under the independent government of Yucatán. The war was not a result of those distinctions themselves but rather of the state's failure to play by the rules they implied. As in Oaxaca, indígenas developed an understanding of the responsibilities of the state in reference to both new institutions and new iterations of the political role of indigenous people. But unlike Oaxacan officials, representatives of the Yucatecan state increasingly found themselves either unwilling or unable to share indígenas' vision of proper government.

Yucatán's New República de Indios: *Federalism and Centralism, 1821–1839*

As in Oaxaca, Yucatecan indigenous villagers' attachment to the government was based first and foremost on the state's willingness to support the autonomy of indigenous communities. Because in Yucatán this often meant balancing the interests of two ethnic groups within each town, the arrangement was constantly in danger of collapse. Overall, in the first fifteen years after independence, the government's responsiveness to the demands of indigenous communities would keep a significant breakdown of state legitimacy at bay. The fragile peace that the Yucatecan state sought to maintain would be constantly challenged, but it would not fall apart. Yet the events of these years established the lines along which the Yucatecan peace was soon to fracture. Yucatán's relationship with the Mexican government was particularly tumultuous; the state seceded twice from Mexico, first in 1830 and then in 1839. In addition, land use was becoming an increasingly contentious issue in Yucatán. The result was that, by 1839, much of the rural Yucatecan population was politicized in ways that had not occurred in Oaxaca. The creation of expectations and the experience of disappointments set the stage for the final disintegration of good relations between Yucatecan indígenas and the Yucatecan state by 1847.

CREATING THE DIVIDED POLITY: INDEPENDENCE AND THE INSTITUTIONALIZATION OF ETHNICITY

Yucatecans broke officially from Spain in 1821 with specific economic goals in mind. They were initially reluctant to join Mexico in independence. Declaring war on Spain would mean cutting ties with the island of Cuba, Mérida's only direct trading partner. In 1820 and 1821, however, Yucatecan authorities increasingly disagreed with the liberal government in Spain over issues of free trade. Yucatecans ultimately accepted both independence and allegiance to Mexico. But they did so in the expectation that Mexico would be receptive to the region's economic needs, at least to the degree that the Spanish had been if not more. In 1823, when Iturbide fell, Yucatán, like Oaxaca, set up its own "federal republic," pending the confirmation of Mexico City's commitment to a federalist system that would ensure the new states' autonomy. When that system was declared, Yucatán confirmed its existence as a state in the federal republic of Mexico.[5]

The regional government's agitation for free trade was intimately linked to its aspirations for the development of new local products and thus to its designs on the indigenous villages. The products that it hoped to export—dyewood, sugar, salt, rice, and henequen—required a fundamental reorganization of the Yucatecan social structure. Indigenous people, who lived primarily in autonomous subsistence-based villages, would have to be either convinced or forced to provide labor for this project. The most vocal proponents of this change were self-identified liberals, members of a political group known as the *sanjuanistas*.[6] Liberals argued that indigenous communal production was not as efficient as wage labor and that it was thus crucial to gain control over indigenous resources.

The Spanish constitutional ayuntamientos established in 1812 seemed to offer a tool to gain that control. When controlled by nonindígenas, ayuntamientos could undermine indigenous autonomy. At first, this seemed to work; as hoped for, the ayuntamientos elected in 1812 had fallen largely into nonindigenous hands. As they observed the functioning of those ayuntamientos, however, the political elites who would eventually determine the shape of state law lost their enthusiasm for the ayuntamiento as a complete solution. In seeking an institutional remedy for the problem of town administration, the Yucatecan state congress, like the Oaxacan, would attempt a compromise that borrowed heavily from the past. It did so, however, with very different intentions.

Legislators' first criticisms of ayuntamientos denounced them as tools for exploitation through which new town authorities siphoned off resources from the villages.[7] When the constitutional congress met in late 1823, congressmen expressed concern about abuses of power, calling the recent administration of public funds "scandalous" and noting that the election of ayuntamientos had become a spoils system.[8] But the problem was not simply that the ayuntamientos were poor and corrupt administrators. It was also that they had replaced a system that legislators now understood to have worked quite well. In particular, ayuntamientos were much less effective in the collection of taxes than had been the repúblicas. In September 1823, deputy Juan N. Rivas compared the new state of affairs with the colonial system:

The experience of those years since the erection of the Intendencies in New Spain until the establishment of the Constitution has confirmed in an incontestable and grievous manner that the so-called casiques aided by the officials of the repúblicas collected the tributes with ease, to their own profit and the convenience of the community of tax-payers . . . and without corruption. Compare this conduct with that of the present alcaldes, councilmen and clerks: add to this the amount that these have swindled from the most recent contributions and the ancient *pósitos* . . . and you will find that the changing of hands and the manner of tax-collection and the administration of public funds has only served to promote vice . . . converting these functionaries not only into true vagos but also into demoralizers of the Indians. . . . Being more ignorant, corrupt and insolent than the Indians themselves, what can the *patria* expect from them, what civilization can they give to the Indians?[9]

Rivas argued that the ayuntamientos both harmed the indigenous population and were less efficient at funneling revenue to the center. Putting town government directly in the hands of the local nonindigenous elite, he suggested, was a risk to the revenue of the state.

Yet Yucatecan legislators were not as willing as their Oaxacan counterparts to return complete local political control to indígenas. Rather, a central aim of the Yucatecans was to *reduce* indigenous control. Legislators relied on indigenous officials to collect the taxes that were the lifeblood of the Yucatecan state, but they also wanted the towns to have nonindigenous figures with the political authority to check the autonomy of indigenous government and open up the possibility for further nonindigenous enterprise. The challenge was introducing such officials without entirely alienating the indigenous population.

Legislators pursued these goals with three major decisions. First, Congress retained the ayuntamiento as a universally elected body but approved a measure suppressing ayuntamientos in towns that were not cities, *villas*, or political cabeceras, thus limiting their election to towns that had considerable nonindigenous populations. This law ensured that ayuntamientos would be nonindigenous whenever possible. Next, Congress created a second kind of universally elected municipal body, the *junta municipal*, to be elected in the towns where ayuntamientos had been suppressed. Many of these towns had significant indigenous populations. But these juntas, too, were explicitly intended to be nonindigenous institutions. State legislators wished to avoid the formation of municipal juntas in entirely indigenous towns where they were likely to consist of indigenous councillors. Such towns, which the new legislation described as "small settlements included in the vicinity of the towns that have Ayuntamientos or Municipal juntas and are located at some distance from them" were to be governed by *alcaldes auxiliares* (auxiliary mayors) appointed in the closest town with a council.[10] These smaller villages were generally those known as ranchos or *sitios* and were often inhabited by groups of indígenas who had emigrated from larger villages nearby. People living in these settlements retained the right to vote in the junta or ayuntamiento elections in those larger towns, but they had no universally elected government of their own.[11]

The third step Yucatán's congress took was more controversial. In May 1824, four congressmen proposed the following:

That for the collection of the established taxes, and only for this objective, respecting the indígenas, the old repúblicas de indios should be reestablished. This proposition, which seems scandalous in a republican system, is not, given the total lack of funds in our accounts and our precarious way of supporting ourselves without any type of . . . industry among the indígenas of Yucatán.

Congress justified this unorthodox suggestion by looking to history. Under the Spanish regime, they asserted, collecting taxes had always been difficult, requiring a great deal of coercion. Indígenas had often fled to escape the exactions and the punishment that accompanied nonpayment. But under the monarchy, the Spanish state had access to these dispersed members of the community through the repúblicas. Independent Yucatán, without such indigenous mediators, did not have this advantage regarding errant villagers:

> Their reduction, which did not cost the Spanish government anything, would now be very expensive to this Free State, as the same causes cited above still exist and the same contributions cause them to flee, but the same punishments and the vigilance of those authorized to impede the flight no longer exist.[12]

Aware that it did not have the resources or the authority to control indigenous villagers and keep them within the taxpaying community, the Yucatecan government tapped the repúblicas once again to fulfill this function.

On July 26, 1824, Congress officially reestablished the repúblicas. The stated motive was "to remove the obstacles that thwart the collection of public contributions, contain the dispersion of the indígenas in the forests and find them an honest occupation that makes them useful to society." The indigenous authorities were thus exhorted to keep their communities contained, productive, and subservient to the state. Beyond that, the primary responsibility of the repúblicas would be the collection of taxes. All other official administrative tasks belonged to the ayuntamientos and municipal juntas.[13] Thus, rather than setting up a system with one clear source of local authority, the Yucatecan state congress had created dual structures, often both within the same town, one explicitly indigenous and the other ostensibly open to anyone. Retaining the universally elected councils allowed Congress to preserve the notion of universal popular sovereignty established in 1812 and reaffirmed with independence; the reestablishment of the repúblicas allowed them to retain legal differences between indígenas and nonindígenas as political actors.

Between 1824 and 1829, Yucatecan villagers embarked on the creation of a system that created a clear demarcation between the political practices of Yucatán's two ethnic communities. In general, ayuntamientos existed only in towns with large nonindigenous populations, in many cases close to 50 percent of the total number of inhabitants. Juntas, on the other hand, were elected in a wider variety of situations. Pocboc, for example, was an almost entirely indigenous town, while Tizimín was heavily nonindigenous. Both elected municipal juntas by 1827.[14] Most of the towns electing juntas had small but significant nonindigenous communities. Yet, in those towns that did elect juntas, the local indígenas, often the majority, would have little chance to serve on them. It would have been politically impossible for the legislature to ban indigenous people explicitly from serving on the universally elected councils; but, in practice, a literacy requirement kept many if not most indigenous aspirants out. In the end, most of those serving in juntas and ayuntamientos in Yucatecan towns after 1824 had Spanish, not Maya, surnames. There were some exceptions, such as the junta of the village of Tinum in 1825, which described itself as being composed of "indígenas." Some towns had councils with at least one member with a Maya name; in others, indígenas served as members of the junta that ran the electoral proceedings. But, in most towns, the juntas were controlled by the nonindigenous minority. Alcaldes and councilmen serving on the ayuntamientos or juntas had to fulfill strict residence requirements—three years of local residence and employment—to serve on the councils. Drawn from this pool, the councils were most often composed of small farmers and businessmen and sometimes of larger landowners who lived in the area.[15]

If indigenous service on the councils was limited, indigenous voting in their election was not. Yucatán's suffrage was broad, including all "citizens," a category that encompassed resident male individuals above the age of twenty-one, or eighteen if married. As in other parts of Mexico, one could lose these rights for not having a "known home, occupation, or way of life," a vague distinction that in practice likely eliminated some potential indigenous voters but also affected nonindigenous people. Illiteracy was not an obstacle to citizenship; the 1825 state constitution postponed any consideration of a literacy requirement until 1835.[16] The indigenous population thus dominated the electorate.

It is clear, however, that indigenous participation in the election process was understood to be distinct from that of nonindigenous villagers. When indígenas voted, nonindígenas characterized their participation as uninformed or uninterested. For example, in 1825 the alcalde of Temax, José María Samada, was accused of deliberately manipulating the recent junta elections. While not precisely denying the substance of the charge— that he had failed to publicize the elections properly—he noted that he had strategically planned the event to occur during a public festival so that nearly the entire population would be present. Everyone, then, had had the opportunity to vote: soldiers, the indigenous population, and the "vecinos" of the town and its haciendas, ranchos, and sitios. Samada claimed that "the natives have no interest in these activities; anyone who has the least knowledge of them is well persuaded of this truth" and that there was little point in improving publicization because "those who did not want to vote did not, and those who were absent would not have come even with two proclamations."[17] If indigenous townspeople still did not vote, Samada argued, it simply could not be said to be his fault.

Indigenous votes were also considered to be easily bought. In Maní in 1825, for instance, the local priest was accused of offering relief from religious taxes for members of the república who would vote for his favored

candidates, presumably also providing votes from the indigenous community.[18] The illiteracy of much of the indigenous population also allowed
for manipulation of the indigenous vote. In Maxcanú in 1829, for instance,
Juan José Novelo was surprised to discover that he had been elected, as
he had not been aware that any elections had taken place. Apparently, no
proclamation had been published, and thus no nonindigenous townspeople had voted; only members of the indigenous community had cast their
ballots, again presumably because their votes could be manipulated by the
organizers of the election. After an investigation, the elections were nulli-
fied. When held again a month later, Novelo attended with the intention
of protecting illiterate voters but was prevented from this duty by men
who "usurped the will of a multitude of citizens, who in voting for one,
were set down [as voting for] another."[19]

It is impossible to judge whether indigenous people were indeed uninterested or manipulable. Certainly, it may have seemed far more advan-
tageous to many to sell their vote in exchange for privileges that could
alleviate poverty, and the evidence suggests that this occured with some
frequency.[20] But even where it is clear that indigenous people took an
active interest in local politics, nonindigenous behavior could stand in
their way. In February 1832, during the brief federalist interim of 1832–
1833, thirty-four indigenous citizens from the small town of Xcupilcacab
complained to the governor about the recent elections for their municipal
junta. They indignantly asserted that Tomás Sándobal had abused his position as president of the electoral committee, imprisoning several indígenas who refused to vote according to his wishes, closing the elections two
hours earlier than required by law and sending a number of citizens—
including the entire population of a nearby rancho called Hoctún—home
without casting their votes. By these actions, the petitioners wrote, he had
"scorned the will of the majority of the inhabitants of the pueblo."[21]

This political separation of indígenas and nonindígenas apparent in
elections for ayuntamientos and juntas was reinforced by the existence
of the repúblicas. The distinction between the two councils within each
town was deeply rooted in Yucatecan understandings of ethnic difference.
If they considered indigenous people to be political creatures at all, nonindígenas expected them to limit their participation to their own councils. And in turn, many indigenous people believed that those councils
represented their interests more effectively. Repúblicas de indígenas, like
juntas and ayuntamientos, were elected popularly, but only members of
the indigenous community could vote. These councils were headed up by
a cacique who, in practice, usually served in that office until he resigned,
died, or was forced out. Below him were the members of the council—
including a *teniente* (cacique's lieutenant), several alcaldes and regidores,

and a scribe—who were elected yearly.[22] As Rugeley has noted, the decree that reestablished the repúblicas pointedly ignored the function that the repúblicas had traditionally served as institutions of self-government, representation, provision of justice, and reproduction of social hierarchy.[23] But these functions were not likely to disappear on their own, and the repúblicas remained crucial institutions in the towns. It was here, rather than in the municipal juntas, that most indígenas were to exercise their political will.

This did not mean that the juntas and ayuntamientos were irrelevant to the indigenous community. Juntas, ayuntamientos, and constitutional alcaldes were in charge of activities that affected the population as a whole: policing, protecting the persons and goods of the townspeople, promoting the establishment and care of primary schools, preserving common supplies of grain, taking care of construction and maintenance of streets and public works, and promoting agriculture and commerce. They had the right to collect municipal *arbitrios*, local taxes that the councils devised to pay for their expenses; these could include taxes on transit on roads within the towns' territory and on the transport and sale of certain goods. The alcaldes also had a judicial function, trying cases involving small crimes or small amounts of property. In Motul, a large and ethnically mixed town in central Yucatán with several small indigenous auxiliary villages, the ayuntamiento met twenty-seven times over the course of 1833. In these sessions, they discussed and named commissions to deal with concerns about the maintenance of streets, the local schoolteacher, and other sundry issues, among them provisions for dealing with ownerless animals running free in the village square. The judicial function of the alcaldes made intimate contact with and influence over the lives of all villagers inevitable. Out of thirty-two cases tried by the alcalde of Ticul in 1826, at least eleven involved indigenous litigants. The cases included inheritance disputes, property transactions, minor thefts, marital altercations, disagreements over work contracts, injuries, custody battles, and debts. Finally, the universal councils played an important role in times of crisis. The Motul ayuntamiento in 1833, for instance, acted to mitigate the effects of a grain shortage and a cholera epidemic.[24]

In general, members of both the indigenous and nonindigenous communities viewed an ayuntamiento or a municipal junta as a good thing. Towns composed largely of non-Maya were quick to ask for juntas when they did not have them. The town of Hool, for instance, which was 70 percent nonindigenous, petitioned the government for a junta in 1827. But in the tiny village of Sinanche, the request came from the entire community. The villagers had taken it on themselves to hold junta elections in 1825, only to find that they had been assigned an auxiliary mayor from the nearby town of Yobaín. They sent a petition to the state authorities, signed by both indigenous and nonindigenous villagers. The investigation that followed revealed strong support for the creation of a junta among the indigenous community, including the cacique.[25] Indeed, the universally elected councils were often valued by the community as a whole; and, in the early years of Yucatán's republican government, the relationship between the two representative bodies was fairly free of conflict.

Good relations between the two sets of councils—and between the communities they represented—were, however, reliant on certain clear divisions of duty. In particular, juntas and ayuntamientos were not to collect state taxes from the indigenous community. There were two major taxes to collect. The primary state tax was known as the personal contribution. A fee of twelve reales, or one and a half pesos, was collected in portions throughout the year, usually in June and December, from men between the ages of sixteen and seventy. Although the second tax, the obvención, was a strictly religious exaction, its collection was also regulated by the state after October 1825. The law established an "absolute inhibition" against the participation of alcaldes, ayuntamientos, and municipal juntas in the collection of these taxes. The text of the law mandating the obvención offers one clue as to why. It states that "malicious and disruptive men" were apt to foment discord among the indígenas, prompting them to refuse to pay, and it singled out municipal authorities as a particular problem, as they were often reluctant to give aid to priests in the process of collection.[26] In the case of civil taxes, state officials were skeptical of the ability of nonindígenas to collect taxes from indígenas. This, after all, had been the primary justification for the reestablishment of the repúblicas in the first place.

This arrangement meant that, for Yucatán's indigenous population, the vital relationship of mutual obligation that taxation represented developed directly between indigenous communities and the state government. This direct relationship existed in other areas as well. *Subdelegados*, the regional officials who supervised tax collection, were also responsible for overseeing república elections and for supervising the repúblicas' regulation of the residence patterns of indigenous individuals, reinforcing a direct relationship between the repúblicas and the state that bypassed the juntas and ayuntamientos.[27] Subdelegados were also the first step in a chain of command reaching to the state governor, who had the power to judge the capabilities of elected indigenous officers and, in cases where they were found wanting, to remove them from their posts. All in all, these provisions created a situation in which, despite the existence of local councils that excluded indígenas, indigenous people had a direct relationship with the state government in which the issues most vital to the indigenous community could be worked out.

As in Oaxaca, both parties used this relationship deliberately, indígenas to improve their situation and the government to increase its revenues. The subdelegados' function of judging the capacities of caciques is a case in point. Caciques were frequently accused of a number of abuses, including drunkenness, absenteeism, and whipping, the last a practice that had been illegal since the Spanish constitutional era. Townspeople relied on the state to intervene when conflicts could not be worked out within the village. In and of themselves, however, townspeople's accusations against their cacique were unlikely to move the authorities to act. In a case tried in Izamal in 1825, for instance, the court found that the cacique had ordered twelve and seven lashes respectively for a local husband and wife who had allegedly attacked their parents. The court ruled that the punishment was appropriate: "Taking into consideration the rusticity and ignorance of the indígenas, the punishment given to José Rafael Chan would have been very proportional, even if [the cacique] had applied twenty-five lashes as his father requested." By contrast, the state was quick to act against caciques in cases where the collection of taxes was in question. In 1829, Baltasar Canché complained on behalf of himself and the indigenous community that the cacique of the town of Telá mistreated his constituents, often whipping and imprisoning them without just cause. A lengthy investigation based on interviews of indigenous townspeople revealed that the cacique's abuses were notorious. The decision to remove him was made, however, only after the subdelegado, Antonio Gutiérrez, pointed out that the cacique's drunkenness, presumably the cause of his behavior, also interfered with his ability to collect taxes. On several occasions, Gutiérrez had sought the cacique out to settle accounts and had found him in a state of inebriation.[28]

The removal of the cacique for failure to collect taxes was a common recourse for state authorities. In Yaxcabá in 1827, Lázaro Caamal was accused of failing to collect the personal contribution, largely due to his nearly perpetual absence from the town. After an investigation, Caamal was relieved of his duties. In Tahdzin in 1829, the cacique was removed after a court established that he had failed to collect civil taxes. And finally, the cacique of Pocboc was brought to trial by his own constituents in 1825 for abuses of authority, and the court found that the complaints stemmed from townspeople's unwillingness to turn over the personal contribution that the cacique demanded. After the cacique expressed his own unwillingness to punish them for their refusal, the office of the governor suggested that his tax-collecting duties be turned over to a designated agent.[29]

In all of these cases, the indigenous administrative structure was directly supervised by the state government, whether in the form of the executive administration or the judicial system. Municipal authorities could be involved peripherally, as government representatives were likely to request their observations of the behavior of indigenous officials. In the case in Yaxcabá, it was in fact the constitutional alcalde who brought the problem to the attention of the subdelegado in the first place. But caciques and repúblicas were not answerable to constitutional alcaldes. This had important implications for the relationship between the indigenous community and the universally elected councils.

In the years immediately following independence, conflict over taxes was common. In Nunkiní in 1825, for instance, a group of indigenous villagers angry at the imposition of both civil and religious taxes had made the local ayuntamiento a target of its ire, expelling its members and setting up its own alternative body. The response of both local and state authorities to such events, however, made it clearer to villagers that ayuntamientos and juntas were not responsible for taxation. In the town of Pich in 1827, a group of indígenas wrote directly to the governor to complain about their cacique, Procopio Cocom. Cocom had apparently perpetuated a range of abuses, from illegal imprisonment and punishment to theft of livestock, and, finally, to charging double obventions. The villagers' first recourse had been to complain to the alcalde, Diego Peón, who legally could do nothing about it. Only through a government investigation could the problem be addressed; eventually, the governor ruled that the accusations were valid, and that Cocom should be removed.[30] By 1829, however, most complaints about tax collection were routinely addressed directly to the subdelegado or the governor himself, and conflict among the various bodies within individual towns was largely avoided. As indigenous townspeople began to understand the distribution of authority between elected officials and appointed state representatives, the potential for conflict within the town over the issue of taxes receded.

The dual structure of Yucatán's local politics had important implications for indígenas' understanding of the state and their relationship to it. Theoretically, juntas and ayuntamientos served some state functions: acting as a conduit of information from the government and supervising the electoral process for state and national congresses at the local level. But for indígenas, the most important state function was taxation, and because taxation in no way involved the juntas and ayuntamientos, those councils were not seen as part of the state. This, in turn, had important consequences for the nature of representation. Indígenas believed that they were represented to the government by the república, not the junta or ayuntamiento, whereas the functions of the latter boiled down to their administrative duties. This meant that when indigenous Yucatecans appealed to the state, they almost always did so explicitly *as indígenas*: either through their own representatives or in complaint against them. Unlike their Oaxacan counterparts, they consistently referred to themselves explicitly as indigenous and stressed their indigenousness as a necessary factor in the government's consideration.

The juntas and ayuntamientos were not entirely without a representative function; in crisis situations, they often appealed to the state for aid or intervention on behalf of their villages. But petitions from the junta usually came from the entire community, often explicitly in concert with rather than in place of requests from the república. In the aftermath of an epidemic in Seye in 1825, for example, the members of both the municipal junta and the república signed separate copies of the same petition. Similarly, complaints made about the alcalde were likely to come from the entire community, as they did in 1826 in Yaxcabá. According to the villagers' petition, the alcalde consistently abused his authority. The signatures on this letter were arranged in two large groups, one of Spanish and the other of Maya names, suggesting a coordinated effort between two discrete communities.[31] If the ayuntamientos and juntas served a representative function for the indígenas, it was only in the rare cases in which those communities acted in concert, and even then the distinction was maintained.

Overall, institutions of local government in the first years of Yucatán's statehood provided for relatively peaceful relations between two communities that shared the same space. Within this system, indigenous individuals developed a sense of their ties to the state that was particular to them as indígenas and that was predicated on an understanding of the juntas and ayuntamientos as outside of that relationship. The relative stability of this arrangement relied on the maintenance of a number of good relations: among the indigenous community, their representatives, and the ayuntamientos and juntas and between all of those actors and the state. It also relied on the clear delineation of the limits of those relationships. As long as interests within the towns remained relatively aligned, and as long as neither the state nor outside parties made undue demands on the communities, this arrangement continued to hold fragmented Yucatecan towns together. In effect, it was that fragmentation itself that was responsible for the lack of friction between indigenous and nonindigenous Yucatecans.

YUCATAN UNDER CENTRALISM, 1830-1839

Friction would develop along with transformations at the level of the state. In 1829, Mexican president Vicente Guerrero was forced out of power in a centralist uprising. The national government did not become officially centralist until 1836, and most of Mexico's states retained their federalist institutions until that year. Yucatán, however, reacted to the national disorder in 1829 in a particularly dramatic way. When it seemed clear that Guerrero would lose, the military garrison in the city of Campeche declared for centralism. Despite the opposition of the state congress in Mérida, centralist forces raised the support necessary to take power and named their representative, Colonel José Segundo Carvajal, governor of the province. In March 1830, Carvajal convoked a general assembly, which declared that Yucatán, although an integral part of the Mexican Republic, would in effect remain separate from the nation until certain trade and commercial demands were met. Under the assumption that the national shift to centralism would occur soon, Yucatán's new provincial government convoked elections for deputies to the national congress in December 1830. Not surprisingly, these deputies were excluded from deliberations in Mexico City, where federalism still held sway, and Yucatán found itself politically isolated. By early 1831, it had become increasingly clear to the council in Mérida that the national government would not declare for centralism, and pressure to return to the nation increased. After a series of political maneuvers designed to keep Carvajal's government in office, elections were called, and Yucatán returned to the Mexican fold. Yucatán's independent centralist administration had thus lasted only two short years.[32]

Although the state would remain uneasily within the Mexican union until 1839, its own internal politics remained turbulent. From 1832 to 1834, the federalists held power, but they lost control again after a coup that put the centralist faction back at the head of state. The Yucatecan government peacefully accepted the centralist turn on the national level in 1836, closing its congress and installing an appointed governor and departmental junta.[33] But Yucatán remained dissatisfied with national trade policies, and in 1839 a faction of the Yucatecan military rebelled once again, leading to effective separation from the Mexican central state, this time under the banner of a growing national movement for federalism.

With this political chaos came parallel upheaval in the villages, as new legislation implemented with each political change altered the mechanics of town government and threatened to fracture the relatively peaceful relationship that indigenous villagers and their nonindigenous local governments had developed by 1829. Centralism, the ruling system in Yucatán between 1829 and 1831 and again from 1834 to 1839, did the most to threaten that relationship. It compromised the dual electoral system that had helped preserve stability in the towns and introduced appointed state authorities directly into the villages, thus collapsing the distinctions between local and state power that had developed in the preceding years.

The discontinuous nature of centralism in Yucatán and the eventual return to federalism limited the immediate disruption of the relationship between the state and indigenous villages; centralism itself would not, in the end, provide the impetus for indigenous rebellion. But Yucatán's unique political trajectory in these years did have crucial significance. The events of the 1830s inculcated indigenous citizens with a sense of the importance of certain institutional forms to the maintenance of their own autonomy and thus with a clearer notion of what they desired and expected from the state. By the end of the decade, indigenous Yucatecans began to express their dissatisfaction in a language of rights in which their understanding of the state's responsibilities was increasingly explicit. Because it hardened the definition of state legitimacy for indígenas, the centralist interim was a vital precursor to the Caste War.

The centralist system of appointed jueces de paz was instituted for the first time in Yucatán under the insurgent state administration of 1829–1831. From 1832 to 1834, the old system of elected government briefly returned, but it disappeared again with the advent of centralist government in Mexico City in late 1835. In Yucatán, as in Oaxaca, national centralism would mean that very few towns would have the right to elect their own administrative councils. Large cities were exempted; Mérida retained its ayuntamiento, as did Campeche. Some of the towns that had been political cabeceras, including Maxcanú, Hecelchakán, Valladolid, Espita, Tekax, and Peto, also met the qualifications for having ayuntamientos, but the remaining twelve had fewer than the requisite 8,000 inhabitants. Of all the other towns on the peninsula, only Tiholop and Chemax had more than that number.[34] Thus, for most of the 1830s, the vast majority of Yucatecan towns were governed by appointed officials.

On the surface, local administrations did not always change dramatically. In many cases, the jueces were the same men who had served as alcaldes or members of the municipal juntas under the federalist system, just as Oaxacan jueces had often previously been members of the constitutional repúblicas. The laws of 1836 stipulated that like the elected officials, the jueces should be "vecinos of the pueblo," that is, that they should be locals. Government officials with responsibility for a large number of towns were likely to choose their appointees based on previous elections, for lack of more detailed knowledge of the towns' populations. This was reflected in villagers' use of terminology for the towns' administrators, as petitioners would sometimes refer to their juez de paz as their "alcalde" even after alcaldes no longer existed in law.[35] Nevertheless, the fact that they were appointed by the government rather than elected by the townspeople had important repercussions. In Halachó, for instance, many townspeople were outraged by the government's choice of a man who had served as their alcalde nine years before with disastrous consequences. They wrote:

This pueblo and its region exceed 5,000 inhabitants and in its numerous population there are twenty-five or thirty people of . . . honor who know how to read and write, and thus it is not difficult to find someone who can fulfill the duty of Juez de Paz without it being necessary to seize just anyone for this purpose and as the system that fortunately governs us does not allow the pueblos to elect their Juez or Alcalde by voting, electing the best for their government, at least [they should] not choose the worst for it.[36]

It is obvious why nonindigenous villagers would want their own elected officers; less immediately apparent, however, is why this was so important to indígenas, whose participation in the election of those authorities had always been marginal and who did not view universally elected officials as their representatives. And yet, all in all, jueces de paz caused considerably more dissatisfaction than elected officials, especially among the indigenous population. Indigenous villagers repeatedly accused the new authorities of working against the interests of the community or of violating their rights. This occurred because under centralism the distinction between state authority and the authority of local nonindigenous officials that was so crucial to the balance of power in the villages disappeared. Not only were jueces de paz allowed to perform vital state functions that ayuntamientos and juntas had been barred from, they were also, because they were appointed, explicitly understood to be representatives of the state—again, as the ayuntamientos and juntas were not. Thus, many indigenous complaints stemmed from a blurring of the previously clear distinctions that had governed their relationship with the state government. In Yucatán, where local peace had long depended on those distinctions, centralist government made town politics increasingly volatile.

Cracks in the stability of the system began to appear when jueces involved themselves in the tax-collection process. Although repúblicas de indígenas continued in practice to be the primary tax collectors in indigenous towns, jueces de paz, unlike the officers of the municipal juntas, were not prohibited from involvement. Often, the jueces' intrusion into the process of tax collection was manifested in demands for labor service. Jueces, like the alcaldes before them, were responsible for arranging periodic labor drafts on state projects such as roads or pest control. After 1831, villagers began to complain that the officials were also compelling townspeople to perform service on private projects specifically as compensation for tax debt; presumably, the recipient of the services would then cover the taxes of the workers. The indigenous villagers of Cholul, for instance, complained in 1831 that their juez de paz was forcing them to work illegally, imprisoning them without cause and then sending them to work on labor projects in the city of Izamal. They wrote:

We, Excellent Sir, do not doubt that if we were vagrants, badly behaved or without having paid our duties they could obligate us to external work in order to pay our debts; but on the contrary, not only are we extremely busy in our own labors, we have the satisfaction of saying that we do not owe on our contributions.[37]

As they saw it, if the villagers had fulfilled their tax obligation to the state, the juez de paz had no right to interfere in their affairs. Similarly, the juez of the coastal town of Chicxulub arranged in 1831 for the indigenous villagers to perform work service in the milpas of Don José Mequita, claiming that the cacique's ineptitude at collecting obventions made some kind of compensatory arrangement necessary. The villagers were scandalized by the low half-real salary they received for their work, and the cacique and república refused to agree to the contract. Their refusal was followed by a public gathering of eighty indígenas expressing their dissatisfaction with the demands of the juez, who promptly put the cacique and most members of the república in the local jail.[38]

Based on their long-standing direct relationship with the Yucatecan state government, indigenous villagers expected that the governor would step in when their autonomy was violated in this way. In Quelul in 1831, the indígenas complained to state authorities several times, claiming that their juez had forced them to perform compensatory labor service cutting sugarcane at nearby farms, an activity they looked on as "by nature unhealthy." Certain that his actions were illegal, they had sought and gained an order for him to stop from the authorities in Campeche. Now that he had ignored that order, they were appealing to the governor, stressing the direct obligations of the state government to the indigenous community:

Excellent Sir, for all classes of private service you should preside and mediate . . . between the parties; without this prerequisite no one can be compelled or rewarded . . . to ignore this would be to trample upon the sacred rights of liberty so recommended by the laws.[39]

And, in Yaxkukul in 1838, when villagers accused their juez de paz of having intimidated and perhaps killed a local woman in the context of a property dispute, they expressed their certainty that the governor would answer their appeal, based on their claim that their pueblo "breathes . . . the air of liberty."[40]

While villagers could still expect a certain amount of responsiveness from state authorities in these situations, now the juez de paz himself often stood between the villagers and the state government. This was particularly problematic when villagers wished to complain about the jueces themselves. Thus, if the villagers of Chicxulub were outraged by their juez's arrest of the república, they were also concerned that he was blocking their direct access to the state. Apolonio May, the only member of the república who had avoided arrest, complained that the juez had posted guards to prevent him from sending complaints out of the village: "Where is the individual security of the citizens so recommended by the law?"[41] Any seeming reluctance on the government's part to address these issues seemed to violate that law; thus the frustration of a group of villagers from a small town near Motul who found it difficult to get justice against the abusive "alcalde" of their town. Apparently, appeals that the cacique and república had made to the subdelegado, the governor, and the alcalde of Motul had all gone unanswered.[42]

For caciques and repúblicas, these incidents were particularly galling. As the parties who had provided the direct link between villages and the state, they saw their privileges—and, in many cases, their livelihood as tax collectors—eroding and their role as mediator becoming less important as nonindigenous officials took over more and more direct control in the villages.[43] As for villagers, while they may have resented the power of traditional indigenous authorities in some cases, the subordination of those authorities in the new system left them with no direct link to the state. All in all, these incidents reflect the fundamental challenge that the appointed local administrations posed to the villagers' conception of the rights of the pueblos. Villagers associated direct access to the state government through appeal with the nature of citizenship itself—with "sacred liberty," "law," and "rights." During the centralist era, they repeatedly used these terms in protest against their jueces de paz. Certainly, they were upset about the particular actions of the jueces. But abuses on the part of local officials were nothing new. It was not the actions of the jueces de paz in and of themselves that caused problems but rather the institutional context in which they were performed. In effect, the "right" to which indigenous villagers appealed was not one to a particular kind of treatment but rather to a particular kind of system—one in which there was direct and legal recourse to the state in cases of violation of village autonomy. Centralism threatened the distinction between local administration and state government, and it prompted villagers to articulate the importance of that distinction.

The Kind Hands of the Superior Government: Land Legislation under Federalism and Centralism

That centralism did not fundamentally upset stability within Yucatán's towns is particularly remarkable given the fact that it occurred simultaneously with increased pressures on village land. But the potential crisis that this pressure implied was softened by the state's seeming support of villagers on the land question during these years. While villagers did lose land and see usufruct rights restricted throughout the 1830s, circumstances made it possible for them to perceive these pressures as the result of the attempted incursion of outside individuals and to understand the state as consistently working to protect them against these people. The land situation, then, actually helped to offset growing dissatisfaction regarding municipal authority.

Before the 1830s, legal imprecision regarding land use, ownership, and distribution tended to favor indigenous villagers. Due to the semiarid nature of Yucatán's soil, individual farmers relied on a far greater expanse of terrain than they and their villages could conceivably own. Because land had to be left fallow for long periods of time, often several years, farmers were forced to establish at least tentative control over a large and frequently changing number of plots, known as *milpas*. Thus, villagers were likely to use a good deal of land that lay outside of either their villages' common holdings or their own private property. Villagers used land that they did not technically own for a variety of reasons, including the gathering of firewood and the grazing of livestock. As long as their claims to usufruct were not countered, the haziness and relative unimportance of land titles could work to the villages' advantage.

This imprecision would eventually create problems for indígenas, however, when combined with state attempts at rationalization and a growing demand for land from nonindígenas. Many of the lands that villagers used were *baldíos*, technically land that was neither private property nor part of any town's common holdings. Ownership of these lands had passed from the Spanish crown to the Mexican government with independence, and under federalism they were administered by the state governments. From 1813 through the 1850s, baldíos would be at the center of agrarian controversy in Yucatán. As the property of the government, baldíos were a potential source of income for the state. They were also a source of conflict because of their vital importance to the pueblos and their potential worth to agricultural entrepreneurs.[44] For the state, the temptation to sell the lands was supported by liberal ideology that promoted private ownership. The first legislative attempts to transform the use of land in Mexico occurred under the Spanish constitutional regime, which passed various measures promoting the alienation and sale of both baldíos and village lands. These measures were inherited by the independent Mexican state, and in 1824 the national congress published its own law of colonization. This decree provided in a general way for the alienation of public lands to private individuals, but it left the details to the states, exhorting them to produce their own colonization decrees as soon as possible.[45]

Accordingly, the Yucatecan state congress passed its first law of colonization in 1825. An aspirant to any piece of public land had to prove both the plot's availability and his or her own claim on it, established by demonstrating at least four years of peaceful possession. These provisions made it quite difficult to acquire baldíos. The onus fell entirely on the aspirant, who was likely to have problems proving the plot's availability. The proof of four years of peaceful possession was difficult to establish, given the temporary demand for baldíos on the part of a wide variety of rural agriculturalists. There were at least enough attempts to gain title to baldío lands to warrant the reform of the law in 1827 in response to abuses, particularly claims for more land than the aspirant was actually using. On the demand of the governor, the Yucatecan congress ordered the review of all titles granted since 1825 and the nullification of those considered to be illegal. A similar series of decrees, reviews, and retractions occurred in 1832. In 1833, another colonization law was passed, and it stayed in effect until 1837, when the government once again declared the grants of baldíos made under the previous administration to be null. Under all of this legislation, some land alienation did occur, disputes over the process disrupted rural life, and the transformation of land into large-scale rural estates advanced gradually. The overall result of the Yucatecan government's land alienation policies until the early 1840s, however, was the maintenance of the status quo. The difficulty in establishing claims to baldíos, the incomplete commitment of the state to a plan of privatization, and various strategies of peasant resistance meant that villages were often successful in maintaining access to the land that they used.[46]

Adding to the limited effects of these early alienation laws was that local nonindigenous authorities were often no more eager to see their villages' lands alienated than were the indigenous villagers themselves. For the most part, local government officials, whether elected or appointed, were interested in protecting lands in the vicinity of their villages from outsiders. Often, such interests were personal. Claims on village lands could threaten officials' individual holdings, especially if ownership was not clearly established, as was often the case. Alcaldes and jueces de paz were members of the community and were often small farmers themselves, and as such they and their families benefited from the use of both the village commons and of the baldíos that lay within each community's resource base. Local officials were generally concerned for the prosperity of their constituents, which in many ways determined their own.

Over the course of the 1830s, various local administrations decried the effects of the laws of colonization. The municipal junta of Tekantó, writing in 1834, demanded the reform or repeal of the alienation laws, claiming that their implementation had had a terrible effect on the pueblo, greatly increasing the number of people living in poverty. In the same year, the juntas of the towns of Yobaín, Dzilám, Buctzotz, and Telchac, in a concerted effort, wrote to the governor to protest the laws. Their campaign stemmed from a meeting of the junta in Yobaín, in which a local man explained the problem:

Citizen Luis Flores . . . demonstrated the ruinous effects that the law of Dec. 28 of last year have caused to the common good, not only in this municipality, but in the entire *Partido*; [the law] has obstructed the few means of subsistence that are found among the inhabitants of La Costa, in working the *montes* that exist between Dzilam, Buctzotz, Sucilá, Panabá and Senotillo, and [has made] it pathetically clear, that far from achieving the avoidance of scarcity of grains of first necessity [and] protecting and facilitating resources for the opening of croplands, in view of the few products that the hardworking laborers collect . . . , it has promoted difficulties in their labors.

The harmful effects of the laws were widespread: "The result that this unfortunate law has brought to laborious agriculture is manifest, [and] difficulties grow for the poor farmer, which is the immense majority of the partido, in order to benefit those few who have the means to found Haciendas." Jueces de paz under centralism could be as concerned as their elected federalist counterparts. In 1837, the juez of Sudzal, in concert with that of Xanabá, wrote to complain that a recent survey had resulted in harm to the commons of both pueblos.[47]

Villagers were quick to point out the responsibilities of the state. In late 1837, for instance, the indigenous representatives of the town of Kinchil protested the threat to their lands on the part of local hacendados. In their petition, they cited a number of laws, including regulations dictating the necessary space between properties and colonial laws on the provision of *ejidos* (common lands). Most importantly, however, they argued for the obligation of the Yucatecan state to protect the rights of towns, offering their own interpretation of the colonization laws:

If the pueblo of Kinchil has grown in the number that compose it: if from its ejidos the vecinos supply themselves with firewood, coal and other necessities for life: if its lands are still few . . . ; is it not evident that it is opposed to the liberty offered by a free and philanthropic government like the one that we enjoy? [And] to the possession from time immemorial that the pueblo has of its croplands, and what's more to the will and spirit of the legislator[s] who with the goal of supplying the national wealth want the alienation of baldíos, that is, of those lands of the common which are not worked nor are they inherited?

The state, these villagers believed, had the responsibility to help the towns maintain their subsistence. The laws were not the problem; rather the problem was with those who misidentified the lands that villages were using as baldíos. In this case, villagers' expectations of the government were fulfilled; the prefect of the region ordered the suspension of the sales in question.[48]

A similar set of demands and responses occurred in a dispute involving the towns of Muna and Opichén in 1836–1837. The conflict began when Sebastián Avila requested that the state sell him a piece of land located near Muna that he wished to use to graze cattle. The municipal junta in Muna supported his claim, hoping to be granted some of the proceeds for public works in the village. The process stalled, however, when it became clear that the land in question was also claimed by the nearby town of Opichén. That village was not nearly so enthusiastic about the sale of the land, which they claimed would "leave their commons a skeleton." Opichén's junta accused the townspeople of Muna of deliberately attacking their holdings, using "papers of Conquest and other ridiculous documents" to prove their possession of land that Opichén had used for years. Central to Opichén's claims was the responsibility of the government to protect the villagers. Without the land, the junta wrote, the villagers would be forced to take refuge elsewhere, a situation that should be unacceptable in the government's eyes:

This sad portrait for an agricultural town demands the greatest attention from the Superior Government, which wishing to extend its kind hands to it, dictates measures that will protect it from the ambushes of a neighbor whose intentions and continuous machinations cause the unhappiness of a population (*común*).

Juan Pablo Talavera, the political chief of the partido of Camino Real Bajo, which encompassed Opichén, came down strongly on the side of that town, promoting its retention of the lands under dispute. Talavera's protest was successful, as the government decided that the lands in question were part of Opichén's commons and should not be sold.[49] In both Opichén and Kinchil, then, the government answered appeals to its responsibility to uphold such rights with effective protection of village lands. Such vindication was not uncommon.

These rulings, however, often reflected the government's desire to protect *private* landowners who already had title to Yucatecan land rather than a particular concern for indígenas. Because large-scale agriculture was not feasible on most of the peninsula, most aspirants for the new land titles—like Avila in Muna and Opichén—were prospective cattle ranchers, not farmers. As Arturo Güemez Pineda has shown, laws that made it difficult to acquire baldíos were aimed primarily at shielding already existing private landowners from the encroachment of cattle entrepreneurs, not at maintaining village access to land.[50] A case from Ucú is instructive. After lands near the pueblo were requested in 1837, the juez de paz asserted that their alienation would hurt no one. The cacique and república, however, disagreed: "Not only can the montes not be sold as [the juez] claims, because the individuals have nowhere to make their milpas . . . but also in order to avoid the raising of cattle, as the crops will be destroyed by [them]." After an investigation by the prefect, it was found that the lands, "far from being baldíos, as it was supposed, fell visibly within the commons of that pueblo, very close to it, *and to other haciendas in the area, whose owners would without doubt oppose the establishment of another population of cattle within its limits.*"[51]

As in this case, laws aimed at protecting private landowners coincidentally provided substantial protection to the towns as well. Cattle entrepreneurs were a serious threat to the subsistence of the villages, both because they needed land and because their cattle could damage crops. Villagers' relatively free use of large areas of land was possible only as long as no one put up fences. The incursion of cattle entrepreneurs, whose animals had to be stopped from entering farmland, left villagers with the untenable choice of accepting fences or allowing free-range cattle to destroy their crops. Thus, any law designed to stop that incursion worked to the benefit of the villages. Regardless of intentions, a combination of state and local officials' actions seemed to villagers to reflect a broad commitment to protect village integrity.

Land legislation could, however, be turned against the villages, especially when a long-standing hacienda owner wished to have access to lands used by townspeople. Hacendados who raised cattle resented the presence of indigenous settlements on or near their lands, both because they impeded their free use of the area and because they believed that indígenas were prone to cattle theft.[52] This could lead to conflict. For instance, a group of indígenas from the town of Hunucmá planted milpas on common land in the vicinity of the property of Doña Manuela Solis. In 1831, Solis, who ran a cattle ranch, repeatedly burnt the outbuildings that the indígenas had built to protect their crops, claiming that they were doing harm to her cattle. Atanacio Canul, the spokesman for the farmers, claimed that their settlements were at least six leagues from the hacienda, more than the law required, and that any harm that came to the cattle was no fault of their own but rather of Solis's careless cattle hands and foremen, who allowed the animals to wander too far from home. The court, however, ruled that the farmers were harming not only Solis's property but also that of others nearby and that the location of their settlement violated colonization laws.[53]

The state did not, thus, indiscriminately support village claims. When existing powerful hacendados were involved, their interests tended to come first. The state instituted at least one policy that made their support of hacendados clear. In 1836, jueces de paz were empowered and encouraged by the state to identify and destroy indigenous settlements that lay outside of the control of village authorities, a policy specifically aimed at reducing the impact of small farms and ranches on surrounding enterprises. In many cases, such actions lay outside of the practical capacity of local authorities. But their implementation of the policy was widespread enough to warrant the governor's issuance of a warning against abuses less than a month later. Outside of Teabo in 1837, for instance, an alcalde ordered the destruction of the homes of José Moo, Nasario May, Tomás May, and Manuel Colli. Even after the victims complained that they inhabited land that their families had owned and worked for generations, the subdelegado defended the official's actions.[54]

Throughout the 1830s, however, the state, hacendados, and the villages had a shared interest in keeping new cattle entrepreneurs from making significant inroads into Yucatecan territory. State actions convinced villagers that the government supported the essential right of villagers to land. This significantly mitigated the threat to stability that came with centralism. While indigenous Yucatecans may have felt that centralist structures violated their political and personal rights, they could still, it seemed, rely on both local and state authorities to protect them from threats to their capacity for subsistence. Shifts in municipal and land policies in the 1820s and 1830s destabilized indigenous villagers' relationship with the state on several fronts, but they did not fundamentally delegitimize the authority of the government.

And yet, the experience of these years did prompt changes in indigenous villagers' conceptions of their relationship to the state that would prove vital in the years to come. First, for indígenas, federalism was clearly preferable to centralism. Whereas the circumstances of the Oaxacan countryside had allowed for the reshaping of centralism to resemble its predecessor, constant pressure from the relatively large nonindigenous population in Yucatán prevented a comparable transformation. And second, because the experiences of federalism and centralism were so different, indigenous villagers increasingly articulated the privileges they believed federalism brought in a language of rights. The experience of federalism and then centralism suggested to Yucatán's indigenous citizenry a connection between federalism, village autonomy, and the responsibility of the state. As long as the state held up its end of the bargain, especially in disputes that involved land, those connections persisted. As Rugeley puts it, Yucatecan indígenas "seemed prepared to accept a large amount of exploitation provided that certain traditional rights remain intact."[55] But the escalated conflict of the 1830s suggested that both the state's ability and its desire to honor its obligations were always in question.

The Return to Federalism and the Breakdown of State Authority, 1839–1847

Between 1839 and 1847, Yucatán seceded repeatedly from Mexico, result-ing in its effective independence from the central government for almost an entire decade. This series of events began with a rebellion against the Mexican government in the late 1830s. The immediate causes of the up-rising, led by reserve battalion captain Santiago Imán, were Yucatecan ob-jections to Mexican demands spurred by the war with Texas. Strapped for funds, the national administration tightened trade regulations. Tariffs in-creased on both internal and external trade, which led to considerable dis-satisfaction among Yucatecan government officials, who were forced more and more to rely on undependable and often scant income from state taxes for both government expenses and their own salaries. At the same time, the Texas campaign prompted increased military recruitment throughout Mexico, resulting in the drafting for the first time of local militias to serve in other parts of the country, an unwelcome imposition for Yucatecans reluctant to leave the peninsula.[56]

By late 1840, Imán made an explicit demand for Yucatecan independ-ence.[57] A newly elected state congress proceeded to produce its own con-stitution for Yucatán, which was approved in 1841. For the next seven years, Yucatán would be in and out of the Mexican union, as state leaders tried often unsuccessfully to negotiate their obligations to the Mexican government. Mexico's unwillingness to promise Yucatán control over its trade led one prominent politician to complain that Yucatán was being treated "like a colony."[58] Conflict with the Mexican government over trade and other issues thus led to de facto local control over the internal organization of the state just as central control was tightening over the rest of the country.

Yucatán's independence altered its leaders' relationship with indigenous villagers in three ways. First, the new state was outspokenly federalist and thus brought the reinstitution of local elected town administrations. Vil-lagers, who had learned from their recent experience to associate fed-eralism with certain benefits and privileges, began the independent era with heightened expectations. Second, the process of secession brought expectations of tax relief. After early defeats during his rebellion, Santiago Imán had made the fateful choice to recruit actively among Yucatán's in-digenous population by offering to abolish church taxes in exchange for military service. He may also have hinted that he would abolish civil du-ties as well and would distribute land to indígenas.[59] Third, the rebellion had been costly, and it nearly bankrupted the state. Thus, not only would

Imán's promises of tax relief and land restitution go unfulfilled, but the state would actively subvert them in an effort to replenish its treasury. Ultimately, this combination of rising expectations and government intransigence resulted in a sense among indígenas that the state had betrayed the contract that had long governed their relationship.

It was not, however, only these circumstances that would lead to indigenous Yucatecans' disillusionment after 1840. Embedded in the laws and provisions of the new Yucatecan federalism was an explicitly liberal reformism that has been described as precocious in Mexico.[60] The independent state legislature pushed through liberal reforms in political administration, church-state relations, and especially land regulation. Many of these reforms, when put into practice, had the potential to upset the tenuous peace between the government and its mostly indigenous constituency. Increasingly, indígenas would find that even a federalist constitution was not enough to guarantee the relationship they wished to have with the state in the crucial arenas of municipal politics, taxation, and land.

The link between the liberal administration of Yucatán's independent government and the Caste War seems in some ways to be obvious. Clearly, the rebellion was triggered in part by new land legislation that struck at the heart of indigenous subsistence. But the relationship between the implementation of that legislation and the breakdown of state legitimacy and authority was not direct or inevitable. Rather, relations between the state and the indigenous citizenry broke down in very specific ways that were tied to indígenas' longer experience of changing administrative practices in the towns. The Caste War cannot thus be said to be a result of liberalism per se but rather of the specific experience of its institutions that indigenous Yucatecans had had since 1812.

THE RETURN OF FEDERALISM AND MUNICIPAL GOVERNMENT

In an application for the restoration of its village's elected officials after the return to federalism, the república de indígenas of the settlement of Telá outlined the history of the governments that had affected villagers' lives since the Spanish constitutional era:

We do know that from time immemorial our rulers were those formerly called *justicias* [and] *cabos de justicia españoles*, and the authorities of the municipality were Spaniards until our glorious emancipation from Spain threw off the yoke of the mother country, with authorities of distinct denominations beginning to govern and rule us through the shocks suffered by the Mexican Republic, and because of its bad government our peninsula has had its . . . political transactions governed alternatively by central and federal government, and [now] this [one] of absolute democratic liberty to which the people aspire.[61]

The indígenas of Telá believed that under the new independent federalist administration, they would finally get the autonomy that they deserved.

It soon became clear, however, that local institutions of federalism as reestablished in 1841 were not the same as those of the federalism of 1824–1829. The laws passed in 1841 established no numerical requirements for various types of town government. Instead, cities, villas, and all district cabeceras were to have ayuntamientos, regardless of population. All other settlements with the status of pueblo would elect alcaldes municipales—municipal mayors whose duties were similar to those of the municipal juntas of the first federalism. For settlements not considered to be pueblos, a literacy requirement limited access to electoral politics. The new laws defined these settlements as "those ranchos which are not establishments subject to private dominion" and those "small towns where there are not at least ten citizens in the exercise of their rights who are able to read and write." Here, the local administration would consist of a juez de paz. According to the letter of the law, jueces de paz, like alcaldes municipales, would be popularly elected.[62] But having a juez de paz still meant not having a truly autonomous administration, as the authority of the jueces was directly subject to that of the nearest town with alcaldes or an ayuntamiento. Towns could easily be disenfranchised by the literacy requirement. In Becanchén, for example, one of the alcaldes wished to install a juez de paz in the nearby rancho of Xcabihaltún rather than allowing it to elect alcaldes, citing the fact that there was no one there able to read and write or administer justice. Despite the fact that jueces de paz were technically elected, a dissenter in the town administration accused his colleague of wishing only to deny the inhabitants of the rancho—"an immense pueblo . . . of more than five thousand souls"—their right to vote. In this case, the governor ruled that it was indeed correct to install jueces de paz in areas that were outside of any town's particular jurisdiction, regardless of size, and he ordered the alcaldes of Becanchén to proceed.[63]

The literacy requirement was intended to fine-tune the government's methods for avoiding universal elections in entirely indigenous towns. In May 1840, the comments of the parish priest of Hoctún reflected this intention. The nearby towns of Xocchel and Tahmek, he wrote, had been electing their own municipal authorities despite the fact that they were "inhabited entirely by unfortunate Indians who do not know how to read or write nor are enlisted in the civil militia." A commission named to investigate agreed with the priest, and the elected authorities were replaced with an auxiliary mayor who governed from Hoctún.[64] In and of itself, a large indigenous population was not an obstacle to having an elected administration. Pisté's successful request for a council came from two sets of townspeople, one explicitly identified as the república de indígenas.[65]

But state authorities assumed that the officials themselves would have to be nonindigenous. This disqualified entirely indigenous towns and often those with very small nonindigenous populations. In the town of Tekal, for instance, the nonindigenous population was limited to a father and his son and son-in-law, who together made up the municipal junta. Authorities who argued for the abolition of this junta cited concerns about regulations against family members serving together. In doing so, they revealed their assumption that among the entire remaining population of the town, there was simply no one else who could conceivably serve.[66] During Yucatán's first federalism, certainly, towns with no nonindígenas had often been administered by appointed auxiliary alcaldes rather than elected authorities. But the new provisions, which depended on literacy rather than numbers, were much more efficient at avoiding the election of authorities in indigenous towns.

None of this stopped indigenous villages from trying; the return to federalism prompted numerous requests from towns to have their own elected authorities. These towns were quick to pick up on the literacy requirement. Kinbilá, a town of a thousand people, and Citilcum, with 400, claimed to have "more than ten citizens in exercise of their rights and able to read and write," as did Chacsinkín. It was quite possible for villages such as these to be turned down, however. Although Chacsinkín, Pisté, and Mocochá got the administrations that they asked for, Kinbilá and Citilcum were shown not to meet the literacy requirements.[67] And Telá, whose petition is cited earlier, was also denied. An investigation of conditions in the town revealed that it had none of the legal requirements for autonomous administration. The building that the townspeople claimed could house the local governing body was a crumbling structure that had once belonged to either a hacienda or a local confraternity. Most importantly, while their overall numbers warranted the status of pueblo, not one individual in the community could read or write. Even their república was substandard, as it had no scribe, and the indígenas of Telá were thus forced to pay taxes through the indigenous authorities of neighboring Chikindzonot.[68]

The government's denial of requests for elected administrations did not always go uncontested. In 1841, the townspeople of Cholul were turned down after an investigation revealed that the village lacked ten literate citizens. The original request had been signed by twelve men whom the townspeople claimed fulfilled the literacy requirement, but when examined they proved to be either not from the town, unable to do more than sign their names, or, in some cases, unable to speak Spanish at all. Unsatisfied, the townspeople tried again in 1842, claiming the investigation had been biased. In doing so, they challenged the validity of the law itself. "It is true, Excellent Sir," they wrote, "that some vecinos do not write with perfection, but this is an evil that all the pueblos suffer, and how many times have we seen subjects whose signature one cannot understand occupying high posts, because they have fulfilled the object of the law, which is that they know how to sign?" Indígenas in particular, they argued, had long held authoritative positions despite illiteracy: "We constantly see [of] the caciques that one can hardly understand their signature despite the fact that the law insists that they know how to read and write." This tactic did not prove fruitful. A new examination of the individuals in question, all of whom had Maya surnames, found that they were able to read and write only with "clumsiness" and "fear," and the request was turned down.[69]

Of course, the literacy requirement affected mostly individuals in entirely indigenous towns. There were many indigenous men who voted for local councils because they lived in towns with significant nonindigenous populations. But, as always, the mere fact of voting did not necessarily entail substantive participation in the process of selecting village officers. Indigenous voters proved well able to make this distinction. In Chichimilá, a group of twenty indigenous villagers protested in early 1842 that the entire process of election for their municipal authorities had been illegal. First, the electoral committee had been named without popular participation, and then this committee proceeded to threaten the citizens, forcing them to vote according to its will. The townspeople reportedly resisted, and, in the end, only the "*tímidos*"—the shy and fearful who could not stand up to pressure—actually cast their votes. These ballots, of course, were fraudulent: "On [them] they put the names of the people they wished, against the will of the voters." As a result, those elected were both unwanted and unqualified to serve.[70]

Other indígenas complained of being turned away from elections if they were not willing to vote as directed. When the cacique and two others were arrested in Yaxkukul after trying to cast their ballots, the alcalde claimed that they had been disorderly; the indígenas asserted that he was merely trying to violate their right to vote, for which they took him to court.[71] José Patricio Pat complained that he and a group of indígenas he had brought to the polls in Baca were repeatedly turned away over the course of several days.[72] The falsification of votes was another common complaint. Under the new system, voting was done on ballots, whereas previously it had been out loud. Many indígenas depended on help from literate nonindígenas and were thus unable to verify for whom they were in fact voting. Votes could also be invented out of thin air. Juan Zun, an indígena of the town of Tekit, claimed that his name and a vote were recorded in the official register, despite the fact that he had not voted.[73]

Certainly, that indigenous villagers had difficulty asserting their opinion at the polls was nothing new; the same had been true during the first
federalist period. But both the frequency of difficulties and indigenous
concerns about them had reached a new intensity; conflicts over the indigenous vote were much more common in the second federalism than
they had been in the first. This was in part due to the fact that nonindigenous townspeople had increased interest in town politics after 1841. Since
the conflict with Mexico had begun, two opposing political factions, the
Mendistas and Barbachanistas, had solidified around the issue of Yucatán's
independence.[74] The rapid division of much of the Yucatecan population
into political factions made town politics a site of conflict. Although the
content of such conflicts is often impossible to discern in individual cases,
it is clear that town politics were increasingly politicized. In Komchén
in 1840, for instance, elections were interrupted by a *"caudillo"* who attacked individuals with whom he disagreed. In Espita, the elections for
ayuntamiento were disrupted by partisans of centralism. One subdelegado
reported that the town of Dzemul was split into two political camps, one
composed of "some few vecinos [who are] enemies of the federal system."
The town of Xul was divided into two *"bandos"* who intervened violently
in elections. Finally, in Saban in 1840, Justo Pavia wrote that he was legally elected as one of the members of the municipal junta but that "as
my election did not combine with the ambitions of the aspirants to the
mayorship, I was separated."[75]

Town politics, then, had become a site at which the larger political
struggles of Yucatán were played out. The stakes of local political office
were raised as service on the municipal level became linked to the privileges of belonging to the ruling party. Accordingly, the motivation for
manipulating votes increased as well. The most available—and presumably the most manipulable—votes were those of indigenous townspeople.
Votes could be "bought" primarily through using patronage relationships.
The parish priest, the hacienda owner, and the cacique and república were
all targeted as parties that could deliver indigenous votes for a particular
candidate. Caciques and priests could serve as members of the electoral
committee, giving them control over the voting process. Priests could influence the committees even when they were not a part of them by convincing them to invalidate elections the results of which did not meet
their criteria. The participation of caciques could be either voluntary or
involuntary, but everyone understood that they could influence the voting behavior of their indigenous constituencies.[76] Indigenous individuals
who lived on the haciendas could be rounded up and brought to the polls
en masse, as they were in the elections in Baca in 1840 and Peto in 1841.

Sometimes these indígenas would be the only voters. In 1840 in Chapab, the outgoing alcalde, Tomás Alcocer, held an election with only the indigenous workers from his own hacienda an hour earlier than he had previously announced.[77] By 1841, then, it was increasingly clear to indígenas that nonindigenous aspirants to power would go to extreme lengths to manipulate the indigenous vote.

While many indigenous villagers were angry that they were not being given an opportunity to participate effectively, many nonindígenas were concerned that their own political ambitions were undermined by the manipulability of the indigenous community. In 1840, Clemente Vásquez protested that elections in Tekit had been a farce, largely because only indígenas had voted. The election had been extremely poorly publicized, with the convocation posted on a door of a public building where it could be seen only when the door was closed. On the day of the elections, most nonindigenous townspeople thus did not know to attend. By contrast, the committee actively sought the participation of the town's indígenas, forcing them to attend the elections by bringing them into town en masse from the fields. This situation, Vásquez opined, violated "the most sovereign act that the pueblos exercise."[78] Similarly, Santiago Osorio registered a complaint about elections in Dzemul. The townspeople had met for the election; but, because of disorder manufactured by the outgoing alcalde, the voting did not actually occur until most had left, leaving only a crowd of "drunken indígenas" to cast their votes.[79]

By May 1841, concern about irregularities in elections had reached the highest levels of state administration. In that year, the council of state, a body that advised the governor on legal matters, issued a general proclamation. The council recognized problems with elections but was reluctant to take measures to improve the situation. Townspeople's behavior, it argued, was only natural:

A new system, new laws, a new order of things is not easy to expedite in one single blow, and thus it is that one should not attribute too much force [to the fact that] on receiving and putting into execution the recently published institutions, the pueblos are agitating, their vecinos enter into a ruinous fight, and at the time of exercising one of the rights which flatters them most, they dispute the preference of their candidates and procure that they be in immediate contact with their interests.

To interfere now would only cause trouble: "Prudence dictates that we not enter into a scrupulous examination of these unimportant faults that ignorance produced or malice extols." The council's suggestion for dealing with these "unimportant faults" was to encourage concerned citizens to make use of the existing laws. It cited statutes that regulated the process of protesting an election in which the electoral committee was enjoined to consider any protests of immediate importance. Any protests that had not been brought before the committee at the proper time—during the elections themselves—would not be considered.[80] In most ways, the council's response amounted to very little. The vast majority of protests about electoral practices were complaints about the committees themselves, which could hardly be expected to undermine their control over the electoral process. Thus, in effect, this proclamation was a tacit acceptance of electoral fraud.

The state was reluctant to intervene because it derived certain benefits from the conflict in the villages. The establishment and strengthening of patronage ties provided a network of power that the government could manipulate. Elections were an important site at which such networks were worked out and reinforced, and if this resulted in conflict or illegal activities, the state was prepared to look the other way. The rulings of the state on cases that it did consider were notably inconsistent, perhaps reflecting the partisanship of state officials. But such machinations could get out of control when state politics were out of control as well; at such times, the state was forced to step in. The state congress's stock response was to simply remove the threat of disorder that elections could pose. At the end of 1842, as Yucatán prepared once again for war with Mexico, the legislature deferred municipal elections for an unspecified amount of time. In September 1843, it convoked new town elections but suspended them anew in November 1844. The electoral year of 1843–1844 may thus have been the last time that Yucatecan towns actually held elections before the outbreak of the Caste War.[81]

Not surprisingly, many indígenas were dissatisfied with the people who had been elected since 1840. The content of their complaints was not dissimilar to that of those that they had made about the appointed jueces de paz during the centralist administration. In most ways, they understood the federalist alcaldes of the years after 1840 to be imposed, just as had been the jueces. Thus, villagers complained about alcaldes forcing them to work on illegal projects, such as a road from Kinchil to Sisal, or forcing them to provide free services for the alcalde personally. Alcaldes were increasingly accused of abuses committed specifically against a village's indígenas, as in Tinum in 1844. In a case in Xcan involving accusations of abuse of authority on the part of an elected official, the investigator noted that it was impossible to find out the truth in such cases because many indigenous villagers feared the alcaldes of their pueblos.[82]

By 1844, then, indigenous villagers could not expect to exert real influence over universally elected village government. While this may have also been the case between 1824 and 1829, the situation now came as a bitter disappointment. The experience of federalism and then centralism had taught indigenous villagers the importance of particular institutions of local government; the experience of renewed federalism taught them that even the system they had come to prefer was deeply flawed.

THE RETURN OF FEDERALISM AND THE ADMINISTRATION OF TAXES

The words of the villagers of Sicpach, written to the governor in protest of the abuses of their alcalde, Don Santiago López, demonstrate the collapse of villagers' faith in local government:

How sad it is, Excellent Sir, that when we sacrifice ourselves and our small interests for our adored liberty [the alcaldes] exercise with us acts of the highest despotism and tyranny. But trusting in the paternal protection of your Excellency we do not doubt for a moment that as soon as these clamors of cruelly tyrannized humanity reach your ears you will place a barrier before the arbitrariness and vile greed that move our oppressors.[83]

Faced with the failure of Yucatán's restored federalist institutions to provide the protection they had expected, the townspeople came to rely even more on their direct relationship with the state government to ensure the integrity of their villages and thus their capacity to subsist. For a while at least, Yucatán's government would prove up to the task of protecting indígenas. But increasingly, as economic pressures forced the government to accede to demands from nonindígenas, even the governor himself began to appear as less than a friend of Yucatán's indígenas.

The first betrayal came in the administration of taxes, where the relationship of villagers to the state was most direct. In 1840, Santiago Imán offered relief from religious taxes in exchange for military service. As a recruitment strategy, Imán's promises were extremely effective, but the new soldiers would be disappointed when the new government took power. Legislators made dire predictions about the elimination of any kind of taxes for the indigenous population. Juan de Dios Cosgaya, Yucatán's elder statesman and a former governor, insisted that the government make it clear that any reduction in taxes was not a reward for service to the state, which was after all an obligation. The danger that indígenas would misinterpret tax relief doubtless did not loom as large, however, as the dangers of not fulfilling the promise at all. The government could not entirely abandon the promises Imán had made to the indigenous masses. It could, though, significantly reduce their effects. In 1840, Congress officially abolished the religious taxes known as obventions and replaced them with a new tax of one real monthly. This tax was to be paid only by indigenous males, a significant change from the older taxes that had been levied on both members of indigenous couples. But this was far from the total abolition that indígenas had been led to expect. And when the war with Mexico began in 1842, the state demanded an extraordinary war contribution from all its citizens.[84]

In 1843, renewed war with Mexico forced the government to make another offer of tax relief in return for military service, and both civil and religious contributions were briefly suspended for all soldiers. Like Imán's promises, this measure specifically targeted indigenous Yucatecans. In introducing the bill, Governor Miguel Barbachano wrote that he was offering this tax relief "in order to satisfy the noble desires of the indígenas who, with the most ardent patriotism, wish to augment the number of the worthy defenders of the state." Later in the year, Congress permanently abolished obventions and made the state responsible for providing resources for the church. Not coincidentally, however, the government issued a new civil tax code on the same day, raising the personal contribution for indígenas to two reales monthly to finance the new church stipend. Finally, indígenas were asked to participate in a "voluntary contribution" to the war effort.[85]

Not surprisingly, in the 1840s conflict over the collection of taxes from indigenous citizens increased sharply. The first round of difficulties involved religious taxes. In response to the incomplete execution of Iman's promise, some indígenas refused to pay obventions, as did the inhabitants of the rancho San Antonio in 1843. Others, such as the indígenas of the rancho Yalkuk and several men in Tiholop, refused to pay *civil* taxes as well. Officials, taken aback at such actions, observed that indígenas, given an inch, were wont to take a mile. In Dzitnup in 1841, the cacique was brought up on charges of inciting rebellion by claiming that "soon he would do away with these robberies," meaning taxes in general. In court, the public defender argued that the cacique had merely misunderstood Imán's "just revolution," which had offered to mitigate the many burdens suffered by the indígenas, by concluding that the personal contribution was no longer required at all. And in Ebtún, after an investigation of nonpayment, one official found that many of the indígenas in the village believed themselves to be entirely exonerated from religious taxes and that "this sinister idea has those of this class in movement."[86]

Yet tax complaints came only after the new laws themselves had been violated. In the above case in Ebtún, Marcelo Uc viewed the situation differently, complaining that his wife was being charged obventions despite their abolition for women and that similar practice throughout the town was forcing people to flee.[87] Such abuses seem to have been widespread. In 1841, the caciques of four towns surrounding Motul wrote to complain that their parish priest was ordering them to be whipped for not paying obventions. They claimed that they had always done their best to collect the church taxes, but that the priest was now illegally demanding that the república members themselves pay, "when it is known that we have never paid them as is customary from time immemorial in all our State."[88]

Caciques, who received a portion of the taxes they collected, were also prone to abuses when those taxes were reduced. The indígenas of Hopelchén complained that their cacique's abuses were causing significant outmigration from the town and the abandonment of two local ranchos. In 1840, a group of indigenous residents of Cuzumá wrote that

> our cacique and justicias are summarily extorting us, saying that they will finish with us in order to pay the charges of our poor wives and sons in order to stay in their vigor and power, and having arrived to our notice that, in virtue of the act celebrated in the city of Valladolid the 12th of January of this year, upon which the payment of these charges ceases.[89]

Even alcaldes, who legally had never had any right to collect taxes, got in on the act. When the alcalde of Chichimilá imprisoned several indígenas for owing money on their civil and religious taxes, the accused were quick to point out that he lacked the authority to do so. In another case of a local official overstepping his bounds, the alcalde of Dzibalchén was accused of contesting the notion that the cacique and república should turn tax money directly over to the subdelegado.[90]

After 1843, the state government was again faced with ubiquitous tax conflicts, usually precipitated by claims of service in the campaign. That year, the government had briefly suspended all taxes for those who fought for Yucatán, but most indigenous soldiers thought the suspension should last longer than three months. In 1844, the subdelegado of Mérida reported "hindrances in the collection of the personal contribution from the indígenas who served during the war in the public security battalion." Similar claims were made as late as 1845.[91] Indigenous communities were likely to demand tax relief for the whole town because sacrifices for the war effort, including contributions of soldiers, were understood to affect the entire community. In 1843, the political chief of Izamal wrote that *all* of the indígenas of the town of Tixcocob refused to pay civil contributions in exchange for some of them having served in the army. The same official wrote that the indígenas of Hoctún refused to pay and noted the statewide problem that authorities were having with that "class of individuals." Villages demanded repayment for all kinds of war-related sacrifices. The cacique and república of Telchac asked for exemptions on the basis of "the misfortunes that they suffered upon the invasion of the Mexican army." In Izamal, the indígenas demanded indemnification for the weapons that they had provided for the cause. And finally, the villagers of Lerma asked for exemption on the basis of unspecified "suffering."[92]

The government was reluctant to grant all of these requests while money was so tight. As early as 1843, it was demanding clear documentation of service in order to authorize exemptions. As the council of state wrote that year,

> Although it is certain that justice obliges [us] to give to each the reward for his services, it is also necessary on dictating measures that can harm the treasury of the state, that there be all necessary circumspection in order not to be overloaded with charges, perhaps unjust, in the case of finding [some individuals] already rewarded enough.

The council effectively admitted the injustice of its actions by claiming, in the case of volunteers from Sisal in 1843, that "in other less afflictive circumstances we would not vacillate an instant" in fulfilling their demands. The problem, they made clear, was that if the government granted exemptions to some, it would be forced to grant them to everyone. Groups and individuals who could not decisively prove their participation in the war, like the indígenas of Bokobá, would have to continue paying taxes as before.[93]

The conflict surrounding the tax system was significant on three fronts. First, it was clear that local nonindigenous officials, who often found themselves adversely affected by attempts to grant exemptions, would not be effective representatives for the villagers, and this reinforced the perception that local institutions of government were essentially bankrupt under the new federalism. Second, caciques and repúblicas found themselves in an uncomfortable position, caught between the two groups—government officials and villagers—that legitimized their power. And third, the state government no longer served as an effective counter to local administrations' abuses, and in fact it became increasingly obvious that the state itself was the source of much of the problem. Villagers reacted accordingly. In 1847, the subdelegado of Ticul reported that it was nearly impossible to collect the contribution in his partido, largely because debtors had fled the villages to avoid payment.[94] By that year, it was clear that a large part of the indigenous population had opted out of the tax system completely, the result of years of broken promises.

THE RETURN OF FEDERALISM AND THE ADMINISTRATION OF LAND

But the betrayal went far deeper than one partially fulfilled promise. By late 1843, Yucatán's indígenas were probably paying less in taxes than they had been in 1839, but they were doing so on a drastically limited resource base. The new independent government passed land legislation in 1841 that, by the mid-1840s, significantly reduced the amount of land available to Yucatecan villages. Like previous land laws, the 1841 decree focused on baldíos. This time, however, the legislature established limits on how much land could be considered immune from this designation by demarcating the extent of each village's ejido. The 1841 law defined the ejido of each pueblo as a square plot of land measured one league in each direction from the church, which was usually located in the center of town. Once these lands and those privately owned had been set aside, any remaining plots would be actively claimed by the state.[95] Some of the lands would be reserved to relieve the pressure of paying soldiers' back pay. In August 1842, in an attempt to protect its meager funds, Congress decreed that soldiers could claim their wages in the form of land, each one receiving a square quarter league of the state's baldíos. And in November 1843, the government authorized the treasury to pay back loans made to the government during the war with land grants rather than money.[96] The remaining land would then be available for purchase at low prices.

On paper, the new land reform reiterated the state's commitment to the integrity of indigenous villages and to the general notion of communal property. Not only did the laws explicitly protect ejido holdings, the state also stressed the importance of other pueblo lands. After three years of land alienations, the legislature issued a statement in 1844 clarifying the distinction between "communal lands" and the ejido:

Communal lands are those possessed by the pueblos in full and absolute dominion by title of purchase and sale, *donación* or *real merced*. No pueblo can alienate these lands other than for justified causes, or with the object of completing its ejidos, buying or exchanging them for those they need. All the inhabitants of the town to which community lands of this nature belong can use and take advantage of them, requiring of the municipal authorities the rent that corresponds whenever inhabitants of other pueblos introduce themselves in order to work these lands.

The governor ordered the departmental assembly to stop considering requests for such "communal land," stressing "the necessity that, aside from the egidos, the possession of the lands they work, or part of them, is left to the pueblos."[97] But, in practice, the requirement that only titled land would be protected limited this provision. State officials were well aware that all Yucatecans—and especially indigenous villagers—used a lot of land that was not properly titled. The legislation was intended to eliminate the uncertainty that existed in Yucatecan land tenure by sharply delineating lands legally owned—whether in common or not—from those available for private use.

The ideas behind this law were apparent in the words of Juan Pablo Talavera, the appointed government official in the district of Camino

Real Bajo. He believed that the problem lay in inconsistent and inaccurate documentation:

A vulgar error has confused the classification of lands that are divided in ejidos, commons or baldíos, and . . . because of an abuse or lack of conformity in this material the archive of Maní, to which everyone who proposes to sustain some question of lands usually goes, gives these [documents], or takes them away, according to the affectation or interest in which its directors are moved. From which it results that an industrious and agricultural pueblo of four or five thousand souls that wishes to extend its cultivations finds itself without the means to [do so], because of the opposition of [a pueblo] with perhaps less elements and population, who comes to the fore with these documents, which in truth only serve to foment discord and to slow down not only the advances of the pueblos, but also the administration of justice.

As Talavera saw it, Yucatán suffered from dismal, ineffective, and ambiguous distribution of land, which stifled productive impulses. It had become customary, he opined, for villages to claim the baldíos in their vicinity as their property, despite the complete absence of legal title to the land. All too often, the laudable desires of a town to expand its production were stymied by the ridiculous claims of neighboring villages. The result was disastrous for both the political and economic prosperity of the state:

Under these obscure principles the territory of the country has been distributed, suffocating industry and individual prosperity, so that each pueblo seems more like a tiny independent nation, happy or miserable, according to the extension of its lands, than it does a fraction of a province subject to the obedience of the same laws and with the option of the same rights and privileges.

For Talavera, the aim of land legislation should neither be to promote the integrity of the villages nor to protect the rights of large landholders; rather it should be to promote efficient and productive agricultural practices on the peninsula as a whole.[98] According to Talavera, "true village lands"— those acquired by purchase or royal grant—were "sacred." He made no explicit mention of the importance of private property to prosperity, dwelling instead on the necessity of promoting the productive inclinations of the pueblos. His argument rested ultimately on the imperative to redirect the attention of Yucatán's primary producers away from land disputes and back toward the use of the land itself. Talavera's suggestions were intended as a corrective measure, not a fundamental transformation. The specifics of the 1841 law reflect a similar intention on the part of the state.

And yet the new law, unlike earlier ones, touched off a land grab of which Yucatán's indigenous villagers were the principal victims. The implementation of previous land laws had reflected the state's ambivalence about "upstart" cattle entrepreneurs; the 1841 law cleared the way for those entrepreneurs to purchase previously disputed lands. To be sure, many indigenous individuals claimed land as well, most citing their service in the war. Of those making larger claims, most were caciques. But most large claims, and all claims of the maximum size (two square leagues), went to nonindigenous officers, entrepreneurs, and priests. All in all, 459,923 hectares of public land were sold or granted under the new laws. Almost three-quarters went to purchasers rather than to soldiers, and much of the land was quickly consolidated in land deals made soon thereafter.[99]

The new laws were so devastating for the indigenous villages for several reasons. The state actively promoted the alienation of public lands to fill its empty coffers. Land prices dropped, as did the standard of proof for establishing the baldío status of particular plots of land. Conspicuously missing from the new legislation were the complicated requirements found in earlier laws for establishing that the land was not in use. Instead of respecting tradition, the new procedure relied entirely on written titles, which many villages simply did not have. Villages could and often did own land outside of the one-league square now called the ejido. But, in practice, the land they held title to was usually only a small portion of the land they used. For the villages, then, a drastic turnover of state land could block their access to croplands, water, and supplementary goods necessary for subsistence. Even the newly delineated ejidos were often unavailable for village use, as private property held within the square league reserved for the villages was to be respected. Fairly typical was the case of the town of Maní, where in 1842 the mayor reported that all but a small piece of land within the prescribed limits was owned by either individuals or the church.[100] Where indigenous villages managed to maintain their access to public lands, they were now required to pay rent. Indigenous Yucatecans had long relied on the flexibility of the system of baldío use. Over the course of the 1840s, that flexibility was disappearing.

This attack on the bases of village integrity did not go uncontested; at least fifty-two communities filed legal actions against land alienations in the years after 1841.[101] But by the latter half of the decade, many if not most Yucatecan villages had lost their access to much of the land they had used for generations. Neither the court system nor direct appeals to government officials proved effective in procuring protection. As they had in the past, villages claimed that they had the right to enough land to provide for their subsistence. But contrary to past experience, such claims now fell on deaf ears unless they could be supported by titles. Thus, when the república of Maxcanú complained in 1844 that a claim made by Lorenzo Peón would leave the town without adequate milpas, the sale went through because of the absence of a title. And in Tecoh the same year, the indigenous authorities objected to the claims of José Dolores Espinosa, who was owed money by the government. Even after the pueblo was found to have no ejido at all, the lands in question were turned over to Espinosa with the vague suggestion that someone should find some lands for the pueblo to use. If the village actually held the titles, they could expect more success. When Cristóbal Espinosa made a claim on the island of Tayna in 1845, the república of Pocmuch protested that its village had owned the land for at least two centuries. When it was able to produce titles and a map, the ayuntamiento, the political chief, and finally the state government all supported the claim.[102] But the requirement of documents was not only a legal obstacle that many villages could not surmount. It was also a direct violation of the understanding that indígenas had developed about their rights to land, an understanding that state action had seemed to support in the past.

The case of Nunkiní in 1844 demonstrates both the determination of pueblos to hold on to their land and their difficulty in doing so. When the Nunkiní república perceived that the village's lands would soon be threatened by outside claims, it moved to take advantage of the new laws by filing its own claim to a piece of land that the villagers had long used. "What stimulates the exponents to make this request," the officers wrote, "is the lack of sufficient land for our farming, taking into account the numbers of our population and that our egido is extremely rocky and sterile and does not produce the grain necessary for our subsistence." But despite their intentions and the findings of a government commission that the land was indeed available for sale, the república officers were unable to come up with the money that was necessary to buy it: "On denouncing the land on the 28th of August, [we] believed that the inhabitants of the vecinity would happily contribute in gathering the amount needed; but having made various insinuations . . . , we have not found more than a small portion of individuals who offer to pay."[103] The laws no longer took into account the special needs of indigenous Yucatecans, and indigenous Yucatecans were beginning to see that this meant the loss of their villages' autonomy, integrity, and capacity to survive.

In the final analysis, the sense of betrayal that indigenous Yucatecans felt at the failure of the state to provide effective local administration or to fulfill its promises of tax relief was undergirded by a larger and more profound realization of the government's breach of faith. A resurgent federalism had failed to offer the autonomy and protection that villages felt to be their right. Effective participation in village government had ceased to be a possibility as village administrative councils became a battleground of partisan politics that deliberately and blatantly manipulated indigenous votes. Indigenous citizens derived little or no benefit from these new networks of party patronage, largely because they soon found their livelihood to be under direct attack. Over the course of the 1840s, it became increasingly clear that this attack would not be staved off by the villages' erstwhile protectors in the Yucatecan state and that, indeed, the assault emanated from the state itself.

Before the passage of the 1841 land law, the Yucatecan state had tacitly contracted with its indigenous constituency in various ways. In a general sense, the government derived its legitimacy from its ability to protect its citizens. This responsibility had particular weight in the case of indígenas, who depended on the government for protection from the nonindigenous population. Government officials were particularly successful in convincing indígenas that they were committed to the continued access of villages to the land that they needed. After 1841, however, after the economic devastation of two major military campaigns, the state was increasingly unable and in some ways unwilling to fulfill its side of the bargain. By 1847, the two pillars of state legitimacy among indígenas—village autonomy and its protection by the central government—had begun to crumble.

In June 1843, *El Siglo XIX*, the official newspaper of the Yucatecan government, reprinted an article that had been published in the Mexico City newspaper *El Pacificador*. A reporter had ruminated on the possibly tragic results of Yucatán's recent separation from the Mexican nation:

Among the innumerable unfortunate consequences that the recent rebellion has brought to this wretched peninsula, thinking men worry that they have put the Indians . . . in arms, exasperating them, so to say; because five of six parts of the population being composed of this class of people, it would not be strange if they were to become proud in the future, and resist their subjugation to other rulers than those of their own qualities and customs; and if by misfortune this political prediction should come into effect, what will become of Yucatán?

In response, the Yucatecan newspaper reassured its readership, claiming that "all the consequences and results of our just revolution, are well calculated . . . ; liberty, guarantees, useful reforms, civilization, equality, stimuli: I have here some of them." As for the indígenas, those with arms in their hands were merely defending their own rights, which were the same as those of other citizens. The Yucatecans accused the Mexican journalist of implying that the indígenas did not in fact have these same rights: "Do the Mexicans perchance wish that this unhappy class not breathe, that they not arise from their abjection, that they lack rights, that they not enjoy protection, that they not be considered as the other Yucatecans?"[104]

The Yucatecan response was disingenuous on several counts. First, Yucatecan politicians were quite concerned about the consequences both of arming the indigenous population and of making promises of tax relief to potential indigenous soldiers. In 1840, in the context of deliberations on what to do about religious taxes, ex-governor Juan de Dios Cosgaya had made a prediction that would long be cited as prophetic. In his address to Congress, he asserted the following:

It is necessary not to lose sight of the natural stupidity of the Indians. This, united with other circumstances, could one day be the cause of many misfortunes, if we do not today take the preventative measures that prudence advises. [Because of this stupidity, the indígenas will] understand, that if a revolution provided them with relief from their obventions another will relieve them from the rest, and another will convert them into Lords of their country. Because of [their stupidity], they still see us as their conquerors and will not lose an opportunity to throw off the yoke that their ignorance presents to them as a result of Spanish invasion.[105]

Second, Cosgaya's concerns were reflected in a political and administrative system that consistently distinguished between indigenous and nonindigenous Yucatecans. Returning to the words of the columnist for *Siglo XIX*, then, indigenous Yucatecans did not "lack rights," nor did they not "enjoy protection." They had these things, but they had them in a way specific to their indigenous status. There was, therefore, no way to defend the statement that they were "considered as other Yucatecans."

Between 1825 and 1847, through negotiation, observation, and experience, Yucatán's indígenas had built an understanding of their relationship to their government that was based on mutual obligation and the specific rights of indigenous people. This was an understanding that the state did not always share but that nevertheless appeared workable until the 1840s, when government actions made its essential bankruptcy painfully clear. By 1847, as the Caste War began, many indigenous Yucatecans were prepared to jettison their attachment to the Yucatecan state. What's more, the indigenous elite, their privileges and resource base seriously eroded, were willing to provide the leadership necessary to do so. As the year progressed, all Yucatecans could see that Yucatán's divided polity was coming apart. The dire predictions of the skeptical Mexican columnist and the pessimistic Yucatecan ex-governor had thus come true. But their simplistic understanding of the manner in which indigenous Yucatecans related to the state, in which indigenous people awaited any opportunity to throw off an oppressive yoke, could not begin to explain the conflagration. Yucatán's indígenas had made a good-faith effort to become Yucatecan citizens, even if this was a uniquely *indigenous* kind of citizenship. It was only when the government removed that option that that effort, for many indígenas, came to an end.

Oaxaca and Yucatán Compared, 1825–1847

Between 1825 and 1847, the states of Oaxaca and Yucatán put the governing systems devised after independence into practice. In the process, new institutions and structures acquired meaning for the two states' citizens. In both places, the structures laid out in the first state constitutions allowed for the maintenance of a direct and unique relationship between the state and indigenous people. Through the constitutional repúblicas in Oaxaca and the repúblicas de indígenas in Yucatán, the state carried on a process of negotiation and legitimation directly with the indigenous population. Yet there were also significant differences between the two systems. In Oaxaca, because indígenas controlled local administration, negotiation between the state government and the indigenous towns was the central administrative activity of most Oaxacan officials. In Yucatán, by contrast, the state governed by maintaining relations with both indigenous *and* nonindigenous administrations within the same town. As the economic interests of nonindigenous rural residents in Yucatán became more and more pressing for the Yucatecan state, the potential for conflict developed. That conflict would begin to unfold in the late 1830s, when Mexico opted for a centralist administrative structure. It intensified through the 1840s and erupted into war in 1847.

The Yucatecan government's pact with its indigenous population was in some ways not fundamentally different from that between the Oaxacan government and Oaxacan indígenas. Both governments drew on colonial notions of justice and obligation while adapting them to the liberal institutional context. In both states, the pact was deeply imbued with a sense of what was moral and just. But the different economic goals of the two nonindigenous populations meant that the two governments were not equally committed to upholding their side of the pact. Oaxaca's nonindigenous elite did not have the impetus to challenge indigenous autonomy because it had no prospects for changing the structure of the economy. Into the 1840s and beyond, the elite continued to depend heavily on the taxation of indígenas and on the marketing of products from indigenous villages. Yucatán's elite, on the other hand, was eager to make changes. It saw itself as poised to conquer new and broader markets, if only it could gain control over indigenous land and labor. So although representatives of the Yucatecan state knew it was necessary to maintain a pact with the indigenous population for the sake of social peace and a minimum level of governability, the economic aspirations of the nonindigenous population led them simultaneously to take actions that undermined it.

Oaxacan state officials and their indigenous constituents shared and consistently reinforced a language about poverty and state obligation that the Yucatecan government was increasingly rejecting. Oaxacan indígenas, in exchange for certain concessions, were willing to accede even to some of the state's harshest demands, at least in principle. Yucatecan indígenas, by contrast, were increasingly unable to see the state as working in their interests at all. Even demands that had been acceptable in the past became unbearable as the 1840s wore on.

The differing experiences of the first twenty years after independence are also reflected in the use of the category of "indigenous." Certainly, indigenousness was a central part of political culture in Oaxaca, where indígenas and nonindígenas held differing positions in the economic and political structures of the state and where the political and moral relationship between the state government and the villages had its roots in the legal distinctions made between indígenas and nonindígenas in colonial New Spain. But in Oaxaca, where *villager* nearly always meant *indigenous* and where there was fundamental agreement about what both the state and villagers could and could not demand, neither party explicitly used ethnic categories extensively to make claims on the other. In Yucatán, by contrast, economic and demographic circumstances led the state to stress indigenousness in its relationship with villagers and to make distinctions between those villagers who were indigenous and those who were not. In turn, indigenous villagers were quick to stress their *own* indigenousness and to use the distinctions made by the state to reinforce their claims. When the Caste War began, even though there were evidently significant numbers of nonindígenas fighting with the rebels, the racial divide at the heart of the war was explicit and clear to all.[106]

The comparison of Oaxaca and Yucatán between 1824 and 1847 illuminates the way that liberalism in Mexico's states developed in reference to both institutional requirements and local concerns. Common assumptions about what liberalism did and did not mean guided state legislators in each place as they wrote and implemented their constitutions. But at the same time, local exigencies meant that the content and meaning of liberalism could vary according to the nature of the population and its distribution, the economy, and preexisting assumptions about the role of government and the reponsibilities of those it governed. Under Mexico's radically federalist first administration, Mexicans could agree that they were participating in "liberalism," but there was no common liberal model asserted for the nation. Mexico's liberalism—or rather Mexico's liberalisms—was built locally from the ground up around shared institutions. They incorporated colonial moral economies, new economic aspirations, and new notions of citizenship in ways that were unique to each place. And yet, if Oaxacans and Yucatecans did not share common assumptions about the nature of citizenship and did not thus create common political cultures, they did share some common institutions and languages. And the systems they created were understood by all—by indígenas, the nonindigenous elite, and government officials—to be part of the common project of the new independent Mexican nation.

In the years to come, the commonility of that project would be put to the test, as reform, rationalization, and standardization became explicit goals of both national and local governments. By the late 1840s and early 1850s, both Oaxaca and Yucatán seemed poised for change. Oaxaca, after the return of federalism in 1846, elected a liberal reformer named Benito Juárez to its governorship, a man whose ideas about citizenship and the indigenous population would challenge what were now long-standing agreements between indígenas and the state. Yucatán, meanwhile, entered a period of protracted war that would force its government to rethink its relationship to the indigenous population. But as agents of both states reworked political relationships, they would have to negotiate the complicated compromises achieved in previous years. Oaxaca's government would enter the era of reform with its legitimacy deeply rooted in everyday politics. Yucatán's would make its changes having lost its mandate to govern the indigenous population. They would each have to make reforms with an eye to both the nature of their own local political cultures and, as the 1850s wore on, the developing national consolidation of liberalism.

CHAPTER 5

"The Shadow of Liberty"

THE POLITICS OF REFORM IN OAXACA TO 1858

IN MAY 1835, THE SUBPREFECT of the Oaxacan district of Tlacolula complained that he was having trouble complying with state government mandates regarding the draft, schools, road maintenance, and tax collection. To enforce government orders, he wanted to establish an armed unit made up of "honorable"—that is, nonindigenous—citizens of the district's cabecera. Otherwise, he feared,

laws and Superior orders will be the plaything of the pueblos of this district, that little by little are demoralized in the shadow of liberty, as they are accustomed to the rigor of the Alcaldes Mayores who made them obedient with whippings and punishments of that sort.[1]

For this appointed government official, memories of the colonial system that had collapsed fifteen years before provoked nostalgia. As he remembered it, alcaldes mayores—the regional colonial officials responsible for the administration of indigenous affairs—had been able to keep the population in check with punishments that were now unconstitutional. By contrast, "liberty"—the rules and regulations of the new republican government—was a "shadow"; it "demoralized" villagers by distancing them from the influence of the state.

While this indictment of liberalism was unusually blunt, it captured many officials' essential ambivalence about the regimes that had governed Oaxaca in the years since independence. Liberal structures of governance seemed to offer a long-term solution to the myriad administrative problems involved in governing indigenous communities where traditional modes of village administration persisted. But, at the same time, officials in republican Oaxaca were torn between potentially disruptive attempts to force indigenous villagers to behave like liberal citizens and the peaceful continuation of colonial-like relationships. It was out of this ambivalence, in the first twenty years of republican rule, that Oaxacan officials and Oaxacan villagers had forged an arrangement based on the compatibility of republican and colonial forms, practices, and ideas. Embedded in this arrangement was the notion that, despite adherence to liberal institutions, indígenas could continue to enjoy a special relationship with the state.

After 1847, the increasing power and focus of the liberal movement on both a local and a national scale would raise questions about this unique Oaxacan arrangement, giving further voice to officials' doubts. Oaxaca's governor between 1847 and 1852 was Benito Juárez, later an architect of national liberal reform and Mexico's president in the 1860s and 1870s. As governor, Juárez would use his home state of Oaxaca to experiment with liberal reformism, especially with the challenge of integrating the largely indigenous population into an undifferentiated citizenry. The reforms that Juárez promoted potentially struck at the core of Oaxaca's unique political culture because they asked officials to separate the elements of the hybrid system that had developed since 1824. What was liberal was to remain, and what was colonial—or "customary"—was to be replaced with liberal institutions. During Juárez's regime, local Oaxacan officials would struggle once again to accommodate new government demands in order to produce a system that was acceptable to all parties.

Before 1855, reform occurred mostly on the state level. But, after that year, Oaxaca's new local liberalism would come face to face with a developing national liberalism intent on transforming all of Mexico. In Oaxaca, new national liberal legislation would pose a significant challenge; in particular, the land legislation embodied in the Ley Lerdo of June 25, 1856, constituted a conscious attack not just on customary institutions but on indigenous identity itself. The law aimed to create individual property owners whose interests would be separate from those of their communities, an aspiration that had been present in Mexican government since independence, but that, in most places, including Oaxaca, had been deferred. The new national reform promised—or threatened—to make it a reality.

But when national liberalism came to Oaxaca, it would come up against the state's local liberalism, a political culture that in its dedication to indigenous autonomy was at odds with the liberal ideas emanating from Mexico City. The ideological intentions of national reformers were not entirely shared by the Oaxacan officials entrenched in this local culture, and the latter would work to find ways to make national legislation less threatening to Oaxacan political relationships and thus less liable to touch off social conflict and destroy the tenuous legitimacy of the state. In particular, Oaxacan regional officials and indigenous villagers would negotiate an interpretation of the Ley Lerdo that would be acceptable to both. In the process, they reproduced the relationship between state and society on new terms, terms that incorporated the new national liberalism in much the same way that Oaxacans had earlier incorporated liberalism on a state level. The Oaxacan government emerged from the first years of the Reform not as a destructive force for indigenous communities but still as a relatively protective one. It emerged also with a new and crucial role: that of mediator between national forces for change and the interests of Oaxaca's indígenas.

Indigenous Villages and the Politics of Reform, 1847–1855

Benito Juárez's liberal project for the transformation of Oaxaca had, first and foremost, a political objective: "to inculcate," as Brian Hamnett writes, "a sense of popular awareness of the obligations required by civil authority and the advantages that could accrue from complying with them." Juárez wished Oaxacan citizens' primary obligation to be to the state, rather than to a host of groups, institutions, and identities—including villages and the church—that had governed social and political relations in colonial Mexico. Linked to that political goal was an economic objective. The bonds of colonial society, Juárez argued, together with the poverty of the majority of the people, prevented Oaxaca's citizens from taking advantage of economic opportunities. Thus, the state had an obligation both to counteract colonial ties and to combat poverty by improving opportunity. Juárez advocated the improvement of transportation, the building of ports, and the lifting of tariffs as measures toward Oaxaca's economic advance.[2]

Many of these projects were long term, and turmoil in Oaxaca, especially on the isthmus of Tehuantepec, meant that they did not progress far during the four years of Juarez's governorship. The regime was able to make its most cogent demands in the local arena, at the level of the indigenous villages. Juárez was from one of these villages, a Zapotec town in the Oaxacan sierra called Guelatao. His rise to power was thus somewhat unusual. With the help of a local benefactor he was able to attend seminary in Oaxaca City, hoping eventually to gain his own parish. But, in 1828, when the city opened a new secular Institute of Sciences and Arts, he chose to transfer his studies. At the Institute, he studied law and came into contact with some of the most prominent Oaxacan liberals of the time. Through those connections, Juárez eventually served in the state legislature during the reformist regime of 1833–1834. He was elected as one of Oaxaca's deputies to the national congress in 1846 and appointed governor of Oaxaca in 1847. One year later, he won that office through election and proceeded to serve a four-year term.[3]

That Juárez was indigenous is a fact that has garnered much attention. But, as Hamnett writes, Juárez and his counterparts were "first and foremost Liberals rather than Indians."[4] If anything, Juárez's experience gave him a broad justification for his policies regarding indígenas. Separated from his local associations at an early age, educated outside of his village, he saw himself as a testament to the progress indigenous individuals could make if they cut traditional ties and entered the "mainstream" of civic and political life. Given the right opportunities, Juárez's life suggested, all Oaxacan indigenous citizens would come to exhibit the characteristics that he believed were natural to all men. The "right opportunities," according to Juárez's reformist project, meant both providing resources for education, good administration, and economic advance and actively rooting out the customs and practices that stood in the way.

At the level of the villages, Juárez's liberal reforms addressed two major issues: the management and use of communal funds and primary education. The two were, he explained in 1848, intimately linked:

It would be desirable if for the better security of their funds, the . . . treasurers watched over their management, abandoning any recompense for the work they spend in collecting and distributing these funds, which with preference to any other object that is not of absolute necessity, should be invested in the development of the schools.[5]

Thus, the government aimed simultaneously to promote good fiscal management and to sustain the development of a system of rural education. Both had been official goals since 1824. Oaxacan officials charged with administering the reforms were thus intimately familiar with the obstacles to change. Before 1847, education and the management of village finances had been constant administrative problems for officials, as they strove for the most efficient government possible. After 1847, they would suddenly become ideological problems as well. In an era of liberal reform, the aim of primary village education and efficient money management was not just to improve villagers' financial prospects and increase the efficiency of government; these measures were now intended to effect a fundamental change in the political identity of Oaxaca's indigenous population.

This project prompted the articulation of a new discourse about indigenous identity on the local level. In the first twenty years after independence, indigenousness was rarely explicitly invoked by either state officials or villagers in Oaxaca. Now, as the state committed itself to erasing indigenous identity, its political importance came to the fore. State officials began to speak more frequently about what made their indigenous constituents different. And although the term *indigenous* itself would still be used only rarely by villagers, they did find themselves actively defending their differences under the rubric of "custom" and "tradition," which came under explicit attack from the new reformist state.

Doubts came not only from the indigenous population. The Juarista reform promoted a change that many Oaxacan state officials were not sure was possible or even desirable. Regional government officials had limited access to what went on inside indigenous villages and had long depended on indigenous authorities to mediate their relationship with the wider population. The legitimacy of those authorities depended heavily on "custom" and "tradition." While they may have agreed in principle with the long-term goals of liberalism, local government officials thus found it difficult to find ways to implement new policies in the short run without compromising the fragile pact between state and society. Even when they believed, in the abstract, in the efficacy of reforms, their commitment to the political culture that had long governed the practice of administration in Oaxacan villages made their engagement with Juárez's proactive liberalism a distinctly limited affair.

Indigenous Custom and Liberal Practice in Oaxaca's Villages

Even reformists did not always see the customs of local indigenous government as inherently bad. In his first report to the Oaxacan congress in 1848, Juárez himself waxed enthusiastic about the local governments of Oaxaca's towns and villages. "Since before the establishment of the federal system," he wrote,

the pueblos of the State have had the democratic custom of electing their functionaries for themselves, that with the name of alcaldes and regidores take care of policing, the conservation of peace, and the administration of communal funds.

After praising this "beneficial custom," Juárez went on to attribute the downfall of the central republic and its replacement with the new federal government to the "universal disgust" caused by the centralist suppression of local authority. Under the new restored federal republic, "the pueblos have recovered not only their ayuntamientos and repúblicas, but also the right to elect them in conformity with their ancient customs." As of now, he was proud to report, these municipal bodies "are complying exactly with their duties."[6]

Just four years later, in 1852, Juárez was less enthusiastic about the local governments that served Oaxaca's indigenous communities. In part because of the "demoralization" produced by internal unrest in recent years and in part because of "the general ignorance of the indigenous class," many of the local municipal bodies "neglect their obligations." In particular, Juárez worried about local officers' mishandling of communities' treasuries, suggesting that "with very rare exceptions," alcaldes and regidores "took advantage of these products for their personal use or in order to foment vices and customs pernicious to society." He urged the departmental governors and subprefects to take special care in overseeing the activities of the repúblicas—a direct blow to the theoretical autonomy of the pueblos.[7]

There is no evidence to suggest that the indigenous authorities of 1852 were any more or less venal, corrupt, or incompetent than those of 1848. Rather, what had changed in the intervening years was Juárez's presentation of the correlation between liberal institutions and indigenous traditional practice. In his 1848 address, Juárez had assumed that it was possible to equate the local institutions of federalist Oaxaca—ayuntamientos and repúblicas—with Oaxacan indígenas' "ancient customs." Just as indígenas had always elected local bodies, they continued to do so under Mexican liberal policy; in effect, all that had changed was the terminology. Four years later, Juárez no longer referred to "beneficial custom," but rather to "pernicious custom." By that time, Juárez believed that indigenous practices of self-government were harmful rather than helpful for good administration, and that ignorance stood in the way of the ability of Oaxaca's indígenas to take their place in the polity as liberal citizens. Pueblo autonomy was not in and of itself a bad thing—institutionally, it remained at the center of the liberal project as envisioned by Juárez—but the way that it was practiced according to indigenous custom did not conform to liberal ideals. Thus, indígenas must be forced to reject older forms of local government and replace them with new ones.

Without doubt, most Oaxacan officials were well aware by 1848 that indigenous practices were not precisely correlated to the republican institutions the names of which they shared and that the infrastructure of liberalism disguised a host of local indigenous practices that bore little relation to the ideas underlying liberal republicanism. Juárez's 1852 lamentations were thus a sign of his growing acknowledgment of this state of affairs. But Juárez, unlike many regional and local officials, believed that change was possible. To Juárez, "indigenous custom" and "liberal practice" were discrete and identifiable entities. But viewed from the villages, this clarity tended to dissipate for both officials and villagers. Certainly, Oaxacan officials were never satisfied with indigenous authorities' governance of their villages, and they were certain that, even when indígenas followed the letter of the law, they were not necessarily adhering to its spirit. But in their attempt to strike a bargain with the villagers that would maintain the legitimacy of the Oaxacan state, officials participated in the maintenance of both customary indigenous practices and liberal forms and ideas. For government officials, then, the Juárez regime would present the challenge of instituting reform while navigating the complicated terrain of Oaxaca's unique political culture.

A dispute between the villagers and their priest in Cacahuatepec in 1849 demonstrates the difficulty of separating colonial and liberal forms, practices, and ideas in one small Oaxacan town. When investigating a complaint from the priest that the villagers were not paying their ecclesiastical taxes, the governor of Jamiltepec found that there was some confusion about who actually held power in the village. One man, Antonio Ernandes, referred to himself as the "indigenous regidor," acting for the suspended "second alcalde of the indígenas." Ernandes claimed to represent "the Corporation, the ancianos of the Pueblo, and all the indigenous class that composes its larger part," a position that, legally, did not exist. Meanwhile the town's priest, Francisco Parra Salanueva, claimed that the pueblo in fact had no legal second alcalde and that Ernandes's duty was merely to collect taxes and help the real alcalde, Pascual Chabes, "who is . . . nonindigenous (*de razon*) and swears an oath . . . and receives the staff." Apparently, the town had an informal—and extralegal— arrangement in which an indigenous man and a nonindígena shared local authority, with the indígena representing the indigenous population and the other man representing the smaller population of nonindígenas, an arrangement that, while not uncommon in colonial Oaxaca, was antithetical to liberal law.

This was not, however, a simple case of indígenas using newer titles to describe older forms. Despite their investment in an older kind of local authority, the town's indígenas simultaneously made an appeal to new liberal laws and ideas about equality, writing that

not wanting any longer to be subject to the old Custom of contributing to our Parish priest with obvenciones, *limosnas*, and personal services, abolished since the year [18]18 . . . we have agreed of common accord to direct this humble representation to Your Excellency, with no other object but that you exonerate us from this burden, remaining in its place subject to happily paying the charges imposed on the nonindigenous class.

Meanwhile, the priest, who had earlier appealed to liberal municipal forms, refuted the villagers' request to alter their payments to the church with a defense of tradition, citing the colonial notion that "custom, according to a principal of law, not contradicting the law has the force of law."[8] Thus, not only did older and newer forms coexist in the villages, older and newer ideas coexisted as well, and both sets of forms and ideas were available to and used by all parties, often in inconsistent ways. For Oaxacan officials, disentangling the liberal from the customary was a daunting and probably impossible task.

Certainly, there were some "indigenous customs" that officials could identify and unequivocally repudiate. For example, Tehuantepec governor José María Muñoz complained in 1848 about indigenous authorities' practice of calling public meetings to discuss government orders:

Since my accession to this Department I have tried to stop the punishable custom that the Alcaldes of the Pueblos have . . . of gathering all of the inhabitants in order to inform them of every providence that the Government directs to them, as these Juntas result in disobedience to superior orders, insubordination to the authorities themselves . . . , and in sum every kind of disorder.

Muñoz stressed that, while this sort of custom may not have been harmful in the past, it was harmful now, under a liberal government.[9] The assumption that government orders were subject to village deliberation ran counter to an ideal state in which both governors and the governed were bound by the rule of law. And, perhaps more importantly, the suggestion that local authorities were not the ultimate arbiters in village affairs threatened the officials' tenuous control over the villages. Thus, practices similar to that observed in Tehuantepec would continue to be a problem, under both Juárez's regime and the one that followed. In 1854, the prefect of Teposcolula referred to a "vicious custom" among the pueblos whereby "the orders that are communicated to the authorities are published without reservation, among those they call principales, who advise as to their arbitration, rendering them illusory." The same prefect instructed the subprefect of Yanhuitlán to tell the authorities in San Pedro Añañe to stop holding public juntas to discuss communal accounts and rather to make their decisions in private. Decisions should be made, "without the necessity of letting the ancianos and principales know immediately," a practice the prefect referred to as "those tortuous steps against order."[10] Because it undermined the ability of officials to negotiate with local authorities about village affairs, this practice was unacceptable, and officials believed it must be rooted out.

But there were also cases in which clearly illiberal practices tended to help rather than hinder officials' ability to govern. In such cases, officials could be willing, albeit reluctantly, to promote situations and relationships that contained elements of older forms. Consider the governor of Ejutla's 1848 description of the town of Santa Anna Zegache, in which there were two barrios hostile to each other, one called "El Mixteco" and the other "El Zapoteco." The origins of this division lay, according to local custom, in the history of the preconquest wars between Mixtecs and Zapotecs, the town having emerged from an uneasy conglomeration of two encampments of the opposing sides. Despite this hostility between barrios, the town had survived as a single entity but only with a long-standing agreement—sanctioned by now defunct colonial decrees—determining that in the municipal government there should always be one alcalde from each barrio. But when elections were carried out according to the form prescribed by the liberal Oaxacan government, the Zapotecos, who were more numerous, always won both seats, causing

> riots, divisions, hatreds, and hostilities between those of the municipal body, and repeated homicides, and wounds, perpetrated on the persons of the Alcaldes, and Regidores, which has lowered . . . the public morality, and the respect owed to local authorities, [so] that these today, whichever barrio they come from, do not have the liberty to administer justice, nor the prestige necessary in order to be obeyed in their judicial and political providences.

It was clear to the Ejutla governor that, whereas a Spanish colonial law had helped solve the problem, liberal Oaxacan law exacerbated it.[11] The situation was made even worse by the Zapotecos' willing embrace of the new liberal laws. Although the Mixtecos continued to choose an alcalde among themselves, the Zapotecos, following the electoral laws determining that the majority ruled, refused to recognize his authority.

Indigenous "tradition" and "custom" were inextricable parts of Oaxacan life, a situation that could be, in officials' eyes, for better or for worse. On the one hand, the custom of opening all government orders up to community deliberation was potentially harmful to officials' ability to govern; on the other hand, the custom of allowing distinct groups within a unified town to elect their own officials could help maintain order. Both customs ran counter to the liberal ideals that underlay Oaxaca's government, but their differential effects led officials to have very different opinions about them. What's more, it was often impossible to separate such customs from the liberal forms and practices introduced in 1825. For Oaxacan officials serving under Juárez's proactively liberal administration, then, some liberal reforms would seem appealing, but blanket reform that would make clear distinctions between indigenous custom and proper liberal procedure would seem for the most part unworkable.

Reforming the Towns: Communal Funds and Education in the New Regime

One of the areas in which all could agree that liberal reform was most sorely needed was education. In 1847, the council of government issued a report on the state of public education in rural Oaxaca, lamenting that no previous state government had given this issue the thought or resources that it deserved. "No one is unaware," the councillors argued,

that the education of youth, if it produces very happy results in the Cities and Capitals of the States, is of more beneficent consequence in the population of the periphery, which because of its distance from the Center, or because of its small convenience, lacks honorable and capable vecinos to do direct business relative to government.[12]

In its daily relationship with the indigenous population, the hallmark feature of the new liberal regime in Oaxaca would be its policies regarding schools. Education was the primary mechanism through which Oaxaca's indígenas would enter the polity as equal citizens prepared for participation in political life. As Benito Juárez put it in his address to the Oaxacan congress in 1848, "the desire to know and to educate one's self is innate in the heart of man"; according to the liberal ideal, if given the opportunity and the means, even the poorest Oaxacan indígena would rush to take advantage of an education, much as Juárez himself had. Education, liberals argued, would have to reach into the farthest corners of Oaxaca and into its remotest villages. In 1850, Juárez's regime issued regulations enjoining the departmental governors to "procure with special care that in all the pueblos of the department they do not lack primary schools," to ensure that "the children attend them with all possible punctuality," and to make certain that the teachers had "the necessary aptitude for the perfect education of the youth."[13]

To reform education, however, would require significant transformation of Oaxacan "custom" because it demanded a kind of participation and cooperation on a municipal level that did not mesh easily with longstanding practices. First and foremost, to have schools in the pueblos, towns would need the money to establish them. Traditionally, the villages had funded schools directly through their fondos del común. These "common funds" were traditionally derived from a kind of commonly held lands— the *propios*—which were often rented out to pay for community expenses, or from communal sources of revenue such as milling operations or rent from stalls in the marketplace.[14] The fondos del común could be spent on the functioning of the town government, the maintenance of the local priest, religious festivities, and especially on the salary of the schoolteacher. Strapped for resources, Juárez's government continued to rely on the pueblos for school financing. But, increasingly, the government would try to coerce the towns into using these funds *exclusively* for education. Thus, traditional ways of managing local funds and control over how they would be used became major concerns for the Oaxacan government after 1847.

Certainly, officials had long been critical of how pueblos chose to use their funds. State inquiries into the nature and use of fondos del común were carried out for the first time in 1825 and were repeated regularly in the years thereafter.[15] For liberals, who mistrusted the communal politics that they believed to inhibit individual ambition and progress, the funds were an obvious target of attention. But it was not only federalists or even liberals who were concerned about communal finances. Laws regarding the funds were passed for the first time in 1844 by the centralist departmental assembly, requiring pueblos to turn in budget proposals to their subprefects for approval. And in August 1848, a conservative congressional deputy, Juan Bautista Carriedo, called for further attention to the problem:

> Most of the pueblos of the State, with the exception of very few, have funds known as communal or common: it is reasonable that this Honorable Camera should have an exact knowledge of the present investment of these funds, both to decide on measures that free these funds from the many abuses committed against them, and to give them new investment . . . for the benefit and advancement of the pueblos themselves.

Carriedo proposed that the government should produce a report on all the towns that had funds and on how they were administered; then, the legislature would proceed to direct the investment of those funds. In December 1849, the liberal Oaxacan congress passed a law giving departmental governors and subprefects some control over the money. And finally, in 1851, Congress, explicitly noting both the 1844 law and Carriedo's 1848 suggestion, passed a new code ruling that ayuntamientos and repúblicas must turn in accounts and budgets annually and giving the government the power to accept or deny those budgets.[16] With this code, the liberal government gave new life to a proposal that had long been on the minds of Oaxacan politicians, now explicitly in the name of liberal reform.

Right away, officials ran into difficulties in carrying out the new laws, often because there were few funds to administer, let alone to administer well. Indeed, throughout the years leading up to and including the Juárez administration, many towns had no resources from which to derive the funds at all. In 1830, of fifty-one pueblos in Teotitlán, only six had working municipal funds. In 1842, the governor of Huajuapan reported that nearly all the pueblos in his department lacked land and thus funds, despite laws mandating them. And in 1844, out of approximately sixty towns in the department of Jamiltepec, only eighteen had communal resources.[17] Little changed after the transition back to federalism. An 1848 report on the towns of the district of Yanhuitlán revealed that most villages had little or no land to use in the production of fondos del común and had few or no buildings to rent out and thus that most did not have enough to support a school year-round. Similar reports came in over the next few years from Miahuatlán, Tlaxiaco, Huajuapan, Teotitlán, and the Centro.[18]

More importantly, pueblos resisted government interference in the administration of the funds they did have. Villages traditionally used their common funds for a variety of purposes that were not sanctioned by the government. Among the most common of these were contributions to the maintenance of local churches. Under the new laws, common funds were not to be used for the church without explicit permission from authorities, and authorities were less likely to give such permission in the context of the anticlerical liberal regime that came to power after 1848. In the municipality of Don Dominguillo, for example, the townspeople had been given permission to use their funds for the long-term repair of the local chapel in 1843, but the subprefect then required that the villagers request permission anew from the departmental governor in 1852. The villagers complained that if they were not allowed to continue the repairs, all the work they had done up until now would be destroyed in the next rainy season.[19] Similarly, the town of Santa Anna Chiquihuitlán had long used its income from common plantings to pay for church accoutrements, "calculating that in no other manner could they afford any purchases." But in 1852, the government rejected the town's proposed budget because it contained church expenses. As a result, the villagers of Santa Anna were now refusing to work the common lands, arguing that they were not being allowed to spend the proceeds as they desired. They cited their poverty as the reason they could not afford to maintain the church by other means and appealed to the state government to intervene in their behalf.[20]

Under the Juárez regime, then, despite more attention to the matter, officials were no more able to change the way that villagers used their fondos del común than they had been in the past. The resources themselves were extremely small, and any attempt to redirect them could potentially cause outrage on the part of the villagers; few officials were willing to push the point in the service of education or anything else. But the state government's desire to promote schools remained strong, and it continued to seek ways of convincing villagers to pay for them. In 1850, subprefects were to "inform the government . . . about the charges that should be established to create or augment the municipal funds that should cover the costs of the school."[21] These charges were envisioned as minor local taxes levied on market activity or production, above and beyond the revenue from common land and other enterprises that made up the actual community fund.

This was not the first time that the government had made such a suggestion. Dorothy Tanck de Estrada has detailed an increasing state insistence on local schools through the Bourbon era in New Spain as a whole and the intimate connection of the schools to the management of communal finances.[22] In independent Oaxaca, efforts to establish primary schools began in 1825. And in 1834, the departmental governors had sent a circular to all the towns encouraging them to establish new primary schools and inquiring as to what funds might be available to do so. The response of both villagers and officials to this earlier attempt is instructive. Oaxacan officials were well aware that many villages already had schools of a sort, in which a teacher from the village itself taught mostly Christian doctrine on an irregular basis; that irregularity reflected villagers' need to use the labor of their children during plantings and harvests. The government, however, wished to promote consistent attendance at secular primary schools that focused mainly on reading, writing, and the "political catechism," which, in nearly all cases, would require towns to contract a teacher from outside the village to run the school. Thus, the 1834 circular focused on finding solutions to the two major problems with schools as government officials saw them—funding and contracting outside teachers—by suggesting that town governments charge a small fee from each villager to bring in a qualified instructor.[23]

In response, villagers were puzzled and defensive. In the department of Huajuapan, for example, many villagers could not understand why existing schools were not sufficient. According to its alcalde, the town of Santiago Huajolos had a school "established at the expense of the Parents . . . , who are required to pay one half real in order to form the endowment for the instructor who is a vecino of the pueblo itself." Paying for an outside instructor, meanwhile, would be beyond their means. Similarly, the república of Santo Domingo Yodoyuc reported that the town's school was paid for by the parents, "from whom we cannot squeeze more . . . because they are miserable indígenas who rely on their seasonal crops alone." The república of San Gerónimo Zilacalluapilla wrote simply that applying any further tax would be futile, because the potential taxpayers were "extremely poor and few." And the república of Santa María Sochistlapilco succinctly countered the government's suggestions, saying that

there is no way to create [a tax] because everyone is encountering difficulties that are impossible to solve at this time and at others in which you have wanted to fix our attention on this subject, because the way to conserve instruction is to demand a half real from the parents of families creating with this the endowment of the Teacher . . . whose salary is so inferior that it does not permit the solicitation of a . . . teacher from the outside.[24]

Oaxacan officials were thus often frustrated. In theory, education did seem to many officials to be a likely way of raising indígenas out of poverty and of making them more conscious of political matters. José Mantecón, the prefect of Teotitlán, writing in 1832, had advocated proactive measures on the part of the government regarding schools, because

without this, they will neither be able to acquire a decent education, nor much less will the inhabitants [of the pueblos] have the [ability] required of a Republican; in the multitude of languages that they speak they know no word that can substitute for honor and love . . . ; thus, love of country (*amor patriae*) is totally unknown, and their actions are never accompanied by any sense of honor.[25]

Officials argued that only through education would indígenas acquire the tools necessary to advance. But at the same time, they were certain that indigenous people were not interested in getting the sort of education that the government had in mind. Tehuantepec governor Mariano Conde's 1831 observation that villagers had long "seen [a primary school] with hate and repugnance, such that the priests and judges are not able to persuade them to establish one, [and they are] always eluding it with frivolous pretexts" reflected a deep consensus among nonindigenous officials about Oaxaca's indigenous population. As Ignacio José Ortega wrote of the town of San Juan Guichicovi, "faithful to the customs of their grandparents, the San Juaneros do not wish to be enlightened." Officials claimed that villagers were unlikely to start up schools on their own initiative. In San Juan, Ortega claimed, "there is no school, and nor do I believe there will be one soon, nor children learning their ABCs, until . . . the Government takes energetic measures." Villagers welcomed the existence of local schools taught by local people but wanted to retain flexibility about both the timing and the content of education. For officials, this often translated into laziness, recalcitrance, and a fundamental lack of ambition. In 1837 José Mantecón described the indigenous population with disdain:

[T]he indígenas, without a strong stimulus, are little inclined to work; and as they obtain their food and clothing with two or three months of occupation, they spend the rest of the year in the most pitiful idleness . . . , passing their lives like automatons, free of the cares that surround the other classes of society. It would certainly be desirable [to find] an occupation that would make these Citizens useful and would raise them out of the unfortunate state to which they are reduced.[26]

But even as they criticized the indígenas' unwillingness to educate themselves, officials defended the pueblos' explanations and even their educational practices. The governor of Jamiltepec, for instance, responded to the state government's circular in 1834 by reporting that in his department, the pueblos had recently been ravaged by both drought and war,

such that even in order to pay one real of contribution one sees a thousand conflicts . . . because there is nowhere to get it from. . . . Where, then, can we find [the money] to pay a primary school teacher in the Pueblos? Some of those zealous for the education of the youth established for some time [the custom of using] crops from labor in common, with product of which they maintained their teachers for a time . . . , but this bonanza they enjoyed while Heaven was propitious.[27]

Similarly, the governor of Ejutla, Mariano Antonio Casas, believed that "although in some Pueblos there are products, and in others dedication to manufacture on which one could levy a tax, if one were to be established, aside from being harmful to the farmer and the artisan the collection of the tax would be very difficult because of the novelty [of it]." As far as Casas was concerned, there was little that the government could do: "There is no other measure more secure and less harmful to the pueblos in this Department . . . than that they have already adopted."[28]

This response was consonant with officials' prevailing attitude toward indígenas. Officials were deeply invested in a political relationship that put the hardship of the pueblos at center stage. Thus, they were willing to accept that education—like taxes and the draft—put undue burdens on the indigenous population. They could support the pueblos' claims to exemption from new education regulations based on the same discourse of poverty that permeated other administrative concerns. To do otherwise was to risk reprisals from the villagers. In short, Oaxacan officials faced a quandary; education was certainly a good idea, they felt, but forcing it on the indígenas had the potential to upset the fragile legitimacy of Oaxaca's state.

In 1850, sixteen years later, little had changed. The government's plan for villagers to pay for education was the same, and the villagers were still not able to do so. Officials continued to balance their desire to improve Oaxacan administration with their dependence on a relationship that supported the status quo. After the passage of the 1850 regulations, a number of schools opened in the villages. Official ceremonies were held, consisting of the presentation of the teacher, a listing of the students, and a solemn blessing. In the department of the Centro, for example, the governor reported twenty-one new municipal schools in the district of Santa María Oaxaca, ten in Etla, six in Zachila, fourteen in Zimatlán, and thirty-one in Tlacolula. But of the schools hastily opened with much fanfare, many if not most closed just as quickly. In the district of Juquila in 1852, the governor reported that the twenty-three schools he had recently opened were now all closed because there was no way to pay a teacher. As of now, those twenty-three pueblos were back to holding Christian doctrine classes taught by an indigenous teacher from the town itself.[29]

Most villagers rejected the 1850 regulations; not surprisingly, villagers were no more willing or able to establish extraordinary charges to pay for schools in the 1850s than they had been in the past. The villagers of Yxtepeji, for example, resisted orders to use their common planting profits for schools, and the subprefect worried that there would be a riot.[30] And in

Logocho, when the subprefect tried to force the villagers to establish fees for using spots in the town plaza during the market, the vendors objected. When he went to investigate, the subprefect found himself confronted by "an army of women watched over by another of men," upset, as the town's alcaldes told him, "because they are being harassed in [the matter of] schools, taxes, and others; and that the governor and I are nothing but thieves." According to his account, the subprefect barely escaped with his life.[31]

This was a frustrating and even dangerous experience for Oaxacan officials. But, as in 1834, even these officials recognized the very real obstacles to school establishment. Increasingly, the obstacles that they pointed out were not all internal to the villages themselves; some had to do with the approach of the state. In a rare request to found their own school, the town officials of Santa María Petapa wrote in 1852 that it was "desirous today of doing what is possible in favor of [education] so that the young people can advance." But they were too poor to pay for it themselves, and they asked for help from the government. The governor of Tehuantepec found the village's request particularly compelling because Santa María had never before expressed an interest in education and, of the pueblos of the department, was "one of the least civilized." But despite the villagers' interest, there was no mechanism for the government to help them establish a school, ensuring that they would remain sunk in "the highest ignorance."[32]

Officials were certain that without an active commitment to help pay for schools, the Oaxacan government would never accomplish its educational goals. Under the government's various funding plans since 1824, education had for the most part become simply one more administrative burden to be negotiated with the villagers. And as an administrative burden, it was less important to most officials than tax collection or the draft, because the latter two required that they produce tangible results, whereas education could easily fall by the wayside. In an era of purported reform, the contradiction between the government's stated aims and its methods was painstakingly clear. Nicolás Tejada, the governor of Jamiltepec, expressed his frustration in 1852 when he lamented the lack of resources devoted to rural schools:

Despite my eagerness to . . . improve [the schools] in all ways, as the principal organ of society that exists in tendency toward progress, nothing has favored me. The near complete lack of municipal funds in these pueblos, and the tenacious resistance that in general the common classes oppose to devoting their sons to them, have been such constant and invincible obstacles to my duty, that many times they have made me feel the bitterness of despair.

To have schools, Tejada stressed, it was vital to have men of "capacity and knowledge," but such men had to be paid. Left to their own resources, pueblos would never be able to pay them because of "their common ignorance on the one hand, and their necessity on the other." Tejada thus called upon the government to act: "as I see the Supreme Government is highly interested in [the schools'] protection and development, I do not doubt that nothing would serve as an obstacle" to creating means to pay for schools. The people of Jamiltepec, he wrote, "do not lack intellectual capacity, only the means to develop it." If the government could provide for "solid and sufficient funds," he would be able to establish teachers' colleges in each parish seat so that all of the pueblos would be properly served by qualified teachers.[33]

As far as village administration was concerned, Juárez's liberal reforms introduced little that was new into the experience of Oaxaca's officials. The Juárez regime, by making old administrative problems into new ideological problems, failed to solve the administrative problems first and thus provided no way of getting beyond old obstacles. As they had since independence and even before, attempts to reform the administration of communal funds and to promote the establishment of rural primary schools came up against the relationship between villagers and the state that made governance possible. Officials understood this relationship quite well. If anything, the effect of the attempt to implement Juárez's reforms was to point out the disjuncture between the politics of liberal reform and the politics of governing actual indigenous villages.

Protecting the "Government of the Indígenas": Oaxaca under Santa Anna, 1852–1855

In the mid-nineteenth century, reform came not only from the liberals. From 1852 to 1855, Mexico—and Oaxaca—was governed by a conservative regime under General Antonio López de Santa Anna. The movement that would culminate in the conservative Santa Anna presidency of 1853–1855 had its first Oaxacan repercussions on the isthmus of Tehuantepec, where José Gregorio Meléndez proclaimed for the conservative Plan of Jalisco on December 26, 1852. General Ignacio Martínez Pinillos, the state's military commander, headed for the isthmus to confront Meléndez's forces but, after a quick defeat, decided to proclaim for the Plan himself. In short order, the Oaxaca City garrison and the National Guard joined Meléndez and Martínez; and, by February 1853, the Oaxacan government had signed the Plan, with Martínez named the new state governor. From that time until the defeat of Santa Anna at the hands of Juan Álvarez, Martínez would govern Oaxaca without a state constitution, overseeing the implementation of the conservative reforms of the Santa Anna government. Martínez's tenure in office was characterized by the persecution and exile of many of the state's prominent liberals; Benito Juárez himself was arrested and deported on May 27, 1853, to settle eventually in New Orleans for the duration of the regime.[34]

Despite far-reaching goals, the conservative government would never gain firm control over Mexico, and most of its reforms were never fully put into practice. Oaxacan officials' reaction to them is nevertheless instructive. The Santa Anna regime's reforms were diametrically opposed to the tenets of Mexico's national liberalism. Most important for Oaxaca, the regime's conservatism allowed for distinctions between indígenas and nonindígenas in a way that liberalism could not. This might have been appealing to Oaxacan officials, who had long recognized that governing indígenas often meant accepting their difference. But the precise distinctions made by Santa Anna's legislation were not always the ones that Oaxacan officials wished to make. As they reacted to the conservative vision of state-indigenous relations, Oaxacan officials made increasingly clear what they believed was possible in the environment in which they worked. The encounter of Oaxacan officials with conservatism made apparent exactly where their liberalism lay.

Santa Anna's reforms regarding taxation and the draft would seem quite fitting for Oaxaca, as the unofficial linkage between the two in Oaxaca's political culture became explicit under national conservative law. The new regime abolished the personal contribution known as the capitación. But after further consideration, Santa Anna's government decided that, in the highly indigenous states of Yucatán, Oaxaca, and Chiapas, the personal tax was a necessary evil, "because it is the only resource for covering public costs."[35] In November, the government issued a new law regulating the collection of the capitación, stipulating that it should be paid only by indígenas, and in August of the next year it confirmed that Oaxaca should continue charging the tax as it had in 1845, before the restoration of federalism.[36] For indígenas, however, the payment of the capitación was not without its compensations. The new laws made the responsibilities of indigenous citizens explicit, with the personal tax serving as a substitute for the obligation of registering for the draft:

The Excellent Señor President, whose paternal intentions are well known, considers that those called Indians of the primitive race, who have not mixed with others, [who] are poor and destitute, who cultivate our fields, who employ themselves in other occupations no less useful to society, who pay capitación in various States, has resolved that pure indígenas with no mixture at all are excepted from the lottery.[37]

This logic, whereby the payment of taxes—but not military service—determined good citizenship, was familiar to both indígenas and state officials in postindependence Oaxaca.

Some officials did protest the new laws, complaining that they were having difficulty finding recruits for the armed services. Even though the law reduced the number of men required from each state to make up for the shortfall caused by the exemption of indígenas,[38] officials had difficulty finding men to fill their quotas without tapping the indigenous population. The prefect of Teposcolula, for instance, complained in 1854 that in order to fill his quota (sixty-seven men), he would have to draft them all from the cabecera of Tlaxiaco, the only large nonindigenous settlement in the prefecture.[39] But finding recruits had always been difficult, and Oaxaca's own state laws had mandated that they speak Spanish, a requirement that had eliminated a large part of the indigenous population even before 1853. Moreover, Oaxacan indígenas' objections to being drafted had always made it hard for officials to force them to join the military forces and had discouraged officials from pushing too hard to get them to do so. The new laws certainly made the draft more difficult, but the effects of their provisions were not entirely new.

If the conservatives' tax and draft reforms were relatively compatible with Oaxacan political culture, their reform of town administration was not. The Santa Anna regime explicitly rejected the trappings of pueblo autonomy that had lay at the heart of liberal ideas about administration. Early on in the regime, Lucás Alamán, the conservative movement's most prominent ideologue, had declared of Santa Anna's conservative supporters: "We are decided against . . . the elected ayuntamientos and against all so-called popular elections, as long as they do not rest on other bases." Conservatism posited that not only were indígenas different, they were also less able to administer their own affairs. As such, although they were welcome to their customs in other areas, indígenas would not be allowed to use their customs of town government. Early on the regime eliminated most elected town councils, replacing ayuntamientos and other bodies in all but a few large cities with appointed jueces de paz. As a conservative Mexico City journalist noted, "It was necessary to put an end to the multitude of these corporations, that composed in large part of ignorant persons, resulted in failure in all the business in which they intervened."[40] Most Mexican townspeople, the conservatives were certain, were unqualified to hold local positions of authority and should be replaced by people who would rationalize and improve local administration; in short, they should be replaced by people who were not indigenous.

On the surface, many Oaxacan officials would no doubt have agreed. They had long complained about indigenous officials, bemoaning "the inexact management of the Repúblicas in complying punctually" with orders and claiming that "generally the individuals who serve in the Municipalities are all useless."[41] Some officials welcomed changes in municipal legislation. Manuel Ortega, the subprefect of Yautepec, for instance, saw the new law as an opportunity to replace the present local officials, of whom he disapproved: "The circumstances of the present functionaries in the majority do not lend much confidence, as much because of their indigence as their many vices, or better their apathy and little intelligence." He blamed this situation on a combination of popular elections and indigenous customs of sharing responsibility in the villages. According to those customs, Ortega claimed, the "most well-off" people in the town were exempt from participation in the cargo system, including elected office, and thus those actually elected were "the most unlucky and vice-ridden" people in town. Now, he would have the opportunity to name the proper people for the job.[42]

But to most Oaxacan officials, Ortega's optimism would seem ill founded. First of all, the new provisions seemed impossible to carry out. Because most towns did not have significant nonindigenous populations, officials knew that there was no reliable way to guarantee that the new appointed municipal officers would be nonindigenous; in most cases, there was no choice but to appoint the very people who would probably have been elected in any case. But more importantly, officials knew that indígenas would not easily accept outsiders as town administrators and that to attempt to force them to do so would be inviting disaster. Under similar legislation in the 1830s, officials had proven willing to negotiate ways of allowing indigenous villagers to continue selecting their own governments, and the new conservative legislation seemed fated to have the same limited effect as its centralist predecessor. Officials began to turn in lists of jueces de paz for the pueblos in their districts in late 1853. Many assumed that the jueces de paz would have to be indigenous and made little effort to see that they were not.[43]

If the Santa Anna municipal reforms had a limited impact on indigenous villages, they caused a considerable stir in towns with small but significant nonindigenous populations. Here, it was the minority nonindigenous villagers—those who ostensibly gained power under the new laws—who complained. Nonindígenas were concerned that their exercise of such local power would be harmful to them and their villages. In the past, they explained, local people had made arrangements to share power. Under both the federalist and centralist systems, the flexibility of the laws had made it possible to split authority in "mixed" villages between the indigenous and nonindigenous communities. The townspeople would choose two alcaldes or two jueces de paz; and, in practice, one represented the indígenas and the other the nonindígenas. As Francisco Baños Peña, one of the new nonindigenous authorities in the town of Pinotepa Nacional, put it, "since very remote times . . . it has been a given [that] there have always been two [local authorities], one for each class, that with absolute independence have governed their respective citizens."

Under the new laws, there were also two officers chosen in each town, a "municipal commisary" and a "juez de paz." But there was no assurance that one would be an indígena, and, in practice, indígenas were usually excluded. In Amusgos, for instance, despite the nonindigenous community's explicit suggestion that one of the two officers be indigenous, the government had failed to name an indígena to either post.[44] Although little direct evidence exists for the indigenous reaction to this change in the "mixed" towns, the nonindigenous response is suggestive. Nonindígenas were certain that, without official municipal representation, indígenas would be unwilling to perform important town duties. Indígenas had been responsible for charging taxes, managing municipal funds, distributing laws and circulars, providing aid to passing military agents and mail carriers, developing schools, and supporting the church; nonindígenas had been responsible for providing soldiers for the army and militia (from which indígenas were now excepted) and for overseeing the indigenous authorities in the collection of taxes and the management of funds. Without indigenous participation, the commissaries warned, few of these vital activities would happen. The nonindígenas were few in number and had never participated in the responsibilities long managed by indígenas; nonindigenous "habits," the commissary of Amusgos wrote, were "totally different." What's more, without the indigenous authorities' aid in tax collection, it would be impossible to carry out. Baños Peña, in Pinotepa Nacional, explained that a nonindigenous commissary did not "possess the language that is necessary to make [the indigenous villagers] understand and obey and he does not know personally more than a small number of indígenas." Nonindigenous officials would not be obeyed, because the indígenas would not

have among themselves a representative, because the meetings of the council no longer exist, [the villagers] will not hear their language in order to obey the laws that govern the nation, nor their customs under which they have always been subject in the good of the State and the Church.[45]

Thus, the nonindigenous authorities in these towns wished for a return to a system in which indígenas were responsible for most administrative tasks.

Oaxacan state officials agreed. In January 1855, José Mariano Abrego, the prefect of Jamiltepec, sent a collection of commissaries' complaints to the governor of Oaxaca, strongly supporting their request that the indígenas retain "the prerogative of conserving their Jueces de Paz in the same form that they have always had in order to protect among them order and customs to which they are strongly tied by their habits and traditions." The Santa Anna government's rulings, Abrego claimed, had not been founded in "a practical knowledge of the . . . Government of the Indígenas, under which and in conformity with their customs they have always governed all their Pueblos in peace." Elected indigenous authorities, he wrote, were not antithetical to conservatism because they constituted "nominal representation that cannot be called judicial or even political" but rather "without much interest in public order but that of conserving harmony between them and the gente de razón." He warned of dire occurrences if this "representation" were to be taken away from the indígenas: "They already know that this law that deprived them of that nominal representation exists, and the disgust that they have manifested because of it has come to my ears in various ways and with various meanings." Abrego predicted that many indígenas would abandon their towns or fail to cooperate with nonindigenous authorities, refusing to pay or collect taxes and to take care of the church. Finally, he reported that "many fear that this is the origin of the fomentation of a rivalry between one and the other that will end in a Caste War."[46]

The words of Abrego and the nonindigenous people of these towns confirm the deeply engrained persistence of indigenous forms and practices in village life and the willingness of nonindigenous people, both villagers and representatives of the state, to accept and even defend it. As far as nonindigenous townspeople were concerned, reliance on indigenous custom had always been perfectly legal and beneficial. The new commissary of Amusgos, Lázaro Martínez, explicitly pointed out that indígenas were bound strictly by their own customs, which covered even "the most trivial things." But these very customs, he argued, although "rustic," facilitated governance in a particularly effective way. "The indígena," he wrote, "naturally laborious in the area of agriculture and in some arts, although with imperfection, lends great aid to humanity and always lives submissively, if one does not alter his laws."[47] As nonindígenas in a Jamiltepec town put it, "the customs of the Indians are a firm support for the sustenance of government," a system that "in no way conflicts with any that could be established, as it has not conflicted with the diverse [systems] that we have had since the glorious days of our independence."[48] The "juez indio," as the commissary of Santa María Asunción Huazolotitlán called the highest indigenous official in a town, "carries out his duty with entire subjection to the laws, and with decided obedience to the system of government that reigns," while also carrying out "the ancient customs, established among them, and that in all times and under all circumstances have always conspired for the sustenance of their political and religious being."[49]

Prior to 1855, the political culture that had developed in Oaxaca since independence proved remarkably impervious to reform, both liberal and conservative. This was not just because the reforms were difficult to carry out but also because Oaxacan officials and other nonindígenas actively participated in that culture and increasingly found themselves defending it from change. Often, this occurred out of necessity, as officials in particular were concerned that change could only make governance impossible and bring about violent conflict. But their own attachment to the way things were seemed at times to run deeper, as their fear of rebellion bled into their understanding of and relationship with their indigenous constituency. The result was official reluctance to force a transformation of Oaxaca's indigenous population, a reluctance that proved capable of stopping reform in its tracks.

Land and Social Peace in Oaxaca, 1854–1858

After 1854, land became a major focus of national reform. For liberals, this meant encouraging private ownership, which they believed provided incentives both to improve one's property and to participate meaningfully in a larger political community. But liberals were not the first to promote land reform in Mexico. Under Santa Anna, the conservative national government had attempted to "rationalize" land tenure practices by converting baldíos—the "unused" lands that legally belonged to the nation—into private property. In Oaxaca, this posed a significant threat to land-poor villages that depended on access to baldíos for survival. The Santa Anna government's reform would never be carried out in Oaxaca. But, like their response to Santa Anna's municipal reform, the reaction of Oaxacans to the conservative assault on land foreshadowed and helps clarify their response to the much further-reaching liberal reform that would be instituted two years later.

For the Santa Anna regime, baldíos offered an untapped and potentially huge resource for the national treasury. Many baldíos, conservatives observed, were being used illegally by individuals or communities, or alternatively were being sold. To stave off these losses, functionaries throughout the country were instructed to identify baldíos and reclaim them for the nation.[50] The ministry of development was to produce a statistical survey of all the baldíos in the Mexican territory. In February 1854, the minister wrote to Ignacio Goytía, his agent in Oaxaca and a former state governor, to request information. The minister stressed Mexico's failure to take advantage of its resources and suggested that the answer lay in European immigration. To encourage potential immigrants, Mexico must be able to offer them land. But in Oaxaca, Goytía was not enthusiastic about the plan to use baldíos in this way. "It is true," he wrote, "that in this Department baldío lands abound . . . ; and there are also those known as *realengas*. The first are the property of the pueblos, and regarding their conservation, and expansion, they are vigilant with an enthusiasm difficult to express." To appropriate these lands, he argued, the government would have to use force because Oaxacan towns would fight tooth and nail for even the most "small and sterile piece of land." Appropriation would cause "grave disgust," and "an alarm that it is not easy to conceive of quieting." Indígenas would make common cause among themselves, and no colonist attempting to use the lands granted to him would ever be able to count on his personal security or on the use of the fruits of his labors. Goytía warned that, in Oaxaca, to mitigate the effects of the process, the identification of baldíos should be done not by a commission but by prefects and subprefects, and even then the repúblicas should be consulted. To do otherwise was to risk rebellion.[51]

Oaxacan officials proceeded with caution. Although some did send requests for information about baldíos to the pueblos, they were careful to avoid asking villagers for titles to lands belonging outright to the villages, asking only for information about the baldíos that they used (a request unlikely to produce results from townspeople who viewed their access to baldíos as a right). In June 1856, when one subprefect wished to send an armed unit to enforce a land transaction, the governor of Ejutla objected; the most important thing, he wrote, was "to avoid the disturbance of the best tranquility that is now found in the state," and villagers would be quick to claim their rights to "the only patrimony on which they subsist." Officials' response to the possibility of land reform suggests not only fear but also an understanding of and even sympathy for villagers' objections. Goytía, for instance, exhibited a thorough knowledge of how the villages used baldío lands—not just for cultivation but also for grazing, cutting wood, and renting out. He also observed that, in practice, there was little difference between baldíos and lands belonging to the pueblos; according to him, baldíos were pueblo "property," a claim that, while not legally correct, reflected the arrangement that pueblos had long lived by. The governor of Ejutla suggested that villagers had good cause to object to what they saw as unfair judicial decisions about their land, as it was all that they had to live on. And the governor of Huajuapan, in 1856, explicitly stated that he understood the protection of communal lands to be one of his duties.[52] The notion that villages had an inalienable right to the lands that they used was deeply embedded in Oaxacan political culture, and those who participated in that culture, both indígenas and representatives of the state, were resistant to the Mexican government's attempts to change the nature of land tenure.

Such attempts were a central part of the platform of the liberal government that replaced Santa Anna in 1855. For liberals, land reform was inextricably linked to ideology. The government in Mexico City saw the transformation of the nation as its major goal and the transformation of the indigenous population as crucial to fulfilling it. Indígenas, along with the church, were the target of the Ley Lerdo passed on June 25, 1856, by the national congress, which outlawed communal landholding and called for the distribution of common lands to individual property owners. Ideologically, the Ley Lerdo fit well with Benito Juárez's earlier Oaxacan reforms, which had also been aimed at drawing indigenous villagers into a new kind of citizenship. But the new law reached further and was potentially far more destructive for indigenous communities than previous reforms, both liberal and conservative. Juárez did not make a concerted effort to reform land tenure. And Santa Anna, despite his policy on baldíos, explicitly upheld the right of villages to hold land communally,[53] while the new national government quickly legislated against that right itself. In Oaxaca, where vast amounts of land were held communally by hundreds of villages, and where disputes over land were a daily affair, the law could be expected to—and did—cause a major commotion.[54] But what was most striking was the role that representatives of the Oaxacan state played in mitigating the effects of the law on indigenous pueblos and the extent to which the new laws became subsumed into a long-standing regional agreement about the responsibilities of the state.

While land had always been a preeminent issue in Oaxaca, before the 1850s its distribution had been an administrative problem, not an ideological or even an economic one. Land disputes between villages were a constant source of conflict and violence and a constant drain on both community and judicial resources. But in the vast majority of cases, these small-scale land disputes did not spill beyond their localities. Land disputes served a productive as well as a disruptive purpose; the role that the government played as a mediator between villages and between villagers helped it maintain legitimacy among the indígenas. Certainly, Oaxacan officials complained about these endemic land disputes. On paper, the state government made several attempts to eliminate communal landholding, none of which, before 1856, had much effect.[55] Still, neither the Oaxacan state government nor its regional officials showed any significant desire to overhaul the system. In most of the state, although land was at a premium for the indigenous villages, it was not in great demand among the nonindigenous elite, who continued to rely on the indirect exploitation of goods produced in the indigenous communities. Even after 1856, there were few interest groups in Oaxaca that stood to benefit greatly from the Ley Lerdo. In Oaxaca, there was no large bloc of powerful land speculators and landowners waiting in the wings, eager to take control of land that belonged to the pueblos. Certainly, there were elite families, such as the Esperóns and the Fagoagas, who made relatively large purchases after 1856 and whose intervention after that year would cause conflict. But in the late 1850s, agriculture was not the primary interest of most of Oaxaca's elite families, who instead had long pursued a strategy of diversification in the face of indigenous control over production.[56]

Without powerful and united interest groups calling for the universal privatization of land, the Oaxacan state had no strong impetus to facilitate outside access to the villages' communal property. This did not necessarily reflect unequivocal good will toward the villages on the part of the government. Where land was particularly suited to direct commodity production, such as in the salt beds of Tehuantepec, the state was quick to act in favor of present and potential landowners. In such cases, the legitimacy of the state could indeed collapse. Notably these cases were rare in Oaxaca. In most of the state, the balance of the government's interests tipped toward the villages. There were, of course, a number of small-scale nonindigenous farmers in Oaxaca, many of whom rented their land from indigenous communities, who stood to benefit from any reform that would allow them to purchase the land they rented. But these did not constitute a powerful interest group. In many ways, the most powerful interest group in Oaxaca in the 1850s was in fact the indigenous pueblos, who controlled much of the state's production and dominated numerically.

Research has shown that, in many of Mexico's states, the implementation of the Ley Lerdo was deferred until after 1867 or even later; local circumstances determined when state governments became willing and able to enforce the laws.[57] In Oaxaca, it appears that the law was implemented in the 1850s but that its effects were similarly deferred, in some ways indefinitely. The provisions of the Ley Lerdo were taken quite seriously by both villagers and officials, who spent considerable time and resources on the process of privatization. After June 26, the legal process began, and numerous transactions were completed in the next few years. But although there are no clear and reliable figures, indigenous pueblos do not seem to have lost significant amounts of land during the initial implementation of the law in the late 1850s.[58] The process was confusing, tendentious, and often produced violent conflict. It does not, however, appear to have undermined indigenous autonomy, nor does it seem to have damaged indígenas' relationship with the state. If anything, the process of working out ways to apply the Ley Lerdo would strengthen that relationship, as the state served to arbitrate disputes that occurred between villages, between villagers, and between villages and outside aspirants to land.

Again, this occurred despite a significant threat. When implemented in villages with communally held land, the Ley Lerdo was supposed to provide for the division of that land into individual parcels, which would then become the property of the various members of the community. But, in practice, the provisions of the law were unlikely to produce this result. The law divided communal property into two types: that which was rented out and that which was not in use. In the former case, tenants had preferential rights to purchasing the land, and in the latter the land was to be sold at auction. Indigenous villagers who worked parcels of communal land could claim that land as tenants and thus, for a fee, gain legal title to the land through the process of "adjudication." Most villagers, however, did not see themselves as tenants, but rather as "*usufructuarios*," members of the community who occupied village land as part of an agreement with town authorities, a relationship that was not acknowledged by the Ley Lerdo. The law required that "tenants" claim their land within three months after the publication of the legislation; after that time they would lose their preferential rights, and the land would be considered to be not in use, making it vulnerable to public sale.[59] Some Oaxacan villages did distribute land to "various sons of the pueblo" within the allotted time. But others failed to act because of confusion about whether villagers were "tenants." By October, as the three months drew to a close, one state official noted that "the larger part of the pueblos of this partido, because of their apathy and habitual delinquency, have not applied to this office for adjudication of their lands, nor have they celebrated conventional sales."[60] All of these villages now stood poised to lose their land entirely.

The Ley Lerdo had not been designed to harm indígenas. Ideally, liberals hoped it would provide them with the tools necessary for economic and political progress.[61] Thus, some national officials were dismayed when many villagers began to lose their lands. By October, they worried that indigenous villagers were being disenfranchised en masse. On October 9, the ministry of hacienda issued a circular amending the Ley Lerdo and explicitly addressing its intended consequences for "the most destitute classes," especially poor laborers and indígenas. The circular noted that many of these people had not been able to claim lands to which they had a right, either because they could not afford the fees or because "speculators" had put obstacles in their way. President Comonfort had thus ruled that any piece of land worth less than 200 pesos would be automatically distributed among its users without the expensive procedures laid out by the law. At the same time, because three months had already passed, the president decreed that no land could be sold to outsiders without the present users having explicitly renounced their rights, and no agreements made previously should be ratified by state officials.[62]

In Oaxaca, the October decree was welcomed. Some officials had already expressed similar concerns. Governor Juárez himself, in response to conflict between the wealthy Esperón family and the indigenous community from whom they rented land, wrote to President Comonfort to ask for permission to let the villagers distribute the land among themselves. Chassen-López notes that Juárez and many other Oaxacan liberals were "genuinely determined to transform the indigenous *comunero* into a private owner," belying the assumption that the midcentury privatization laws were merely a front for an attempt to wrest land from the indigenous population.[63] But some officials seemed to go even further, doubting both the efficacy and the plausibility of the reform itself. In September, the governor of Teposcolula predicted that the land laws would be impossible to carry out in Oaxaca. He pointed out that most villagers could not afford the procedure of adjudication itself because it required the production of official documents and thus involved the purchase of paper and the payment of fees for scribes and judges. The governor suggested that if villagers had had the money, they would gladly have spent it to protect even meager amounts of land, in effect "spending four pesos to acquire a property that is worth one." Similarly, the subprefect of Etla did not consider the June 25 law to be "plausible" for the indigenous population; before the October revisions were passed, he had applied for a postponement of the implementation, to protect the indígenas in his district, and had been officially denied. After October 9, he felt vindicated. When he explained the new provisions to the alcaldes in his district, they rejoiced, calling for town fiestas, setting off fireworks, and asking for permission to solemnify the circular in a religious ceremony. The subprefect's "true weight of sorrow" at official blindness to the plight of the indígenas had been converted into "the opposite, and in union with the Indians of my partido, I pray to the Heavens to preserve the life of Señor Comonfort for many years and perpetuate him in Government, in order to receive all the goods we expect from his beneficent hand." The new circular, he noted, unlike the previous laws, took the indígenas into account: "They leave no doubt for the indígenas and other unfortunate people, that the desires of our present government, tend in a sure manner toward the well-being of this class of men submerged always by our ancestors in obscurantism."[64]

Indígenas in Mexico as a whole were quick to take advantage of the real protection the October 9 revisions offered. In Oaxaca, indígenas cited the revisions consistently, both to reverse adjudications that had occurred in favor of individuals before the three-month deadline and to argue that their rights to retain their property stemmed from their being poor indígenas. In Ayoquesco in 1856, for instance, a hill that the alcalde José Godines claimed belonged to the ayuntamiento had been sold to two individuals, despite the fact that 200 villagers used that land as usufructuarios. "In virtue of what the circular of last October 9 orders," Godines wrote, "this should not be firm and binding." Similarly, the villagers of San Pedro el Alto complained about a sale of village land to Gregorio Valencia, who lived in the nearby pueblo of Lachixio. Four men who believed they had a right to the land cited the October 9 decrees, noting that they were well aware of the "ideas and sentiments that animate the Supreme Government with respect to the indígenas and other miserable people" and that "being poor indígenas and farmers," they were thus deserving of the protection of the law.[65]

The October 9 revisions, then, seemed to offer some relief. But, for many, a deeper concern about the new laws still existed. Many villages objected not only to the loss of land to outsiders but also to the very idea of privatizing communal land at all. In late October 1856, when one official in Villa Alta tried to explain the benefits of the Ley Lerdo to the villagers of Logocho, he soon found that the villagers were rising up in arms and threatening to murder alcaldes who went through with the process. Other towns argued for an exception, as did Juchitán, which complained that its lands were too scarce to subdivide among all the villagers. And the authorities of the barrios of Tehuantepec similarly explained their objection to the law in terms of pueblo survival. For as long as they could remember, each year, they had divided their land among the villagers. But because that land was scarce, not all villagers could always have land. Rather, they received it in recompense for community duties; and, as those duties revolved among members of the community, so too did rights to use the land. This system would collapse if the land were permanently subdivided, to the great detriment of the barrios:

It is beyond doubt that the adjudication or auction [of these lands] in favor of determined individuals would benefit [those individuals], while the others would be harmed, as they would only have personal burdens and no enjoyment or recompense. In addition, the principal object of the law is to benefit the needy class; and this will not occur in the present case; on the contrary, there will be a kind of monopoly.[66]

Given such constraints on their resources, it is not surprising that many villages objected to being forced to transform their property regimes entirely in favor of private landholding. But it is striking that some Oaxacan officials shared their view. The governor of Huajuapan, for instance, criticized the Ley Lerdo's impact on indígenas from the start. Citing article 8 of the law, which excepted "buildings, egidos, and lands dedicated exclusively to the public service of the towns to which they belong," the governor had suspended *all* land alienation in his department. His objections were not a result of his misinterpretation of the law but rather his concern for maintaining public peace; changes in land tenure "would be the motive for grave and continual discussions and repeated disquiet that could be harmful for the public cause." He was also worried that the allocation of any land at all to private individuals—"even if these are themselves vecinos"—would have detrimental effects on the communities that he supervised. Echoing the remarks of the barrio authorities in Tehuantepec, he explained that the distribution of common lands among villagers "has come to serve as a scarce but well accepted recompense for work in community duties and public benefit that each one offers." If the lands were adjudicated permanently to individual villagers, those vecinos would cease to have any incentive to perform those duties. Thus, he worried about the adjudication process not only because it tended to favor outsiders who could afford to pay the fees involved but also because it struck at the heart of the arrangements that made Oaxacan indigenous communities function.[67] Again, a dynamic and a discourse existed that allowed Oaxacan officials to defend "illiberal" practices from the inroads of liberal reform.

Of course things were rarely so clear cut in practice. Not all officials favored the maintenance of communal property, and not all villagers were blatantly opposed to the implementation of the Ley Lerdo. Many villages—and many individual villagers—saw ways to use the land laws to improve their situation. San Miguel Tilquiapam, for instance, found itself losing in a land dispute against the hacendado Nicolás Tejada and in need of land for subsistence. The local authorities proposed that the town should buy a piece of land that had become available as a result of the Ley Lerdo; they would then, they claimed, distribute that new land among individual villagers.[68] Other towns saw the laws as a way to settle disputes with other villages over who owned pieces of territory. Ayoquesco, for instance, wished once and for all to settle its claim on a piece of land called El Zape that had been in dispute for over 200 years.[69] Indeed, in many disputes over the implementation of the law, it is clear that villagers were using its provisions either to get title to land claimed by another village or to refute similar claims on land they believed to be theirs. When the town of Huajuapan asked for the adjudication of a piece of land it claimed, the authorities of nearby San Agustín Yataruni pointed out that ownership of the land was in dispute and thus suggested that it be put up for auction instead of giving preference to people from Huajuapan; this would give San Agustín a chance at regaining the land through purchase.[70]

In many of these disputes, the lines between private property and communal ownership were not entirely clear, either for officials or for villagers. Private property did exist even within the pueblos, but the haziness of land titles often made distinguishing it from common lands extremely difficult. But, clearly, in the tumult that followed the passage of the Ley Lerdo, both ways of making claims on land were available to nearly everyone. In the case of San Pedro el Alto, Tomás, Narciso, and José Gaspar and José María Luis claimed a piece of land after the subprefect arranged for its sale to an individual named Gregorio Valencia. Valencia claimed the land as an usufructuario from Lachixio, a town from which San Pedro had split sometime in the past. The Gaspars and José María Luis claimed it as "private property," as part of a previous agreement with their town of San Pedro. But the Gaspars' letter failed to have any effect because the subprefect who brokered the deal claimed that the lands in question had "belonged to the común" of the combined village and that

they did not lose this character because their possessors located themselves in other pueblos, as it is well known, that the lands that indígenas had possessed while they formed a pueblo, even in the case of dividing themselves to form or belong to another, remain in common, and do not pass to private ownership . . . unless they acquire titles recognized by existing legislation.

Within days, however, the authorities of San Pedro el Alto countered the subprefect's defense of communal landholding. They were claiming the land not as communal property, they insisted, but as their own *private* property; by treating the land as communal, the subprefect, they argued, was responsible for "the sale of our pueblo, and all of its lands."[71] Similarly, in another case involving San Pedro, the subprefect of Zimatlán officiated in the adjudication of a piece of nearby San Miguel Sola's common land in favor of José María Péres, a villager and the son of the alcalde. But then two individuals from San Pedro claimed that they owned the land as private property. Péres then insisted that he, in fact, owned the land. For the San Miguel authorities, whether the land in question was common land or private property seemed secondary to finding a way to keep it within the community. Furthermore, disagreement could also exist within communities; after Péres made his claim for private ownership, several other residents of San Miguel Sola claimed the same land as usufructuarios.[72]

In these cases, the language and logic of private property coexisted with the language and logic of communal property, both for villagers and for officials. Whether or not land titles actually changed hands seemed to have had much more to do with local conditions than with commitment on the part of either party to a particular legal model of property. What officials and villagers shared was a common commitment to finding a way to implement the law without causing fundamental disruptions. For officials, this meant being open to "illiberal" forms of property holding; for villagers, it meant—at least on paper—being open to "liberal" ones.

In 1861, Oaxaca's governor, Ramón Cajiga, would be able to write that "the pueblos . . . possess lands without measure: The least observant [person] would be surprised to know that there are municipalities in whose territories an entire State could fit."[73] Certainly, this was an exaggeration. But that Cajiga's observation could be made at all, five years after the Ley Lerdo was promulgated in Oaxaca, attests to its limited immediate effect on property distribution in the state. This was not because the law was ignored. Villagers, smallholders, and hacendados initiated claims on each other's land and tried to use the law to their advantage.[74] In its first few years of implementation, the Ley Lerdo prompted negotiation between state officials and indigenous villagers as to how that particular law would affect Oaxacan society. This conversation was the continuation of one that had been taking place between those parties at least since independence over how changing institutions and structures of government could be incorporated into Oaxaca's state system without destroying state legitimacy or threatening social peace. But the implementation of the Ley Lerdo did introduce new terms and prompt new adjustments. It contributed to the reproduction of the legitimacy of the state, but it did so around new institutions and on new terms. In addition, the Ley Lerdo also strengthened that relationship by making the Oaxacan state government a mediator between the national government and local society. In the encounter between national and local liberalisms, the Oaxacan state's role for the indigenous population was confirmed and expanded.

The history of reform—and of the Reform—in Oaxaca begins not with the Ley Lerdo and the other legislation attached to the Constitution of 1857 but rather much earlier, with the formation of the state's unique political culture. Oaxaca's local political culture was one in which indigenous villagers, nonindigenous Oaxacans, and Oaxacan government officials all participated, as the relations of power between them translated into ideas about government, its role, and its limits and into ideas about citizens, their rights, and their responsibilities. Between 1847 and 1858, both state and national reformist movements came up against this local liberalism. By the end of the period, those movements would be aimed explicitly at regularizing practices within the nation. But Oaxaca's experience with the Ley Lerdo speaks to Oaxaca's relative imperviousness to national reform. It did not make sense to Oaxacans, either villagers or state officials, to separate tradition and custom from liberal law. The two things had been, at the outset, linked in their minds, as a result of the compromises they had made with each other in implementing laws passed after independence. As Oaxacans carried out the Ley Lerdo, they demonstrated a belief that it was acceptable to interpret the new liberal reforms in ways that were compatible with custom—this despite the fact that, from the national ideological perspective, "custom" was one of the central targets of "reform." In such a climate, it would be hard for the framers of the law to effect the deep changes they had intended. In Oaxaca, national consolidation foundered in part because it tried to impose its own version of liberalism on a place that already saw itself as liberal but defined its liberalism in a very local way.

CHAPTER 6

The Transformation of Indigenous Citizenship

POLITICS IN YUCATAN DURING THE CASTE WAR

THE YEARS THAT were marked by the negotiation of reform in Oaxaca were dominated by violence in Yucatán. In 1847, an indigenous rebellion began in the east, in towns that had long been relatively isolated but were now being partially integrated into the new economy. The rebellion, known as the Caste War, was extraordinarily violent and nearly successful. It spread rapidly over the peninsula, eventually drawing support from isolated communities in the south. At the war's height in 1848, an estimated 100,000 people were involved in the rebel movement, including between 30,000 and 45,000 males "active in or directly supporting the fighting." Within a year of the onset of the war, indigenous rebel groups controlled three-quarters of the peninsula. Over the next decade, the state government, with the eventual help of the Mexican army, slowly reestablished control over the majority of the state. The rebellion would continue through the 1850s and beyond, dividing the peninsula into government- and rebel-controlled territory. By the war's end, between 200,000 and 300,000 Yucatecans had died.[1]

The Caste War, along with several other revolts in rural Mexico in the 1840s and 1850s, prompted a nationwide debate on the "Indian problem" and spurred a national movement for liberal reform.[2] Yet in Yucatán itself this discussion had little immediate resonance. Certainly, it was in Yucatán that problems with the indigenous population were most obvious and in which the need for a solution was most pressing. But nonindigenous Yucatecans could not await the outcome of debate to address the crisis with institutional reform. Faced with an emergency, the Yucatecan state acted on its own to try to make the peninsula safe for the nonindigenous population. Convinced that the years of universal participation since 1812 had been a terrible mistake, legislators and state officials sought a new way of defining the political membership of the peninsula's indigenous population. Between 1847 and 1850, the Yucatecan government passed a series of laws that disenfranchised the peninsula's Maya inhabitants, transforming them in a legal sense into a subject population. Over the course of several years, the government made indígenas' citizenship not only second class but also contingent on good behavior as defined by the state itself. This entailed a near complete transformation of the basic assumptions that had undergirded the state's legitimacy among indígenas. Yucatán's government built its legitimacy after independence around the idea that the state had unique responsibilities to its indigenous citizens. To break faith with those responsibilities by disregarding indigenous needs and demands was to risk the collapse of consent. Indeed, this was exactly what had happened in Yucatán by 1847. The new laws governing indigenous citizenship after the outbreak of the Caste War did not reproduce the foundation for negotiation between indígenas and the state that had been crucial to the legitimacy of previous regimes.

In the end, they did not have to. As the government began to gain the upper hand against the rebels, the Caste War effectively removed the possibility of future uprisings by making the futility of rebellion clear. As it rebuilt its relationship with the defeated rebels and the rest of the indigenous population, the Yucatecan state could act with much more freedom than it had before the conflict. Ultimately, the war allowed the Yucatecan government to eliminate the necessity for negotiation with the indigenous population in matters of policy. While this could not be a permanent or a complete solution, it allowed for fundamental changes in social and economic relations that tipped the balance of government rule away from negotiation and toward force.

Foremost among those changes were transformations in the structures of land and labor, the long-standing issues that had dogged the Yucatecan government since before independence. By the time of the Caste War, more and more Yucatecan nonindígenas were living in rural areas and using indigenous labor to produce for the market. But in 1847 the transformation to a wage labor economy was incomplete. In some parts of Yucatán the plantation economy was quite advanced, while in many others indígenas remained tied to their villages and worked only part-time for nonindígenas if they did so at all. Even where working for wages was the norm, indígenas could not be counted on to provide a permanent labor force.[3] Wartime legislation opened the door for nonindigenous Yucatecans to lobby successfully for the forcible reorganization of the Yucatecan countryside, putting the indígenas and their labor power more firmly under nonindigenous control. The changes that took place during the Caste

War would, over the course of the next half-century, allow nonindigenous Yucatecan landowners to develop an extremely lucrative trade in henequen, a fiber crop that would be planted, tended, and harvested by indigenous hands.

This transformation of Yucatán's economy too often appears as a fait accompli, the simple result of the labor needs that the henequen industry created.[4] Historians disagree on whether the henequen boom was a direct result of the Caste War or whether technology and demand were the vital factors.[5] But either way, long-standing ideas about the state's obligation to protect indígenas and their autonomy had to be overcome before the government would participate unequivocally in forcing labor supply to meet the new demands. Before the Caste War, those ideas were already deteriorating; the war broke them down rapidly and decisively.

This process did not, however, mean either the end or the beginning of "liberalism" in Yucatán. Rather, it signified a shift in what liberalism meant and in who could participate in it. In Oaxaca, although indigenous and nonindigenous citizens approached politics with very different objectives and interests, they participated in a shared political culture that made those objectives and interests compatible. Yucatecan liberalism, by contrast, had always been fractious, in large part because the interests of indigenous communities and the emerging nonindigenous entrepreneurial elite could not be easily reconciled. The state government had walked a fine line between the demands of the elite for land and labor and the demands of the communities for autonomy and protection. Both sets of demands could be—and had been—understood as "liberal." But they contradicted each other; and, increasingly, the state found itself having to choose which liberalism it would participate in. What the Caste War did was to invalidate the liberalism that had previously governed the relationship between villages and the state, and to clear the way for the economically oriented free-market liberalism of the entrepreneurial elite. In the process, it shut down most of the avenues by which Yucatán's indígenas had defended themselves against both nonindígenas and the state.

Indigenous Citizenship and the Caste War

The Caste War began in earnest on July 30, 1847, when indigenous forces under the command of Cecilio Chi attacked the eastern town of Tepich and slaughtered its nonindigenous residents. A tremendous backlash against the entire indigenous population followed. Quickly, the conflict came to be represented as an all-out war of civilization against barbarism. Pedro Regil y Estrada, a Yucatecan emissary to the Mexican government, explained: "The cause of Yucatán is the cause of humanity." By the end of 1847, the newspaper *Revista Yucateca* had a regular section detailing the events of the war that it called, simply, *"Bárbaros."*[6] Immediately, the insurrection was labeled a race war, one in which not only the rebels but *all* indígenas were complicit because of their inherent hatred for the nonindigenous population.

To nonindígenas, indigenous Yucatecans had demonstrated their total incapacity to behave as proper Yucatecan citizens. Yucatán's political leaders thus felt it necessary to consign them once again to colonial-like subordination. On August 27, 1847, less than one month after the attack on Tepich, Yucatán's government issued a decree stating that the indigenous population did not "have the aptitude necessary to continue in the enjoyment of the rights consigned to citizens in the constitution of 1841." The merciless race war they were now waging against Yucatán's nonindígenas was, legislators argued, only the culmination of the events of the years since independence, in which indígenas had misused their rights in a way both "harmful to their persons and interests and offensive to society." There was no time to observe the formalities of a constitutional amendment. The state congress thus felt justified in using its legislative power to reduce indígenas to "the pupilage in which they found themselves before they were granted the free use of the rights conceded to citizens."[7]

The August 27 decree ranged widely. Aside from reestablishing the colonial relationship between indigenous Yucatecans and the state, the new law retooled the repúblicas de indígenas. The government took on the responsibility for naming caciques and placed the repúblicas under the authority of municipal administrations.[8] The new legislation also reestablished religious taxation and gave priests sweeping powers over indigenous cultural life. It prohibited "vagrancy and idleness" among indígenas and ruled that all indigenous settlements of fewer than fifty families be broken up and their inhabitants forcibly moved to nearby towns or haciendas. It took away the indígenas' right to bear arms, called for the forced collection of what weapons they presently possessed, and prohibited their participation in military activities of any kind. When they broke the rules, indígenas were to suffer the corrections that their "indolence and customs" required.[9] With one decree, the state imposed the unrelenting rule of the República de Españoles over that of the República de Indios.

Four days later, the secretariat of war ruled that any suspected "conspirators," or even anyone thought to be a bandit or thief, should be tried not in a civil setting but rather in a military court, including that of the local militia. This opened the door to the persecution of indigenous individuals, prompting a proliferation of local trials in which indigenous leaders were commonly jailed and even executed. It also touched off seemingly groundless targeting of noncombatants. In the words of historian Eligio Ancona, "under cover of these laws, and above all with the pretext that they were conspiring . . . , there developed a wicked persecution of a multitude of Indians who surely for the most part were innocent."[10]

The content of one of these local trials reveals the tenor of the early response to the rebellion. In August 1847, a district judge ruled on the accusation that several indigenous town officials had conspired to rebel against the government. The caciques and scribe of the western towns of Euan and Noló, Valentín Chale, Patricio Ake, and Santiago Ek, had allegedly taken part in planning an attack, serving as conduits of information from eastern organizers. At the trial, the judge claimed that there was no doubt that a conspiracy existed among the peninsula's indígenas:

Bloody conspiracy, because it is one of extermination: immoral, because it aims to destroy men of all ages, its authors lewdly calculating to reserve for themselves the invaluable enjoyment of the . . . charming sex: sacrilegious, because in their insane furor they break the sacred immunity of the holy temples, and the respectable character that the priesthood carries: infamous, because it exercises in every sense vile usurpation: and absolutely odious, [because it is] enemy to all the rights that give life to cultured society, and it aspires to sacrifice it under a dagger infested with the vices inherent in the origin of the barbarous agitators.

For their crimes against civilization, the judge believed, Chale, Ake, and Ek deserved the harshest of sentences:

He who has put his resources toward destroying society, should die without forgiveness, because only under this guarantee and express convention, has he been able to live securely in society. In the educated judgment of a notable author, every delinquent who openly attacks social law, becomes because of his excesses a traitor to the *patria*, ceases to belong to it [by] violating its laws, declares himself at war with it, and finishes by making his existence incompatible with that of the state, creating the hard necessity that one of the two perish.

According to the judge, the rebels had forfeited their rights; a criminal such as this, he opined, should die, "not as a Citizen, but as a public enemy."[11]

The harsh words of this local trial judge were aimed at active rebels. But their argument about indigenous citizenship was easily extended to all indígenas after 1848. In the face of what they quickly recognized as a threat to their presence on the peninsula, Yucatecan nonindígenas and the Yucatecan state abandoned some of the fundamental bases of Mexican republicanism. The dire emergency of the early years of the war allowed Yucatán to sidestep national political requirements and to effect a major shift in its relationship to the indigenous population, one that would have important repercussions for indigenous claims both during and after the war. The measures that the Yucatecan state took, in the long run, drastically limited indigenous people's political options. Before the war, the government had struggled to establish its legitimacy in the eyes of the indigenous population while constantly trying to avoid the threat of rebellion. The war revealed the ultimate failure of that struggle. But it also offered the state the opportunity to reestablish its control based more on outright coercion than on consent. In effect, the war reduced the state's dependence on its own legitimacy, and the government took advantage of the situation in order to assert its control.

"POLITICAL MEASURES": THE LEGISLATION OF INDIGENOUS CITIZENSHIP

The August 27 decree would not be the Yucatecan government's last word on indigenous citizenship. Over the course of the next ten years, stopping the war and preventing its recurrence would be the state's primary focus. The government wanted a peace that would last, and it became increasingly clear that the blanket subordination of indígenas decreed on August 27 was unlikely to produce this. At the same time, the government was unwilling to restore the prewar situation in which indígenas were theoretically the equals of their nonindigenous neighbors. And so the Yucatecan government experimented with ways to find a compromise that addressed indigenous needs while denying them equal citizenship. Indigenous citizenship would no longer be a universal right but would rather depend on indigenous actions. It would also no longer be the same for all indígenas. In making these changes, the Yucatecan state ultimately devised a system that effectively controlled the indigenous population.

First, the government had to stop the fighting; and, in the first months of the war, things did not go well. By October rebels had taken the towns of Tixcacalcupul, Tihosuco, and finally, in February 1848, the important town of Peto. By May, rebels controlled the majority of the peninsula, leaving only the northwestern area around Mérida and the southeastern environs of Campeche firmly in government hands. Even these strongholds were in danger; the council of state ordered extraordinary sessions for the congress, noting that if the rebel advance made it impossible to meet in Mérida, Congress would have to convene in Calkiní, northeast of Campeche. According to the governor, writing to Congress in late 1847, the indígenas had the military advantage; their larger numbers, their superior knowledge of the terrain, and the vulnerability of frontier towns like Peto, Yaxcabá, and Valladolid all gave them a vital edge. What's more, the governor suggested, the indígenas were satisfied with less, and thus remained "robust and sated" while government troops suffered from hunger and lack of proper clothing.[12]

The words and actions of state officials reveal their desperation. In late 1847, Governor Méndez suggested that any captured rebel ringleaders should be hung, and that

all the others who are not females, or males of less than fourteen years, will be reduced to servitude, selling them at public auction, marking them with an iron on their right cheek with an "S" for *"sublevado"* (rebel). All of their goods would then be confiscated and sold to pay for the campaign.[13]

Although there is no evidence that his suggestions were carried out, the government did authorize the expulsion of prisoners of war, most to Cuba with fabricated "contracts" obligating them to serve on sugar plantations. When the Mexican government objected, claiming that this practice amounted to Mexican citizens being sold into slavery, Governor Barbachano insisted that "the stubbornness of the indigenous race gave no hope for true pacification," making the removal of indígenas from the peninsula necessary. By July 1849, swayed by Yucatecan arguments and by the continuation of the war, the Mexican government decided that the expulsions were "liberal and humane," as the indígenas "could not expect anything but the most severe punishment for their atrocities."[14] One historian has estimated that between 1847 and 1861, close to 2,000 indígenas and mestizos were forcibly transported to Cuba.[15]

By late 1847, however, it was clear that these measures would not be sufficient to win the war. A public debate among elites and journalists developed over the proper path to take. Arguments ranged from the insistence that there was no hope for any kind of incorporation of indigenous people into nonindigenous society to calls for a greater intensity of military effort.[16] Government officials were more willing to innovate and compromise. The state's highest officials increasingly urged that the government turn away from a single-minded focus on defeating the indígenas through force. Instead the state should begin, in the words of the secretary of government, to instigate "political measures" in its fight against the insurrection, measures that "without offending decorum or the dignity of Governments, nor demonstrating weakness, would attract the common enemy." Similarly, the commission of justice argued that

equity, politics, and public convenience urgently demand that the measures of blood, fire, and destruction that until now have been dictated uselessly, be substituted with those of humanity, sweetness, and benevolence with this unfortunate race whose extreme ignorance and the pernicious examples of the other classes have made form this horrible plan.[17]

The government's first "political measure" was a traditional attempt to forge a peace treaty. In early 1848, Governor Méndez named a commission to meet with rebels fighting under the leadership of Jacinto Pat, a cacique from Tihosuco. The commission, headed by ex-governor Miguel Barba-chano, established communication with the rebels in mid-February. In a letter sent to several rebel leaders, Barbachano stressed his willingness to consider their demands. After an interim during which hostilities in-creased, Barbachano, now governor once again, reintroduced negotiations in a letter to Pat, claiming that he would "procure that there will no longer be motives to fight or to sow discord among your descendents, from now on." To accomplish this, he was willing to consider the aboli-tion of religious taxes, the withdrawal of troops from Tekax, a lowering of fees for religious services, and the return of indígenas' weapons, which had been confiscated under previous laws. These negotiations resulted in a treaty, signed at Tzucacab on April 19, that called for, among other things, the abolition of the personal contribution, the elimination of rent on pub-lic land, the cessation of alienation of that land, the return of weapons, the release of indebted workers, and a measure of sovereignty for indígenas under Pat himself.[18]

There were several problems with this treaty. First, it failed to take into account deep divisions within the rebel forces, especially between Pat and Cecilio Chi; the government's assumption that Pat represented the whole of the rebel population was quickly proven incorrect when both Chi and many of Pat's own followers refused to accept the agreement.[19] Second, although there was and is much disagreement about actual rebel aims, it is clear that there were various and conflicting grievances behind the war. No one treaty was likely to satisfy all; in the end, it satisfied almost none. And finally, the government was not committed to real change, as was clear when Barbachano, as he negotiated with the rebel leaders, stressed the brotherhood of all Yucatecans in terms that revealed his assumptions about Yucatecan social hierarchy. Yucatán's lamentable state, he claimed, put it at the mercy of foreign forces, whose reign would surely be worse than that of the Yucatecan government. "Wouldn't it," he asked,

be better if we were as brothers and loved each other? Would it not be good if all were pacified, and being so, each one returned to his house to protect his children, be with his spouse, take care of his fields, recuperate his forces and feed himself along with his children? What is there to look for in prolonging this war?; *the whites will teach your children, and the noble Christians of this land will teach them the word of God, Our Lord*. Once this is accomplished . . . , we will once again be able to buy and sell, and he who works will have money in his hands; [with] all of us united we can repair and exalt the name of our land.[20]

Barbachano described a world in which the nonindigenous population continued to serve as tutor and leader to the indígenas. Not surprisingly, the treaty of Tzucacab collapsed almost as soon as it was signed.

The government was then forced to seek other methods of stopping the insurgency and turned its attention toward the rank and file.[21] The second "political measure" taken to stop the war was to offer a practical incentive—tax relief—for the rebels to lay down their arms. According to Governor Méndez, the primary goal of the rebels was to secure the abolition of taxes of all kinds, a claim he based on letters and other papers purportedly found in captured rebels' possession. Many officials worried that tax relief would look like a concession. But despite these reservations, over the course of the next ten years the government repeatedly used tax relief as an incentive for rebels to leave the field. Both the religious tax and the civil tax—"one of the principal branches that constitutes the public treasury"—were fair game.[22] Taxes could be used not just as a carrot but also as a stick. For unyielding rebels, the fiscal consequences were high. In an 1848 amnesty offer, for instance, Governor Méndez declared that any captured rebel who did not turn himself in would pay a fine of fifty pesos—to be paid off with six years of personal service—and would be subject to double taxes for the rest of his life.[23]

The penalties for rebellion were extreme, but the government was consistently willing to waive them in the face of surrender. A decree passed in September 1847 declared an amnesty from the death penalty for all indígenas who had taken part in the rebellion excepting the leaders of the insurrection. In February 1848 Governor Méndez declared an amnesty for all rebels who turned themselves in. And in August Governor Barbachano offered a new amnesty to those who surrendered within the next sixty days, allowing them to return to their pueblos provided that the towns were not under the control of the rebels. In offering these new incentives, Barbachano wrote that "at no time could the rebels complain that they had not been called once and again by the paternal voice of the government to retrace their steps, with the objective of avoiding the terrible fate that awaits them." The "paternal voice" would be forced to call out again and again before the war was over. In September 1849, February 1850, April 1851, and as late as December 1858, the government would pass measures offering amnesty to rebels who surrendered.[24]

Any government attempt to stop the war would have to address not only the indígenas who had taken up arms but also those who had not. This was a large group; most of the indígenas of the more densely settled northwestern towns did not rebel initially. But according to the prevalent nonindigenous interpretation of the rebellion, the problem was universal, not specific, and so the solution should be as well. "In a word," one 1847 government report stated, "the decree of the 27th of August has as its objective subjecting the Indians with a strong yoke, without any distinction between the rebels and those who have not made any attempts at conspiracy." And yet, the report went on, persecuting nonrebels might kindle a spirit of revenge in those who had not rebelled, causing the revolution to spread.[25] The solution, then, appeared to lie in large part in solidifying the relationship with those indígenas who had remained at peace. The attempt to do so was the third "political measure" the government took to stop the war, and, in the end, it was the most far reaching and effective.

The obvious approach to the noncombatants was to recruit them to fight on the government side. This was understood to be risky. Many non-indígenas believed that the Caste War itself was the result of having armed Indians during the Imán rebellion. The *Revista Yucateca* argued that:

> it is the most dangerous step to avail one's self of those who have given such proof of their ferocity, and who trained by those who later must be their victims, will wait for the moment [in which they] see us most divided, so that [in our weakness] we cannot resist them.[26]

For this reason, indígenas had long been exempt from official participation in Yucatán's armed forces. But the government had never been above tapping this vast human resource in times of emergency, and the Caste War, in the end, was no exception. As hostilities escalated, Yucatecan officials hoped to fill their reduced military ranks and supporting forces with indígenas. To attract them, they would have to offer extraordinary benefits. But in doing so, they would themselves reap the benefits of preventing many indígenas from joining the rebels and of strengthening noncombatant indígenas' ties to the Yucatecan state.

As early as December 1847 Governor Méndez suggested that any indígena who fought against the rebels be exonerated from the civil tax and exempted from the effects of the August 27 decree. A decree passed in February of the next year ruled that those who participated in the war effort would both be exempt from taxation and "enjoy the rights of citizens," adding that they were welcome to a portion of the goods that they took from any vanquished rebels.[27] By 1848, the government began calling the indígenas fighting on its side "*hidalgos*." *Hidalgo* was a colonial term that referred to a class of Maya who paid the tithe and was similar in status to Spaniards. Since independence, the term had come to mean, more generally, the hereditary indigenous elite.[28] But early in the course of the Caste War, the government began using the title in a new way, bestowing it on indígenas who lent extraordinary support to the government's war effort. In January 1848, for instance, Felipe Cauich, the cacique of Saban, was made an hidalgo "for not having acceded to the suggestions of the rebels of that pueblo, and for having fled from the ranks of the rebels of Tijosuco." As a result of his new title, Cauich would be exempt from the personal contribution for the rest of his life. Similarly, three months later, Governor Barbachano granted the title and its privileges to the cacique and "other indígenas" of Tunkás after they defended their pueblo against invaders. And on April 27, the governor presented a list of twenty-nine new hidalgos from Dzidzantún and Dzilam, all of whom had fought for the state at the hacienda of Dzitax.[29]

At least in theory, the above cases had been instances of spontaneous support for the government, as villagers sought to defend their homes from invaders. In May 1848, however, the government circumvented laws prohibiting indígenas from serving at arms by formally approving the creation and use of hidalgos for direct service in the campaign. Any indígena who wished to serve should present himself to the proper authority with his axe and machete, a coat, and a *calabazo* and *mecapal* (a gourd for carrying water and a yoke for carrying items over one's shoulders). He would then be given his title and a band to wear around his hat. From that time on, he was at the government's disposal.

The position of hidalgo was demanding and dangerous, but it held great benefits for indígenas as well as for the state. Not only were hidalgos exempt from the personal contribution, but in exchange for their services they would receive rations along with the other troops. Their families would get government support while they were away, and any existing debts to their employers would be paid.[30] For rural indígenas struggling to feed themselves and their families in the midst of a vast war zone, *hidalguía* was an attractive option. Not surprisingly, many indígenas offered their services and requested the title. By August 1848, Governor Barbachano reported that three or four thousand hidalgos were now in military service and that this aid was turning the tide of the war.[31]

The creation of hidalgos meant the reintroduction of certain indígenas into the political community as citizens. But their citizenship was not a simple restitution of equality as defined before the war; hidalgos were citizens, but they were marked as indigenous. Certainly, both the government and indigenous people had long explicitly used notions of ethnic difference along with notions of equality. But the Caste War exacerbated and changed the content of ethnic difference. Across the board, ethnic differentiation became more explicit. For the first time, the state made an unequivocal *constitutional* distinction between the rights of indigenous and nonindigenous Yucatecans. The original 1825 state constitution had ruled that anyone entering into citizenship after 1835 would have to be literate. A new constitution passed in 1850 moved that year up to 1858 for most new citizens but explicitly suspended the rights of citizenship for all "indígenas who did not know how to read and write." Even hidalgos were not excepted "because this title does not change their nature. . . . The indígenas to whom [the government] conceded the title of hidalguía, do not thus cease to be indígenas although ennobled with respect to their class."[32] Hidalgos were not just different citizens, they were explicitly lesser citizens.

Equally important was the introduction of explicit and extensive divisions *between* indigenous people. For if hidalgos were not the equals of nonindigenous citizens, other indígenas were not the equals of hidalgos. Nor were all other indígenas equal to each other. This kind of differentiation lay at the heart of the state's strategies. In its attempt to pull indigenous people back into the political community, rather than offering blanket concessions to indígenas as a whole, the government made controlled concessions to different groups of indígenas, based on the kind of commitment those groups had made to the state. By the beginning of the 1850s, Yucatecan indígenas could have one of five different official relationships with the government. Active rebels, of course, were considered enemies of the state. Captured rebels were subject to deportation or forced labor; in 1851, Congress ruled that those taken in enemy territory should be distributed among Yucatán's agricultural property owners, who were then to treat them as they would their servants.[33] Indígenas from rebel-controlled territory who surrendered to the Yucatecan government were also put to work, usually in the military garrisons that guarded the far-flung areas under government control. As the government began to regain lost ground, thousands of these *presentados* streamed in from enemy territory.[34] Noncombatant indígenas in government-controlled territory were citizens, but their citizenship was limited by literacy requirements. Finally, hidalgos were citizens as well, but they had both a number of special rights and privileges and a continued obligation to serve the state. All indigenous people were unequal to nonindígenas, but they were unequal in different ways.

What had held indigenous people together as a community before the Caste War was not just a clear sense of ethnic identification but also a shared political identity. By fracturing that political identity while retaining its implication of inferiority, the Yucatecan state during and after the Caste War diluted the potential for shared grievance in the future. It also diluted the basis for shared claims. By 1857, the political rights of any given Yucatecan indígena would be determined not by his status as a free individual in a liberal republican state, or even by his status as an indígena within that state, but rather by his particular actions toward that state. Even the status that brought the most rights and privileges, that of hidalgo, was contingent on extraordinary acts. The political field on which Yucatecan indígenas addressed the state had thus changed dramatically. As the initial chaos of the beginning of the war began to fade and Yucatán's indigenous residents began to piece together their lives, they did so in a new and considerably more hostile legal context.

This arrangement was not strictly legal according to Mexican law, but a combination of extraordinary circumstances and inconsistent concern on the part of the national government allowed Yucatán to do what it wished with the indigenous population during the first ten years of the war. The newspaper *El Fénix* worried in 1850 that if the government formalized categories like that of hidalgo, the national congress would react negatively, "for the simple reason that in a republican system, these hierarchies are impossible." But because the hidalgo system was "very good and praiseworthy, and one could say that it has been one of the various acts that has changed the aspect of the war," *El Fénix* suggested that it operate informally in order to avoid recriminations from Mexico City.[35] After 1853, racial distinctions would not have to be hidden from Mexico, as the conservative national regime that took power that year had few qualms about formalizing such distinctions in law.[36] But regardless of the regime in Mexico City, without a strong or clear mandate from the national government, Yucatán would act in what it believed to be its own best interests in a time of dire emergency. Yucatán's governmental system from 1847 until 1857 was not federalist or centralist, and barely democratic. Accordingly, there were very few institutional restraints on its actions. Several years into the Caste War, new kinds of ethnic distinctions permeated not only custom but also law; in other words, in its rush to its own defense, Yucatán's government reacted by instituting law where it had previously believed that tradition was sufficient.

INDIGENAS AND THE POSTWAR STATE

In 1853, the hidalgos Baltasar Cob and Luciano Canul, of the town of Timicuy, wrote to the commander general offering a suggestion for how he could accomplish the seemingly impossible task of ending the war in Yucatán. "This measure, Sir," they wrote, ". . . is extremely easy, as it consists only of Your Excellency imposing your influence on the Government of this State with the end that in all or the greater part of the pueblos that compose it the alcaldes or jueces de paz be removed." According to Cob and Canul, these local officials were responsible for a host of abuses. Soon after receiving his appointment, each juez set himself up like a king in his village, quickly amassing "his own houses, lands, and money in savings, but all at the cost of the sweat of the poor unfortunates of our race, who have no sin but that of being Indians." For Cob and Canul, this amounted to a fundamental breakdown in the political process: "It is true that according to the laws of the country we have legal resources to turn to;

but whether because of a defect in the laws or because of their poor application in practice, they are nothing more than illusions." And yet, Cob and Canul still believed that they had a vital bargaining chip. Hidalgos like themselves, they claimed, had served the state only because of their knowledge that, in the Yucatecan government, there were was always someone "who was interested in protecting their fortune and remedying their ills." They would refuse to serve, they warned, if the government left them "abandoned to the caprice of our oppressors."[37]

Cob and Canul, in their petition, drew on two distinct models of indigenous citizenship. One was derived from years of experience before the war, during which indígenas came to expect responsiveness from the government. The other came from the war itself, when one's political identity came to rest not on one's abstract political character, one's place of residence, or even one's ethnicity but rather on the kind of services one did or did not provide for the state. As Cob and Canul saw it, the two models need not have been contradictory. Both seemed to assert the government's responsibility toward its citizens. For noncombatants in particular, the new laws seemed to offer distinct advantages, and they were quick to use them. But Yucatecan federalism and centralism were no more, and the notions that had underlain them had largely been replaced. The new system made no blanket promises, and the new arrangement offered none of the potential for institutionalized protection of indígenas that had characterized Yucatecan federalism, nor even the coherence of Yucatecan centralism. Many claims made in reference to the government's promises of privileges in exchange for certain acts would be met with refusal; Cob and Canul, for instance, were rebuffed with the response that "the appointments of the jueces de paz always fall on persons who according to the political chiefs and others are qualified."[38] In the years after the outbreak of the caste war, noncombatant indígenas struggled to find a way to make sense of their new political situation, one in which universal citizenship was no longer a central tenet and in which indigenous opinions and needs seemed to have little significance.

As Cob and Canul's complaint suggests, municipal government had changed dramatically. Elections of all kinds were suspended as the war broke out. In August 1848, when Governor Barbachano decreed the reincorporation of Yucatán into Mexico, he called for local, state, and national elections, to comply with national federalist law. Only a month later, however, the governor suspended elections again, citing the war's endurance. Many parts of the state were still under rebel control, and Yucatecans lacked "the quietude indispensable for occupying themselves with the designation of persons who can best represent them in the direction of public affairs." Elections, the governor feared, would cause "agitations that complicate and worsen the state of the war." After 1848, elections for state and national congresses would be held only erratically. Local elections disappeared almost entirely. In January 1848, following the provisions of the August 27 decree, the government issued an emergency ordinance redesigning municipal administration until peace could be established. As under centralism, each village would have a juez de paz named by the government rather than an elected municipal junta. Also as under centralism, this would prompt protests from the indigenous population.[39]

Unlike the centralist laws, however, the new decree set up an explicit hierarchy for who should serve as juez. Preference would be given to married and literate nonindígenas who lived in the towns in question; if these were not to be found, outsiders, unmarried men, and even illiterates were acceptable. Only when these possibilities had been exhausted should officials consider naming indígenas to the posts, with preference given to those who had been considered nobility under the Spanish administration. This system was to last throughout the 1850s. In November 1849, the Yucatecan congress officially suspended the elections of municipal juntas and ruled that the appointed jueces de paz set up immediately after the outbreak of the war would continue to function. And in 1850, a new literacy requirement eliminated most indígenas for consideration as jueces. So while elections in at least some large towns continued to occur, indígenas living in most Yucatecan villages would not vote for or serve as local officials until constitutional reform in 1862.[40]

Few indígenas saw their new town governments as representing them in any way. But new laws still seemed to offer an alternative. Many indigenous Yucatecans understood the categories of indigenous citizenship created by the government to be new and different conduits for representation. Being an hidalgo, a presentado, or even a surrendered rebel allowed indigenous individuals to make claims on the government, compensating in some ways for the loss of participation in municipal administrations. Indeed, indígenas immediately began to make claims based precisely on the distinctions that the government had created. In response to the abuses of tax collectors in Campeche, the caciques of the city's four repúblicas declared:

Faithful to the S[uperior] Governments of the State and the cause of humanity and civilization, the indígenas of this city were the first to throw themselves into its defense . . . , and had conducted the war of the savage to the state of agony and imminent termination in which it happily is today. Since this memorable and glorious day they have not ceased lending their services in the campaign in the military cantonments of this district, suffering with humble resignation the miseries and penalties of the war without more recompense than a small ration, many times earned at the savage expense of one's own blood.

In charging the personal contribution to the indígenas in the city, local officials were "confusing the faithful hidalgo of Campeche with the rebel Indian." In June 1852, Francisco and Aquilino Pech petitioned the government, writing:

Since the year of 1848 when the barbarous Indians wanted to invade the pueblos closest to us, with the objective of repelling them and enthusiastic to defend the common cause of the state, we added ourselves to the columns of the valiant troops . . . with arms in hand so that when they retired we could return to the bosom of our beloved families to sustain them in their necessities. . . . [W]e have complied with our principal duties as good citizens.

Having been assigned to work duty in Tihosuco after their participation in the war, they wished to return home; the governor found in their favor. Many other indígenas simply took what they thought they deserved, especially in the area of taxation. According to the subdelegado in Campeche, by 1849, many of the indígenas under his jurisdiction considered themselves to be exempt from taxes because of their services, and he admitted that, according to the letter of the law, many of them were. In the town of Chiná, townspeople who had served as hidalgos, worked in the garrisons and in the cantonments, or directly defended the town expected to receive tax exemptions from the government. The priest in Tixmeuac reported in 1852 that there were many presentados in the area who did not pay taxes because they had worked in the cantonments in Tekax.[41]

If indígenas were quick to take advantage of the new categories, they also pushed at their limits by ignoring the finer distinctions between them. In essence, in the eyes of indígenas, the various distinctions boiled down to a basic difference between rebel indígenas and those who did not rebel. Indígenas thus attempted to turn the government's complicated system into one on which almost anyone could make a claim. Hidalgos, presentados, and those who had served in other capacities presented themselves as more or less equally deserving of the government's largesse. Noncombatant indígenas of all kinds were quick to point out the vast difference between them and the rebels. The town of Tekom, for instance, had been occupied by rebels in 1854, and the indígenas living there described their acts as "the most horrendous crimes and disorders to which human perversity can arrive." They, in contrast, had never done anything of the sort: "Taking into consideration the firm adhesion that we have always had to the government," the villagers wished to be excused from taxes for the next two trimesters.[42] They deserved the government's consideration, they argued, for their failure to rise up against it.

It helped, certainly, to make claims on the basis of being an hidalgo. But even the term *hidalgo* lost its specific meaning in many of the indígenas' claims. When Juan José Mex, Felipe Ek, Anastacio Xool, and Vicente Canul requested the title of hidalgo in 1852, they did so not because they had fulfilled the specific requirements the government had established for that position but simply because they were not rebels. Similarly, another group of indígenas asked for the title in the same year not only because of their services but also because of their "good behavior."[43] Because the rebels were so very bad, other indígenas felt that their own loyalty, even if it was basically passive, deserved consideration. And anyone who had not rebelled, whatever his status in the eyes of the government, felt sure that he could still expect the government to pay attention to his needs.

Herein lay a fundamental misinterpretation of the new laws. In appealing to the state in this way, indigenous Yucatecans treated the new system as they had treated federalism—as a coherent set of rights and government responsibilities theoretically available to any loyal indígena who claimed them. They assumed that the new set of laws overlay a relationship of reciprocity between state and citizen not unlike that which had been part of Yucatán's system of governance since independence and even before. But, in reality, the new regime had no such coherence. It was not based on fundamental assumptions about what a loyal indigenous citizen deserved. Instead, the way that government officials dealt with indígenas depended on what the state believed was necessary to keep the peace.

As such, the government's response to claims was not consistent. At least some of the claims reaped their intended benefits. The Campeche caciques received the tax relief that they requested, as did the townspeople of Tekom. But others were not so lucky. Pedro Vicab, on returning from service in the cantonment at Conkal in 1848, came home to tax demands from his juez de paz, and the government supported the juez's claims. Over time, the government was less likely to honor such requests, even when they were based in the very promises that the state had made, because state officials saw concessions as no longer necessary. In 1852, indigenous presentados from Xcan, Nohku, and Santa María, all small towns near Tizimín, complained that they should not be asked to pay taxes because "they lack resources, they don't have what is necessary to subsist, they have no fields, and finally, they have no houses." They wanted time to "establish themselves" in their new towns without having to worry about the added expense of taxes. The council of state, in response, ruled that it was no longer necessary to grant this exception to presentados because the tide of the war had changed since the time of the original concessions.[44] Faced with this kind of inconsistency, the old tools that the indígenas tried to use on the new system simply did not work.

Thus, the new complex of Yucatecan laws offered no fundamental guarantees for indígenas. Forged in a moment of war, they were by nature contingent on circumstances. As late as 1857, the war was still going on, and the laws had not been replaced by a more coherent political structure. This left noncombatant indígenas vulnerable to the whims of the state, without a larger set of concepts according to which they could make claims on the government. In 1853, the government had hoped that indígenas would believe the concessions it was making to surrendered rebels were "a true pardon and not a rope to hang themselves with."[45] And many indigenous Yucatecans, whether or not they actually believed this promise, strove to make the concessions work in their favor. But by 1857, the government's concern began to ring false. Noncombatant indígenas during the Caste War in Yucatán found that the kind of citizenship the government offered was contingent, limited, and out of their control. This kind of citizenship, many indígenas found out, was not really citizenship at all. Unlike in 1847, however, this disappointment was not met with outright belligerence. Noncombatant indígenas saw little hope in an insurrection that could not seem to prevail. Instead, those indígenas found themselves increasingly vulnerable to the actions of state officials.

Building a New Yucatán: The State, the Nonindigenous Population, and Indigenous Labor

Even as it instituted emergency measures, the state also looked to the future. By late 1848, the government managed several important victories against the rebels and established control over much of northeastern Yucatán. In early 1850 a peace commission reached an agreement with a faction of rebels in the far south. In much of the peninsula, a stalemate had set in; government forces could not proceed any further east, and rebels could not reestablish control over territory to the west.[46] Frustrating as this stalemate was, it meant that the government could now put some of its energy into rebuilding. Nonindigenous property owners, whose own livelihoods were threatened by the war, were also eager to rebuild Yucatán. The government depended deeply on these people, whose presence in the countryside often made state control possible. Yet the government and nonindigenous property owners did not have precisely the same idea of what the new Yucatán should look like. The government remained committed to a form of rule based primarily on its relationship with indigenous villages. It aimed to reestablish and conserve those villages so that the state could supervise production in the countryside and protect its traditional tax base. Nonindigenous property owners, by contrast, were primarily concerned with improving their access to labor and did not see the villages as fundamentally necessary to that project; indeed, villagers' access to their own lands made it difficult for landowners to draw them onto the haciendas. Landowners hoped that the war would open the door to a transformation of Yucatán's social structure about which the state had always been ambivalent.

In the end, the massive dislocation of indígenas caused by the war combined with the state's own policies to tip the balance in favor of the landowners. The assault on indigenous citizenship fundamentally altered the relationship between state and indigenous society. And many of the specific policies it entailed, especially those regarding the distribution of labor, ultimately compromised the ability of the government to control the nature of indigenous citizenship. In response to the Caste War, the state had claimed increased power over the indigenous population. But the events of the war and the increasing influence of nonindigenous actors outside the state limited the government's role in the process of rebuilding Yucatán.

GOVERNMENT POLICY IN RECOVERED TERRITORY

When they sat down in 1850 to deliberate on a new state constitution, delegates to the Yucatecan congress hoped that they could solidify control over the indígenas and ensure indigenous passivity and obedience in the future. As the state's official newspaper proclaimed during the deliberations,

The political reorganization of society is difficult in all times, and much more so, when grave and consequential events, like the rebellion and rising of the indígenas of this peninsula have been, totally change the face of the people, creating necessities previously unknown.

It was thus vital for the new constitution to change "the essence of the authority that the agents of the government exercise in the interior."[47] That interior, however, had changed dramatically. The population of the territory that the government nominally controlled had dropped by as much as 40.66 percent between 1846 and 1850.[48] Previously existing administrative arrangements had crumbled, as town structures deteriorated in the face of constant war and the fluctuation of the population. In this context, making changes in the "essence of authority" often meant first reestablishing control.

This would not be easy. The power of the state in the countryside was compromised by the mass exodus of nonindígenas from the regions affected by the war. In November 1847, the political chief in the district of Peto reported that the entire nonindigenous populations of the pueblos of Dzonotchel, Sacalaca, and Ichmul had left their towns and fled to the cabecera. In Dzan the following year, the juez de paz noted that the local nonindígenas had abandoned their homes. By early 1848, the council of state lamented that numerous towns had been abandoned and left in the hands of the "barbarians." This state of affairs worried the government profoundly because reestablishing control over the countryside would depend on the continued presence of nonindígenas. Most important, the government needed nonindígenas to serve in local village administrations. But if it was difficult to get nonindigenous people to live in the villages, it was even harder to get them to serve in local office. Nonindigenous town authorities simply fled the villages along with everyone else.[49] As the emigration continued, state officials found it increasingly difficult to find anyone to take on these jobs. The political chief of Hecelchakán in December 1847 could not comply with the laws regarding jueces de paz because there were not enough nonindígenas to choose from. And, in late 1852, the chief of Motul was forced to allow a number of men to stay on in their positions longer than legally permitted "because of a lack of suitable individuals."[50]

Several years into the war, whole regions of the peninsula were apparently without government-sanctioned authorities. An official in Valladolid, in the war-torn east, noted that there were no jueces in many of the partido's pueblos "because [the towns] are purely of Indians . . . and for now are subject only to the respective caciques." In 1853, the vice-governor ruled that the problem with the 1850 interior regulations had been that there were not enough people qualified to serve as jueces de paz and that those there were would be more useful to the state as members of the National Guard. He thus reduced the number of jueces from two in each pueblo to two in each cabecera and one in every other town. As late as 1857, many towns in Motul had no jueces "because," one official wrote, "in said pueblos there are found very few who know how to read and write, [the] circumstance that is required for that position."[51]

The government responded by trying to present emigration from the villages as a sort of treason. In February 1848, the governor ruled that no one over sixteen years of age could leave his pueblo and move to another as long as the rebellion continued. Villagers could leave only "when they are threatened and they lack a garrison for their defense, [or] when the number of vecinos is so small that they cannot resist the barbarians." This ruling had little effect. As early as May 1848, the governor reported that Mérida and Campeche were flooded with refugees from the countryside, putting a massive strain on the cities' resources. In 1852, the government was still calling for nonindígenas to return to their villages. One year later, the official newspaper lamented that

unfortunately . . . , some of the pueblos that are in continuous alarm find themselves abandoned by the vecinos, because they flee with their families and go to establish themselves in other pueblos . . . with the end of eluding compliance with the sacred obligation that the laws and the patria impose upon them.

And, as late as 1856, Governor Méndez wrote that it was vital to avoid what one juez de paz had called "furtive emigration" from the pueblos. "I know," wrote the governor in a letter to the council of state,

> that this emigration is unfortunate in its consequences, and I know at the same time that all citizens have the liberty to vary their residence and locality when it is convenient for them . . . But I also recognize that it is necessary to reconcile this liberty with the exceptional state in which we find ourselves as a result of the malign influence of the war.

It was necessary for the government to devote its resources to preserving residence in the pueblos, Méndez wrote, because "otherwise and giving full extension to the exercise of that liberty," the population, including the large portion of it who were serving the government in some capacity during the war, would be free to live where it chose, even outside of Yucatán itself.[52]

Of course nonindígenas were not the only Yucatecans who felt themselves free to live where they chose as the war spread over the peninsula. Many indígenas also chose to leave the towns, removing themselves both from state authority and from their ties to the nonindigenous farmers and ranchers who sometimes employed them. Many families were living in improvised ranchos, afraid to return to towns that may or may not have still existed. These settlements were often far from any other villages and, for nonindígenas, finding them could be difficult; as one official put it, "one only arrives there because in the silence of the north one hears the song of the rooster and the bark of the dog."[53] Officials worried that if indígenas were permitted to continue to live unsupervised, they would never return to government control. As Father José Antonio García, a government-appointed peace commissioner traveling through the region around Tekax, noted,

> If there were some way to convert these ranchos into pueblos, introducing some police into them, putting in their little churches, you can believe that it would be one of the best means of pacifying this region, but the ill luck is that no one would dare [to do] this, at the immense distance they are from quick assistance.[54]

The problems for the government were obvious. Vast parts of the population were effectively out of state control. The absence of jueces de paz—and the jueces' tenuous hold on power where they did exist—made taxes increasingly difficult to collect. In May 1848, the subdelegado of Yzamal reported that, in his partido, "the collection of taxes has ceased entirely because there is neither anyone to tax nor anyone to tax them."

The nonindígenas were all gone, as were many of the indígenas, having either emigrated or joined the rebellion. What had already been a difficult duty to impose on the indígenas was now nearly impossible. As the sub-delegado of Campeche put it in 1849, "the collection of the personal contribution that for so many years has constantly presented many obstacles, in this day, accumulates unconquerable difficulties." There was nothing new about the dispersal of indigenous people per se; the state had always had difficulty controlling indigenous residence patterns. But the war had greatly exacerbated the problem. To make matters worse, officials worried that villagers who lived in isolated settlements could not be prevented from maintaining contact with the rebels.[55] Without resident nonindígenas, without functioning town governments, and without taxes, the state had little presence in many Yucatecan towns as the 1850s began and, accordingly, a dwindling resource base on which to draw.

The government had begun to address these problems with the decree passed on August 27, 1847, which had set the stage for government control over the movements of the indigenous population. Among the decree's provisions was a call for the forced removal of all indígenas living in settlements of fewer than fifty families. These people would be moved to "the towns or haciendas that suit them most." In November of the next year, Congress expanded this provision and tied it directly to the war effort by authorizing the transport of all noncombatant indígenas found living in the countryside to villages firmly under government control. And the law on local government published in conjunction with the state constitution of 1850 stated that regional officials should "not permit vagrancy and unemployment among the indígenas" and should force indígenas in settlements of fewer than twenty-five families to move. Any indigenous settlements that had been destroyed in the war could not be resettled without a government license, and villagers who had been displaced were not allowed to create new towns. The government justified these actions in part with old arguments about drawing indígenas into society. As the political chief of Mérida explained when faced with the complaints of a group of indígenas who were being forced to move,

The spirit of this law, without doubt, has as its objective avoiding the indígenas' dispersal in the montes, without immediate vigilance, for lack of a certain number of inhabitants, living without subjection, in an independent way and without learning or complying with religious duties . . . like savages.

But now the war offered new justifications. These small unsanctioned settlements, this same official was certain, "cannot be called places of residence in an organized society that pursues the savages."[56]

While the displacement of much the population was an enormous problem for the state, the circumstances created by the war also presented the government with new opportunities. State officials hoped, once and for all, to accomplish the long-held goal of controlling the residence patterns of the indigenous population. What government officials wanted was a system in which the state continued to supervise indígenas inside indigenous towns. Changes in citizenship rights for indígenas offered new tools for realizing this goal. They allowed the government to pass laws, such as those dictating indigenous residence, with provisions that would have been both ideologically unacceptable and unenforceable before the war. And the war machine, with its traveling garrisons and cantonments, provided an excellent tool for enforcement. In effect, the government continued to promote an idea of administration that came out of the federalist and centralist experiences rather than proposing an entirely new vision of governing the indígenas.

But the government's interests conflicted with those of nonindigenous property owners, who saw the war as an opportunity to improve their own access to indigenous land and labor. Certainly, the kind of control the state was working to establish was crucial to this goal. But landowners wished to use that control to force indígenas to make labor on nonindigenous haciendas their primary activity, a goal that ran contrary to the government's aim of preserving the towns. The government's freedom of action was limited by its increasingly heavy dependence on this nonindigenous interest group. The government relied on nonindígenas' participation in and support of the military. And more important, without the return and cooperation of the nonindigenous population, state control was an impossibility. As state officials tried to tempt nonindígenas back to rural Yucatán, they found that they had to contend with those people's own vision for the peninsula. Appeasing the nonindigenous population was an enormous priority, and it proved difficult to resist nonindígenas' demands. Between 1849 and 1857, the government's concessions to nonindigenous Yucatecans caused it, ultimately, to cede much of the responsibility for controlling indígenas to the nonindigenous property owners themselves.

"THE TRUE VICTIMS OF THE HORRIFIC RISING
OF THE INDIGENAS": THE STATE AND THE
NONINDIGENOUS POPULATION

In 1849, at least one prominent figure, Justo Sierra O'Reilly, was convinced that land outside of the sure control of the nonindigenous population should simply be abandoned. "Which families," he asked, "will wish in the future to live almost isolated in the heart of the barbarous pueblos?"

A year later, Sierra O'Reilly was still convinced that the government should concentrate its resources in the territory over which it had firm control:

Fix for now a dividing line between the rebel Indians and ourselves, concentrate our forces and means of defense, and say a last goodbye to our favorite projects of absolute submission and permanent conservation of pueblos which cannot sustain themselves alone.[57]

Many nonindigenous Yucatecans saw the prospect of returning to their previous homes as a risky and perhaps fruitless proposition. They wanted government assurance not only of their safety but also of their access to and control over the indígenas who, to varying degrees, labored in their fields, tended their cattle, and served in their households. In fact, they wanted better access than they had had before. And because they had sacrificed so much for the war effort, nonindígenas believed that the government owed them special consideration.

   That special consideration would have to include tax relief. The war had eroded the state's ability to collect the personal contribution from the indigenous population. As the government approached total bankruptcy, it was forced to tap the nonindigenous population with ever-increasing property and capital taxes. In February 1848, the government raised the property tax 1.5 percent until the end of the year, stressing the desperate situation of a state in which the "indigenous race . . . is trying to exterminate those who do not correspond to its class" and in which funds were rapidly dwindling. By raising the tax on capital and property to four reales per month for every hundred pesos, the government hoped to "save the existence of society" in Yucatán. In November, the tax was extended for another year, although at a slightly lower rate. Late in the next year, Congress imposed a tax of 10 percent on all capital.[58] Each time a new tax was passed, local authorities began immediately to compile lists of those who were required to pay. The vast majority of the names on the lists were not Maya; and, in most towns, their numbers were quite small, representing the small numbers of nonindigenous residents.[59]

   Many nonindigenous Yucatecans refused to concede to what they saw as exorbitant tax demands that did not take into account their own suffering during the course of the war. Many nonindígenas had lost a large portion of their property in the fighting. On returning to their homes, many, like the vecinos of Dzidzantún, "only found . . . remains of their past fortunes."[60] Buildings had been destroyed, land had been burnt, and many of the indígenas who had served nonindígenas in the past were gone. It was inappropriate, they argued, to use tax rolls produced before the war— often the only ones available—because people shouldn't have to pay taxes on what they did not have. Furthermore, nonindígenas were unable to produce capital at the level they had before the war because they no longer had sufficient land, employees, or markets. In March 1848, the juez de paz of Tekit reported that he had collected only 20 percent of the new tax, claiming that the nonindígenas of his town had been under direct threat from the rebels for close to two months. At least three leagues of the land in the area had been burnt, the farms were not producing, emigration had led to a shortage of farm workers, and no one was buying cattle.[61]

Nonindígenas believed that some of their labor problems resulted from government policies themselves. The use of hidalgos and other indígenas in war service drew many people out of the villages and haciendas and thus out of their personal pools of labor. María Dolores Correa complained in 1850 that she had been left with only a third of her hacienda servants because so many men were serving in the garrisons as hidalgos. In 1851, Domingo Tenreiro had lost his nonindigenous servants to the war, and he reported that he was no longer able to maintain a productive farm enterprise. And the nonindígenas of Dzidzantún complained specifically about the cantonments, which were "still more atrocious than the barbarous indígena" because of the demands in labor and resources that they made on the towns.[62] Finally, nonindígenas worried that some of the concessions that the government was making to the rebels could prove disastrous for the labor supply. In April 1848, one group of property owners and farmers from the area around Seybaplaya wrote to the government to complain about the provision of the Tzucacab peace accords that called for the forgiveness of debt for agricultural workers. Without these workers, they warned, there was no way to run the farms. To grant debt forgiveness would be to guarantee that none of the workers would stay, a calamitous move no better than the prospect of losing the war: "What else would the barbarians have done if they triumphed?" "In such a case," they wrote,

It would have been better for us if the war had continued, because then, triumph or death would have liberated our families from the horrors of misery that threaten. . . . There is no example in history, Your Excellency, of such an attack on private property.

Instead, these landowners wanted the state to obligate the workers to stay at least until the crops were planted, which would give them ample time to "indebt their servants anew."[63]

Nonindigenous Yucatecans stressed that their inability to comply with the government's demands was a matter of poverty and hardship, not of disobedience. As the subdelegado of Campeche put it, "in the present circumstances even the bad citizen tries to be a good patriot." But it was precisely the sacrifices that they had already made for Yucatán that made nonindigenous Yucatecans question the justice of the government's demands.

One group of hacendados, in response to the requirement that they pay the taxes of their employees, wrote that "the hacendados . . . have been the true victims of the horrific rising of the indígenas, and those who did not lose all their goods of fortune and the well-being of their families, have experienced every [other] kind of reversal" because of heavy taxation to support the war effort. As late as 1856, many vecinos refused to pay the capital tax, claiming that it was high time they be reimbursed for the forced "loans" they had repeatedly made to the government since the war began.[64]

For the government, it was imperative to address the doubts and concerns of the nonindigenous population. The needs of the treasury were insurmountable, and nonindígenas were still the only reliable tax base available; the state remained fairly inflexible on this point. But the state government did take steps to address the labor problem. Between 1849 and 1857, Congress passed a series of laws that laid the basis for the distribution of indigenous labor on the peninsula. These laws, ultimately, gave the nonindigenous population far more access to indigenous labor than they had had before the war. In some ways, the laws were a formalization of a situation the war itself had brought about. Many indigenous people had been separated from their pueblos; the laws aimed to make this separation more or less permanent and thus to tie indigenous fortunes to their employers rather than their towns.

The most obvious source of labor was that of the newly titled hidalgos. Technically, these indígenas were supposed to perform military service, either by providing support to divisions, garrisons, and cantonments or by participating in the fighting itself. But hidalgos soon proved to be just as if not more useful for replacing the hands missing from the labor force since the war had begun. Some officials began making use of them as agricultural workers as early as 1849. For instance, when the political chief of Tizimín complained about the lack of resources he had with which to feed the families of absent soldiers, he requested the services of fifty hidalgos to work in the fields. In April 1850, the government made it clear that this was an acceptable practice by authorizing regional officials to send hidalgos presently working in the cantonments to perform agricultural work in lands that had belonged to the rebels. There were, the secretariat of government noted, many "milpas of the rebels that are not planted for lack of laborers," and it thus called for a new list of hidalgos who could be dispatched to work on those lands. The governor allowed the political chief of Maxcanú to use hidalgos to tend the crops of absent farmers in 1851.[65]

The number of hidalgos was still small in relation to the indigenous population as a whole, and their services were not enough to ensure a steady labor supply. As cantonments carried out sweeps of rural Yucatán in an attempt to control the dispersal of the indigenous population, they also produced a displaced potential labor force of indigenous people living outside of government-sanctioned settlements and without homes and occupations. In April 1851, the government ruled on what should be done with these people:

Those collected in enemy territory, who are turned in to the government of the state, will be employed in field labors, distributing them among the property owners, with the condition that they contract them and pay them in the same terms that the law requires for servants of their class.

The first opportunity to employ these indígenas would go to their previous employers, then to farmers whose lands had been burnt by the rebels, and finally to any others who solicited their services.[66] Soon, this new potential labor force began to grow. The vast numbers of people brought in by government forces were augmented by presentados, indígenas who put themselves at the government's disposal in the hope of escaping war zones in which they could no longer provide for their families. Like "those collected in enemy territory," the presentados were put to work both in the fields and for the military.[67]

From 1851 on, nonindigenous Yucatecan employers took full advantage of the sudden availability of large numbers of unattached workers. Technically, the new laws made distinctions among prisoners of war, noncombatants who were forcibly taken in by government troops, noncombatants who presented themselves willingly, and those who surrendered. And, technically, the government was in charge of their distribution. But, in practice, all of these people became part of a largely undistinguished pool of labor available to private individuals. After surrendering or presenting themselves, indígenas were subject to claims on the part of nonindígenas purporting to be their former "masters (amos)." In Bolonchenticul in 1851, a local official provided a list of sixteen individuals, "a Nominal Relation of the indígenas of this Pueblo, having taken refuge in the pardon—I distributed them to the vecinos of this pueblo, preferring the old masters in accord with the decree of April 1 of this year." Similarly, one division colonel reported that most of his prisoners of war "were taken from the jail by their masters." It is quite likely that some claims to be previous employers of specific indigenous individuals were fraudulent. The juez de paz of Hopelchen, for instance, complained in 1851 that private individuals, little by little, had spirited away the laborers assigned to him under the pretext that the indígenas were debtors. "One can say," he lamented, "that in this area they have established a veritable commerce."[68]

In many parts of Yucatán, especially where the rebels were most powerful, there were few presentados, and even where they were more numerous, they still represented a relatively small part of the indigenous population.[69]

But there is little doubt that the policies the government instituted to appease the nonindigenous population set significant change in motion. By the mid-1850s, many indígenas claimed to be working against their will on the lands of private individuals. In 1852, nineteen indígenas presented themselves to the political chief in Cármen, claiming that Francisco Rosado had forcibly taken them to work for one Don Manuel Galera. Indígenas in Izamal claimed the same year that they had been made to work to the detriment of their own crops.[70] The government did not respond consistently to such claims. In the case of Cármen, the state official noted that despite the fact that Rosado had a passport to transport the indígenas for this purpose, the condition the workers had arrived in—sick and without their families—indicated that his actions were illegal. But in Izamal, the judge who reviewed the case adamantly denied the validity of the indígenas' claims.

Officials worried that this could go too far. They were well aware that the longer an indígena had to work for a nonindigenous property owner, the less time he would have to plant his own crops and maintain his own property. The longer he was separated from his property, the more likely it was that he would lose it. Because many government officials believed that the attack on indigenous land tenure in the 1840s had been a central cause of the Caste War, they feared the ultimate consequences of the hacendados' actions, and they did their best to counteract them where they could. In 1856, in response to various complaints, the government issued two prohibitions of the practice of forcing indígenas to work against their will.[71] In 1857, it issued a decree reiterating the rights of pueblos in their village ejidos, stressing that no one individual should use an undue share of the land and its resources.[72] And that same year, Governor Méndez explained why he had promoted the repeal of the 1841 land law that permitted the alienation of "unused" common lands. He was behind the suspension, he claimed, "in favor of the indígenas." The sale of lands must be limited because to do otherwise would be an "ingratitude" for the indígenas' important services in the war and would also provoke them to join the rebels. Even if indígenas did not make the most efficient use of the land, Méndez noted, the Yucatecan state could not afford to irritate them, as "one should not doubt that this was one of the causes of the horrific war from which the State is still suffering." In his statement, Méndez made an explicit connection between the alienation of land and the alienation of labor:

It is well known, that in many of the measurements practiced by order of the Supreme Government in order to effect the sales, there has been opposition from the indígenas established in sites formed within the lands or in pueblos in whose immediate area they are located, one can even assure that almost only lands in this condition are those solicited, because regularly the objective of the buyers is none other than monopolizing them and reducing to servitude those who are accustomed to working them, without desire to extract any other class of advantages, improving, or better said establishing a true cultivation in said lands.[73]

The government did make an effort to limit nonindigenous entrepreneurs' access to land. During the war, at least some indigenous land had passed to nonindigenous Yucatecans. In 1851, for instance, Pablo Antonio Gonzáles, in exchange for his service in the war, received a piece of land that had belonged to the ex-cacique of Tekit and to Felis Puc of Chapab. But, more often, the government was reluctant to allow villages to sell the land even of indígenas who had abandoned the villages. When the juez de paz of Dzitbalché wanted to make use of the plots left abandoned by rebel villagers, the government turned him down. In 1856, there were still many lands in the vicinity of Hopelchen that lay empty and unused because their owners had never returned to claim them, and the government would not allow them to be sold. In some cases, the government actually defended village lands against nonindigenous property owners. In May 1853, three hacendados complained about a nearby indigenous settlement called San Antonio. Its inhabitants, the landowners opined, could be "useful dedicating themselves to the labors of the field in our plantings as well as their own," but instead, "they live almost in vagrancy." The hacendados wanted the indígenas forced off the land in question. But the political chief of Mérida, after investigating, found that the forty indigenous inhabitants of San Antonio had been there for years and thus enjoyed undeniable usufruct rights. They had no title to the land, "but they enjoy what for them is equivalent, which is possession in good faith . . . transmitted from their ancestors, the first founders of this site." The political chief turned down the hacienda owners' request.[74] Even in the absence of title, the government wished to support these villagers against claims not just on their land but also on their labor.

Yet in most cases there was little that the government could do to curb the actions of local landowners. In many instances, the person arranging for indigenous labor service was the juez de paz, the very individual the government depended on for establishing state authority in the villages. Many jueces de paz were themselves landowners, or related to them, and they often participated in the formation of labor contracts involving the villagers under their charge. In 1852, José Tomas Kolloc, Pedro Kuk, and Simon Uc complained about Nicolas Flota, the juez de paz of Kopomá. Flota, they claimed, "has set us up in perpetual service without allowing us a moment to plant our own fields that furnish us with sustenance for our families, and what's more without giving us the legitimate price for our work . . . , obligating us only through his authority to serve almost gratis." The juez de paz denied this charge, claiming that "what is happening is that those who are complaining, they do not want to perform any services." The indígenas had worked three days for the juez, three days for the priest, six days for the cacique, and eleven days in Maxcanú, a demand that local officials saw as well within acceptable limits. In 1853, the indígenas of Yaxkukul complained that "we are sold against our will to labor in the fields of private individuals without even respecting the female sex." The juez de paz had contracted with Don Luis Silveira to make such arrangements, to the detriment of the villagers' own crops and without proper payment. And two years later, the members of the república of Tekantó claimed that the juez de paz was making them work against their will, "as if by way of an order as in the time of the Spanish Government, without paying attention to the great harm that such conduct causes us." Most of the indígenas in the village were now under contract to private individuals and owed them service; the república insisted that they also needed time to work on their own land.[75]

In some cases, the government took action against jueces de paz. When the indígenas of Chocholá complained in 1853 that the juez was claiming their labor, that local official was found guilty and removed from his post. Similarly, after the villagers of Yaxkukul complained that their juez had made them work illegally on a road-building project, the juez lost his position. But jueces de paz were central to the government's project for the rebuilding of Yucatán, and it was not in state interests to antagonize them. When the hidalgos Baltasar Cob and Luciano Canul claimed in 1853 that the biggest problem with the jueces de paz was that they had connections in high places and that cases against them always ended in the officials' favor, they identified a central reason for changes in the Yucatecan countryside.[76] Increasingly, local officials—and thus local landowners—could do what they wished with the villagers they were supposed to represent.

Ten years after the Caste War began, many relationships of service that may have been tenuous, temporary, or occasional before the war were beginning to become permanent and binding. For many Yucatecan indígenas, the war meant loss of control over their own labor power. By the mid-1850s, a combination of indigenous displacement, nonindigenous demands, and the government's grudging willingness to facilitate those demands had transformed labor relations on much of the Yucatán peninsula. This transformation was by no means complete in 1857; and, indeed, the autonomy of the pueblos would never entirely disappear. But the Caste War and the policies it engendered had instigated changes that would accelerate as the nineteenth century drew to a close.

In May 1856, a Yucatecan journalist defended his state against a writer from Mexico City in response to an article that had appeared in *El Monitor*

Republicano. The Mexico City newspaper had implied that all of Yucatán's indígenas lived on haciendas and that their mistreatment there had led to the Caste War. According to the Yucatecan paper, this could not have been further from the truth:

One can divide the Indians of Yucatán into three classes. The first (but not the most numerous as the writer believes) is that which is dedicated to agricultural cultivation on the haciendas, the *colonos* or servants of the owners. The second is that which lives in the pueblos from their own farms or their own industry without depending on any master or lord, in immediate communication with the great towns of the State. The third [is] that which lives with very little contact with the other residents of the country in distant pueblos, or in camps hidden in the forest.

It was this last category, the author claimed, that had produced the vast majority of the Caste War rebels.[77]

The Yucatecan journalist was closer to the truth. In 1847, although their numbers were growing, relatively few indigenous Yucatecans had lived and worked permanently on haciendas, and it was in fact from Yucatán's eastern frontier that most of the rebels had come. But, by 1856, many nonindigenous Yucatecans believed that it was only by transforming independent rural villagers into hacienda servants that peace could be regained on the peninsula, and many of the mechanisms that would allow this transformation were already in place. By the late nineteenth century, the words of the Mexico City journalist would ring far truer, as Yucatán began to resemble the exploitative labor system that John Kenneth Turner would immortalize in 1911 in *Barbarous Mexico*.[78] As international demand for henequen cordage increased, its production would come to dominate the Yucatecan economy, becoming both enormously lucrative and enormously exploitative. Thus, in 1856, the Yucatecan journalist may have been correct to say that the Mexico City paper's description of Yucatán's indigenous population was inaccurate, but he neglected to say that many nonindigenous Yucatecans were at that very moment working to make it a reality.

That reality would come about, though, not just as a result of nonindigenous efforts. It was also facilitated by the state's decisive rejection of any kind of universal citizenship for the peninsula's indigenous population. After the initial blows from the rebels in 1847, the state had been prepared to take drastic action against indígenas, regardless of the implications for the democratic political system to which Yucatán had long adhered in one form or another. The government saw itself as having "the immense responsibility for the salvation of the country that lies in imminent danger of perishing under the weapons of the common enemy," and no measure was too extreme to avoid that terrible fate.[79] Even in 1859, when the emergency had receded, some nonindigenous Yucatecans defended the state's actions, including the sale of prisoners of war into virtual slavery, on the basis of "the right of self-conservation."[80]

But the actions of the government had paved the way for far more than self-conservation; they had opened the door to a far-reaching transformation. When the government chose to disregard the rights of indígenas and its own responsibilities to them as citizens, it created the mechanisms for nonindigenous property owners to push for and accomplish changes in social and economic structures that would ensure their access to a captive labor force. The government was not entirely convinced that these changes were a good thing; Governor Barbachano suggested in 1853 that what was most important for lasting peace was "generous treatment of the indigenous servants of the field and industry," something the government was increasingly unable to provide.[81] But by the late 1850s, the government had lost its ability to control effectively the rate and nature of change in the countryside.

For Yucatán's indígenas, these changes were a violation of what they had come to see, since 1812, as their rights of political membership in the state. They believed in the government's responsibility to protect these basic rights because, until the 1840s, notions of rights had indeed limited the power of the government, allowing indígenas to maintain both their village autonomy and their access to land despite the nonindigenous population's designs on both. In 1853, the indígenas of Yaxkukul, in complaining about their juez, wrote, "we believe that the deeds of which we are complaining are without doubt criminal because they attack our liberty and individual security guaranteed by the wise institutions that govern us."[82] Here, they drew on notions of "liberty" that they had come to understand in the years since 1812 but that the government no longer seemed to honor. Indígenas were also disappointed by the state's failure to carry out the promise it had made during the war, which now rang increasingly empty. Eusebio Mex, for instance, a former captain of hidalgos and ex-cacique of Ytzimná, was told to leave his small farm, known as Poxcheina, in 1857, based on the 1850 law that prohibited indígenas from living outside of towns. For him, this was a breach of the government's obligations to him as a good citizen:

Just as I thought to pass a quiet life with my family on my property, satisfied in having cooperated in the defense of my patria and that this same behavior gave me an individual guarantee, not without horror did I receive an order to leave my habitation for some hacienda or pueblo.[83]

Ultimately, Mex would be allowed to stay, despite one investigator's insistence that he was not fulfilling his obligations as a citizen in any town. But in most cases, the government would be unable to protect its indigenous citizens, and it was often unwilling. In the wake of the war, indigenous Yucatecans would increasingly find that there were, for them, no individual *or* collective guarantees and no basic structure of government responsibility underlying the new regime.

In 1847, when the government frustrated indígenas' expectations of protection and rights, many indigenous Yucatecans had taken up arms against the state. Ten years later, this was no longer a feasible option. For most of the indígenas living in the territory controlled by the government, war had brought dislocation, hunger, and loss of autonomy. The rebels, although not yet defeated, were held mostly at bay. Certainly, the war would continue; it would only reach its final conclusion in 1901 when the national government decisively stepped in.[84] But few indígenas in government-controlled territory would be willing to take up arms again after the 1850s.

The nonindigenous population had, indeed, made most of the peninsula safe for itself. But it had also made it safe for a kind of liberalism. First, it had paved the way for an economic liberalism that stressed private ownership of land and efficient production for the market. But by eliminating the need for the state to recognize the unique demands of indígenas—a need that had been at the root of the state's first local liberalism—it had also made Yucatán safe once again for the political liberalism that had come under attack after 1847. In 1862, Yucatán's government would sign a new constitution in reaction to the national liberal Reform. Its full implementation would be delayed by the French Intervention and ensuing war, but its provisions would finally take effect when the empire fell. The 1862 constitution, following national law, restored full citizenship to all Yucatecans, reintroduced participatory town government, and reestablished the electoral system. It made no distinctions of any kind between indigenous and nonindigenous Yucatecans.[85] Six years later, in 1868, Yucatán's unique legal sanction of those distinctions would come to an end when the government officially legislated the abolition of the repúblicas de indígenas.[86] With this final stroke, the older system of government legitimization disappeared, replaced by a system that was outwardly liberal but that lacked the essential elements that had, before the Caste War, made the relationship between indígenas and the state one of mutual obligation. Without doubt, Yucatán's indigenous population would seek and find ways to make the best of the tools available to it in the years to come. In the wake of the Caste War and its dislocations, however, the range of those tools was increasingly limited and circumscribed. The Caste War had been a near disaster for Yucatán's nonindigenous population. But, in the long run, it was far more disastrous for indígenas, as it opened the door to exploitation on a scale previously unimaginable.

Local Liberalisms: Oaxaca and Yucatán Compared

In both Oaxaca and Yucatán, the events of 1847 threw into question the compromises that indígenas and state officials had worked out in the preceding decades. In Oaxaca, a proactively liberal and reformist state government posed an ideological challenge to the de facto terms of indigenous citizenship negotiated between indígenas and the state. In Yucatán, the Caste War threatened the very foundations of indigenous citizenship. In the years that followed, the governments of both states would decide what they wanted to change about the citizenship of indigenous people and what they would maintain from the past. They did so based on their knowledge of what had come before and based on their perception of what might be possible in the future. The legitimacy of the government in both states had been built through the participation of both indígenas and nonindígenas as they negotiated a way to make their demands on each other acceptable. In Oaxaca, that negotiation would continue; in Yucatán, it would come to an abrupt end. The "reform" of the years after 1847 in Oaxaca was a change in which both parties took part, while that of Yucatán was a decidedly one-sided affair.

The states pursued different paths in part because they had different understandings of the distinction between indígenas and nonindígenas. Oaxaca's government both relied upon and was limited by the notion that the state had a unique responsibility to villagers. National liberal reformism asked the state to more consciously define those villagers as indigenous and then to make an effort to eliminate that indigenousness. But this threatened the fundamental bases of the Oaxacan state's legitimacy. As agents of that government attempted to put liberal reforms into practice, they found themselves making compromises regarding a basic tenet of liberal reformism: the notion that "indigenousness" was an obstacle to progress. In concert with indígenas themselves, Oaxacan officials sought and often found ways to make liberal reform compatible with "indigenousness" and "custom." They promoted liberal issues—such as primary education, efficient town finances, and even land privatization—while simultaneously acknowledging and negotiating indigenous rights and privileges. Where officials could not find workable compromises, they tended to let reforms fall by the wayside.

In Yucatán, by contrast, after the Caste War began the government openly advocated the idea that indígenas had different rights, not to accommodate them but rather to strengthen the state's control. After 1847, the government promulgated laws and decrees that essentially eliminated the participation of indígenas in the legitimization of the government and that limited the claims that they could make on the state. Importantly, the government was not the only actor with an interest in this change; nonindígenas outside of the government exercised an increasingly broad influence. In the long run, the government's retooling of indigenous citizenship would facilitate an economic transformation that loosened the ties between indígenas and their villages, making their land and labor available to the market. It would also solidify the distinction between indígenas and nonindígenas that liberalism hoped to erase.

In neither state did the changes of the 1840s and 1850s conform to any recognizable liberal ideal. In Oaxaca, to be sure, liberalism was officially the blueprint for political change, while in Yucatán, political liberalism seemed to many politicians to be the root of local problems. But Oaxaca's liberalism was based in many ways on distinctly illiberal notions, and in Yucatán, if an expansive political liberalism had lost its validity, economic liberalism was clearly on the rise. As the era of national reform dawned, then, both states still had local liberalisms. But crucially, Oaxaca's local liberalism remained one in which indigenous people, nonindígenas, and the state all participated. Yucatán had had such a local liberalism in the years before 1847. It had always been conflictual, and by 1847 it had collapsed. The liberalism that replaced it, though far less inclusive, was no less idiosyncratic. It, too, had been shaped by local circumstances and in particular by the precise failures of the political culture that had come before. When liberalism triumphed on the national stage in the late 1850s, Oaxacans and Yucatecans had notions of liberalism that were unique and locally specific, a reality that would always effect the ways that they approached and responded to national institutional demands.

Conclusion

THE EXPERIENCES OF Oaxaca and Yucatán suggest that it is impossible to identify a singular Mexican "liberalism" in the early nineteenth century. Mexican liberalism was never a consolidated ideology with clear and predictable aims. Moreover, liberal policies and liberal institutions affected Mexico's various regions in different ways because local circumstances shaped and influenced those policies and institutions on the ground. As this and other studies demonstrate, there was no one "liberalism" in early nineteenth-century Mexico but rather many unique "liberalisms." This book demonstrates, nonetheless, that liberalism produced common processes, even if those processes did not have common outcomes. In the years between 1812 and 1857, the tenets of liberalism, as formulated and adopted first in Spain and then in Mexico, forced Mexicans, both inside and outside of the government, to rethink the mutual obligations of states and citizens. Liberal policies directly challenged colonial institutions. In their universalizing tendencies, they discouraged or rejected associations and institutions that had defined the boundaries of Spanish subjects' autonomy and established the limits of the government's legitimate sphere of activity. As colonial institutions came under attack, both governments and citizens faced the challenge of replacing them and of endowing the new institutions with content and legitimacy.

As a result, Mexican liberalism in the early nineteenth century was simultaneously fractured and universal. It was fractured in large part because in the earliest years after Mexico's independence, the process of state formation took place first and foremost at the level of the individual states and their systems of constitutional law. State legislators and administrators, faced with locally unique situations, found themselves able and willing to manipulate the institutions presented to them to address pressing needs. In turn, the interests, needs, and desires of the new citizenry—and especially the indigenous population—could be incorporated into local systems in a variety of ways, depending on the situation that prevailed.

Yet the multiple interpretations of national institutions across Mexico did not result in arrangements that were simply local. Mexicans knew themselves to be engaged in a shared liberal project, even if, in this period, most citizens may not have identified strongly with the nation. Each local system was also a local liberalism, understood by all parties to be such. Mexico would, over the course of the rest of the century, see a concerted attempt to consolidate national government and promote progress under the name of liberalism. When this occurred, the existence of profoundly local and often profoundly different systems and political cultures—all understood to be "liberal"—would matter deeply. The development of local liberalisms in the early nineteenth century would, in the long run, compromise the ability of the reformist national state to effect real and uniform change. Like local and early national reformers before them, the liberals of the latter nineteenth century would come up against complicated local arrangements, built around liberal institutions but based on peculiar combinations of liberal practice, colonial concepts, and local exigencies. Their reforms would thus be subject to local interpretation and transformation by elite and "subaltern" people alike.

The history of Mexico's latter nineteenth century would not, however, be merely one of endless reinterpretation and failed attempts to consolidate power. By the 1870s, it seemed increasingly clear that institutional change alone was failing to produce a "modern" nation in which property-owning citizens facilitated economic progress. Liberals, especially under the extended regime of Porfirio Díaz that began in 1876, thus adopted new strategies. Increasingly, they turned to repressive practices to force change. They backed up the desire to transform land tenure with force in the form of the rural police and resorted more and more to outright electoral fraud. Such practices could, in the short run, make possible what institutions had not. Mexico at the end of the nineteenth century *was* far more consolidated than it had been in the years under consideration here. Far more land was in the hands of private owners, allowing for an unprecedented transportation revolution and export boom. This was true in Oaxaca and Yucatán. In Oaxaca, both local and international investors expanded the production of a number of export crops—especially coffee and tobacco—and developed Oaxacan mining and industry. And in

Yucatán, the henequen boom transformed much of countryside into a collection of private estates on which indigenous people lived as dependent wage laborers.[1]

Certainly, this expansion of export-oriented capitalism in the states was made possible by the national politics of the Porfiriato. But within this larger national story, what was economically and politically possible in both states was determined in large part by the state and local politics that had developed in the first half of the century. Here the differences between Oaxaca and Yucatán are important. Even in 1910, much of the Oaxacan countryside had changed little since Mexican independence. The indigenous population far outnumbered the nonindigenous. Outside of Oaxaca City, indígenas were still widely dispersed in villages rather than living on landed estates, and available research suggests that these indigenous townspeople continued to control much of their land.[2] Even new products like coffee and tobacco were sometimes produced by indigenous communities—much as cochineal and cotton had been— as well as directly by nonindigenous entrepreneurs. Much of the nonindigenous elite, meanwhile, continued to live primarily off of the profits from trade.[3] The limits on change did not result from lack of trying to bring it about. Both Chassen-López and McNamara have detailed the high hopes of Oaxacan entrepreneurs for developing their "land of tomorrow." Their failures cannot be understood without comprehending the close relationship between the Oaxacan government and the indigenous constituency that would have to provide both the land and the labor for many of the hoped-for enterprises. Oaxaca's postindependence political culture, in which the government and indígenas worked together to facilitate basic governability, persisted into the twentieth century and limited the capitalist transformation of the state.

In Yucatán, by contrast, the collapse of the local political culture built after independence opened the door to a near-complete transition to an export economy. Or, more precisely, the belief that nonindígenas and indígenas could share a political culture at all collapsed with the Caste War, and this collapse facilitated the elites' economic goals. Yucatecan nonindígenas emerged from the Caste War with the conviction that indigenous political participation—not to mention indigenous military service—had been a terrible mistake. The government's eventual triumph in the war made it possible for nonindígenas to act on this conviction and allowed them to create a Yucatecan political culture that was optimistic, "modernizing," and liberal but that excluded indigenous people—and thus indigenous concerns—almost entirely. Elites were determined to prevent the resurgence of indigenous political demands, and this led them to redesign the way land and labor were distributed and used and to create networks of control and surveillance that were remarkably successful. Increasingly, the arena in which indigenous people acted politically was circumscribed by the borders of the hacienda.[4]

The story of local liberalisms does not end with its persistence in Oaxaca and collapse in Yucatán. The narrative of the latter nineteenth century is also a narrative of the increasing importance of national as well as local citizenship. In midcentury civil wars, the emerging Liberal party struggled with Conservatives for control. Yucatán remained largely disconnected from the conflict, but Oaxacan indígenas participated in large numbers on the Liberal side, acting both on the learned expectation that liberals would protect their land and on personal loyalty to native sons Benito Juárez and Porfirio Díaz. In addition, villagers participated as members of National Guard units that, as McNamara shows, were structured to mirror and reinforce community hierarchies. In this sense, the Guard units reiterated the autonomy and unique identity of each town and reinscribed Liberal commitment to the maintenance of "custom" that was essential to Oaxacan indígenas' pact with the state. In the process, Oaxacans cemented both a new obligation to serve the national Liberal state—once it triumphed—and a new claim on that state's obligations to them as citizen-soldiers.[5] This pact mirrored the one they had long insisted on with the Oaxacan state, in form if not in content.

After 1876, the Liberal state would be personified in the figure of Porfirio Díaz. And with his consolidation of power, a new kind of national Liberal politics developed. Increasingly, the national government—and in particular Díaz himself—became an indispensable party to negotiations over resources, and the distribution of positions of political power in the states came to depend increasingly on agreements made with Mexico City. In Yucatán, where indigenous people had been excluded from formal politics, that negotiation went on between the Díaz government and the state's economic and political elite. In Oaxaca, indigenous villagers participated actively. At times, this allowed villagers to retain privileges and especially autonomy. But the new national orientation coincided with—and perhaps helped facilitate—the gradual withdrawal of the *state* government from the process of negotiation. A new generation of state politicians less committed to the political culture that bound the state government to indígenas came to power in the 1890s, and conflict between the two parties increased. In response, villagers turned to Díaz, calling on the national government to respect the pact they still believed in. Díaz, though, was committed to economic and political change that was difficult to reconcile with indigenous needs. This left Oaxacan villagers—in some ways not unlike their Yucatecan counterparts—without a party with whom to negotiate.[6]

The consolidation of national liberalism thus produced the collapse of local liberalisms. If in Yucatán this had already occurred suddenly and violently by midcentury, in Oaxaca indígenas' insistence on the maintenance of local political culture meant that the collapse would be longer in coming and that the path to it would be more complex. But nationwide, national liberalism was incapable, in the end, of reflecting all the things that liberalism had come to mean locally, and national liberals could not play the role that state governments had in maintaining a reciprocal pact with local populations. Increasingly, national liberals relied on the brute exercise of force and fraud both to maintain control and to promote "progress," and an increasing range of Mexicans, from indígenas to small private farmers to sectors of the national elite, were dissatisfied. It would be incorrect to assume that this dissatisfaction in and of itself produced revolution, at least among the popular classes. Neither Yucatán nor Oaxaca was, after all, a center of proactive revolutionary activity, and neither Yucatán's nor Oaxaca's indígenas initiated the fall of the Porfirian state. And yet, ultimately, because it eroded the practices and beliefs that had made daily governance possible in local places—in other words, because it caused local liberalisms to collapse—national liberalism also contributed to its own eventual demise.

Was Mexican liberalism, then, a failure? The question can be addressed from the viewpoint of both nineteenth-century liberals and modern critics. In the era this book addresses, elite liberalism, to the extent that it was a consolidated set of ideas, promoted political inclusion, individual ownership, and free markets. Oaxaca's government allowed a large number of citizens to participate in the political process but failed to replace communal ownership with private property. The Yucatecan state ultimately eliminated much communal ownership but only by denying political rights to the majority of the population. Based on these criteria, neither Oaxaca's nor Yucatán's liberalism was either a clear success or a clear failure on nineteenth-century terms. The modern critique of liberalism focuses on the harm it did to indigenous people in particular. According to this argument, liberalism did not create a nation of smallholders but rather disenfranchised the indigenous population and forced indígenas to labor for inadequate pay for the nonindigenous elite. But the experiences of Oaxaca and Yucatán suggest no such direct path. In Oaxaca, despite the government's embrace and implementation of liberal land laws at midcentury, many indígenas retained their land; in Yucatán, where those laws were not immediately implemented, indígenas increasingly lost their holdings. Liberalism, as this book demonstrates, contributed to both results.

Modern critics concerned with liberalism's effects on indigenous people might thus be tempted to call Oaxaca a liberal "success" and Yucatán a liberal "failure." Certainly, in the context of the years covered in this study, Oaxacan indígenas were more able to shape the parameters of liberal politics and were thus more able to retain control over their land and labor. And, certainly, the Yucatecan Caste War was tremendously destructive to indígenas there, and opened the door to a liberalism in which indigenous people took no part and in which land and labor were controlled by the haciendas. But Oaxacan indigenous villagers were—and would remain—extraordinarily poor. While the government was responsive to their needs, it was not fundamentally committed to finding a way to combat their poverty; indeed, indigenous poverty was a key element in maintaining the flexible relationship between indígenas and the state. The government's willingness to compromise did not shift the balance of power between nonindígenas and indígenas; it was only through their sheer demographic and economic weight that Oaxacan indígenas could force concessions from a state controlled by a tiny minority. So while circumstances for indígenas were undeniably bad in Yucatán, it is a stretch to say that in Oaxaca they were good. To ask whether liberalism succeeded or failed yields us little. In neither Oaxaca nor Yucatán did liberalism fulfill its promise to open up the political process or to create property-holding citizens. And it certainly did not erase ethnic distinctions. But it is also not correct to suggest—regarding *either* state—that the broad political franchise was entirely a sham or that attempts at creating individual smallholders out of villages with communally held land led directly to the impoverishment and exploitation of indígenas.

Of course, Mexico's nineteenth-century liberal experiment ultimately *did* fail. The contradictions that it produced nationwide led to its collapse in the Mexican Revolution that began in 1910, and the nation would, thereafter, struggle to find an adequate set of assumptions and ideas to replace it. But that failure was not a failure of "liberalism," per se. Rather, it was a failure of national liberals to understand the ability of the Mexican population—"subalterns" and local officials alike—to interpret political ideology and use political institutions in ways that were flexible and, often, expansive. Mexicans had, in the first half of the century, worked to make the seemingly incompatible compatible. They had embraced liberal ideas and institutions while insisting that they must incorporate and allow for select elements of older systems. They had done this not to produce utopian societies that met everyone's needs but rather to maintain a basic level of governability, sustenance, and social peace. The failure, in the end, was the attempt to consolidate the local systems that developed after independence, each one liberal in its own way, into one unitary national liberalism. The Revolution was not the result of the imposition of liberalism onto a colonial world. It was, rather the result of the imposition of a particular kind of liberalism onto a collection of local liberalisms, local systems with varying underlying structures and assumptions but with shared origins and, crucially, systems in which those who participated shared the understanding that what they were doing was liberalism.

Despite its insistence on attention to the local, this book also argues, then, for attention to the national. For despite the fact that Mexico's states in the early nineteenth century each had discrete political, ideological, and economic structures, they nonetheless participated in a national process. Only by examining both the local *and* the national can we begin to comprehend the history of liberalism in the early nineteenth century. And only by understanding this early history can we understand the history of liberals' later attempts to gain control over their movement by making states and citizens conform to a national norm. In the latter nineteenth century, liberal reformers, conservative ideologues, and political dictators would search for ways to make local practice conform to national mandates. As they did so, they would face a Mexico in which people in towns, villages, and state capitals had already spent years making national ideas and institutions adapt to ways of doing politics that were both liberal and local.

Reference Matter

List of Abbreviations in Notes

AGEO: Archivo General del Estado de Oaxaca, Oaxaca City
RI: Ramo Real Intendencia y Periódo de la Guerra de Independencia
G: Ramo Gobernación
    GD: Sección Gobierno de los Distritos

AGEY: Archivo General del Estado de Yucatán, Mérida
Col.: Ramo Colonial
PE: Ramo Poder Ejecutivo
PE*: Ramo Poder Ejecutivo 1841–1843
    G: Sección Gobernación
    A: Sección Ayuntamientos
    J: Sección Justicia
M: Ramo Municipios
J: Ramo Justicia
C: Ramo Congreso
    D: Sección Decretos

AGN: Archivo General de la Nación, Mexico City
A: Ramo Ayuntamientos
G s/s: Ramon Gobernación sin sección

AHMO: Archivo Histórico Municipal de Oaxaca, Oaxaca City
AC: Actas de Cabildo
DGM: Decretos del Gobernador Murguía

ASRE: Archivo de la Secretaría de Relaciones Exteriores, Mexico City

CAIHY: Centro de Apoyo á la Investigación Histórica de Yucatán, Mérida
CCCA: Colección Crescencio Carrillo y Ancona
    LM: Sección Libros Manuscritos
    F: Sección Folletería

M: Sección Manuscritos
D: Sección Documentos

INAH: Instituto Nacional de Antropología e Historia
AHM: Archivo Histórica en Micropelícula
O: Oaxaca
AJT: Archivo del Juzgado de Teposcolula
AMT: Archivo Municipal de Tlacolula
CGO: Colección González Obregón

SMGE: Sociedad Mexicana de Geografía e Estadística

Notes

NOTES TO CHAPTER I

1. Jefe Político de Motul, Apr. 23, 24, 25, 26, and 28, 1846, AGEY, PE, Box 52, G, Jefatura Política de Motul.

2. I have used the word *Indian* only when directly translating the Spanish word *indio* or when referring to a direct quotation. In all other cases, I have used the word *indígena*, meaning an indigenous person. Although both terms were in common use in the early nineteenth century, among both indigenous people and nonindigenous people, *indígena* was a more neutral, descriptive term, while *indio* was often used in a derogatory manner. *Indígena* was used more often by government officials and by indigenous people in describing themselves. As for people who were not indigenous, the Spanish term would, in most cases, have been *gente de razón*, or people of reason; often, it was *vecino*, but this term was also applied to *indígenas* and used by them in some circumstances. To avoid confusion—and terms that are laden with implications of indigenous inferiority—I have used *nonindígena*, my version of the more modern Spanish *no-indígena*.

3. Nils Jacobsen, "Liberalism and Indian Communities in Peru, 1821–1920," in *Liberals, the Church, and Indian Peasants: Corporate Lands and the Challenge of Reform in Nineteenth-Century Spanish America*, ed. Robert H. Jackson (Albuquerque: University of New Mexico Press, 1997), 124.

4. This broad definition of liberalism is derived in large part from Norberto Bobbio, *Liberalism and Democracy*, trans. Martin Ryle and Kate Soper (London: Verso, 1990).

5. The classic study of liberalism in early nineteenth-century Mexico is Charles A. Hale, *Mexican Liberalism in the Age of Mora, 1821–1853* (New Haven, CT: Yale University Press, 1968). More recent attempts to categorize and analyze the political beliefs and affiliations of Mexico's early nineteenth century include Michael P. Costeloe, *La primera república federal de México (1824–1835). Un estudio del los partidos políticos en el México independiente* (Mexico City: Fondo de Cultura Económica, 1975) and *The Central Republic in Mexico, 1835–1846*: Hombres de bien *in the Age of Santa Anna* (Cambridge, U.K.: Cambridge University Press, 1993); Donald Fithian Stevens, *Origins of Instability in Early Republican Mexico* (Durham, NC:

Duke University Press, 1991); Will Fowler, *Mexico in the Age of Proposals, 1821–1853* (Westport, CT: Greenwood Press, 1998); and Torcuato S. DiTella, *National Popular Politics in Early Independent Mexico, 1820–1847* (Albuquerque: University of New Mexico Press, 1996).

6. On the church, see Brian Connaughton, "The Enemy Within: Catholics and Liberalism in Independent Mexico, 1821–1860," in *The Divine Charter: Constitutionalism and Liberalism in Nineteenth-Century Mexico*, ed. Jaime E. Rodríguez O. (Lanham, U.K.: Rowman & Littlefield, 2005), 183–202; and "La larga cuesta del conservadurismo mexicano, del disgusto resentido a la propuesta partidaria, 1789–1854," in *El conservadurismo mexicano en el siglo XIX*, ed. William Fowler and Humberto Morales Moreno (Puebla, Mexico: Benemérita Universidad Autónoma de Puebla, 1999), 169–186. For an interesting discussion of the compatibility of Catholicism and liberalism, see Pamela Voekel, *Alone before God: The Religious Origins of Modernity in Mexico* (Durham, NC: Duke University Press, 2002). For an example of the conflation of federalism and centralism with liberalism and conservatism, see John Tutino, *From Insurrection to Revolution in Mexico: Social Bases of Agrarian Violence, 1750–1940* (Princeton, NJ: Princeton University Press, 1986), 221. And for discussions of the origins of Mexican political thought in the Spanish liberal experiment, see Jaime E. Rodríguez O., "Introduction: The Origins of Constitutionalism and Liberalism in Mexico," in *The Divine Charter*, ed. Rodríguez O., 1–32; William Fowler and Humberto Morales Moreno, "Introducción: Una (re)definición del conservadurismo mexicano del siglo diecinueve," in *El conservadurismo*, ed. Fowler and Moreno, 22–36; and François-Xavier Guerra, *Modernidad e Independencias: Ensayos sobre las revoluciones hispánicas* (Madrid: Editorial MAPFRE, 1992) and "El soberano y su reino: Reflexiones sobre la génesis del ciudadano en América Latina," in *Ciudadanía política y formación de las naciones: Perspectivas sobre América Latina*, ed. Hilda Sabato (Mexico City: El Colegio de México, Fideicomiso Historia de las Américas, and Fondo de Cultura Económica, 1999), 33–61.

7. The exception is the Santa Anna regime of 1852–1855.

8. Josefina Vázquez calls the political ideology of the centralist era "liberal centralism"; it "maintained the division of powers, restricted representation (like the French, the North American, and the English) and autonomous administrative and even political space in the departments" (Josefina Zoraida Vázquez, "Centralistas, conservadores, y monarquistas 1830–1853," in *El conservadurismo*, ed. Fowler and Morales, 115–121, quote is from 117). For a different perspective on centralism, see Reynaldo Sordo Cedeño, "El pensamiento conservador del partido centralista en los años treinta del siglo XIX mexicano" in the same volume, 135–168. Michael Costeloe writes that by the 1830s most Mexicans with political and economic influence—"of both liberal and conservative convictions"—were disappointed with the results of the nation's first constitution and had come to believe that its provisions had been too radical and that federalism was a failed experiment (Costeloe, *The Central Republic in Mexico*, 29).

9. James Dunkerley, "Preface," in *Studies in the Formation of the Nation-State in Latin America*, ed. James Dunkerley (London: Institute of Latin American Studies, 2002), 4.

10. For a discussion of the historiographical usefulness of the notion of political culture, see Nils Jacobsen and Cristóbal Aljovín de Losada, "The Long and the Short of It: A Pragmatic Perspective on Political Cultures, Especially for the Modern History of the Andes"; Alan Knight, "Is Political Culture Good to Think?"; and Jacobsen and Aljovín de Losada, "How Interests and Values Seldom Come Alone, or: The Utility of a Pragmatic Perspective on Political Culture," in *Political Culture in the Andes: 1750–1950,* ed. Nils Jacobsen and Aljovín de Losada (Durham, NC: Duke University Press, 2005), 1–73. See also Patrick J. McNamara, *Sons of the Sierra: Juárez, Díaz, & the People of Ixtlán, Oaxaca, 1855–1920* (Chapel Hill: University of North Carolina Press, 2007), 11–12.

11. See in particular Guerra, *El soberano y su reino.*

12. Antonio Annino, "Ciudadanía 'versus' gobernabilidad republicana en México: Los orígenes de un dilema," in *Ciudadanía política,* ed. Sabato, 63.

13. As María del Carmen Salinas Sándoval writes, "any work on the municipality should begin with an analysis of the interior of the states that formed the federal pact" (María del Carmen Salinas Sándoval, *Política y sociedad en los municipios del estado de México, 1825–1880* [Zinacantepec, Mexico: El Colegio Mexiquense, 1996], 13).

14. "New liberals" comes from Rodríguez O., "Introduction," 23–25.

15. Hale, *Mexican Liberalism,* 1–3.

16. The quote is from Stanley J. and Barbara H. Stein, *The Colonial Heritage of Latin America: Essays on Economic Dependence in Perspective* (New York: Oxford University Press, 1970). For an exploration of the notion of colonial heritage in Latin American history and historiography, see the essays in Jeremy Adelman, ed., *Colonial Legacies: The Problem of Persistence in Latin American History* (New York: Routledge, 1999).

17. This was the argument of Mexican liberals in the second half of the nineteenth century, when it became apparent that liberalism had not transformed Mexican society in the expected ways. For a review of these ideas, see Charles A. Hale, *The Transformation of Liberalism in Late Nineteenth-Century Mexico* (Princeton, NJ: Princeton University Press, 1989). According to this argument, doctrinaire liberalism had been inappropriate for Mexico, both because it did not take into account the deep roots of colonial notions of government and because colonialism had stunted the political potential of the majority of the population. This "culturalist" explanation survives in reworked form in the work of modern scholars who seek to explain Latin America's apparent failure to sustain stable democracies and prosperous economies by identifying a unique political tradition rooted in, among other things, the Catholic monarchy. See Glen Caudill Dealy, *The Public Man: An Interpretation of Latin American and Other Catholic Countries* (Amherst: University of Massachusetts Press, 1977) and *The Latin Americans: Spirit and Ethos* (Boulder, CO: Westview Press, 1992); Claudio Véliz, *The New World of the Gothic Fox: Culture and Economy in English and Spanish America* (Berkeley: University of California Press, 1994); and many of the essays in Howard Wiarda, ed., *Politics and Social Change in Latin America: The Distinct Tradition* (Amherst: University of Massachusetts Press, 1974), which was revised and reissued in 1992 as *Politics and*

Social Change in Latin America: Still a Distinct Tradition? (Boulder, CO: Westview Press, 1992).

18. E. Bradford Burns, *The Poverty of Progress: Latin America in the Nineteenth Century* (Berkeley: University of California Press, 1980), 11–12. See also Manuel Ferrer Muñoz, "El estado mexicano y los pueblos indios en el siglo XIX" and "Pueblos indígenas en México en el siglo XIX: La igualdad juridical, ¿Eficaz sustituto del tutelaje tradicional?" in *Los pueblos indios y el parteaguas de la independencia de México,* ed. Ferrer Muñoz (Mexico City: UNAM, 1999), 65–83, 85–103. The literature on the negative effects of liberalism/capitalism on peasant society is huge and varied. For some foundational examples, see Barrington Moore, *Social Origins of Dictatorship and Democracy: Lord and Peasant in the Making of the Modern World* (Boston: Beacon Press, 1966); Eric R. Wolf, *Peasant Wars of the Twentieth Century* (New York: Harper and Row, 1969); Joel S. Migdal, *Peasants, Politics, and Revolution* (Princeton, NJ: Princeton University Press, 1974); and James C. Scott, *The Moral Economy of the Peasant: Rebellion and Subsistence in Southeast Asia* (New Haven, CT: Yale University Press, 1976). Latin American history saw a boom in the 1970s and 1980s in social history, much of which shared this critique. For overviews of this literature, see William Roseberry, "Beyond the Agrarian Question in Latin America," in *Confronting Historical Paradigms: Peasants, Labor, and the Capitalist World System in Africa and Latin America,* ed. Frederick Cooper et al. (Madison: University of Wisconsin Press, 1993), 318–363; and Steven Topik, "Mexico's Southern Liberals in the Post-Independence Decades," *Mexican Studies/ Estudios Mexicanos* 18:2 (Summer 2002), 399–403. For works on Oaxaca and Yucatán that emphasize the critique of liberalism, see Rodolfo Pastor, *Campesinos y reformas: La Mixteca 1700–1856* (Mexico City: El Colegio de México, 1987), 12–13; Nancy M. Farriss, *Maya Society under Colonial Rule: The Collective Enterprise of Survival* (Princeton, NJ: Princeton University Press, 1984), 355–388; and Marcello Carmagnani, *El regreso de los dioses. El proceso de reconstitución de la identidad étnica en Oaxaca. Siglos XVII y XVIII* (Mexico City: Fondo de Cultura Económica, 1988), 227–238.

19. For a synthetic overview of this process, see Tutino, *From Insurrection to Revolution.* On the Reform, see Richard N. Sinkin, *The Mexican Reform, 1855– 1876: A Study in Liberal Nation-Building* (Austin: University of Texas Press, 1979), 22, 172–173. Alan Knight has detailed the changes in historiography on the Mexican Revolution in "Revisionism and Revolution: Mexico Compared to England and France," *Past and Present* 134 (1992): 159–199. He traces three major stages. First, the "revolutionary orthodoxy," which, roughly speaking, portrayed the Revolution as "a broad popular movement, strongly agrarian in terms of both social composition and political agenda, progressive, egalitarian, and nationalist," in strong contrast with the Revolution's Porfirian predecessor. This was a position taken by participants, Mexican nationalist historians, and some American observers, perhaps most famously Frank Tannenbaum (see, for example, *Mexico: The Struggle for Peace and Bread* [New York: Alfred A. Knopf, 1950]). Next, in the 1960s, revisionists produced work critical of the orthodox stance, questioning the "popular, progressive and egalitarian" nature of the Revolution. These two positions can perhaps be seen most starkly in the two works of John Womack Jr.—

Zapata and the Mexican Revolution (New York: Vintage, 1968) and, later, "The Mexican Revolution, 1910–1920," in *Cambridge History of Latin America*, ed. Leslie Bethell, Vol. 5, c. *1870 to 1930* (Cambridge, U.K.: Cambridge University Press, 1986), 79–153, the first an account of agrarian revolution in the state of Morelos and the second an account of the Revolution as a "bourgeois civil war." Knight himself has promoted a reinterpretation of the Revolution that takes both into account. See Alan Knight, *The Mexican Revolution* (Lincoln: University of Nebraska Press, 1986).

20. The "favorable conjuncture" Thomson refers to was the disgrace of conservatism after the French intervention and the rise of a young liberal leadership with "ideological clarity and military prowess." Guy P. C. Thomson, "Popular Aspects of Liberalism in Mexico, 1848–1888," *Bulletin of Latin American Research* 10:3 (1991): 265–292. The quotations are from page 265.

21. Peter F. Guardino, *Peasants, Politics, and the Formation of Mexico's National State: Guerrero, 1800–1857* (Stanford, CA: Stanford University Press, 1996); Thomson with David G. LaFrance, *Patriotism, Politics, and Popular Liberalism in Nineteenth-Century Mexico: Juan Francisco Lucas and the Puebla* Sierra (Wilmington, DE: SR Books, 1999); McNamara, *Sons of the Sierra*; and Florencia E. Mallon, *Peasant and Nation: The Making of Postcolonial Mexico and Peru* (Berkeley: University of California Press, 1995). The quotations from Mallon are from page 141.

22. Guardino, *Peasants, Politics*, 44; Mallon, *Peasant and Nation*, 9, 17.

23. Guardino addresses this issue in Peter Guardino, *The Time of Liberty: Popular Political Culture in Oaxaca, 1750–1850* (Durham, NC: Duke University Press, 2005), 281–284. Here, he discusses the differences between his work on Guerrero and on Oaxaca.

24. Eric Van Young, *The Other Rebellion: Popular Violence, Ideology, and the Mexican Struggle for Independence, 1810–1821* (Stanford, CA: Stanford University Press, 2001). For a refutation of Van Young's approach, see Guardino, *Peasants, Politics,* 58 and *Time of Liberty*, 286. Guardino writes that "historians who believe that the peasants who formed the mass of the rebels and the priests, muleteers, and even landowners who led the insurgents had very different goals may very well be correct. However, these different aims were not expressed in radically different ways." Guardino draws here on James Lockhart's notion of "double mistaken identity." James Lockhart, *The Nahuas after the Conquest: A Social and Cultural History of the Indians of Central Mexico, Sixteenth through Eighteenth Centuries* (Stanford, CA: Stanford University Press, 1992), 445–446.

25. For the early nineteenth century, regional histories include Guardino, *Peasants, Politics* and *Time of Liberty*; Salinas Sándoval, *Política y sociedad*; Michael T. Ducey, *A Nation of Villages: Riot and Rebellion in the Mexican Huasteca, 1750–1850* (Tucson: University of Arizona Press, 2004); Antonio Escobar Ohmstede, "Del gobierno indígena al Ayuntamiento constitucional en las Huastecas hidalguense y veracruzana, 1780–1853," *Mexican Studies/Estudios Mexicanos* 12:1 (Winter 1996): 1–26; and Claudia Guarisco, *Los indios del valle de México y la construcción de una nueva sociabilidad política, 1770–1835* (Zincantepec, Mexico: El Colegio Mexiquense, 2003). The articulation of the impulse to focus on Mexico's regions owes much to Luis González y González, whose *Invitación a la microhistoria* (Mexico City:

Secretaria de Educación Pública, 1973) called for the study of Mexico's locally defined *matrias* as well as its national *patria* and spurred the writing of a variety of microhistories. Scholars of the Mexican Revolution have made much of this suggestion, in such collections as Thomas Benjamin and Mark Wasserman, ed., *Provinces of the Mexican Revolution: Essays in Regional Mexican History, 1910–1929* (Albuquerque: University of New Mexico Press, 1990), which have greatly enriched our understanding of the causes and effects of the war. More recently, Timothy E. Anna has called for a return to regional history for the nineteenth century in his *Forging Mexico, 1821–1835* (Lincoln: University of Nebraska Press, 1998), 1–33. For a discussion of some of the possibilities of regional history, see Gilbert M. Joseph, *Rediscovering the Past at Mexico's Periphery: Essays on the History of Modern Yucatán* (Tuscaloosa: University of Alabama Press, 1986), 8–11.

26. In, as Claudio Lomnitz-Adler puts it, "internally differentiated regional spaces." The term is taken from Claudio Lomnitz-Adler, *Exits from the Labyrinth: Culture and Ideology in the Mexican National Space* (Berkeley: University of California Press, 1992). Lomnitz-Adler is concerned with finding a way of characterizing "national culture"; this project has much (although not all) in common with that of defining Mexican liberalism.

27. Few comparisons of states exist for this period. Guardino's brief discussion in *Time of Liberty* of the implications of the differences between Guerrero and Oaxaca is suggestive. Helpful in thinking about the possibilities of comparison for the nineteenth century are Mallon, *Peasant and Nation*, which compares both regions and nations in the latter half of the century, and Brooke Larson, *Trials of Nation Making: Liberalism, Race, and Ethnicity in the Andes, 1810–1910* (Cambridge, U.K.: Cambridge University Press, 2004), which compares Andean countries on a national scale.

28. Josefina Zoraida Vázquez, "De la difícil constitución de un estado: México, 1821–1854," in *La fundación del estado mexicano, 1821–1855*, ed. Vázquez (Mexico City: Nueva Imagen, 1994), 37; and Timothy Anna, "Demystifying Early Nineteenth-Century Mexico," *Mexican Studies/Estudios Mexicanos* 9:1 (1993): 199–137. Fowler surveys the various ways historians have expressed and explained this historiographical lacuna in *Mexico in the Age of Proposals*, 1–2.

29. I have found the concept of "sequencing," developed by historical institutionalist political scientists, to be helpful here. See Theda Skocpol, "Why I Am a Historical-Institutionalist," *Polity* 28 (Fall 1995): 103–106; and Paul Pierson and Theda Skocpol, "Historical Institutionalism in Contemporary Political Science," in *Political Science: State of the Discipline*, ed. Ira Katznelson and Helen V. Milner (New York: W. W. Norton), 693–721.

30. Population information for Oaxaca is from Carlos Sánchez Silva, *Indios, comerciantes y burocracia en la Oaxaca poscolonial, 1786–1860*, Serie Dishá (Oaxaca, Mexico: Instituto Oaxaqueño de las Culturas, Fondo Estatal para la Cultura y las Artes, and Universidad Autónoma Benito Juárez de Oaxaca, 1998), 48. The number for Yucatán is derived from a variety of local statistical documents compiled by Farriss, *Maya Society*, Appendix 1, "The Population of Yucatán," 397–398, and is roughly supported by the calculations of Wolfgang Gabbert, *Becoming Maya:*

Ethnicity and Social Inequality in Yucatán since 1500 (Tucson: University of Arizona Press, 2004), 16–18.

31. Among the many ethnohistories are, for Oaxaca in the precolonial period, Ronald Spores, *The Mixtecs in Ancient and Colonial Times* (Norman: University of Oklahoma Press, 1984); for the colonial period, Kevin Terraciano, *The Mixtecs of Colonial Oaxaca: Ñudzahui History, Sixteenth through Eighteenth Centuries* (Stanford, CA: Stanford University Press, 2001); María de los Angeles Romero Frizzi, *El sol y la cruz: Los pueblos indios de Oaxaca colonial* (Mexico City: Instituto Nacional Indigenista, Centro de Investigación y Estudios Superiores en Antropología Social, 1996); and John K. Chance, *Conquest of the Sierra: Spaniards and Indians in Colonial Oaxaca* (Norman: University of Oklahoma Press, 1989); and for the nineteenth century, Leticia Reina Aoyama, *Caminos de luz y sombra: Historia indígena de Oaxaca en el siglo XIX* (Mexico City: Centro de Investigación y Estudios Superiores en Antropología Social, Comisión Nacional para el Desarrollo de los Pueblos Indígenas, 2004). For Yucatán in the colonial era, see Farriss, *Maya Society*; Matthew Restall, *The Maya World: Yucatec Culture and Society, 1550–1850* (Stanford, CA: Stanford University Press, 1997); and Pedro Bracamonte y Sosa and Gabriela Solis Robleda, *Espacios Maya de Autonomía: El Pacto Colonial en Yucatán* (Mérida, Mexico: Universidad Autónoma de Yucatán and Consejo Nacional de Ciencia y Tecnología, 1996). For the twentieth century, the literature on both states is too voluminous to detail here.

32. Carmagnani, *El regreso de los dioses*, 13. For a thorough discussion of the ways that Oaxaca has been characterized as "backward" in the historiography, see Francie R. Chassen-López, *From Liberal to Revolutionary Oaxaca: The View from the South. Mexico, 1867–1911* (University Park: Pennsylvania State University Press, 2004), 4–7.

33. The historiography on the Caste War is large and is discussed in Chapter 6 of this book. For a classic account of the exploitative nature of Yucatán's labor system after the Caste War, see John Kenneth Turner, *Barbarous Mexico: An Indictment of a Cruel and Corrupt System* (London: Cassell, 1911).

34. Guardino, *Time of Liberty*; Jennie Purnell, "Citizens and Sons of the *Pueblo*: National and Local Identities in the Making of the Mexican Nation," *Ethnic and Racial Studies* 25:2 (Mar. 2002): 213–237; McNamara, *Sons of the Sierra*; Chassen-López, *From Liberal to Revolutionary Oaxaca* (she discusses the notion of "hybrid modernity" on pages 6–11); and Sánchez Silva, *Indios, comerciantes y burocracia*.

35. For an argument for the relative isolation of Yucatán's indigenous population, see Restall, *The Maya World*. See also Farriss, *Maya Society*, and Terry Rugeley, *Yucatán's Maya and the Origins of the Caste War* (Austin: University of Texas Press, 1996).

36. Colin M. Maclachlan, *Spain's Empire in the New World: The Role of Ideas in Institutional and Social Change* (Berkeley: University of California Press, 1988), 28–29; and Magnus Mörner, *Region and State in Latin America's Past* (Baltimore: Johns Hopkins University Press, 1993), 19–21. For a history of the juridical reasoning behind this construct, see Anthony Pagden, *The Fall of Natural Man: The American Indian and the Origins of Comparative Ethnology* (Cambridge, U.K.: Cambridge University Press, 1982).

37. Since the term *cabildo* also refers to nonindigenous town governments, I use the term *república* to refer to indigenous governments in particular.

38. For a detailed description of the role of the *repúblicas*, see Guarisco, *Los indios del valle de México*, 55–72.

39. Tristan Platt, *Estado boliviano y ayllu andino. Tierra y tributo en el norte de Potosí* (Lima: Instituto de Estudios Peruanos, 1982), 40.

40. Interpretations of indigenous government in colonial Mexico have varied according to the extent to which they are seen as continuous from the precolonial era and according to the extent to which the *repúblicas* are understood to be either instruments of repression and exploitation or instruments of self-protection and autonomy. For a sample, see Gonzalo Aguirre Beltrán, *Formas de gobierno indígena* (Mexico City: Imprenta Universitaria, 1953); Charles Gibson, *The Aztecs under Spanish Rule: A History of the Indians of the Valley of Mexico, 1519–1810* (Stanford, CA: Stanford University Press, 1964); Jan Rus and Robert Wasserstrom, "Civil-Religious Hierarchies in Central Chiapas: A Critical Perspective," *American Ethnologist* 7:3 (1980): 466–478; John K. Chance and William B. Taylor, "Cofradías and Cargos: An Historical Perspective on the Meso-American Civil-Religious Hierarchy," *American Ethnologist* 12:1 (1985): 1–26; Arij Ouweneel and Simon Miller, eds., *The Indian Community of Colonial Mexico: Fifteen Essays on Land Tenure, Corporate Organizations, Ideology and Village Politics* (Amsterdam: CEDLA, 1990); Robert Haskett, *Indigenous Rulers: An Ethnohistory of Town Government in Colonial Cuernavaca* (Albuquerque: University of New Mexico Press, 1991); and James Lockhart, *Nahuas*. For Yucatán and Oaxaca in particular, see Restall, *The Maya World*; Terraciano, *Mixtecs*; and Romero Frizzi, *El sol y la cruz*.

41. The fluctuation in the indigenous portion of the population of Oaxaca between 1793 and 1860, based on sporadic census information, was 87 to 88 percent. In the city of Antequera in 1792, only 29.7 percent of the population of 18,008 was indigenous, meaning that the city had 12,623 nonindigenous inhabitants (including peninsular Spaniards, Creoles, "castizos," mestizos, moriscos or pardos, mulattoes, "afromestizos," blacks, and unidentified individuals). The number of nonindígenas in all of Oaxaca one year later was 48,256. This meant that approximately one-quarter of Oaxacans lived in the capital city. Sánchez Silva, *Indios, comerciantes y burocracia*, 48; John K. Chance, *Race and Class in Colonial Oaxaca* (Stanford, CA: Stanford University Press, 1978), 145, 151, 156, and *Conquest of the Sierra*, 39; Romero Frizzi, *El sol y la cruz*, 208; William B. Taylor, "Town and Country in the Valley of Oaxaca," in *Provinces of Early Mexico: Variants of Spanish American Regional Evolution*, ed. Ida Altman and James Lockhart (Los Angeles: UCLA Latin American Center Publications, 1976), 76; and Spores, *The Mixtec in Ancient and Colonial Times*, 107–108.

42. For descriptions of Oaxaca's geography, see Romero Frizzi, *El sol y la cruz*, 21–31, and Chassen-López, *From Liberal to Revolutionary Oaxaca*, 29–39. On languages, see José María Murguía y Galardi, *Estadística del estado libre de Guajaca. Primera parte* (Oaxaca, 1826), 92z–94a, SMGE, Biblioteca Benito Juárez; Carmagnani, *El regreso de los dioses*, 58–59; Colin Clarke, *Class, Ethnicity, and Community in Southern Mexico: Oaxaca's Peasantries* (Oxford, U.K.: Oxford University Press, 2000), 12–15.

43. Guardino, *Time of Liberty*, 57; Marcello Carmagnani, "Local Governments and Ethnic Government in Oaxaca," in *Essays in the Political, Economic and Social History of Colonial Latin America*, ed. Karen Spalding (Newark: University of Delaware Press, 1982), 107–124; Romero Frizzi, *El sol y la cruz*, 125–135; Terraciano, *Mixtecs*, 182–186, 197. Terraciano also notes the limiting effects of the Spanish government's unwillingness to recognize female hereditary leaders.

44. Sanchez Silva, *Indios, comerciantes y burocracia*, 63. For the trend toward proliferation of towns in Oaxaca, see Terraciano, *Mixtecs*, 121–131. For examples from elsewhere in Mexico, see Danièle Dehouve, "The 'Secession' of Villages in the Jurisdiction of Tlapa (Eighteenth Century)," in *Indian Community*, ed. Ouweneel and Miller, 162–182, and Lockhart, *Nahuas*, 47–58.

45. On the uses of and demand for cochineal in Europe, see Susan Fairlie, "Dyestuffs in the Eighteenth Century," *Economic History Review* 17:3 (1965): 488–510. By 1620, one royal ordinance proclaimed that cochineal was "a merchandise equal in estimation to gold and silver." See Philip III's "Cochineal Ordinance" of 1620, cited in Barbro Dahlgren de Jordán, *La grana cochinilla* (Mexico City: José Porrúa e Hijos, 1963), 9. For trade networks in late colonial Oaxaca and information on the cochineal trade in particular, see Brian R. Hamnett, *Politics and Trade in Southern Mexico* (Cambridge, U.K.: Cambridge University Press, 1971) and Jeremy Baskes, *Indians, Merchants, and Markets: A Reinterpretation of the Repartimiento and Spanish-Indian Economic Relations in Colonial Oaxaca, 1750–1821* (Stanford, CA: Stanford University Press, 2000), 93–109.

46. Baskes, *Indians, Merchants, and Markets*, 10–14; Sánchez Silva, *Indios, comerciantes y burocracia*, 96–104. Sánchez Silva speculates that one of the major reasons for nonindigenous reluctance to produce the dye was that nonindígenas would have to pay tithe and the royal sales tax (*alcabala*) on cochineal, which indígenas did not pay. Baskes attributes the situation to the labor-intensive nature of the production of cochineal and the lack of economies of scale. Estimates of the proportion of the population engaged in cochineal production vary. Baskes puts the number at 8 percent of the population, and one-third of the households, while according to Clarke more than one-half of the agricultural laborers in eighteenth-century Oaxaca were engaged in cochineal production (Clarke, *Class, Ethnicity, and Community*, 24).

47. Chance writes that in the district of Villa Alta, a center for textile production in Oaxaca, "much, if not most" cotton was grown by nonindigenous people or under their supervision and then distributed to the villages for weaving. Guardino, by contrast, suggests that indigenous men cultivated most of the cotton in indigenous villages and then distributed it to others who processed it (Chance, *Conquest of the Sierra*, 29; Guardino, *Time of Liberty*, 44). Terraciano points out that in the Mixteca, silk, wheat, and livestock were additional products that did not involve direct Spanish participation (Terraciano, *Mixtecs*, 235).

48. Terraciano, *Mixtecs*, 251. The most common Oaxacan form of the repartimiento, in which the alcalde mayor advanced a prepayment of cash to be repaid with a product, was less common in most of New Spain, where the alcalde would most often advance goods to villages in the expectation that they would be paid back later. Oaxaca's arrangement was intended to facilitate indigenous production,

while the more common form facilitated indigenous consumption. Baskes notes that some indigenous people did sell cochineal on the open market, a fact he links to increasing social differentiation in indigenous communities (Baskes, *Indians, Merchants, and Markets*, 21–27, 128–137).

49. The repartimiento has long been understood as abusive and coerced. Rodolfo Pastor, for instance, argues that "at its origin, the repartimiento is one more trick for obtaining indigenous products and a compulsion of a market, a political annulment, like others, of the effects of supply and demand that originally benefited the Indian." Baskes, on the other hand, is the most vocal proponent of the revisionist idea that the repartimiento was not coerced, arguing, first, that the indígenas wanted to participate in markets and, second, that the colonial state lacked the power necessary to police such an extensive practice; thus, indigenous participation must have been voluntary. He sees the repartimiento not as a repressive instrument but rather as one that "facilitated the widespread extension of credit by Spaniards to Indians that enabled the latter to produce a major export product and become more fully integrated into the market and the world economy" (Pastor, *Campesinos y reformas*, 153; Baskes, *Indians, Merchants, and Markets*, 62–92, and "Colonial Institutions and Cross-Cultural Trade: *Repartimiento* Credit and Indigenous Production of Cochineal in Eighteenth-Century Oaxaca," *Journal of Economic History* 65:1 [March 2005]: 208). Baskes and others do document some coercion from both nonindigenous and indigenous authorities. See Baskes, *Indians, Merchants, and Markets*, 78–85; and Sánchez Silva, "Indios y repartimientos en Oaxaca a principios del siglo XIX," in *Indio, nación y comunidad en el México del siglo XIX* ed. Antonio Escobar Ohmstede (Mexico City: CEMCA and CIESAS, 1993), 108–109. See also Sánchez Silva, *Indios, comerciantes y burocracia*, 102–110, and, for an account of the repartimiento specifically in the cotton trade, Guardino, *Time of Liberty*, 44–47.

50. William B. Taylor, *Drinking, Homicide, and Rebellion in Colonial Mexican Villages* (Stanford, CA: Stanford University Press, 1979), 88–89.

51. For accounts of indigenous people's use of the justice system, see Woodrow Borah, *Justice by Insurance: The General Indian Court of Colonial Mexico and the Legal Aides of the Half-Real* (Berkeley: University of California Press, 1983) and MacLachlan, *Spain's Empire in the New World*, 48. On the role of alcaldes mayores in the administration of the repartimiento, see Carmagnani, "Una institución económica colonial: Repartimiento de mercancías y libertad de comercio," *Historia Mexicana* LIV:1 (2004): 254. Yanna P. Yannakakis details the intermediary role of indigenous authorities in *The Art of Being In-Between: Native Intermediaries, Indian Identity, and Local Rule in Colonial Oaxaca* (Durham, NC: Duke University Press, 2008). On disputes between nobility and macehuales, see Terraciano, *Mixtecs*, 228–231. And on the increase in conflict over land, see William B. Taylor, *Landlord and Peasant in Colonial Oaxaca* (Stanford, CA: Stanford University Press, 1972), 84, and María de los Angeles Romero Frizzi, "Época colonial (1519–1785)," in *Historia de la cuestión agraria mexicana. Estado de Oaxaca. I. Prehispánico—1824*, ed. Leticia Reina and José Sánchez Cortés (Mexico City: Juan Pablos Editor for Gobierno del Estado de Oaxaca, Universidad Autónoma Benito Juárez de Oaxaca, and Centro de Estudios Históricos del Agrarismo en México, 1988), 173–178.

Both Taylor and Romero Frizzi see an increase in land disputes in the eighteenth century.

52. Taylor, *Landlord and Peasant*, 84, 87.

53. Taylor, *Landlord and Peasant*, 85; Baskes, *Indians, Merchants, and Markets*, 72; and Taylor, *Drinking, Homicide, and Rebellion*, 140. On the Oaxacan alcaldía mayor, see Hamnett, *Politics and Trade*, 16–17; of a list of the values of twenty-six alcaldías mayores in 1718 and 1719, nine are in Oaxaca. Oaxacan alcaldías occupy the first, second, sixth, seventh, eighth, tenth, eleventh, thirteenth, and seventeenth places on the list. On the role of alcaldes mayores in Oaxaca and elsewhere, see María de los Angeles Romero Frizzi, *Economía y vida de los españoles en la Mixteca Alta: 1519–1720*, Colección Regiones de México (Mexico City: Instituto Nacional de Antropología e Historia and Gobierno del Estado de Oaxaca, 1990), 253–260; Taylor, *Drinking, Homicide, and Rebellion*, 117–118, 133–136, and *Magistrates of the Sacred: Priests and Parishioners in Eighteenth-Century Mexico* (Stanford, CA: Stanford University Press, 1996), 396–423; and Alicia M. Barabas, "Rebeliones e insurrecciones indígenas en Oaxaca: la trayectoria histórica de la resistencia étnica," in *Etnicidad y pluralismo cultural. La dinámica étnica en Oaxaca*, ed. Alicia M. Barabas and Miguel A. Bartolomé (Mexico City: Instituto Nacional de Antropología e Historia, 1986).

54. On the Spanish intendency system, see D. A. Brading, *Miners and Merchants in Bourbon Mexico 1763–1810* (Cambridge, U.K.: Cambridge University Press, 1971), 33–92; and John Lynch, *Administración colonial española 1782–1810. El sistema de intendencias en el Virreinato del Río de la Plata* (Buenos Aires: Editorial Universitaria de Buenos Aires, 1962), 51–64. For details of Oaxaca's political boundaries, see Peter Gerhard, *A Guide to the Historical Geography of New Spain* (Cambridge, U.K.: Cambridge University Press, 1972), 50. For the circumstances surrounding the abolition of the repartimiento, see Hamnett, *Politics and Trade*, 56–71; Baskes, *Indians, Merchants, and Markets*, 56–60, 96–101; Guardino, *Time of Liberty*, 96–101; and Silke Hensel, "Las orígenes del federalismo en México. Una perspectiva desde la provincia de Oaxaca de finales del siglo XVIII a la Primera República," *Ibero-Amerikansches Archiv* 25:3/4 (1999): 221–222.

55. Hamnett, *Politics and Trade*, 122–126, 128–131; Ana Carolina Ibarra, *Clero y política en Oaxaca. Biografía del Doctor José de San Martín*, Serie Dishá (Oaxaca, Mexico: Instituto Oaxaqueño de las Culturas, Universidad Nacional Autónoma de México, and Fondo Estatal para la Cultura y las Artes, 1996), 64–69; Guardino, *Time of Liberty*, 127; and Hensel, "Las orígenes del federalismo," 222–224.

56. Population figures for before the late eighteenth century in Yucatán are quite incomplete. Based on extant evidence, Robert Patch estimates that in 1639 Maya outnumbered Spaniards forty-seven to one. This calculation does not take into account the numbers of people who belonged to neither group: mestizos, Africans, and mulattos. Cook and Borah estimate that the entire nonindigenous population came to only 5.5 percent of the population as a whole, also in 1639. Although it is very difficult to determine with any precision, it seems clear that the very small nonindigenous population, before the eighteenth century, was located primarily in the cities (Robert W. Patch, *Maya and Spaniard in Yucatán, 1648–1812* [Stanford, CA: Stanford University Press, 1993], 94; Sherburne F.

Cook and Woodrow Borah, *Essays in Population History: Mexico and the Caribbean* [Berkeley: University of California Press, 1974], II:83; Manuela Cristina García Bernal, *Población y encomienda en Yucatán bajo los Austrias* [Seville, Spain: Escuela de Estudios Hispano-Americanos de Sevilla, 1978], 149–158, and *La sociedad de Yucatán, 1700–1750* [Seville, Spain: Escuela de Estudios Hispano-Americanos de Sevilla, 1972], 21–22; and Farriss, "Indians in Colonial Yucatán: Three Perspectives," in *Spaniards and Indians in Southeastern Mesoamerica: Essays on the History of Ethnic Relations*, ed. Murdo J. MacLeod and Robert Wasserstrom [Lincoln: University of Nebraska Press, 1983], 16–19).

57. The quote is from Farriss, "Indians in Colonial Yucatán," 33. See also Farriss, *Maya Society*, 30–33; Restall, *Maya World*, 53; and Patch, *Maya and Spaniard*, 96–100.

58. Gerhard, *The Southeast Frontier of New Spain* (Princeton, N.J.: Princeton University Press, 1979), 59; Farriss, *Maya Society*, 88–90.

59. Restall, *Maya World*, 51–56, 61–72, 202; Rugeley, *Yucatán's Maya Peasantry*, 11–13, 32.

60. Nancy M. Farriss, "Nucleation versus Dispersal: The Dynamics of Population Movement in Colonial Yucatán," *Hispanic American Historical Review* 58:2 (1978): 196–199; *Maya Society*, 18–19, 206–210; Restall, *Maya World*, 17, 173–177. Restall stresses that Maya population movement was not necessarily tied to colonial impositions but was in fact part of preconquest patterns of settlement as well.

61. Farriss, "Nucleation," 202; Pedro Bracamonte y Sosa, "El discurso político de los caciques mayas yucatecos, 1720–1852," in *Liberalismo, actores y política en Yucatán*, ed. Othón Baños Ramírez (Mérida, Mexico: Ediciones de la Universidad Autónoma de Yucatán, 1995), 108–109; Patch, *Maya and Spaniard*, 138–140; Restall, *The Maya World*, 21; 218–220.

62. Patch, *Maya and Spaniard*, 74–81; Rugeley, *Yucatán's Maya Peasantry*, 22–31.

63. Restall, *Maya World*, 220–225; Patch, *Maya and Spaniard*, 138–148; Farriss, *Maya Society*, 366–375. Rugeley also describes a process by which, where nonindigenous properties were growing, Maya batabs obtained small privately owned plots and sometimes employed Maya laborers. These plots, not in mayorazgo, led to multiple inheritance, which led to sale and exacerbated land loss (Rugeley, *Yucatán's Maya Peasantry*, 18–21).

64. Patch, *Maya and Spaniard*, 148–150. The areas around the cities of Mérida and Campeche were the most intensive, while the eastern portion of the peninsula remained largely composed of autonomous indigenous pueblos.

65. Rugeley, *Yucatán's Maya Peasantry*, 18; Farriss, "Nucleation versus Dispersal," 213–214; Patch, *Maya and Spaniard*, 149–151.

66. Victoria Reifler Bricker, *The Indian Christ, The Indian King: The Historical Substrate of Maya Myth and Ritual* (Austin: University of Texas Press, 1981), 70–76; Rugeley, *Yucatán's Maya Peasantry*, 14–16; Farriss, *Maya Society*, 69. I use the word *arguably* because it is not entirely clear what the rebellion was about, and some authors doubt that it represented a "rebellion." Rugeley suggests that it may have been based in concerns about changes in the practices of a local hacienda, and Farriss calls the rebellion a "historical accident" that had as much to do with Canek's personal circumstances as it did with any new Maya tendency to rebel.

67. Farriss, *Maya Society*, 68, 108; Restall, 53.

68. Howard F. Cline, "The 'Aurora Yucateca' and the Spirit of Enterprise in Yucatán, 1821–1847," *Hispanic American Historical Review* 28:1 (1948): 32; Alejandra García Quintanilla, "En busca de la prosperidad y la riqueza: Yucatán a la hora de independencia," in *Los lugares y los tiempos. Ensayos sobre las estructuras regionales del siglo XIX en México*, ed. García Quintanilla and Abel Juárez (Mexico City: Editorial Nuestro Tiempo for COMESCO, Universidad Veracruzana, and Universidad Autónoma de Nuevo León, 1989), 93–97; and Rugeley, *Yucatán's Maya Society*, 34–37.

69. Bracamonte y Sosa, "El discurso político," 109; Restall, *Maya World*, 318.

70. There is copious literature on both the blurriness of racial boundaries in colonial Latin America and the ambiguities of identity. For Mexico, see in particular R. Douglas Cope, *The Limits of Racial Domination: Plebeian Society in Colonial Mexico, 1660–1720* (Madison: University of Wisconsin Press, 1994); and Laura A. Lewis, *Hall of Mirrors: Power, Witchcraft, and Caste in Colonial Mexico* (Durham, NC: Duke University Press, 2003).

71. In following this framework, I do not intend to minimize the importance of differences among indigenous groups, something that permeates the culture of Oaxaca in particular. The identity of individual ethnic groups was clearly important, especially because it affected the ways in which indigenous people were likely to view collective action against the state; notions of ethnic difference among indígenas can help, certainly, to explain the near absence of "caste war" in most of Oaxaca, its presence on Oaxaca's isthmus of Tehuantepec where most indígenas were Zapotec, and its relative ease of organization in Yucatán where all indígenas were Maya. Yet in both states, on a day-to-day level, when indigenous people engaged the state, they did so as indigenous villagers first, rather than as Maya, Zapotec, or Mixtec. That different ethnic groups engaged the state differently is by no means impossible, but this book concurs with Guardino's assertion that the evidence does not support the existence of distinct political cultures in different indigenous groups (Guardino, *Time of Liberty*, 41).

72. See Peter Guardino's excellent discussion of this issue in *Time of Liberty*, 9–11. James Scott's discussion of "hidden transcripts," is from *Domination and the Arts of Resistance: Hidden Trasncripts* (New Haven, CT: Yale University Press, 1990). For a now-classic discussion of the ability to discern the thoughts of the "subaltern," see Gayatri Spivak, "Can the Subaltern Speak?" in Cary Nelson and Lawrence Grossberg, eds., *Marxism and the Interpretation of Culture* (Urbana: University of Illinois Press, 1988). For a discussion of the importance of Subaltern Studies for Latin American historiography, see Florencia E. Mallon, "The Promise and Dilemma of Subaltern Studies: Perspectives from Latin American History," *American Historical Review* 99 (1994): 1491–1515.

NOTES TO CHAPTER 2

1. "Representación de Ceferino Domínguez, alcalde de Nohcacab, sobre la conducta delictuosa de unos indios, 1813," AGEY, Col., Varios, vol. 1, exp. 17. Wherever possible, I have modernized the names of towns. In doing so, for Yucatán,

I have used the spellings found in Gerhard, *The Southeast Frontier.* For Oaxaca, I have used, whenever possible, the map of the state, "Oaxaca. Plano Cd. De Oaxaca y Mapa General del Edo," Serie Mapas de México (Dist. De Edic. Independencia Mayoreo y Menudeo). If there was any doubt about the identification of a town, I left its name as written in the documents. There are some towns that I have not been able to correlate with certainty to modern towns, either because their names have changed or because they no longer exist. Portions of this chapter, and of Chapters 3 and 4, were previously published in "The Legal Revolution in Town Politics: Oaxaca and Yucatán: 1812–1825," *Hispanic American Historical Review* 83:2 (May 2003): 255–293.

2. Timothy E. Anna, *Spain & the Loss of America* (Lincoln: University of Nebraska Press, 1983), 29–31; Mario Rodríguez, *The Cádiz Experiment in Central America, 1808–1826* (Berkeley: University of California Press, 1978), 31–38.

3. See the work of William B. Taylor, especially *Drinking, Homicide and Rebellion* and *Magistrates of the Sacred.*

4. Guerra, "El soberano y su reino," 33–61.

5. For the definition of citizenship, see "Constitución política de la monarquía española," in *Leyes fundamentales de México 1808–1982*, 11th ed., ed. Felipe Tena Ramírez (Mexico City: Editorial Porrúa, 1982), 62. For a discussion of the legal mandate for the creation of ayuntamientos under the Cádiz rules see Salinas Sándoval, *Política y sociedad*, 31–36.

6. For the laws concerning elections of deputies to the Cortes, see "Constitución política de la monarquía española," 64–72. See also Charles R. Berry, "The Election of the Mexican Deputies to the Spanish Cortes, 1810–1822," in *Mexico and the Spanish Cortes, 1810–1822: Eight Essays*, ed. Nettie Lee Benson (Austin: University of Texas Press for the Institute of Latin American Studies, 1966), 17–21.

7. Guerra, "El soberano y su reino," 49–56; Rodríguez O., " 'Ningún pueblo es superior a otro,' " 76.

8. Alicia Hernández Chávez calls the ayuntamiento "the essential cell of the new political order" (Alicia Hernández Chávez, *La tradición republicano del buen gobierno* [Mexico City: El Colegio de México, Fideicomiso Historia de las Américas, and Fondo de la Cultura Económica, 1993], 33). For a general overview of elections in Mexico during the Spanish constitutional period, see Berry, "The Election of the Mexican Deputies." For Mexico City, see Virginia Guedea, "Las primeras elecciones populares en la ciudad de México. 1812–1813," *Mexican Studies/Estudios Mexicanos* 7:1 (1991): 1–28; and Richard Warren, "Elections and Popular Political Participation in Mexico, 1808–1836," in *Liberals, Politics, and Power: State Formation in Nineteenth-Century Latin America*, ed. Vincent C. Peloso and Barbara A. Tenenbaum (Athens: University of Georgia Press, 1996), 31–40. For Yucatán, see Marco Bellingeri, "Las ambigüedades del voto en Yucatán. Representación y gobierno en una formación interétnica 1812–1829," in *Historia de las elecciones en Iberoamérica, siglo XIX*, ed. Antonio Annino (Mexico City: Fondo de Cultura Económica, 1995), 227–290.

9. For an account of the municipal institutions of Spanish liberalism in Spain itself, see Concepción de Castro, *La revolución liberal y los municipios españoles* (Madrid: Alianza Editorial, 1979). On the participation of American deputies

at the Cortes, see Marie Laure Rieu-Millan, *Los diputados americanos en las cortes de Cádiz (igualdad o independencia)* (Madrid: Consejo Superior de Investigaciones Científicas, 1990). See in particular the arguments of Miguel Ramos Arizpe, a deputy from New Spain, at the Cortes of Cádiz, in *Diario de sesiones de las córtes generales y extraordinarias* 374, Oct. 11, 1811, 2050–2051; 464, Jan. 10, 1812, 2593. On ayuntamientos in colonial New Spain, see Roger Cunniff, "Mexican Municipal Electoral Reform, 1810–1822," in *Mexico and the Spanish Cortes*, ed. Benson, 60–63. And for the laws establishing ayuntamientos in constitutional New Spain, see "Constitución política de la monarquía española," 95–97, and "Decreto de 23 de mayo de 1812. Formación de los ayuntamientos constitucionales," in *Colección de los decretos y órdenes de las cortes de España, que se reputan vigentes en la república de los Estados-Unidos Mexicanos* (Mexico City: Imprenta de Galván, 1829), 28–30.

10. Historians have estimated that, between 1812 and 1814, almost 900 ayuntamientos were established in New Spain as a whole; in 1820, with the reestablishment of the Constitution of Cádiz, some 630 ayuntamientos were formed. Divided by intendencies, the numbers of ayuntamientos by 1814 ranged from three (Zacatecas) to 200 (Oaxaca), and in 1820 from six (Veracruz), to 200 (again, Oaxaca) (Hernández Chávez, *La tradición republicana*, 25; Annino, "Cádiz y la revolución territorial de los pueblos mexicanos 1812–1821," in *Historia de las Elecciones*, ed. Annino, 209).

11. There is disagreement about the extent to which indigenous Oaxacans participated in the conflict, which was led for the most part by Creole merchants and landowners, and about whether those who did fight did so only at the behest of their patrons or exploiters or for conscious reasons of their own. Leticia Reina stresses that although some Indians were coerced into fighting, "the indígenas also acted on their own account" amounting to veritable "social agitation" "motivated by the recuperation of their lands and against abuses." Pastor, on the other hand, argues that indigenous villagers had little enthusiasm for either side (Leticia Reina, "De las reformas borbónicas a las leyes de reforma," in *Historia de la cuestión agraria mexicana*, ed. Leticia Reina and Sánchez Cortés, 213–216 and *Caminos de luz y sombra*, 95; Pastor, *Campesinos y reformas*, 415–420). Guardino details an interesting incident of possible peasant support for the insurgents in Villa Alta in 1812 in *Time of Liberty*, 140–142.

12. Some Spanish liberal policies were put into effect in Oaxaca between 1810 and 1812, including the first declaration of the end of distinctions between Spaniards, Creoles, mestizos, and Indians. The Spanish constitution itself was in effect only from March until May, during which time elections were held for an ayuntamiento in Antequera but not in any other towns or villages. For accounts of the events of the first period of constitutional rule and the subsequent insurgent occupation of Antequera, see José Antonio Gay, *Historia de Oaxaca*, 3rd ed. (Mexico City: Editorial Porrúa, 1990 [1881]), 481–501; Rodríguez O., "'Ningún pueblo es superior a otro,'" 70–74; and Guardino, *Time of Liberty*, 133–144.

13. For records of república elections in the villages from 1812 to 1818, see AGEO, RI, serie I, leg. 2, exp. 38; and serie II, leg. 15, exps. 11 and 38; leg. 38, exps. 10 and 11.

14. Pastor, *Campesinos y Reformas*, 420–425. The quotes are on pages 421 and 423–424. Pastor's argument is based in part on a misreading of the laws passed after independence, explained in Guardino, *Time of Liberty*, 230. Among the works that have contributed to the new understanding of Oaxaca are Sánchez Silva, *Indios, comerciantes y burocracia*, and Guardino, *Time of Liberty*. More similar to Pastor is the work of Marcello Carmagnani, which argues for a "second conquest" of the Oaxacan indígenas in the nineteenth century; he, however, sees this process as beginning later, after 1846 (Carmagnani, *El regreso de los dioses*, 230–238).

15. Manuel Megía to Don Diego Antonio González, Oct. 20, 1820, INAH, AHM, O, AJT, Roll 33.

16. Mar. 29, 1821, "Erección de Ayuntamientos en los Pueblos de . . . ," INAH, AHM, O, AJT, Roll 33.

17. Mar. 10–Apr. 3, 1821, "Creación del Ayuntamiento de los Pueblos de S. Juan, S. Andres de la Laguna, y S. Pedro Mártir Yucunama," INAH, AHM, O, AJT, Roll 33. For a similar arrangement, see March 21–23, 1821, "Creación del Ayuntamiento de los Pueblos Unidos de San Francisco Nuzaña, Magdalena y San Pedro Tidaa de la Doctrina de Tilantongo," INAH, AHM, O, AJT, Roll 33.

18. This was markedly *not* the case in Villa Alta, where towns were dealt with as individual entities (Chance, *Conquest of the Sierra*, 75; Guardino, "'Me ha cabido en la fatalidad': Gobierno indígena y gobierno republicano en los pueblos indígenas: Oaxaca, 1750–1850," *Desacatos* 5 [2000]: 122).

19. Apr. 7–12, 1821, "Sobre que el Pueblo de S. Antonio Monteverde quiere separarse del de S. Marcos, y unirse al Ayuntamiento del de Chilapilla que es su Cavecera," INAH, AHM, O, AJT, Roll 33.

20. Governador y demas oficiales de República del Pueblo de San Francisco Nuzaña, no date, in "Creación del Ayuntamiento de los Pueblos unidos de San Francisco Nuzaña . . . ," INAH, AHM, O, AJT, Roll 33.

21. April 26, 1821, INAH, AHM, O, AJT, Roll 33.

22. March 21, 1821, INAH, AHM, O, AJT, Roll 33.

23. Aguilar, March 10, 1821, in "Creación del Ayuntamiento de los Pueblos de S. Juan, S. Andrés de la Laguna, y S. Pedro Mártir Yucunama," INAH, AHM, O, AJT, Roll 33.

24. República de Yucunama in "Creación del Ayuntamiento de los Pueblos de S. Juan, S. Andrés de la Laguna, y S. Pedro Mártir Yucunama," INAH, AHM, O, AJT, Roll 33. The term *vecino* denoted someone who inhabited a town and participated in its activities. It was also often used specifically to mean *nonindigenous* townspeople in colonial Mexico. But I have found that in many cases, both nonindígenas and indígenas used the term to describe *all* villagers. In this particular case, for example, the term was used by indigenous authorities to refer to indigenous villagers.

25. El Governador y demas oficiales de república del Pueblo de San Pedro Tidáa, no date, in "Creación del Ayuntamiento de los Pueblos Unidos de San Francisco Nuzaña . . . ," INAH, AHM, O, AJT, Roll 33.

26. El Governador y demas oficiales de República del Pueblo de San Francisco Nuzaña, no date, in "Creación de los Pueblos Unidos de San Francisco Nuzaña . . . ," INAH, AHM, O, AJT, Roll 33.

27. Aguilar, Mar. 10, 1821, in "Sobre que se crie Ayuntamiento en el Pueblo de San Bartolomé Soyaltepec," INAH, AHM, O, AJT, Roll 33.

28. There were certainly villages left out of this process, especially very small ones. In Villa Alta, where almost no villages reached the 1,000 mark, Guardino estimates that over 100 villages did not make the transition from colonial república to constitutional ayuntamiento (Guardino, *Time of Liberty*, 230).

29. Francisco Rendón to Diputación Provincial, Nov. 4, 1820, "El Yntendente de Oaxaca haciendo varios consultas sobre elecciones," AGN, A, vol. 183. This is not dissimilar to the process by which Oaxacan villagers accommodated various ethnicities within a town by formally alternating groups in power positions or by formally splitting those positions among the ethnicities (Carmagnani, "Local Governments and Ethnic Government," 112).

30. See Pastor's description of the election of the ayuntamiento of Tlaxiaco in 1821 (Pastor, *Campesinos y Reformas*, 423–424).

31. Joaquín Péres to Juan Ygnacio de Eyzaguirre, Sept. 20, 1823, "El Yntendente de Oaxaca haciendo varios consultas sobre elecciones," AGN, A, vol. 183; Ricos Bermúdez to Intendent of Oaxaca, Oct. 21, 1820, "El Yntendente de Oaxaca haciendo varios consultas sobre elecciones," AGN, A, vol. 183; and Francisco Rendón to Diputación Provincial, Nov. 4, 1820, "El Yntendente de Oaxaca haciendo varios consultas sobre elecciones," AGN, A, vol. 183.

32. Rugeley, *Yucatán's Maya Peasantry*, 34.

33. Farriss, *Maya Society*, 105–106; Patch, *Maya and Spaniard*, 232–240; and Restall, *Maya World*, 16. Hernández Chávez identifies the chance to usurp indigenous power as the fundamental element of attraction of the ayuntamiento for mestizos, those *"orillados y avecindados"* who had been previously left out, and suggests that participation in the ayuntamientos, for these people, could function as an alternative to participation in the wars of independence. The process Hernández Chávez posits, in which the ayuntamientos "almost definitively [eliminated] the extant division between indigenous and Spanish cabildos" and became "interethnic" did not, however, occur in Yucatán, as this chapter details (Hernández Chávez, *La tradición republicana*, 23–25).

34. Rugeley, *Yucatán's Maya Peasantry*, 45–46; Bellingeri, "Las ambigüedades del voto," 253. Bellingeri found that out of forty-six new ayuntamientos, twenty-one had at least one Maya member, with two towns electing Maya alcaldes. Using names as an indication of ethnicity is by no means a foolproof method. Whenever possible, I have depended on self-identification, which fortunately occurred with some frequency. Also fortunately, the correspondence of Maya surnames and indigenous civil status seems to have held quite firm in Yucatán. Don E. Dumond established that in the very early nineteenth century, "of men in the legal and taxable category of Indian, 22 or four-tenths of 1 percent have Spanish names; of those legally *vecinos*, 106 or nearly 8 percent have Indian names. Put another way, of men with Indian names, nearly 1.8 percent are *vecinos*, while of men with Spanish names the same percentage are legally taxed as Indians. In demonstrating this relatively small overlap, the figures . . . lend credence to the Yucatecan expectation that civil status could be predicted on the basis simply of the paternal surname. For with any given male of Indian name the chance was only about one

in 55 that he would not be a legal Indian, and for a male with a Spanish name the chance is almost exactly the same that he would not be a *vecino"* (Don E. Dumond, *The Machete and the Cross: Campesino Rebellion in Yucatán* (Lincoln: University of Nebraska Press, 1997), 41–43).

35. "Comunicando a la Diputacion Provincial la instalación de ayuntamientos en Sahcabchén y Chicbul, pueblos de esa cabecera, 1813," AGEY, Col., Ayuntamientos, vol. 1, exp. 11, and "Expediente promovido por los vecinos para probar que dicho pueblo reune las condiciones para tener Ayuntamiento, 1813," AGEY, Col., Ayuntamientos, vol. 1, exp. 7a. For population percentages, see "Non-Indians in the Villages of Yucatan, 1777–91," Appendix B in Patch, *Maya and Spaniard*, 259–263, unless otherwise noted.

36. "Acta de instalación del Ayuntamiento, 1813," AGEY, Col., Ayuntamientos, vol. 1, exp. 16. In modern Yucatán, there are two towns with similar names, Tahdzibichén and Tandzibichén. Patch has records for only the former, and those are the numbers I am using, based on the presumption that the other town's foundation dates from a later period. This presumption is supported by the existence of a 1655 encomienda at the site of the former town, known as "Tacchebilchen," which was the spelling used in the AGEY document (Gerhard, *The Southeast Frontier*, 86).

37. Feb. 6, 1814, CAIHY, CCCA, LM, Libro de Acuerdos de la municipalidad de Ucú, 1814–1824. Santos Chan, with a Spanish paternal name and a Maya maternal name, could easily have been mestizo as well.

38. For cases involving land, see "Representación del Ayuntamiento del pueblo del Hampolon . . . , Julio 10 de 1822"; "Sobre el perjuicio que reciben los labradores con el ganado . . . , Abril 21 de 1823"; "Expediente promovido por don Francisco Polanco, natural y vecino de Cenotillo . . . , Mayo 26 de 1823"; "Expediente promovido por Dn. José María Andrade, vecino de Cenotillo . . . , Mayo 26 de 1823"; and "Concediendo la propiedad del pozo Ixtepal . . . , Septiembre 2 de 1823," AGEY, PE, T, vol. 1, exps. 4, 7, 8, 9, 11. See also "Instrucciones a Dn. Francisco Genaro Cicero, subdelegado del partido de la Costa . . . , sin fecha," AGEY, PE, A, vol. 1, exp. 5 and "Presupuesto de obras presentado por el Ayuntamiento de Tenabo . . . , Septiembre 9 de 1823," AGEY, PE, A, vol. 1, exp. 9.

39. "Representación del Ayuntamiento del pueblo de Hampolon . . . , Julio 10 de 1822," AGEY, PE, T, vol. 1, exp. 4.

40. Rugeley, *Yucatán's Maya Peasantry*, 45 and Escobar Ohmstede, "Del gobierno indígena al Ayuntamiento constitucional," 12. Rugeley does note some instances in which indigenous villagers took advantage of the reforms to reject repúblicas that they saw as exploitative; it seems likely, though, that these were complaints against those particular repúblicas, not against the notion of the república in general.

41. "Cuenta de cargo y data de la Contribución Patriótica en el pueblo de Hoctun . . . , Septiembre 20 de 1822," AGEY, PE, A, vol. 1, exp. 4, and "Concediendo la propiedad del pozo Xtepal . . . , Septiembre 2 de 1823," AGEY, PE, T, vol. 1, exp. 11.

42. Bellingeri, "Las ambigüedades del voto," 276.

43. "Representación del Ayuntamiento a la Diputación Provincial, solicitando el repartimiento de las tierras comunales, 1818," AGEY, Col., Ayuntamientos, vol. 1, exp. 6.

44. Rugeley, *Yucatán's Maya Peasantry*, 40–57.

45. "Representación de Fray Pedro Guzman, cura de Vayma, sobre la conducta observada por los indios al otorgarles su libertad la Constitución," AGEY, Col., Varios, vol. 1, exp. 18.

46. The text of the questionnaire was as follows: "Tell me how much the Parochial fees amount to in [the pueblos] in your charge, those that were charged from January first to the end of December of last year, and those that remain to be paid, and if there are some that have not been paid the motives that have impeded their collection; [tell me also] if some Yndios are absent in the wilderness and ranchos or have come down from the Haciendas to live in the town [*en poblado*], and of those moved there how many attend Mass and *Doctrina*, if the Lamp in your Residence remains and how you maintain it, if the Churches are well-served, if the Casa Cural also has some service and how you acquire it, and if there is someone who is seducing the people, if he is from the same area or another" (Jose Gmo. Espinola, May 25, 1814, Carol Steichen Dumond and Don E. Dumond, eds., *Demography and Parish Affairs in Yucatán 1797–1897: Documents from the Archivo de la Mitra Emeritense, Selected by Joaquín de Arrigunaga Peón*, University of Oregon Anthropological Papers no. 27 [Eugene: Department of Anthropology, University of Oregon, 1982], 380). This letter is a copy, sent by a priest to his *tenientes*.

47. Don Juan Pio Albarado y Dominguez, Mar. 10, 1814; Br. Bart.e Jose Granado Baeza, Mar. 5, 1814, Dumond and Dumond, eds., *Demography and Parish Affairs*, 444; 450. The wording of these two letters is very nearly the same, suggesting the two *curas* may have been using a template or stock letter.

48. Rugeley, *Yucatán's Maya Peasantry*, 43–44.

49. Fernando Rosado to Francisco Bravo, Feb. 4, 1814, Dumond and Dumond, eds., *Demography and Parish Affairs*, 363–364; Josef Gmo. Espinola to Lorenzo de Castro, Jun 1, 1814, Dumond and Dumond, eds., *Demography and Parish Affairs*, 379–381.

50. Feb. 25 and May 12, 1814; CAIHY, CCCA, LM, Libro de Acuerdos de la municipalidad de Ucú, 1814–1824.

51. "Representación de Fray Pedro Guzman, cura de Vayma, sobre la conducta observada por los indios al otorgarles su libertad la Constitución," AGEY, Col., Varios, vol. 1, exp. 18.

52. "Representación de Ceferino Domínguez, Alcalde de Nohcacab, sobre la conducta delictuosa de unos indios, 1813," AGEY, Col., Varios, vol. 1, exp. 17.

53. Antonio Annino, "Cádiz y la revolución territorial," 177; 209–210. See also Hernández Chávez, *La tradición republicana*, 28–38.

NOTES TO CHAPTER 3

1. For accounts and analysis of the rebellion in Tehuantepec, see Chassen-López, *From Liberal to Revolutionary Oaxaca*, 315–327; Brian Hamnett, *Juárez* (London: Longman, 1994), 40–45; Howard Campbell, *Zapotec Renaissance: Ethnic*

Politics and Cultural Revivalism in Southern Mexico (Alburquerque: University of New Mexico Press, 1994), 37–43; Francisco M. Abardía and Leticia Reina, "Cien años de rebelion," in *Lecturas históricas del estado de Oaxaca. Volumen III. Siglo XIX*, ed. María de los Angeles Romero Frizzi (Mexico City: Instituto Nacional de Antropología e Historia and Gobierno del Estado de Oaxaca, 1990), 457–469; John Tutino, "Rebelión indígena en Tehuantepec," *Cuadernos Políticos* 24 (1980): 94–99 and "Ethnic Resistance: Juchitán in Mexican History," in *Zapotec Struggles: Histories, Politics, and Representations from Juchitán, Oaxaca*, ed. Howard Campbell, Leigh Binford, Miguel Bartolomé, and Alicia Barabas (Washington, DC: Smithsonian Institution Press, 1993), 53–58; and Víctor de la Cruz, "Rebeliones indígenas en el Istmo de Tehuantepec," *Cuadernos Políticos* 38 (1983): 64–67 and "La rebelión del Che Gorio Melendre," in *Oaxaca. Textos de su historia, II*, ed. Margarita Dalton (Mexico City: Instituto de Investigaciones Dr. José María Luis Mora and Gobierno del Estado de Oaxaca, 1990), 371–394. For documents on local events in Juchitán in 1849 and 1850, see Benito Juárez, *Esposición que en cumplimiento del Art. 83 de la constitución del Estado hace el Gobernador del mismo al noveno congreso constitucional al abrir el primer periodo de sus sesiones ordinarias, el día 2 de julio de 1850* (Oaxaca, Mexico: Ignacio Rincón, 1850), INAH, CGO, Vol. 26, 12.

2. In the words of one historian, the rebellion represented "the eruption of foreign elements originating from nascent Mexican capitalism" (De la Cruz, "La rebelión del Che Gorio Melendre," 393).

3. Chassen-López, *From Liberal to Revolutionary Oaxaca*, 337. The first, a tax revolt in the Mixteca in the mid-1840s, was intimately associated with events in neighboring states; its origins were not primarily Oaxacan. And the Isthmian wars resulted from a combination of circumstances unique within Oaxaca, including relative geographical and demographic unity and the relatively advanced nature of capitalist agriculture on the isthmus. For the tax revolt, see Guardino, *Peasants, Politics*, 147–177. For riots and revolts in colonial Oaxaca, see Taylor, *Drinking, Homicide, and Rebellion*, esp. 113–151. For a study of unrest in Oaxaca during the nineteenth century, see Abardía and Reina, "Cien años de rebelión," 435–492.

4. The quote is from Clarke, *Class, Ethnicity, and Community*, 27–28. Clarke suggests that this occurred because of the collapse of the cochineal and cotton economies; his interpretation, however, assumes that market-based economic activity was the only impetus for contact with the state.

5. Sánchez Silva, *Indios, comerciantes y burocracia*, 55, 217–218. "Los poseedores de la riqueza" is the title of chapter three. For more on the fall in the price of cochineal, see Clarke, *Class, Ethnicity, and Community*, 28; and Baskes, *Indians, Merchants, and Markets*, 185–188. By the 1820s, Oaxaca had been superseded by Guatemala as the primary producer of cochineal for European markets. On the decline of cotton in Villa Alta in particular, see Guardino, *Time of Liberty*, 225–226.

6. José María Murguía y Galardi, Governor of Oaxaca, AHMO, AC, Aug. 20, 1824.

7. The other states that installed their own legislatures were Yucatán, Jalisco, and Zacatecas (Jaime E. Rodríguez O., "La constitución de 1824 y la formación del

estado mexicano," *Historia Mexicana* 40:3 (1991): 520). Oaxaca declared itself to be a free state on July 28, 1823, in the "Bases Provisionales," in which the state pegged its eventual participation in the Mexican republic to federalism. For the Oaxacan laws, see "Bases Provisionales," "Ley orgánica para el gobierno del estado libre de Oaxaca," and "Constitución particular del estado de Oaxaca" in Gustavo Pérez Jiménez, ed., *Las constituciones del estado de Oaxaca*, ([Mexico City]: Ediciones Técnicas Jurídicas del Gobierno de Oaxaca, [1959], 32–34, 42–58, and 71–103. The quote from the *Ley orgánica* is on 51. For a narrative of the process of independence in Oaxaca, see Jorge Fernando Iturribarría, *Historia de Oaxaca, 1821–1854: De la consumación de la independencia a la iniciación de la reforma* (Oaxaca, Mexico: Ediciones E.R.B., 1935), 7–58.

8. "Constitución particular del estado de Oaxaca," 42–58. For a discussion of how the failure to consider this provision affects Rodolfo Pastor's interpretation of municipal politics, see Guardino, *Time of Liberty*, 230.

9. "Se prescriben las condiciones necesarias para el establecimiento de ayuntamientos y repúblicas en los pueblos del estado," Jan. 25, 1825, and "Ley que arregla el gobierno económico de los departamentos y pueblos del estado," Mar. 13, 1825, *Colección de leyes y decretos del estado libre de Oaxaca* (Oaxaca: Imprenta del Estado, en el Ex-Obispado, 1879), 106–109; 206–212.

10. "Se prescriben las condiciones."

11. Chassen-López, *From Liberal to Revolutionary Oaxaca*, 301.

12. "Noticia de los Pueblos comprehendidos en la demarcación . . . ," Mar. 27, 1837, AGEO, G, GD, Tehuantepec, Estadística (This is a copy of a report that was first done in April. The original does not put an ayuntamiento in Guichicovi, but the copy does.); Feb. 23, 1837, AGEO, G, GD, Teotitlán; "Division y arreglo de los partidos que componen el estado libre de Oaxaca," May 6, 1826, *Colección de leyes . . . de Oaxaca*, 256–296; 1826, INAH, AHM, O, AMT, Roll 4. Another document in this collection reports 153 towns in Teposcolula, the vast majority of which reported fewer than 500 townspeople (INAH, AHM, O, AMT, Roll 33). For a discussion of the proliferation of municipalities in Oaxaca in this era as compared to other states, see Guardino, *Time of Liberty*, 230–231. For an overview of the forms of pueblo administration in postindependence Oaxaca, see Ronald Spores, "Relaciones gubernamentales y judiciales entre los pueblos, los distritos y el estado en Oaxaca (siglo XIX)," in *Lecturas históricas del estado*, ed. Romero Frizzi, 239–289.

13. Nicolás Fernández to Secretario del Despacho Universal del Estado, May 3, 1829, AGEO, G, GD, Villa Alta, Elecciones; José María Pando to State Governor, 1830, AGEO, G, GD, Zoochila, Elecciones.

14. For the cargo system in Oaxaca, see Guardino, *Time of Liberty*, 50–56, and Chance, *Conquest of the Sierra*, 132–137. For the Mixteca in particular, see Terraciano, 191–195, and for Mexico see Chance and Taylor, "Cofradías and Cargos," 14–17. For a discussion of the "youth movement," see Guardino, *Time of Liberty*, 234–235. After independence, the law on repúblicas determined that all men in exercise of their rights as citizens could vote; the constitution determined that this meant males over twenty-one or over eighteen if married ("Constitución particular del estado de Oaxaca"; "Se prescriben las condiciones necesarias . . .").

15. "Se prescriben las condiciones necesarias. . . ." If anything, the group of electors was smaller; after independence, the number of final decision-makers was to be three times that of the number of councilmen to be elected. In colonial Villa Alta, according to Chance, "the number of nobles eligible to vote could be large. . . . In 1816, it ranged from lows of seventeen and eighteen in Yojovi and Yaviche to highs of fifty to fifty-nine in Choapan and Yovego" (Chance, *Conquest of the Sierra*, 134).

16. Chance, *Conquest of the Sierra*, 137–146; Pastor, *Campesinos y Reformas*, 201–208; Terraciano, *Mixtecs*, 195–197.

17. Guardino, *Time of Liberty*, 238; "Sobre la nulidad de elección municipal del pueblo de Santa María Roaló, Dec. 26, 1831–Feb. 11, 1833, AGEO, G, GD, Centro; Dec. 16–24, 1831, "Diligencias practicadas sobre anular una junta parroquial," INAH, AHM, O, AJT, Roll 26. For Villa Alta, Guardino suggests that the principales continued to act as advisors in village governments well into the 1840s (Guardino, *Time of Liberty*, 242).

18. See, for example, República Constitucional de Santos Reyes Suchiquilasola, Jan. 16, 1826, AGEO, G, GD, Silacayoapam; and Jose Vernardo to Subprefect of Tlacolula, Sept. 22, 1831, AGEO, G, GD, Tlacolula.

19. For examples of violent interpueblo disputes, see Apr. 28–June 18, 1823, "Criminal, por heridas que resultaron del Tumulto que formó el Pueblo de Magdalena del Peñasco contra el de San Agustin Tlacotepeque, ambos de esta Jurisdicción de Teposcolula," INAH, AHM, O, AJT, Roll 20; Ignacio Antonio Ojeda to State Vice-Governor, June 6, Apr. 19, Apr. 24, and Apr. 28, 1826, AGEO, G, GD, Tehuantepec; Vicente Castellejos to State Governor, Dec. 30, 1826, AGEO, G, GD, Yanhuitlan; and Mariano Conde to Secretario del Despacho Universal del Estado, Aug. 31, 1827, AGEO, G, GD. Out of 214 land disputes between 1770 and 1830, 109 were town versus town, with the rest distributed among town versus hacienda, individual versus individual, town versus cacique, measurements of lands, recognitions of cacicazgos, and cacique versus cacique (Reina, "De las reformas borbónicas a las leyes de reforma," 209).

20. 1825–1827, "Expediente sobre tierras entre los Pueblos de Xicotlan, Tulansingo, Santiago las Plumas, y San Francisco Tiapam, ó el Casique de estos Pueblos Don Bonifacio Pimentel," INAH, AHM, O, AJT, Roll 24; 1832, "La Republica del Pueblo de la Consepcion Buenavista solicita se le ampare en posecion de los terrenos que se haya despojado por el común de Santiago Plumas," INAH, AHM, O, AJT, Roll 30; Vicente Rodríguez, Jefe de Policía of Plumas, to Departmental Governor, Nov. 30, 1844, AGEO, G, GD, Centro.

21. For examples, see Aug. 31, 1825, "Espediente en Testimonio sobre despojo de tierras entre San Juan Ixcaltepeque y San Bartolomé Sotula de esta Jurisdicción de Teposcolula"; 1830, "Espediente que la República del Pueblo de Santiago Nexapilla del Partido de Nochistlán sigue contra la del Pueblo de Yodocono de este Partido sobre introducción de tierras y otros ecsesos"; 1832, "Diligencias de Información dada por el apoderado del Pueblo de San Pedro Nopala sobre despojo de terrenos y cansamiento de ganados inferidos por los del de Santiago Teotongo ambos de este partido"; 1836, "Información producida por la República del Pueblo de San Miguel Tizá sobre provar el despojo que le he inferido en sus

terrenos, el de la Magdalena Canadaltepeque," INAH, AHM, O, AJT, Roll 26; and 1840, "Sobre tierras entre el pueblo de San Juan Teposcolula y el de Tejupan," INAH, AHM, O, AJT, Roll 29.

22. Aug. 3, 1835, AGEO, G, GD, Centro.

23. Manuel José Schiafino Norutia, Feb. 26, 1826, AGEO, G, GD, Huajuapan. There were some "towns" that did *not* gain their independence under the new federalist laws. Communities that were considered to be "barrios" of larger settlements and some agricultural settlements known as ranchos or haciendas continued to depend on other towns for administration and judicial services. That these communities often considered themselves to be separate, however, would be a constant source of conflict and a constant subject for petitions to the state each time the system changed and new opportunities presented themselves, as this and the following chapter show.

24. Miguel Antonio Rojas to Departmental Governor, Mar. 24, 1827, AGEO, G, GD, Teotitlán, Juzgado de Primera Instancia; Mariano Conde to Secretario del Despacho Universal del Estado, Aug. 31, 1827, AGEO, G, GD, Tehuantepec.

25. Francisco Casimiro Morales, etc., to Departmental Governor, Jan. 1834, AGEO, G, GD, Huajuapan.

26. Ayuntamiento of Tlacolula, Aug. 2, 1831, AGEO, G, GD, Tlacolula.

27. José María Murguía y Galardi, Governor of Oaxaca, AHMO, AC, Aug. 20, 1824.

28. Sebastián de la Cruz to Francisco Estevez, Jul. 6, 1825; Pascual de Najeza, Jul. 24, 1825, AGEO, G, GD, Jamiltepec; José María Pando to Ramón Ramírez de Aguilar, Aug. 26, 1831; José María Pando to Secretario del Despacho Universal del Estado, Nov. 8, 1831; AGEO, G, GD, Zoochila, Justicia; Jimenes to Prefect of Teposcolula, Sept. 6 and Sept. 13, 1839; INAH, AHM, O, AJT, Roll 31.

29. The quotation is from the town of Calihualá, in Manuel José Schiafino to Secretario del Despacho Universal del Estado, Aug. 14, 1827, AGEO, G, GD, Huajuapan. This town requested land again in 1831, (AGEO, G, GD, Centro. See also the example of Juchatengo, in José María Regules to Secretario del Despacho Universal del Estado, Sept. 6, 1831, AGEO, G, GD, Centro, in which the *república* requested particular *baldío* plots because the town's own land was infertile.

30. Antonio Salbador de Vargas to Prefect of Villa Alta, Oct. 15, 1840, AGEO, G, GD, Villa Alta, Tranquilidad Pública.

31. "Ley para el arreglo y cobro de la contribución personal que antes se ha llamado capitación," AHMO, AC, Aug. 20, 1824; "Ley que reglamenta la contribución personal del estado," Sept. 28, 1826, in *Colección de leyes . . . de Oaxaca*, Appendix, 55–62. The latter of these two laws stipulated that the tax would be based *either* on property or on income, broadly understood. This law would remain in effect until the implementation of the national capitación in 1841.

32. Ignacio de Larraz., May 7, 1830, AGEO, G, GD, Teotitlán, Contribución Personal. See a similar report from Huajuapan, Miguel Castaneyra to Secretario del Gobierno del Estado, July 8, 1831, AGEO, G, GD, Huajuapan, Juzgado de 1a Instancia; June 4, 1835, AGEO, G, GD, Ejutla, Contribuciones; June 16, 1835, AGEO, G, GD, Tehuantepec, Contribuciones. See also complaints from Jamiltepec and Teposcolula, José María Parada to Secretario del Despacho Universal

del Estado, Mar. 11, 1835, AGEO, G, GD, Jamiltepec, Contribuciones; Ygnacio Suárez to Secretario del Despacho Universal del Estado, AGEO, G, GD, Teposcolula, Juzgado de 1a Instancia.

33. Technically, others could be included in the committee that determined who owed what, but in practice the decisions usually fell to the municipal officers alone. The 1824 tax code specified a "*junta de clasificación*" composed of three members of the república or ayuntamiento, the priest, "the most experienced employee in rents," a merchant, and a farmer, depending on the productive structure of the town in question. In 1826, a new law expressed it in the following rather confusing way: The juntas clasificadoras could include "two individuals from inside or outside" of the junta itself. The farmer should have "the necessary property and knowledge," and the merchant and state employee were included only if they were available, which, in most Oaxacan towns, they were not ("Ley para el arreglo y cobro de la contribución personal que antes se ha llamado capitación," AHMO, AC, Aug. 20, 1824; "Ley que reglamenta la contribución personal del estado," Sept. 28, 1826, in *Colección de leyes . . . de Oaxaca*, Appendix, 55–62). For examples of the documentation produced, see the *estados de clasificación* included in 1829, AGEO, G, GD, Juquila.

34. José Mariano Valle to State Governor, Apr. 1, Apr. 3, and Oct. 6, 1827, AGEO, G, GD, Teotitlán.

35. "Sobre la acusación que el Juez de primera Instancia del Partido de Teposcolula hace contra el Ayuntamiento . . . ," June 22, 1824, AGEO, G, GD, Centro; José Mantecón, June 5, 1832, AGEO, G, GD, Tehuantepec, Estadística; José María Pando, Mar. 6, 1840, AGEO, G, GD, Villa Alta, Estadística. For the role of the subprefects, see "Ley que arregla el gobierno económico de los departamentos y pueblos del estado," *Colección de leyes . . . de Oaxaca*, 214–217. Essentially, both subprefects and departmental governors were enjoined to make sure that the pueblos followed the tax laws.

36. José María Herrera to various pueblos, Sept. 25, 1829, AGEO, G, GD, Teotitlán, Contribución Personal; Mariano Conde to Secretaria de Gobierno, Nov. 1, 1829, AGEO, G, GD, Tehuantepec, Contribución Personal.

37. "Decreto sobre la ley que reglamenta la contribución personal del estado del 28 de septiembre de 1826," cited in Sánchez Silva, *Indios, comerciantes y burocracia*, 120; Aug. 3–Dec. 24, 1836, INAH, AHM, O, AJT, Roll 26.

38. Manuel José Schiafino Norutia to State Governor, Feb. 17, 1826, AGEO, G, GD, Huajuapan, Contribución Personal; Ramón Ramírez de Aguilar to Secretario del Despacho Universal del Estado, July 6, 1829, AGEO, G, GD, Centro.

39. See, among numerous others, República of San Martín el Real to Governor, Dec. 25, 1825, AGEO, G, GD, Silacayoapam; República of Santiago [Tinoc], 1825, AGEO, G, GD, Centro; República of San Pedro Martir, Dec. 31, 1825, and República of Santa María, 1825, AGEO, G, GD, Huajuapan.

40. Miguel Billagomes, Alcalde of Santos Reyes Michiapa, Dec. 12, 1825, AGEO, G, GD, Huajuapan; Martín de la Cruz, Alcalde of Santiago Cuicoyán, Feb. 2, 1826; Antonio Gaspar, Alcalde of Santiago Yucuyache, Jan. 1, 1826; and Andres Miguel, Alcalde of San Miguel Peras, 1826, AGEO, G, GD, Silacayoapam.

41. Paulino Antonio, Alcalde of Huautla, to Juez de Primera Instancia, Mar. 21, 1827, AGEO, G, GD, Teotitlán, Juzgado de Primera Instancia; Manuel González, Alcalde of Santa María Ecatepec, to Departmental Governor, Dec. 17, 1827, AGEO, G, GD, Tehuantepec, Contribuciones.

42. República of Tuxtepec to State Governor, Feb. 13, 1848, AGEO, G, GD, Centro.

43. Alcaldes of Nisaviquiti, Agua Blanca, Santiago Tilotepec, San Sebastián Tilotepec, Santa Cruz Tilotepec, San Pedro Tilotepec, and Lachizonase, Feb. 6, 1848; Faustino Rodríguez to Subprefect of Yautepec, Feb. 7, 1848, AGEO, G, GD, Yautepec.

44. Juan Pedro Martínez to Subprefect of Ocotlan, Oct. 27, 1840, AGEO, G, GD, Ocotlan, Subprefectura de Ejutla; Juez de Paz and Corporación of Tepelmeme to Subprefect of Coixtlahuaca, Aug. 28, 1839; "Lista de Ciudadanos de este Pueblo de Santo Domingo Tepelmeme que esistan y estan pagando el ramo de Contribución personal y la Yguala del Presente Año de mil ochocientos treinta y nueve," Nov. 7, 1839, INAH, AHM, AJT, Roll 31. For documents concerning the famine in this region, see Juez de Paz and Auxiliares of Concepción, 1839; Juez de Paz of Concepción to Subprefect of Coixtlahuaca, Aug. 12, 1839; Carrizola to Prefect of Teposcolula, Sept. 5 and 9, 1839; Oct. 20, 1839, INAH, AHM, O, AJT, Roll 31.

45. José María Pando to Secretario del Gobierno del Estado, Jul. 8, 1831, AGEO, G, GD, Zoochila, Comunicados; José María Pando to Secretario del Superior Gobierno del Departmento, Feb. 17, 1836, AGEO, G, GD, Zoochila, Contribución Personal; José María Parada to Secretario del Despacho Universal del Estado, Mar. 11, 1835, AGEO, G, GD, Jamiltepec, Contribuciones; Jimenes to Prefect of Teposcolula, Aug. 18 and 29, 1839, INAH, AHM, O, AJT, Roll 31. For other examples, see Santos de Vera to Comandante General and Juez Político de Provincia, April 19, 1823; Santos de Vera to Jefe Político del Estado, Sept. 13, 1823; AGEO, G, GD, Miahuatlán; and Manuel de Loaeza to State Vice Governor, Jan. 20, 1829, AGEO, G, GD, Jamiltepec, Alcabalas.

46. Junta Departamental, Apr. 24, 1840; Junta Departamental, Aug. 13, 1841; and Cámara de Diputados, Nov. 10, 1834, AGEO, G, GD, Centro.

47. Costeloe, *The Central Republic in Mexico*, 132–133, 163; Guardino, *Peasants, Politics*, 101. For the text of the laws, see "Se establece una contribución personal," Apr. 26, 1841; and "Contribución llamada 'derecho de capitación,'" Apr. 7, 1842, Manuel Dublán and José María Lozano, *Legislación mexicana, ó colección completa de las disposiciones expedidas desde la independencia de la república*, Vol. 4 (Mexico City: Imprenta del Comercio, á Cargo de Dublán y Lozano, Hijos, 1876), 11–21, 147–150.

48. By some accounts, this money did not remain in Oaxaca after all. The departmental government in 1844 complained that the capitación had thus far been usurped by the federal government rather than going to interior departmental costs (Asamblea Departamental, Apr. 2, 1844, AGEO, G, GD, Centro).

49. Camacho to Departmental Governor, June 24, 1841, AGEO, G, GD, Villa Alta, Contribución Personal.

50. Marcelo Herrera to Secretario del Supremo Gobierno del Estado, May 29, 1829, AGEO, G, GD, Teposcolula, Contribución Personal; Camacho to Departmental Governor, June 24, 1841, AGEO, G, GD, Villa Alta, Contribución Personal; Governor of Tehuantepec to Secretario del Despacho, Feb. 13, 1848, AGEO, G, GD, Tehuantepec.

51. Nicolás Fernández to Secretario del Despacho, May 12, 1848, AGEO, G, GD, Villa Alta, Decretos.

52. Juan Martín, Alcalde of Mitla, to Subprefect of Tlacolula, Oct. 1831, and Domingo Lópes, Alcalde of San Juan del Río, to Subprefect of Tlacolula, Oct. 18, 1831.

53. Sept. 16, 1854, AHMO, DGM, 580–584.

54. William A. Depalo Jr., *The Mexican National Army, 1822–1852* (College Station: Texas A&M University Press, 1997), 30–31, 74, 89; "Sorteo General para reemplazar las bajas del ejército," Jan. 26, 1839, Manuel Dublán and José María Lozano, *Legislación mexicana, ó colección completa de las disposiciones expedidas desde la independencia de la república*, Vol. 3 (Mexico City: Imprenta del Comercio, á Cargo de Dublán y Lozano, Hijos, 1876), 582–589; "Arreglo de la milicia local," Dec. 29, 1827, Manuel Dublán and José María Lozano, *Legislación mexicana o colección completa de las disposiciones legislativas expedidas desde la independencia de la república*, Vol. 1 (Mexico City: Imprenta del Comercio, á Cargo de Dublán y Lozano, Hijos, 1876), 49–51.

55. "Primera parte del reglamento para la milicia cívica del estado, Aug. 20, 1828, *Colección de leyes . . . de Oaxaca*, Appendix, 91–110.

56. Guardino, *Time of Liberty*, 253–254; the quote is from 253.

57. Guardino writes that in early nineteenth-century Guerrero militias had no trouble recruiting members, "because of the perceived need to defend the region's coastline and its high degree of mobilization in the War of Independence" (Guardino, *Peasants, Politics*, 88). By midcentury, the attitude toward militias in Oaxaca would change to some extent, when the National Guard units established by Benito Juárez would be called on to defend the liberal state. This process is detailed in McNamara, *Sons of the Sierra*, and is discussed in the conclusion to this book.

58. For examples of these lists, see Mariano Toro to Departmental Governor, Apr. 11, 1828; Visente Gómez to Departmental Governor, Apr. 3, 1828; Juan Santos García to Departmental Governor, Apr. 1, 1828; AGEO, G, GD, Jamiltepec, Congreso; Varios, 1828, AGEO, G, GD, Jamiltepec, Milicia Civica.

59. Felipe de León to Secretario del Despacho Universal del Estado, Sept. 2, 1829, AGEO, G, GD, Huajuapan, Remplazos; José María Pando to Secretario del Superior Gobierno del Departamento, AGEO, G, GD, Zoochila; José María Pando to Secretario del Despacho, May 31, 1839, AGEO, G, GD, Villa Alta, Decretos; Manuel Cortiz, May 9, 1838, AGEO, G, GD, Tlacolula, Subprefectura del Centro; Camacho, Jan. 18, 1842, AGEO, G, GD, Villa Alta, Remplazos; José Mantecon to Secretario del Despacho, AGEO, G, GD, Teotitlán, Remplazos.

60. AHMO, AC, Sept. 16, 1824; Juan Pablo Anaya, June 3, 1830, AGEO, G, GD, Centro; José Mantecón to Secretario del Despacho, July 14, 1839, AGEO, G, GD, Teotitlán, Estadística.

61. Mariano Conde to State Governor, Aug. 18, 1826, AGEO, G, GD, Tehuantepec, Remplazos; Tomás Gallangos to Secretario del Superior Gobierno del Departmento, May 8, 1838, AGEO, G, GD, Jamiltepec, Remplazos.

62. Santos de Vera to Jefe Político del Estado, Sept. 6, 1823, AGEO, G, GD, Miahuatlán.

63. Gregorio Guisado, Apr. 21, 1834, AGEO, G, GD, Nochistlán; José Honorato Rodriguez to Subprefect of Nochistlán, Mar., 1839, INAH, AHM, O, AJT, Roll 31; Juez de Paz of San Baltasar Chuicapam to Subprefect of Ocotlán, Mar. 4, 1838, AGEO, G, GD, Ocotlán, Subprefectura de Ejutla; Marcial Silba to Subprefect of Nochistlán, Mar. 6, 1839, and Mariano Andrés, July 19, 1839, INAH, AHM, O, AJT, Roll 31; José Mantecón, to Secretario del Superior Gobierno del Departmento, Sept. 30, 1836, AGEO, G, GD, Teotitlán, Acontecimientos; José María Pando to Secretario del Superior Gobierno del Departmento, AGEO, G, GD, Zoochila.

64. Miguel Gerónimo, June, 1830; Juan Rey, June, 1830; and Pablo Sánchez, July 22, 1835, AGEO, G, GD, Centro. The state archives are full of such requests. See, for example, files from the Centro and Villa Juárez in 1839 and files from the Centro in 1842, AGEO, G, GD.

65. Diego Pérez, Nov. 28, 1841; Dionisio Favian, 1841, AGEO, G, GD, Centro.

66. Various alcaldes, Jul. 22–28, 1829, AGEO, G, GD, Jamiltepec, Atoyac.

67. Narciso Rojas to Governor, Oct. 3, 1836, AGEO, G, GD, Cuicatlán. The suggestion that abandoned family members would be forced to beg comes from General Francisco Antonio Berdejo, in an attempt to exempt several of his employees in 1838 (Francisco Antonio Berdejo to Governor, May 1, 1838, AGEO, G, GD, Jamiltepec, Remplazos).

68. AHMO, AC, Sept. 16, 1824. De Palo suggests that "by utilizing such coercive measures to fill the ranks, the army came to resemble a large penal institution, a characteristic that did little to enhance its competence and reputation as a legitimate fighting force" (De Palo, *The Mexican National Army*, 31).

69. Gregorio Guisado, Alcalde of Nochistlán, Apr. 21, 1833, AGEO, G, GD, Nochistlán; Juez de Paz of San Baltasar Chuicapam to Subprefect of Ocotlán, Mar. 4, 1838, AGEO, G, GD, Ocotlán, Subprefectura de Ejutla.

70. Victoriano Martín, June 1, 1830; Juan Sárate, June 27, 1830; José Mariano Aguilar, July 2, 1830, and May 10, 1835, AGEO, G, GD, Centro; Juez de Paz of San Pablo Coatlán, Mar. 27, 1842, AGEO, G, GD, Ejutla, Remplazos.

71. Various alcaldes, Jul. 22–28, 1829, AGEO, G, GD, Jamiltepec, Atoyac.

72. Juan Salinas to Prefect of Jamiltepec, Feb. 19, 1842, AGEO, G, GD, Jamiltepec, Jueces de Paz.

73. Baltasar Gómez to Subprefect of Tlacolula, Sept. 17, 1831; Alverto Gutiérrez, Alcalde of Santa María Guelace, to Subprefect of Tlacolula, Nov. 14, 1831; and José Vernardo, Alcalde of San Sebastián Teitipac to Subprefect of Tlacolula, Sept. 22, 1831, AGEO, G, GD, Tlacolula.

74. "Leyes Constitucionales," in Tena Ramírez, ed., *Leyes Fundamentales*, 243–244.

75. "Prevenciones para la renovación de ayuntamientos y establecimiento de jueces de paz," Apr. 24, 1837, Dublán and Lozano, *Legislación mexicana*, III:385–386; José María Parada, July 11, 1837, AGEO, G, GD, Jamiltepec, Jueces de Paz.

76. "Reglamento provisional para el gobierno interior de los Departamentos," Mar. 20, 1837, Dublán and Lozano, *Legislación mexicana*, III:323–338.

77. Juez de Paz of Santa Catarina Yxtepeji, Sept. 28, 1841, AGEO, G, GD, Villa Juárez, Subprefectura de Villa Alta.

78. "Leyes Constiticionales," No. 6, Arts 25–29.

79. Guardino, *Time of Liberty*, 238–239.

80. Juez and República of San Andrés de la Laguna to Prefect, Jan. 21, 1840, AGEO, G, GD, Teposcolula; Pedro Santiago to Departmental Governor, July 9, 1840, AGEO, G, GD, Huajuapan.

81. Fulgencio Martín, Matias Martín, Pedro Martín, and Francisco Dionisio to Departmental Governor, July 11, 1838, AGEO, G, GD, Huajuapan; Interview with Antonio Nicolás, Nov. 25, 1837, AGEO, G, GD, Centro.

82. Sept. 2, 1839, INAH, AHM, O, AJT, Roll 31.

83. Literally meaning "man of property," an *hombre de bien* was, according to Michael Costeloe, "a believer in the Roman Catholic faith, with a strong sense of honour and morality, and of sufficient financial means to maintain a certain lifestyle." Costeloe also cites the definitions of Lucas Alamán—"[a] man of faith, honour, property, education, and virtue"—and José María Luis Mora—"[a man] who has a job which provides him with the necessities of life, or has some productive skill, or some invested capital, or some property." The men chosen as jueces de paz in rural Oaxaca would probably not have been recognizable as *hombres de bien* to either Alamán or Mora, but the term nevertheless denoted a certain kind of elevated status within the village that depended on property, livelihood, and education (Costeloe, *The Central Republic in Mexico*, 17).

84. Mariano González to José Salazar y Rocha, Mar. 20, 1837, AGEO, G, GD, Centro.

85. See "Propuesta en terna para el nombramiento de Jues de Pas . . . ," Dec. 4, 1838; Gaspar Martínez to Juez de Paz of Santiago Plumas, Dec. 19, 1838; Corporación Municipal of Santiago Plumas to Prefect of Teposcolula, Dec. 27, 1838, INAH, AHM, O, AJT, Roll 31; Tribunal Superior de Justicia, Apr. 13, 1841, AGEO, G, GD, Centro; Manuel María Callejas, Jan. 24, 1846; Subprefect of Tuxtepec, June 24, 1846, AGEO, G, GD, Tuxtepec, Subprefectura de Teotitlán.

86. Tomás Gallangos to Secretario del Superior Gobierno del Departamento, Feb. 6, 1838, AGEO, G, GD, Jamiltepec, Jueces de Paz.

87. José Mantecón to Secretario del Despacho, Mar. 16, 1840, AGEO, G, GD, Teotitlán, Jueces de Paz.

88. Jiménes to Prefect of Teposcolula, Dec. 24 and 30, 1839, INAH, AHM, O, AJT, Roll 31.

89. "Propuesta en terna para el nombramiento de Jues de Pas . . . ," Dec. 4, 1838; Gaspar Martínez to Juez de Paz of Santiago Plumas, Dec. 19, 1838; Corporación Municipal of Santiago Plumas to Prefect of Teposcolula, Dec. 27, 1838, INAH, AHM, O, AJT, Roll 31.

90. Guardino, *Time of Liberty*, 239–241.

91. Tribunal Superior de Justicia, Jul. 2, 1838, AGEO, G, GD, Centro; Manuel Ma. Zuñiga to Secretario del Superior Gobierno del Departamento, June 13, 1838, AGEO, G, GD, Cuicatlán, Subprefectura de Teotitlán; Luis Hernández to Secretario del Despacho, June 19, 1838, AGEO, G, GD, Centro.

92. Sept. 2, 1839, INAH, AHM, O, AJT, Roll 31.

93. For examples, see Junta Departamental, Sept. 9, 1838, AGEO, G, GD, Centro; Aug. 27, 1839, AGEO, G, GD, Tuxtepec, Subprefectura de Teotitlán; Junta Departamental, Aug. 13, 1841, and Junta Departamental, July 20, 1840, AGEO, G, GD, Centro.

94. Luis Hernández to Secretario del Despacho, Feb. 18 and July 22, 1840; Junta Departamental, July 27, 1840, AGEO, G, GD, Centro. For other cases of removal for drunkenness, see witnesses' accounts, Apr. 28–May 1, 1838; Manuel Ximénes, May 8, 1838; Ygnacio Goytia to Departmental Governor, May 23, 1838; and Nicolas Dávila Yalindo, May 6, 1839, AGEO, G, GD, Centro.

95. María Domingo, Mar. 26, 1838; Ygnacio Goytia to Departmental Governor, May 23, 1838, AGEO, G, GD, Centro.

96. Junta Departamental, Aug. 26, 1838, AGEO, G, GD, Centro.

97. Carrizola to Prefect of Teposcolula, Feb. 18, 1839, INAH, AHM, O, AJT, Roll 31; Escribano nacional público for República of San Francisco Yucucundo, Oct. 31, 1838; "Padrón de almas del Pueblo de Yucucundo"; Ramón Martínez Zurita, Nov. 10, 1838; Prefect of Teposcolula to Subprefect of Nochistlán, Mar. 8, 1839; José Miguel to Governor, Apr. 1, 1839; Cura of Peñoles, Apr. 11, 1839; Martínez Zurita, Apr. 16, 1838; Ramon Villegas to Governor, Feb. 2, 1840; Manuel Contreras, May. 2, 1840; Ramón Villegas, July 1, 1840; AGEO, G, GD, Teposcolula; Junta Departamental, Nov. 4, 1840, AGEO, G, GD, Centro.

98. Junta Departamental, Mar. 19, 1841, AGEO, G, GD, Centro.

99. Junta Departamental, May 24, 1841, AGEO, G, GD, Centro.

100. The first appointments of jefes de policía were in December of 1844. See, for example, Dec. 19, 1844, AGEO, G, GD, Silacayoapam; José Carraguedo, Dec. 26, 1844, AGEO, G, GD, Centro. But some requests to have jueces de paz date from earlier in the year.

101. Manuel Torres, Máximo Guzmán, Rosalino Contreras, and Luciano Zárate to Subprefect of Juchitán, Sept. 11, 1845; Subprefect of Juchitán, Sept. 12, 1845, AGEO, G, GD, Juchitán, Subprefectura de Tehuantepec; Prefect of Teposcolula, Aug. 9 and Sept. 8, 1844, AGEO, G, GD, Teposcolula, Juzgado de Paz; Jefe de Policía de Capulalpán, Mar. 10, 1845, AGEO, G, GD, Centro; Francisco Franco, Apr. 11, 1845, AGEO, G, GD, Villa Alta, Policía; Francisco Franco to Secretario del Despacho, Feb. 14, 1845, AGEO, G, GD, Villa Alta, Juzgados de Paz.

102. Prefect of Teposcolula, Oct. 4, 1844, AGEO, G, GD, Teposcolula, Juzgados de Paz; Vicente Rodríguez, Jefe de Policía of Plumas, to Departmental Governor, Nov. 30, 1844, AGEO, G, GD, Centro.

103. Común de San Miguel Astatla, Nov. 29, 1844, AGEO, G, GD, Teposcolula, Coixtlahuaca.

104. Benigno Rojas, Oct. 4, 1844; Prefect from Subprefect to Governor, Dec. 26, 1844, AGEO, G, GD, Teposcolula, Juzgado de Paz; Asamblea Departamental, Jan. 3, 1845, AGEO, G, GD, Centro.

105. Manuel José Pérez to Subprefect of Etla, Feb. 8, 1845; Subprefect of Etla to Prefect of Centro, Feb. 11, 1845; Subprefect of Juchitán, Sept. 12, 1845, AGEO, G, GD, Etla, Subprefectura del Centro.

106. For this first set of election records, see Huazolotitlan, Dec. 6, 1846; Cortijos, Dec. 13, 1846; Santiago Pinotepa Nacional, Dec. 13, 1846, AGEO, G, GD, Jamiltepec; Ranchería de San Francisco el Maguei, Dec. 6, 1846 and Juquila, May 1, 1847; "Lista de las nuebas Repúblicas relevadas en 1° de Enero de 1847," AGEO, G, GD, Huajuapan.

107. Juez de Paz, etc. of Yxtlán, Aug. 13, 1846, AGEO, G, GD, Villa Juárez, Subprefectura of Villa Alta.

108. Cámara de Diputados to Secretario del Despacho, Dec. 7, 1846, and Secretario de la Cámara de Senadores, Jan. 27, 1847, AGEO, G, GD, Centro.

109. Ursulo García to Subprefect of Yanhuitlán, Dec. 4, 1848, AGEO, G, GD, Yanhuitlán, Subprefectura de Teposcolula.

110. Manuel Antonio, June 19, 1847; Vice-governor, July 5, 1847, AGEO, G, GD, Huajuapan.

111. Fernando de León to Governor of Centro, Dec. 22, 1846, AGEO, G, GD, Centro. The emphasis is mine.

112. Subprefect of Zimatlán to Governor of Centro, Dec. 26, 1846; Governor of Centro to State Governor, Dec. 29, 1846; Jan. 20, 1847, AGEO, G, GD, Centro.

113. This does not, of course, mean that they did not have these identities, merely that they did not systematically use them in their relationship with the state. There are certainly exceptions. Chassen-López carefully reconstructs the shifting nature of "ethnic identity" in Oaxaca and finds that a range of situations existed and exist and that the use of ethnic self-identification has been and is contingent on circumstances. It is crucial to avoid the pitfalls of "upstreaming," in that more recent circumstances have in many cases produced a resurgence of ethnic self-identification. Overall, my research on the early nineteenth century suggests that the circumstances of most of rural Oaxaca in these years did not prompt the use of broader ethnic identity in villagers' relations with the state. The clearest exception would be Juchitán, on the isthmus of Tehuantepec, where some historians have argued that the Zapotecs shared an identity that was explicitly Zapotec and that this drove not just local relations but also relations with the state through "ethnic resistance"; to the extent that this is true, it reinforces my observations about the rest of Oaxaca, as pressure on the communities was generally much greater on the isthmus. See Tutino, "Ethnic Resistance," 58–60; and Chassen-López, *From Liberal to Revolutionary Oaxaca*, 281–282; 292–294; and 315–347.

NOTES TO CHAPTER 4

1. Lawrence James Remmers, "Henequén, the Caste War, and Economy of Yucatán, 1846–1883: The Roots of Dependence in a Mexican Region," Ph.D. diss, University of California at Los Angeles, 1981, 100–121.

2. Joaquín J. Rejón, *Memoria leida ante la excma. asamblea del departamento de Yucatán, por el secretario general de gobierno el día 7 de mayo de 1845* (Mérida, Mexico: Imprenta de Castillo y Compañia, 1845), xi–xiv; SMGE, Biblioteca Benito Juárez.

3. Miguel Barbachano to Ministro de Relaciones de la República, Apr. 17, 1848, AGN, G s/s, Box 256, Exp. 5.

4. Even after most of the peninsula was regained, the *cruzob*, Maya rebels in the eastern forested areas, maintained an active rebellion from their base at Chan Santa Cruz. At the turn of the twentieth century, the federal government took responsibility for finally vanquishing these rebels, sending in forces and transforming that part of the state into the federal territory of Quintana Roo. For details of these events, see Allen Wells and Gilbert M. Joseph, *Summer of Discontent, Seasons of Upheaval: Elite Politics and Rural Insurgency in Yucatán, 1876–1915* (Stanford, CA: Stanford University Press, 1996), 44–52.

5. García Quintanilla, "En busca de la prosperidad," 86–87; Paul Joseph Reid, "The Constitution of Cádiz and the Independence of Yucatan," *The Americas* 36:1 (1979): 23–25; Rugeley, *Yucatán's Maya Peasantry*, 30–38.

6. Reid, "The Constitution of Cádiz," 23–25; Rugeley, *Yucatán's Maya Peasantry*, 38; Eligio Ancona, *Historia de Yucatán desde la época más remota hasta nuestros días* ([Mérida, Mexico]: Gobierno del Estado de Yucatán, 1917 [1881]), III:15–58.

7. In October 1822, Francisco Bates and José Joaquín Torres reported to the Diputación Provincial, noting that that the ayuntamientos had taken control of the corn repositories in most villages but that their administration was less than scrupulous: "[W]e are advised that many Ayuntamientos have distributed the corn amongst themselves and their partisans, depriving the poor of this benefit, it being very regrettable that they then sell it at inflated prices, and with harm to the [village] funds, resulting from this intrigue that various quantities are lost under the pretext that the debtors have gone bankrupt . . . and thus it seems more convenient that in any case they sell the corn to the public, even when there would be some loss, as the pósito was not established only with the aim of creating, but also of fulfilling the necessities of the pueblos" ("Exposición de los comisionados José Francisco Bates y José Joaquín de Torres . . . , octubre 7 de 1822," AGEY, G, vol. 1, exp. 6).

8. *Gaceta de Mérida*, No. 46, Jan. 21, 1824, Session of Dec. 30, 1823; No. 49, Jan. 29, 1824, Session of Jan. 10, 1824.

9. *Gaceta de Mérida*, No. 14, Oct. 14, 1823, Session of Sept. 25, 1823.

10. *Gaceta de Mérida*, No. 49, Jan. 29, 1824, Sessions of Jan. 12 and 14, 1824; "Sobre el régimen económico y Juntas municipales del Estado," September 20, 1824, *Colección de leyes, decretos y ordenes del augusto congreso del estado libre de Yucatán*, vol. 1 (Mérida, Mexico: Tipografía de G. Canto, 1896), I:310–318. In 1825, only fifteen localities—Bacalar, Campeche, Ichmul, Izamal, Isla del Carmen,

Hecelchakán, Hunucmá, Lerma, Mama, Mérida, Oxkutzcab, Seibaplaya, Sotuta, Tizimín, and Valladolid—met the requirements for having an ayuntamiento. It was not, however, inconceivable for other towns to succeed in petitioning the government for that right; by the end of 1828, Congress had created three new ayuntamientos in the towns of Palizada, Motul, and Yaxcabá. By the same token, the government could rescind privileges dating from previous administrations, as it did in suppressing the ayuntamientos of Oxkutzcab, Hunucmá, Mama, and Tizimín in 1827, when Congress revamped the administrative organization of the state's territory ("Se concede ayuntamiento á Palizada," Sept. 19, 1827; "Se suprimen algunos ayuntamientos," Oct. 13, 1827; "Se concede ayuntamiento á Motul," Oct. 26, 1827; "Se concede ayuntamiento á Yaxcabá," Oct. 28, 1828, *Colección de leyes . . . de Yucatán* II:175, 221, 312).

    11. See, for example, election records from the village of Dzan, in the *comarca* of the cabecera of Ticul (AGEY, M, Municipio de Ticul, Box 248, Vol. 3, Exp. 1).

    12. *Gaceta de Mérida*, No. 92, June 2, 1824, Session of May 28, 1824.

    13. "Sobre Repúblicas de indígenas," July 26, 1824, *Colección de leyes . . . de Yucatán*, vol. 1. (Mérida, Mexico: Tipografía de G. Canto, 1896), I:277–280; "Sobre el régimen económico y Juntas municipales del Estado," Sept. 20, 1824, *Colección de leyes . . . de Yucatán*, I:310–18. For the constitution itself, see "Constitución política del estado libre de Yucatán" (1825), in *Yucatán a través de sus constituciones: Leyes fundamentales 1823–1918*, Colección Historia Legislativa (Mérida, Mexico: Ediciones de la H. Legislatura del Congreso del Estado de Yucatán, 1988–1990), 7–33.

    14. "Nómina de contribuyentes de la Contribución Patriótica, Feb. 25, 1824," AGEY, PE, A, Box 1, Vol. 1, Exp. 15; Patch, *Maya and Spaniard in Yucatán*, Appendix B, "Non-Indians in the Villages of Yucatán, 1777–1791," 259–263.

    15. The literacy and residence requirements are in "Sobre el régimen económico y Juntas municipales del Estado." The general statement about the ethnicity of council members is gleaned from the aggregate of records in the *Ayuntamientos* and *Gobernación* collections of the AGEY. For specific examples see "Tinum. Oficio de la junta municipal de este pueblo, proponiendo una terna para la designación del alcalde conciliador. Aug. 7, 1825," AGEY, PE, A, Box 1, Vol. 1, Exp. 38; the following files in AGEY, PE, A, Box 3, Vol. 4: "Copia certificada del acta de renovación de los componentes del Ayuntamiento de Hool. Dec. 7, 1836," Exp. 8; "Acta del Ayuntamiento del pueblo de Tiholop, para nombrar a su nuevo ayuntamiento, Dec. 8, 1837," Exp. 21; "Copia del acta de la elección del nuevo ayuntamiento de Tiholop, Dec. 2, 1840," Exp. 38; "Copia certificada del acta para la elección del nuevo Ayuntamiento del pueblo de Lerma," Exp. 53; "Copia del acta de la elección celebrada en el pueblo de Chicbul, partido de Seybaplaya para la renovación de su junta municipal, Dec. 8, 1836," Exp. 9; "Acta de elección para la renovación de la junta municipal de Hool, Dec. 9, 1840," Exp. 43; and "Copia del acta del pueblo de Conkal partido de Mérida para la elección de la Junta Municipal, Jan. 1, 1841," PE*, Box 43, Vol. 1, Exp. 19.

    16. "Constitución política del estado libre de Yucatán," 10–11.

    17. "Sumaria averiguación sobre la nulidad de elección de la junta municipal de Temax, denunciada por algunos vecinos, Jan. 11, 1825," AGEY, PE, A, Box 1, Exp. 24.

18. "Diligencias practicadas para dictaminar sobre los cargos de nulidad, en la elección de la junta municipal de este pueblo, May 15, 1825," AGEY, PE, A, Box 1, Vol. 1, Exp. 31.

19. "Información para probar la nulidad de elección del Ayuntamiento de Maxcanú. Mandándose por decreto convocar a nueva elección, Jan. 7, 1829," AGEY, PE, A, Box 2, Vol. 2, Exps. 25 and 28.

20. On the mechanisms of electoral patronage, see Richard Graham, *Patronage and Politics in Nineteenth-Century Brazil* (Stanford, CA: Stanford University Press, 1990), esp. 85–93.

21. "Información producida por el alcalde de Hopelchén, por designación del Gobernador, sobre los hechos ocurridos con motivo de las elecciones del pueblo de Xcupilcacab, Feb. 11, 1832," AGEY, PE, G, Box 10, Vol. 4, Exp. 8.

22. "Sobre repúblicas de indígenas," July 26, 1824, *Colección de leyes . . . de Yucatán*, I:277–280; Rugeley, *Yucatán's Maya Peasantry*, 95–97. See "Oficio de la renuncia del cacique de Chunnuhub y designación de su sucesor, Aug. 4, 1825," AGEY, PE, A, Box 1, Vol. 1, Exp. 36 for an early example of the process of replacing a cacique, in this case written in Maya.

23. Rugeley, *Yucatán's Maya Peasantry*, 94.

24. "Cuaderno de actas del R.A. del pueblo de Motul, Año de 1833," AGEY, M, Box 140, Exp. 1; "Libro de juicios verbales y conciliaciones. 1826, Ticul," AGEY, M, Box 248, Vol. 3, Exp. 7; "Año de 1832. Libro de juicios verbales y conciliaciones," AGEY, M, Box 250, Exp. 1; "Representación del Ayuntamiento de Teabo, sobre que se le permita disponer una cantidad del fondo de pósitos, para pagar sueldos del secretario y del maestro de primeras letras, Jan. 1, 1834," AGEY, A, Box 3, Vol. 3, Exp. 12; "Cuaderno de Actas del R.A. del pueblo de Motul," AGEY, M, Vol. 1, Box 140, Exp. 1. The rules governing the responsibilities of these town administrations are found in "Sobre el gobierno interior de los pueblos," November 19, 1824 and "Reglamento de Policia," Oct. 3, 1825, *Colección de leyes . . . de Yucatán*, I:348–356 and II:18–19.

25. "Información sobre el establecimiento de juntas municipales en los pueblos de Seyba Cabecera, Hool y su agregado Sihochac, Jan. 19, 1827," AGEY, PE, A, Box 2, Vol. 2, Exp. 7; "Sinanche. Diligencias promovidas por los vecinos de este pueblo para probar reune las condiciones para elegir su junta municipal, Jan. 13, 1825," AGEY, PE, A, Box 1, Vol. 1, Exp. 25.

26. The earliest civil tax code that I have is from 1833 (Law of November 23, 1833, "Que arregla el cobro de la contribución personal," Alonso Áznar Pérez, ed., *Colección de leyes, decretos, ordenes o acuerdos de tendencia general del poder legislativo del estado libre y soberano de Yucatán* [Mérida, Mexico: Imprenta del Editor, 1849-1851], I:147–149). For religious taxation, see "Sobre el cobro de obvenciones," October 22, 1825, *Colección de leyes . . . de Yucatán*, II:44–47.

27. "Sobre repúblicas de indígenas."

28. "Diligencias practicadas en averiguación de la persona que mandó aplicar en la villa de Ysamal el atroz y pro[hibi]do castiga de azotes á José Rafael [Chan] y su muger Juana María May, Jan. 14–May 1, 1825," AGEY, J, Penal, Box 1, Exp. 4; "Información promovida por Baltasar Canché, contra el cacique de la república

de indios de Telá, partido de Tihosuco, por conducta escandalosa, dando lugar a su destitución, Mar. 30, 1829," AGEY, PE, J, Vol. 2, Exp. 12.

29. "Sumaria información contra Lázaro Caamal, cacique de Yaxcabá, por ineptitud en el cobro de la contribución personal . . . , Jul. 1, 1827, " AGEY, PE, G, Box 15, Vol. 1, Exp. 29; "Información promovida por Antonio Gutiérrez, subdelegado del partido de Tihosuco, contra el cacique de la República de Indígenas de Tahdzin, por abandono de empleo, Mar. 10, 1829," AGEY, PE, J, Box 24, Vol. 2, Exp. 7; "Sumaria información contra José May, cacique de Pocboc, pueblo del Camino Real Alto, por mal uso de los fondos de algunos ramos, Jul. 8, 1825," AGEY, PE, J, Box 23, Vol. 1, Exp. 9. For more on the ambiguous position of the cacique as tax collector, see Rugeley, *Yucatán's Maya Peasantry*, 104–107.

30. "Autos del proceso seguido contra Francisco Kantun y otros vecinos del pueblo de Nunkiní sentenciados por el delito de tumulto, Aug. 23, 1825–May 19, 1826," AGEY, J, Penal, Box 2, Exp. 2; "Información promovida por los indios de Pich, partido de Beneficios Altos, contra Procopio Cocom, por excesos en su función de cacique de dicho pueblo, Nov. 13, 1827," AGEY, PE, J, Box 23, Vol. 1, Exp. 21.

31. "Seye. Representación de la junta municipal, cacique y justicias, pidiendo no se cobren con rigor las contribuciones mientras no cesen los efectos de la mortal epidemia que las aflige, Aug. 2, 1825," AGEY, PE, A, Box 1, Exp. 35; "Expediente promovido por varios vecinos de Yaxcabá contra el alcalde Claudio Padilla por infracciones a la ley, Oct. 12, 1826," AGEY, PE, A, Box 2, Vol. 2, Exp. 1.

32. Costeloe, *La primera república federal*, 242; Arturo Güemez Pineda, *Liberalismo en tierras del caminante. Yucatán, 1812–1840* (Zamora, Mexico: El Colegio de Michoacán, 1994), 158–160; Eligio Ancona, *Historia de Yucatán*, III:231–242; AGEY, C, D, 8, Nov. 8, 1829; *Exposición que el actual congreso ordinario de Yucatán dirigió a las cámaras de la Unión, participando su instalación y el completo restablecimiento del regimen federativo en aquel estado,"* 1831, and *Examen sobre el actual estado del negocio de Yucatán, y lo que conviene hacer sobre él* (Mexico City: Imprenta de Rivera, 1832), INAH, CGO, Vol. 13, No. 8; AGEY, C, D, 8, Sept. 19 and 21, Oct. 6, and Dec. 20, 21 and 27, 1831; "José Segundo Carvajal, Comandante General y Gobernador Provisional del Estado de Yucatán a sus habitantes" and "Iniciativa de la legislatura del estado libre de Yucatán al Soberano Congreso de la Unión," AGN, G s/s, Vol. 151, Exp. 8; José Segundo Carvajal, *Discurso que leyó el Excmo. Sr. Gobernador Provisional del Estado Ciudadano José Segundo Carvajal hoy 21 de Diciembre en la solemne apertura de las sesiones del 6o congreso constitucional de este estado de Yucatán* (Mérida: Imprenta de Lorenzo Seguí, 1831); and "Representación que eleva la legislatura de Yucatán a las Augustas Cámaras del Congreso General de los Estados Unidos Mejicanos," AGN, G s/s, Vol. 151, Exp. 8.

33. Ancona, *Historia de Yucatán*, III:259.

34. I have not been able to locate the laws from the "illegitimate" insurgent administration of 1829–1831 in Yucatán; thus, my conclusions are based on evidence from the towns themselves. For example, see "Proposición de ternas para la designación de Jueces de Paz y procuradores de los pueblos de Pisté y Chichimilá," AGEY, PE, G, Box 16, Vol. 2, Exp. 48. Census information is taken from

Trabajos hechos por la comisión de la H. Junta Departamental, auxiliada de facultativos sobre la división provisional de este departamento que previene la constitución (Mérida, Mexico: Oficina de Espinosa, 1837), CAIHY, CCCA, F, Box II, No. 20. Although these were the towns that met the prerequisites for having ayuntamientos, I have no direct evidence of the existence of these councils during these years anywhere but Mérida and Campeche.

35. See, for example, a petition from the town of Tabi in 1838, in which Manuel José Aviles is referred to as the town's "alcalde."

36. "Representación de los vecinos del pueblo de Halachó, partido de Maxcanú, protestando el nombramiento de Luis Flores, como Juez de Paz por no tener las cualidades para el desempeño del cargo, Dec. 30, 1837," AGEY, PE, G, Box 20, Vol. 10, Exp. 35.

37. "Averiguación promovida por queja de los indígenas de Cholul, contra el Juez de paz de Conkal, por violentarlos a desempeñar trabajos en las milpas del subdelegado, del cura y las suyas propias, Aug. 4, 1831," AGEY, PE, J, Box 23, Vol. 3, Exp. 13; "Averiguación promovida por queja de vecinos del pueblo de Cholul, contra Marcelo Martin, juez de paz de Conkal, por tenerlos en prisión," AGEY, PE, J, Vol. 3, Exp. 14.

38. "Diligencias para la averiguación de unos hechos que se atribuyen al Juez de Paz del pueblo de Chicxulub contra el cacique y justicias de aquel pueblo, Jul. 20, 1831," AGEY, PE, J, Box 23, Vol. 3, Exp. 12.

39. "Representación de los indios del pueblo de Quelul, acusando a Bernardino Jimenez, Juez de Paz de dicho pueblo, por obligarlos a torcer caña en condiciones injustas," AGEY, PE, G, Box 16, Vol. 3, Exp. 20; "Averiguación promovida por queja de República de Indígenas del pueblo de Quelul, partido de Peto, contra el Juez de paz de Ichmul, por forzarlos a repartimientos y trabajos que consideran abusivos, Apr. 16, 1831," AGEY, PE, J, Box 23, Vol. 3, Exp. 9.

40. "Sumaria promovida por Pedro Nolasco May y otros vecinos de Yaxkukul contra Luis Silveira, Juez de Paz de dicho pueblo, por abuso de autoridad, Mar. 1–May 2, 1838," AGEY, J, Penal, Box 9, Exp. 24.

41. "Diligencias para la averiguación de unos hechos que se atribuyen al Juez de Paz del pueblo de Chicxulub contra el cacique y justicias de aquel pueblo, Jul. 20, 1831," AGEY, PE, J, Box 23, Vol. 3, Exp. 12.

42. "Representación de varios vecinos de la jurisdicción de Motul contra el alcalde Timoteo Bolio, por abuso de autoridad, Apr. 25, 1837," AGEY, PE, G, Box 19, Vol. 9, Exp. 20.

43. This is a central point of Rugeley's work; for a good iteration of it, see *Yucatán's Maya Peasantry*, 115–116.

44. Robert W. Patch, "Decolonization, the Agrarian Problem, and the Origins of the Caste War, 1812–1847," in *Land, Labor & Capital in Modern Yucatán: Essays in Regional History and Political Economy*, ed. Jeffrey T. Brannon and Gilbert M. Joseph (Tuscaloosa: University of Alabama Press, 1991), 57; Nancy M. Farriss, "Nucleation versus Dispersal: The Dynamics of Population Movement in Colonial Yucatán," *Hispanic American Historical Review* 58 (1978): 187–216.

45. Decree of August 18, 1824, cited in Güémez Pineda, *Liberalismo*, 104–108.

46. "Ley de Colonización de 2 de Diciembre de 1825," *Colección de leyes* . . . *de Yucatán*, II:86–89; Güémez Pineda, *Liberalismo*, 133–136; 161; 175; 192–206; 233; Rugeley, *Yucatán's Maya Peasantry*, 64–68.

47. "Representación de la junta municipal del pueblo de Tekantó, pidiendo la derogación de la ley de 28 de diciembre de 1833, sobre la enajenación de tierras baldías, May 27, 1834," AGEY, PE, G, Box 18, Vol. 6, Exp. 15; "Representación de varios municipios del partido de la Costa ante el gobernador del Estado, para que se suspendan los efectos de la ley de 28 de diciembre de 1833 sobre tierras baldías, por los efectos perjudiciales que causa a sus moradores, Mar. 18, 1834, " AGEY, T, Vol. 1, Exp. 25; "Representación de José María Domínguez, juez de paz y representante del comun de Sudzal, sobre un litigio de tierras con Dña. Manuela León y Navarrete, Nov. 8, 1837, " AGEY, PE, T, Vol. 1, Exp. 31.

48. "Información de la república de indígenas del pueblo de Kinchil, en justificación de los perjuicios por la mensura de las tierras concedidas al C. Felipe Peña, Nov. 23, 1837," AGEY, PE, T, Vol. 1, Exp. 32.

49. "Expediente promovido por Dn. Sebastián Avila, relativo a la compra de un pedazo de tierra colindante con su hacienda Techay, en el municipio de Muna, Jan. 31, 1837," AGEY, PE, T, Vol. 1, Exp. 29.

50. This is the central thesis of Güémez Pineda, *Liberalismo*.

51. "Representación de Felipe Gil, sobre que se le conceda la venta de unas tierras baldías pertenecientes al pueblo de Ucú, Jul. 11, 1837, " AGEY, T, Vol. 1, Exp. 30. The italics are mine.

52. This suspicion was likely not entirely unfounded. For an account of Maya cattle theft, see Güémez Pineda, "Everyday Forms of Maya Resistance: Cattle Rustling in Northwestern Yucatán, 1821–1847," in *Land, Labor, & Capital*, ed. Brannon and Joseph, 18–50.

53. "Expediente promovido por milperos del pueblo de Hunucmá, con queja contra doña Manuela Solis, quien los acusa de invasión de sus tierras, Jul. 27, 1831," AGEY, PE, T, Vol. 1, Exp. 20.

54. Güémez Pineda, *Liberalismo*, 224–229; "Representación de José Moo y otros vecinos de Teabo, denunciando abusos de autoridad del alcalde de Cantamayec, May 17, 1837," AGEY, PE, G, Box 20, Vol. 10, Exp. 11.

55. Rugeley, *Yucatán's Maya Peasantry*, 61–90; quote is from 90.

56. For the beleaguered governor, this was a central concern. In explaining widespread dissatisfaction among these soldiers, he wrote, "It is because of the diverse form with which the Yucatecan active batallions are established. These are composed of well-off vecinos, of farmers, artisans and day-laborers in their pueblos: their customs, especially in the matter of dress and food, are very distinct from those in other departments, and from this results the general discontent with which they have constantly seen the orders of the supreme government, when they had taken some troops away from the peninsula" ("Documentos a que se refiere la exposición que hace al Supremo Gobierno, el gobernador de Yucatán sobre su conducta ministerial desde que tomó posesión de este destino hasta su salida de Mérida," AGN, G s/s, Box 249, Exp. 18).

57. Information on the Imán revolt was compiled from the following sources: Ancona, *Historia de Yucatán*, III:260–277; Serapio Baqueiro Preve, *Ensayo histórico*

sobre las revoluciones de Yucatán desde el año de 1840 hasta 1864, ed. Salvador Rodríguez Losa (Mérida, Mexico: Universidad Autónoma de Yucatán, 1990 [1878–1887]), I:21–45; Rugeley, *Yucatán's Maya Peasantry*, 117–123; "Documentos a que se refiere la exposición . . ."; "El consul mexicano en la Habana comunica al Ministerio de Relaciones que el departamento de Yucatán se ha declarado independiente . . . ," AGN, G s/s, Box 247, Exp. 10.

58. Santiago Méndez, *Representación que el gobernador de Yucatán dirige al congreso consituyente de la república mejicana, en cumplimiento del acuerdo de la legislatura del estado, de 2 de junio de 1842* (Mérida, Mexico: Imprenta de J. Dolores Espinosa, 1842), AGN, G s/s, Box 249, Exp. 12.

59. The proclamation is reprinted in Baqueiro Preve, *Ensayo histórico*, I:31-33. On page 28, Baqueiro offers the suggestion that Imán also addressed civil taxes and land, but this is not corroborated elsewhere.

60. Rugeley, *Yucatán's Maya Peasantry*, 123–124.

61. Juez de Paz and República of Rancho de Tela; Asamblea Departamental to Jefe Político of Yaxcabá, May 6, 1845, AGEY, PE, G, Box 59, Secretaría General del Gobierno.

62. "Reglamento para el gobierno interior de los pueblos," March 31, 1841, CAIHY, CCCA, F, Box III, No. 21.

63. "El gobernador, aprobando el acuerdo de los alcaldes de Becanchén partido de Tekax, de elegir un juez en el rancho Xcabihaltún, por ser de conformidad con el Reglamento de Gobierno interior, Dec. 11, 1841," AGEY, PE*, G, Box 44, Vol. 1, Exp. 11.

64. "Información promovida por Dn. Raimundo Pérez cura de Hoctún, para probar la incompetencia de los componentes de las juntas municipales de los pueblos de Xocchel y Tahmek, May 2, 1840," AGEY, PE, A, Box 3, Vol. 4, Exp. 30.

65. "Representación de los vecinos del pueblo de Pisté, pidiendo se establezca junta municipal en dicho pueblo, Apr. 27, 1840," AGEY, PE, A, Box 3, Vol. 4, Exp. 29.

66. "Información del subdelegado del partido de Izamal, sobre que el pueblo de Tekal no tiene las condiciones para tener junta municipal, Dec. 15, 1840," AGEY, PE, A, Box 3, Vol. 4, Exp. 55.

67. For Pisté and Mocochá, see "Representación de los vecinos del pueblo de Pisté, pidiendo se establezca junta municipal en dicho pueblo, Apr. 27, 1840," and "Copia del acta de elección de la junta municipal de Mocochá, Dec. 9, 1940," AGEY, PE, A, Box 3, Vol. 4, Exps. 29 and 41, respectively.

68. Juez de Paz and República of Rancho de Tela; Asamblea Departamental to Jefe Político of Yaxcabá, May 6, 1845," AGEY, PE, G, Box 59, Secretaría General del Gobierno.

69. "El gobernador decretando no hay lugar a lo solicitado por los vecinos del pueblo de Cholul, partido de Mérida, a elegir alcaldes municipales, Nov. 13, 1841," AGEY, PE*, G, Box 44, Vol. 2, Exp. 45; "El gobernador sobre que no hay lugar a la solicitud de vecinos de Cholul, relativa al establecimiento de alcaldes municipales del pueblo, Feb. 19, 1842," AGEY, PE*, G, Box 50, Vol. 1, Exp. 5.

70. "Representación de varios vecinos de Chichimilá, pidiendo la nulidad de las elecciones de sus alcaldes municipales por infracciones a la ley," AGEY, PE*, A, Box 48, Vol. 1, Exp. 16.

71. "Causa instruida contra José Silveira, alcalde del pueblo de Yaxkukul, por abuso de autoridad, con motivo del arresto arbitrario del cacique de la república de indígenas del mismo pueblo," AGEY, J, Penal, Box 16, Exp. 10.

72. "Representación de los escrutadores de la elección municipal del pueblo de Baca, pidiendo su nulidad por no haberse ajustado a la ley, May 11, 1840," AGEY, PE, A, Box 3, Vol. 4, Exp. 31.

73. "Diligencias promovidas por Clemente Vasquez, pidiendo la nulidad de la elección de la junta municipal de Tekit, partido de la Sierra Baja, Dec. 11, 1840," AGEY, PE, A, Box 3, Vol. 4, Exp. 46.

74. Ancona, *Historia de Yucatán*, III:286–287; Baqueiro Preve, *Ensayo Histórico*, I:54–55. Miguel Barbachano, who hailed from Mérida, was a staunch supporter of unconditional independence, in large part because his city depended mostly on trade with Cuba. Santiago Méndez, from Campeche, opposed such a measure, supporting instead provisional independence pending Mexico's return to federal republicanism. Campeche, unlike Mérida, depended on trade internal to Mexico, especially with the ports of Tampico, Veracruz, and Matamoros.

75. "Representación de los vecinos del pueblo de Komchén, pidiendo que se nulifique las elecciones de su junta municipal y se proceda a nuevas elecciones, Apr. 13, 1840," AGEY, PE, G, Box 20, Vol. 11, Exp. 31; "Copia del acta en sesión extraordinaria del pueblo de Espita, relativa a que el Gobierno mandó a don Santiago Iman para cuidar la tranquilidad de estos pueblos, que piden la suspensión de las elecciones, Jan. 10, 1841," AGEY, PE*, A, Box 43, Vol. 1, Exp. 31; "Información practicada por don Juan López alcalde conciliador de Espita, sobre los hechos escandalosos que evitaron la verificación de elecciones del nuevo Ayuntamiento, Feb. 3, 1841," AGEY, PE*, A, Box 43, Vol. 1, Exp. 25; "Representación del subdelegado de Dzemul, informando los sucesos ocurridos en las elecciones de la junta municipal del mismo pueblo, Apr. 12, 1840," AGEY, PE, A, Box 3, Vol. 4, Exp. 25; "Copia del acta de elección del pueblo de Xul del partido de Tekax, para elegir alcaldes municipales, aprobada por el gobernador, Dec. 5, 1841," AGEY, PE*, A, Vol. 1, Exp. 16; "Representación de Justo Pavia, objetando su designación de vocal tercero de la junta municipal del pueblo de Saban, May 8, 1840," AGEY, PE, G, Box 20, Vol. 2, Exp. 36.

76. In Chichimilá, both the cacique and the priest were members of the electoral committee that the protesters claimed was illegally chosen; this is the committee that managed to convince the "tímidos" to vote as it wished. For examples of a priest interfering with electoral results, see Tixcacalcucul, Tekom, and Muchumax, where Father Eusebio Rejón managed to persuade the committee not to accept the elected *vocales*, thus, in the words of the república de indígenas, "trampling with this bad faith the will of the people" ("Decretando como se pide sobre la nulidad de elección de la junta municipal de Tixcacalcupul, Feb. 6, 1841," AGEY, PE*, G, Box 44, Vol. 3, Exp. 88). In Tekit, the members of the república were rounded up and forced to vote against their will ("Diligencias promovidas por Clemente Vasquez, pidiendo la nulidad de la elección de la junta municipal

de Tekit, partido de la Sierra Baja, Dec. 11, 1840," AGEY, PE, A, Box 3, Vol. 4, Exp. 46).

77. For examples of the use of indígenas as controlled voters, see "Representación de los escrutadores de la elección municipal del pueblo de Baca . . . ," AGEY, PE, A, Box 3, Vol. 4, Exp. 31; "Expediente formado por Don Felipe Rosado, alcalde conciliador de Peto, sobre la necesidad de unas elecciones y acta de las celebradas el 28 de febrero para la renovación de su ayuntamiento, Mar. 3, 1841," AGEY, PE*, A, Box 43, Vol. 1, Exp. 26; and "Diligencias promovidas por Dn. Francisco Antonio Pardenilla, pidiendo se declare nula la elección de la junta municipal de Chapab, Apr. 18, 1840," AGEY, PE, A, Box 3, Vol. 4, Exp. 27.

78. "Diligencias promovidas por Clemente Vasquez, pidiendo la nulidad de la elección de la junta municipal de Tekit, partido de la Sierra Baja, Dec. 11, 1840," AGEY, PE, A, Box 3, Vol. 4, Exp. 46.

79. "Sumaria averiguación promovida por Santiago Osorio, vecino de Dzemul, sobre la ilegalidad de la elección de la junta municipal de dicho pueblo, Apr. 18, 1840," AGEY, PE, A, Box 3, Vol. 4, Exp. 26.

80. Such occurrences had always been of some concern to the government. As early as 1824, the state congress had been forced to enact legislation to limit the disruptive potential of electoral complaints ("Sobre vecindad y recursos de nulidad de las elecciones constitucionales," Sept. 20, 1824, *Colección de leyes . . . de Yucatán*, I:273–274). For the 1841 events, see "El Consejo de Estado, aprobando el dictámen sobre un nuevo sistema para la elección de alcaldes municipales presentado por el Gobernador, May 25, 1841," AGEY, PE*, G, Box 44, Vol. 3, Exp. 70. The law that the council cited was "Reglamento para el nombramiento de diputados, senadores, y gobernadores, y para el de ayuntamientos, alcaldes municipales y jueces de paz," March 31, 1841, Áznar Pérez, ed., *Colección de leyes*, II:84–96.

81. "Difiriendo para otro tiempo las elecciones municipales," Nov. 11, 1842, Áznar Pérez, ed., *Colección de leyes*, II:230; "Convocando para las elecciones municipales," Sept. 27, 1843, Áznar Pérez, ed., *Colección de leyes*, II:262; Nov. 17, 1844, AGEY, PE, G, Box 54, Secretaría General del Gobierno. I have no evidence of a decree calling for a new election after 1844, nor is there anecdotal evidence of elections after that date.

82. "Representación de varios vecinos del pueblo de Kinchil, partido de Hunucmá, contra el alcalde de dicho pueblo por obligarlos a cubrir fajinas en la apertura del camino de este pueblo a Sisal, Nov. 9, 1840," AGEY, PE, G, Box 21, Vol. 14, Exp. 1; "Causa instruida contra Andres Kantun y socios por desobediencia a la autoridad del pueblo de Xcupilcacab, Feb. 27-Mar. 18, 1845," AGEY, J, Penal, Box 30, Exp. 28; "Causa instruida contra D. Felipe Ongay, Alcalde 10 de Tinum, por abusos de autoridad, Sept. 20–Nov. 12, 1844," AGEY, J, Penal, Box 27, Exp. 49; "Sumaria instruida contra José Crescencio Moo y Vicente Tun, cacique y teniente de la república de indígenas de Xcan, por suponerse haber liberado a un individuo preso por el alcalde de dicho pueblo, Aug. 14–Sept. 30, 1845," AGEY, J, Penal, Box 33, Exp. 39.

83. "Representación de varios vecinos del pueblo de Sicpach, partido de Izamal, contra el alcalde Dn. Santiago López por abuso de autoridad, Apr. 6, 1840," AGEY, PE, A, Box 3, Vol. 4, Exp. 24.

84. Ancona, *Historia de Yucatán*, I:268–269; 280; "Contribución extraordinaria de guerra," June 3, 1842, Áznar Pérez, ed., *Colección de leyes*, II:186–191.

85. "Dispensando de la contribución civil y religiosa a los que se indican," April 12, 1843, Áznar Pérez, ed., *Colección de leyes*, II:242; April 11, 1843, AGEY, PE, G, Box 51, Consejo de Estado ; "Aboliendo las obvenciones y dejando a cargo del tesoro público atender con la cantidad que se expresa al sostenimiento del culto y sus ministros," June 17, 1843, Áznar Pérez, ed., *Colección de leyes* II:249; June 17, 1843, AGEY, PE, G, Box 51, Consejo de Estado; "Imponiendo las contribuciones que se expresan," June 17, 1843, Áznar Pérez, ed., *Colección de leyes*, II:245-246; June 5, 1843, AGEY, PE, G, Box 51, Consejo de Estado; Apr. 29, 1843. For records of indigenous donations to the war effort, see AGEY, PE, G, Box 53, Correspondencia.

86. Jefe Político Suplente de Bolonchenticul, Apr. 17, 1843, AGEY, PE, G, Secretaría General del Gobierno; "Causa instruida a Bernardino Mex y otras personas, vecinos del rancho Yalkuk, de la juridicción del pueblo de Sacalum, por negarse a pagar las contribuciones que establece la ley, Jul. 13–31, 1843," AGEY, J, Penal, Box 22, Exp. 9; "Causa seguida á Esteban Puc y José N. Moo por resistirse al pago de contribuciones en el pueblo de Tiholop, May 23–Oct. 7, 1844," AGEY, J, Penal, Box 26, Exp. 6; "Causa promovida contra el cacique de Dzitnup, José Sabino Pat, y otros vecinos del mismo pueblo, por el delito de asonada, Apr. 12–May 29, 1841," AGEY, J, Penal, Box 13, Exp. 13; "Representación de Marcelo Uc y otros vecinos de Ebtun, querellándose contra el alcalde auxiliar de dicho pueblo, por los atropellos que cometen al cobrar las contribuciones civiles y eclesiásticas, Jul. 1, 1840," AGEY, PE, G, Box 21, Vol. 12, Exp. 10.

87. For another example of the illegal charging of women, see "Representación de los vecinos del rancho Joteoch, partido de Valladolid, por malos tratos que reciben del alcalde de Chemax, Jul. 20, 1840," AGEY, PE, G, Box 21, Vol. 12, Exp. 17.

88. "Diligencias promovidas por los casiques de Motul, Muxupip y otros, contra Antonio Avila, párroco de Motul, por malos tratos en el cobro de unas obvenciones, Jan. 19, 1841," AGEY, PE*, J, Box 42, Vol. 1, Exp. 8.

89. "Información promovida por la República de Indígenas de Hopelchén, contra el cacique de dicho pueblo, por abuso de autoridad, Oct. 12, 1840," AGEY, PE, G, Box 21, Vol. 13, Exp. 9; "Expediente promovido por Pedro Pascual y otros vecinos de Cuzamá, contra el cacique de dicho pueblo del partido de Sotuta, Jul. 13, 1840," AGEY, PE, G, Box 21, Vol. 12, Exp. 12.

90. "Causa promovida por Miguel Canul y Patricio Noh, vecinos de Chichimilá, contra Dionisio Cervera, alcalde de su localidad, por abusos de autoridad, Jun. 16, 1842–Feb. 17, 1843," AGEY, J, Penal, Box 17, Exp. 5; "Información promovida por el subdelegado de Hecelchakán, contra Eusebio Sánches recaudador de hacienda de Dzibalchén, por alterar el sistema de pago de las contribuciones, Sept. 26, 1840," AGEY, PE, G, Box 21, Vol. 13, Exp. 7.

91. Subdelegado of Mérida to Asamblea Departamental, Jul. 24, 1844, AGEY, PE, G, Box 55, Secretaría General del Gobierno; Subdelegado of Tizimín, Aug. 26, 1845, AGEY, PE, G, Box 59, Secretaría General del Gobierno.

92. Juan de Dios López, Jefe Político Superior de Izamal, Jun. 4, 1843, AGEY, PE, G, Box 51, Secretaría General del Gobierno, Izamal; Cacique and República of Telchac, July 15, 1843, AGEY, PE, G, Box 51, Secretaría General del Gobierno, Mérida; Cacique and Justicias of Lerma, Feb. 6, 1844, AGEY, PE, G, Box 56, Consejo de Estado.

93. Jul. 15, 1843, AGEY, PE, G, Box 51, Consejo de Estado; Dec. 22, 1843, AGEY, PE, G, Box 51, Consejo de Estado; Juan de Dios Henríquez, Jul. 14, 1843, AGEY, PE, G, Box 51, Secretaría General del Gobierno.

94. Carlos Buendía, Subdelegado de Ticul, May 5, 1847, AGEY, PE, G, Box 65, Jefatura Política de Ticul.

95. "Sobre enagenación de terrenos baldíos," April 5, 1841, Áznar Pérez, ed., *Colección de leyes*, II:116–118.

96. "Nuevos premios de campaña," August 26, 1842, Áznar Pérez, *Colección de leyes*, II:215; Patch, "Decolonization," 56; Rugeley, *Yucatán's Maya Peasantry*, 125. For evidence of the difficulty that the government was having in paying back these loans, see Jun. 17, 1843, AGEY, PE, G, Box 51, Consejo de Estado.

97. Nov. 13, 1844, AGEY, PE, G, Box 56, Asamblea Departamental; Nov. 30, 1844, AGEY, PE, G, Box 54, Asamblea Departamental.

98. "Expediente promovido por Dn. Sebastián Avila relativo a la compra de un pedazo de tierra colindante con su hacienda Techay, en el municipio de Muna, Jan. 31, 1837," AGEY, PE, T, Vol. 1, Exp. 29.

99. Rugeley, *Yucatán's Maya Peasantry*, 125, 128. Rugeley found forty-two claims granted to individuals with Maya surnames, most claiming the requisite quarter league for soldiers.

100. "El jefe político de Maní transcribiendo un oficio del gobierno al jefe subalterno, para que investigue sobre si los tablajes de tierras de dicho lugar tienen la documentación correspondiente, Nov. 26, 1842," AGEY, PE*, G, Box 50, Vol. 3, Exp. 53.

101. Rugeley, *Yucatán's Maya Peasantry*, 125–132.

102. República de Indígenas of Maxcanú, Jan. 19, 1844, AGEY, PE, G, Box 57, Consejo de Estado; Dec. 18, 1843; AGEY, PE, G, Box 51, Consejo de Estado; José Dolores Espinosa, Jan. 9, 1844, AGEY, PE, G, Box 57, Consejo de Estado; Cristóbal Espinosa, May 15, 1845, AGEY, PE, G, Box 59, Secretaría General del Gobierno.

103. Cacique and República of Nunkiní, Aug. 28, 1844, AGEY, PE, G, Box 58, Jefatura Política de Nunkiní.

104. *Siglo XIX: Periódico del Gobierno del Estado de Yucatán*, April 8, 1843.

105. Cited in Dec. 28, 1847, AGEY, PE, G, Box 64, Consejo de Estado.

106. Wolfgang Gabbert and Don Dumond both stress the importance of a significant nonindigenous presence in the rebel armies, especially among the leadership (Gabbert, *Becoming Maya*, 54; Dumond, *The Machete and the Cross*, 123).

NOTES TO CHAPTER 5

1. Manuel de [illegible] to Secretario del Despacho Universal del Estado, May 27, 1835, AGEO, G, GD, Centro.

2. Benito Juárez, "Exposición al soberano congreso al abrir sus sesiones, julio 2 de 1848," in Juárez, *Exposiciones (Cómo se gobierna)* (Mexico City: F. Vázquez, 1902), 164–170; Brian R. Hamnett, "Benito Juárez, Early Liberalism, and the Regional Politics of Oaxaca, 1828–1853," *Bulletin of Latin American Research* 10:1 (1991): 10.

3. Hamnett, *Juárez*, 18–37.

4. Hamnett, *Juárez*, 35. Hamnett is referring in particular to Juárez and Marcos Pérez, a fellow indigenous student at the Institute who would be the interim governor of Oaxaca immediately before Juárez and the man who named Juárez to the post.

5. Juárez, "Exposición . . . 1848," 161.

6. Juárez, "Exposición . . . 1848," 159–161.

7. Benito Juárez, "Exposición al soberano congreso de Oaxaca al abrir sus sesiones, Julio 2 de 1852," in Juárez, *Exposiciones*, 367.

8. José Antonio Requera, Governor of Jamiltepec, to Secretario del Despacho Universal del Estado, Mar. 13, 1849; Pascual Chabes, First Alcalde of Cacahuatepec, to Governor of Jamiltepec, Feb. 6, 1849; Antonio Ernandes, Regidor of Cacahuatepec, Feb. 9, 1849; Francisco Parra Salanueva, Cura, to Governor of Oaxaca, Feb. 27, 1849, AGEO, G, GD, Jamiltepec.

9. José María Muñoz, Governor of Tehuantepec, to Secretario del Despacho Universal del Estado, May 19, 1848, AGEO, G, GD, Tehuantepec.

10. Prefect of Teposcolula to Subprefect of Yanhuitlán, July 15, 1845, and Nov. 15, 1854, INAH, AHM, O, AJT, Roll 32.

11. Governor of Ejutla to Secretario del Despacho Universal del Estado, Sept. 2, 1848, AGEO, G, GD, Ocotlán.

12. Consejo de Gobierno, May 1, 1847, AGEO, G, GD, Centro.

13. Benito Juárez, "Exposición . . . 1848," 172–178; "Reglamento para la administración interior de los departmentos del estado de Oaxaca en lo relativo á los gobernadores y subprefectos," Dec. 30, 1850, *Colección de Leyes . . . de Oaxaca*, 716–717.

14. See the "Noticias Circunstanciadas," reports on pueblo organization and resources from 1845 in the Department of Teposcolula (INAH, AHM, O, AJT, Roll 32). For a description of the uses of common lands, see Michael T. Ducey, "Liberal Theory and Peasant Practice: Land and Power in Northern Veracruz, Mexico, 1826–1900," in *Liberals, the Church, and Indian Peasants*, ed. Jackson, 69–73.

15. See various documents in AGEO, G, GD for the year of 1825.

16. The 1844 law is referred to in July 18 and 31, 1851, AGEO, G, GD, Centro. For Carriedo's proposal, see Juan Bautista Carriedo, Aug. 21, 1848, AGEO, G, GD, Centro. For the 1849 law, see "Reglamento para la administración, inversión y seguridad de los bienes municipales," *Colección de leyes . . . de Oaxaca*, 663–666. And for the 1851 law, see July 18 and 31, 1851, AGEO, G, GD, Centro.

17. Manuel Régules, "Espediente de visita practicada por su Governador," Dec. 21, 1830, AGEO, G, GD, Teotitlán; Governor of Huajuapan, Aug. 3, 1842, AGEO, G, GD, Huajuapan; "Estado que manifieste los Pueblos que tienen bienes

comunales, los que persiben arrendamientos de terrenos, por productos de plaza, y de fincas urbanas," Sept. 30, 1844, AGEO, G, GD, Jamiltepec.

18. "Noticia que produce el que suscribe, el Señor Gobernador de este Departamento de Teposcolula, de los bienes de comunidad y fondos de otros tantos pueblos de que se compone este partido, en cumplimiento de lo prevenido en la superior órden de enero anterior que trata sobre el particular," Feb. 4, 1848, AGEO, G, GD, Yanhuitlán, Subprefectura de Teposcolula; May 29, 1848, AGEO, G, GD, Miahuatlán, Subprefectura de Etla; "Noticia de los Pueblos de este partido que tienen bienes y fondos comunales . . . ," Feb. 14, 1848, AGEO, G, GD, Noxistlán; Jan. 29, 1848, AGEO, G, GD, Huajuapan; Jan. 24, 1848, AGEO, G, GD, Teotitlán, Fondos Comunales; "Noticia de los pueblos de este partido que tienen fondos comunales y de los que carecen de ellos con espresión de los que rinden anualmente gastos que de ellos hacen los mismos pueblos, y cantidades sobrantes ó deficientes," May 4, 1852, AGEO, G, GD, Centro; "Noticia que produce la Subprefectura del Partido de Miahuatlán sobre el estado que guardan los ramos de la Admon. pública municipal á virtud de la órden del Superior Gobierno del Estado de 24 de febrero del presente año comunicada el 25 del mismo," 1852, AGEO, G, GD, Miahuatlán.

19. Municipalidad de Don Dominguillo, May 6, 1852, AGEO, G, GD, Cuicatlán.

20. Municipalidad de Santa Ana Chiquihuitlán to Departmental Governor, June 4, 1852, AGEO, G, GD, Cuicatlán.

21. "Reglamentación para la administración interior . . . ," 721.

22. Dorothy Tanck de Estrada, *Pueblos de indios y educación en el México colonial, 1750–1821* (Mexico City: Colegio de México, 1999).

23. José María Guzmán, May 11, 1834, AGEO, G, GD, Huajuapan; Mariano Antonio Casas to Secretario del Despacho Universal del Estado, Apr. 19, 1834, AGEO, G, GD, Ejutla.

24. República of Santiago Huajolos, May 14, 1834; Hipolite López, Alcalde of Santo Domingo Yodoyuc, May 13, 1834; Juan Eustaquio, Alcalde of San Gerónimo Zilacalluapilla, May 13, 1834; José Mariano, Alcalde of Santa María Sochistlapilco, May 13, 1834, AGEO, G, GD, Huajuapan. See also the following letters: Mariano Ambrosio, Alcalde of San José Chichihualtepeque, May 16, 1834; José Gregorio Velasco, Alcalde of Santo Domingo Tehanquistengo, May 15, 1834; Vicente Palma, May 14, 1834, Santa María Camotlán; and José [illegible], San Miguel Amatlán, May 15, 1834.

25. José Mantecón, Comisario de Estadística y Clasificación, June 5, 1832, AGEO, G, GD, Tehuantepec, Estadística.

26. Mariano Conde, "Expediente de visita del Departamento 8o del Estado Libre de Oajaca, formado con arreglo á las prevenciones dictadas por el Exmo. Sor. Vice Gobernador, que me fueron comunicados por la Secretaría del Despacho y Gobierno á 7 de Diciembre de 1830," June 10, 1831, AGEO, G, GD, Tehuantepec; Ygnacio José Ortega, "Notas ó Adiciones al Plan Estadístico," Apr. 12, 1830, AGEO, G, GD, Juchitán; José Mantecón, Governor of Teotitlán, Sept. 1837, AGEO, G, GD, Teotitlán. On local desire for schools, see Florencia E. Mallon, "Reflections on the Ruins: Everyday Forms of State Formation in

Nineteenth-Century Mexico," in *Everyday Forms of State Formation: Revolution and the Negotiation of Rule in Modern Mexico*, ed. Gilbert M. Joseph and Daniel Nugent (Durham, NC: Duke University Press, 1994), 81–89.

27. Julián González, Governor of Jamiltepec, to Secretario del Despacho Universal del Estado, Apr. 22, 1834, AGEO, G, GD, Jamiltepec.

28. Mariano Antonio Casas, Governor of Ejutla, to Secretario del Despacho Universal del Estado, Apr. 19, 1834, AGEO, G, GD, Ejutla.

29. For one of many examples of school openings from 1851–1852, see Jan. 18, 1852, AGEO, G, GD, Choapam. For the school openings in the Centro, see "Noticia de las escuelas que ecsisten en el departamento del centro con espresión de las que nuevamente se han abierto," Dec. 17, 1852, AGEO, G, GD, Centro. For the school closings in Juquila, see "Estado que manifieste el número de Escuelas Municipales que se abrieron en el presente año en esta Cavesera y Pueblos del partido . . . ," Nov. 23, 1852, AGEO, G, GD, Instrucción Pública.

30. Governor of Villa Alta to Secretario del Despacho Universal del Estado, Apr. 29, 1852, AGEO, G, GD, Villa Alta, Capitación.

31. Governor of Villa Alta to Secretario del Despacho Universal del Estado, Feb. 24, 1851, AGEO, G, GD, Villa Alta, Justicia.

32. Ayuntamiento of Santa María Petapa, July 19, 1850; Subprefect to Governor of Tehuantepec, July 20, 1850; Governor of Tehuantepec to Governor of Oaxaca, July 24, 1850, AGEO, G, GD, Tehuantepec.

33. Nicolás Tejada, Governor of Jamiltepec, Apr. 26, 1852, AGEO, G, GD, Jamiltepec.

34. Jorge Fernández Iturribarría, *Historia de Oaxaca*, 408–412; *Los Gobernantes de Oaxaca. Historia (1823–1986)* (Mexico City: J. R. Fortson y Cia., SA, 1985), 77–79; Hamnett, *Juárez*, 43–45.

35. "Sobre que los Gobiernos de Oaxaca, Chiapas, y Yucatán no extingan la contribución de capitación si fuere el único ó principal recurso para los gastos públicos," May 20 and 26, 1853, AGN, G s/s, Vol. 420, Exp. 11. The May 20 letter from the Minister of Government to Martínez can also be found in AGEO, G, GD, Gobierno General. See also the law extinguishing the capitacíon, "Centralización de rentas públicas," May 14, 1853, Manuel Dublán and José María Lozano, *Legislación mexicana, ó colección completa de las disposiciones expedidas desde la independencia de la república*, Vol. 6 (Mexico City: Imprenta del Comercio, á Cargo de Dublán and Lozano, Hijos, 1877), 403–405.

36. "Reglas para la recaudación del derecho de capitación," Nov. 11, 1853, Dublán and Lozano, *Legislación mexicana*, VI:748–752; José Cristobal Bolaños, Jefe Superior de Hacienda, to Governor and Comandante General of Oaxaca, Aug. 3, 1854, AGEO, G, GD, Centro.

37. "Exención del sorteo en favor de los indígenas," Aug. 2, 1853, Dublán and Lozano, *Legislación mexicana*, VI:627. See also "Sobre excepciones para el sorteo," Sept. 7, 1853, Dublán and Lozano, *Legislación mexicana*, VI:663.

38. In Oaxaca, for instance, the number of people required for the permanent army went from 1,826 to 1,050 ("Sobre sorteo para el ejército," May 30, 1853, and "Reglamento para reemplazar las bajas del ejército por rigoroso sorteo," Nov. 30, 1853, Dublán and Lozano, *Legislación mexicana*, VI:435, 793).

39. Prefect of Teposcolula to Governor of Oaxaca, Feb. 11, 1854, INAH, AHM, O, AJT, Roll 32.

40. For the quote from Alamán, see D. Francisco de Paula de Arrangoiz y Berzabal, *Méjico desde 1808 hasta 1867. Relación de los principales acontecimientos políticos que han tenido lugar desde la prisión del Virrey Iturrigaray hasta la caída del segundo imperio*, Vol. 2 (Madrid: Imprenta á Cargo de Estrada, 1872), 337. The new law on *ayuntamientos* is "Se designan los lugares en que debe haber ayuntamiento," May 20, 1853, Dublán and Lozano, *Legislación mexicana*, VI:407. For the conservative quote, see *El Universal*, May 25, 1853.

41. Felipe de León, Governor of Huajuapan, to Secretario del Despacho Universal del Estado, Sept. 23, 1829, AGEO, G, GD, Huajuapan, Comunicado; José Mantecón, Governor of Teotitlán, to Secretario del Superior Gobierno del Departmento, Teotitlán, Acontecimientos.

42. Manuel Ortega, Subprefect of Yautepec, to Superior Government of the Department, Dec. 12, 1853, AGEO, G, GD, Yautepec.

43. "Lista de las Municipalidades nombradas á virtud del Supremo Decreto de 20 de Mayo de 1853," Oct. 27, 1853, AGEO, G, GD, Huajuapan; Various, Oct., 1853, AGEO, G, GD, Silacayoapam; Prefect of Teotitlán, Dec. 18, 1853, AGEO, G, GD, Teotitlán, Nombramientos.

44. Francisco Baños Peña, Comisario Municipal of Pinotepa Nacional, Jan. 20, 1855, AGEO, G, GD, Jamiltepec; Lázaro Martínez, Comisario Municipal of Amusgos, Jan. 9, 1855, AGEO, G, GD, Tuxtepec. The law on the new administrations is "Ley para el arreglo de la administración de justicia," Dec. 16, 1853 (Dublán and Lozano, *Legislación mexicana*, VI:817–861). It is unclear where the decree calling for *comisarios* is found. One official referred to it as the decree of Oct. 9, 1853, but I have not located this law (Prefect of Teposcolula to Governor of Oaxaca, Jan. 5, 1854, INAH, AHM, O, AJT, Roll 32).

45. Lázaro Martínez, Comisario Municipal of Amusgos, Jan. 9, 1855, AGEO, G, GD, Tuxtepec; Francisco Vasconcelos, José María Villa[vano], Ygnacio [illegible], José Romueldo Calderón, and J. Parra Salanueva to Prefect of Jamiltepec, Dec. 31, 1854, AGEO, G, GD, Jamiltepec.

46. José Mariano Abrego, Prefect of Jamiltepec to Governor of Oaxaca, Jan. 2 and 23, 1855, AGEO, G, GD, Jamiltepec. In this statement, the prefect echoes the concerns of the commissaries: Lázaro Martínez, in Amusgos, worries that altering the law by refusing indígenas posts on municipal councils would create a serious risk of "caste war." This was a particular threat for Amusgos, located close to the state of Guerrero, where such a war, Martínez observed, had already broken out.

47. Lázaro Martínez, Comisario Municipal of Amusgos, Jan. 9, 1855, AGEO, G, GD, Tuxtepec.

48. Francisco Vasconcelos, José María Villa[vano], Ygnacio [illegible], José Romueldo Calderón, and J. Parra Salanueva to Prefect of Jamiltepec, Dec. 31, 1854, AGEO, G, GD, Jamiltepec.

49. Felipe Gómes, Comisario Municipal of Santa María Asunción Huazolotitlán, Jan. 12, 1855, AGEO, G, GD, Jamiltepec. See also José Anastacio Merino, Comisario Municipal of Pinotepa de Don Luis, Jan. 10, 1855, AGEO, G, GD, Jamiltepec.

50. "Se declaran nulas las enajenaciones de terrenos baldíos hechas por los Estados," Nov. 25, 1853, Dublán and Lozano, *Legislación mexicana*, VI:776; "Sobre revisión de las enajenaciones hechas en terrenos baldíos," July 7, 1854, Manuel Dublán and José María Lozano, *Legislación mexicana, ó colección completa de las disposiciones expedidas desde la independencia de la república*, Vol. 7 (Mexico City: Imprenta del Comercio, á Cargo de Dublán and Lozano, Hijos, 1877), 228–230.

51. Velásquez de León, Ministro de Fomento, to Ignacio Goytía, Feb. 8, 1854; [Ignacio Goytía to Velásquez de León], Mar. 15, 1854, AGEO, G, GD, Fomento. Ignacio Goytía had been governor of Oaxaca and later president of the Junta Departamental under the centralist regime in the 1830s and 1840s.

52. Governor of Ejutla to Governor of Oaxaca, June 20, 1856, AGEO, G, GD, Ejutla, Tierras; [Ignacio Goytía to Velásquez de León], Mar. 15, 1854, AGEO, G, GD, Fomento; Governor of Huajuapan to Secretario del Despacho Universal del Estado, May 9, 1856, AGEO, G, GD, Huajuapan.

53. The Santa Anna regime placed a premium on the protection of property. It rejected, however, the liberal insistence on individual private property; in an 1853 decree, the government stated that "All property is inviolable, whether it belongs to individuals or to corporations." Lands held in common by corporations, whether the church or indigenous communities, were as inviolable as lands held by private individuals. Communities got special attention, at least on the books; in 1854, the national government passed a law calling for investigation into cases in which communities claimed that their land had been taken away illegally. According to this law, government officials would demand that suspected usurpers produce titles to the land; if they could not, they would have either to formally purchase the land from the community in question or to return it to its rightful owners. Not surprisingly, there is little evidence that such investigations occurred; the law was silent on precisely who should perform them and how they were to be financed. Carmen Vásquez Mantecón offers one example of a community regaining its land; in the Mexico City indigenous *parcialidad* of Santiago Tlatelolco, it was determined that a piece of land was illegally occupied by an industrial firm. But the legislation on communal lands prompted debate in Mexico City, as liberals downplayed the amount of land usurped from indigenous communities, suggested that more land had in fact been usurped from haciendas by those communities themselves, and insisted on the productive advantages of private ownership as opposed to communal ("Ley sobre la expropiación por causa de utilidad pública," July 7, 1853, Dublán and Lozano, *Legislación mexicana*, VI:587; "Sobre terrenos y otros bienes de orígen comunal usurpados," July 31, 1854, Dublán and Lozano, *Legislación mexicana*, VII:283–285; *El Siglo XIX*, Aug. 14 and Sept. 15, 1854; Cárman Vásquez Mantecón, *Santa Anna y el encrucijada del estado. La dictadura [1853–1855]* [Mexico City: Fondo de Cultura Económica, 1986], 150–151).

54. Private property was certainly not unknown in Oaxacan indigenous villages. By the eighteenth century, there was an increasing trend of selling bits of communal land to indigenous individuals as private property (William B. Taylor, *Landlord and Peasant*, 73–75; Sánchez Silva, *Indios, Comerciantes*, 57; Charles R. Berry, *La Reforma en Oaxaca: Una microhistoria de la revolución liberal. 1856/1876*

[Mexico City: Ediciones Era, 1989], 197). But evidence seems to suggest that most pueblo land was still in the hands of the communities themselves. It is also not clear whether land held by indígenas as "private property" during the colonial era would have translated into legal private property after independence.

55. Chassen-López, *From Liberal to Revolutionary Oaxaca*, 89.

56. Esteban Esperón, Sept. 10, 1856, AGEO, G, GD, Centro; Pastor, *Campesinos y reformas*, 475; John Monaghan, "La desamortización de la propiedad comunal en la mixteca: Resistencia popular y raíces de la conciencia nacional," in *Lecturas históricas*, ed. Romero Frizzi, 343–385; Sánchez Silva, *Indios, comerciantes y burocracia*, 168–172.

57. Jennie Purnell observes that, in Michoacán, the civil wars of the 1850s and 1860s delayed implementation and that the government then began to apply "sustained pressure on the Indian communities to privatize their communal landholdings in late 1868" (Jennie Purnell, *Popular Movements and State Formation in Revolutionary Mexico: The Agraristas and Cristeros of Michoacán* [Durham, NC: Duke University Press, 1999], 35). And, in Veracruz, according to Michael Ducey, "governments proved unable to divide peasant land before the 1880s, and in most cases outsiders did not interfere until the last decade of the nineteenth century" (Ducey, "Liberal Theory and Peasant Practice," 78). For other regional examples, see Dawn Fogle Deaton, "The Decade of Revolt: Peasant Rebellion in Jalisco, Mexico, 1855–1864," in *Liberals, the Church, and Indian Peasants*, ed. Robert Jackson, 37–93, and Paul Hart, *Bitter Harvest: The Social Transformation of Morelos, Mexico, and the Origins of the Zapatista Revolution, 1840–1910* (Albuquerque: University of New Mexico Press, 2005).

58. There is very little work specifically on Oaxaca in this early period. The most extensive studies of *desamortización* in Oaxaca—Chassen-López, *From Liberal to Revolutionary Oaxaca*, and Jennie Purnell, "Citizens and Sons of the *Pueblo*: National and Local Identities in the Making of the Mexican Nation," *Ethnic and Racial Studies* 25:2 (Mar. 2002), 213–237—focus on later years. One available source is Berry, *La Reforma en Oaxaca*. The conclusiveness of Berry's research is limited, however, by the fact that he deals primarily with the *Distrito Central*, the area around Oaxaca City. His evidence for other areas is largely anecdotal.

59. "Sobre desamortización de fincas rústicas y urbanas que administren como propietarios las corporaciones civiles ó eclesiásticas de la República" (hereafter referred to as Ley Lerdo), June 25, 1856, Manuel Dublán and José María Lozano, *Legislación mexicana ó colección completa de las disposiciones legislativas expedidas desde la independencia de la república*, Vol. 8 (Mexico City: Imprenta del Comercio, de Dublán y Chavez, á Cargo de M. Lara (hijo), 1877), 197–201.

60. For examples of land distributions that were carried out, see Various, Oct. and Nov. 1856, AGEO, G, GD, Etla; Oct. 8, 1856, AGEO, G, GD, Yanhuitlán. For the description of those that were not, see Oct. 9, 1856, AGEO, G, GD, Etla. For a good discussion of this problem, see Purnell, *Popular Movements and State Formation*, 33–34.

61. For a discussion of the original intent of the Ley Lerdo, see Donald J. Fraser, "La política de desamortización en las comunidades indígenas, 1856–1872," *Historia Mexicana* 21:4 (1972), 615–652. Fraser argues that the law was not intended to

dispossess the indigenous population when it was passed but that this intent only developed during the Porfiriato. Whatever the intent of the legislators, it is clear that they were concerned about indigenous dispossession, either because they did not wish them to be dispossessed or because they worried about their reaction to dispossession. Most likely, both were true to some extent.

62. "Comunicación del Ministerio de Hacienda.—Sobre objetos de la ley de desamortización," Oct. 9, 1856, Dublán and Lozano, *Legislación mexicana,* VIII:264–265.

63. Hamnett, *Juárez,* 67; Chassen-López, *From Liberal to Revolutionary Oaxaca,* 89–91. Quote is from 91.

64. Governor of Teposcolula to Secretario del Despacho Universal del Estado, Sept. 6, 1856, AGEO, G, GD, Teposcolula, Adjudicaciones; Subprefect of Etla to Secretario del Despacho Universal del Estado, Oct. 17, 1856, AGEO, G, GD, Etla.

65. "Ayoquesco, pide una orden de las adjudicaciones hecho a sus terrenos," José María Godines, Alcalde of Ayoquesco, Nov. 22, 1856; Celso Jimenes and José María Godines to Subprefect of Zimatlán, Sept. 26, 1856, AGEO, G, GD, Centro; "San Pedro el Alto. Se declara nula la venta de un terreno de dicho pueblo por el Subprefecto de Zimatlán a favor de Gregorio Valencia," Laureano Gómez, Alcalde of San Pedro el Alto; Manuel Gaspar, Pascual Sánchez, and Antonio Marcos, Regidores; and Juan López, Scribe, Nov. 4, 1856; Tomás, Narciso, and José Gaspar and José María Luis, Oct. 29, 1856, AGEO, G, GD, Centro. For an interesting local interpretation of the revisions, see Mallon, *Peasant and Nation,* 98–101.

66. Oct. 22, 1856, AGEO, G, GD, Villa Alta, Zoochila; Ayuntamiento of Juchitán, Apr. 6, 1858, AGEO, G, GD, Juchitán; Auxiliares of San Blas, Santa María, Guichivere, San Gerónimo, Lavorio, Jalisco, San Jacinto, Diagaveche, Cerrito, Lioza, and Totonilco to Governor of Tehuantepec, Sept. 12, 1857, AGEO, G, GD, Tehuantepec.

67. Governor of Huajuapan to Secretario del Despacho Universal del Estado, Aug. 1, 1856, AGEO, G, GD, Huajuapan.

68. "Tilquiapám, San Miguel pide la aprobación de la transacción de unos terrenos del rancho de San Nicolás"; Gerónimo Medosa, Nicolás Tejada, etc., Nov. 6, 1856, AGEO, G, GD, Centro.

69. Governor of Ejutla to Secretario del Despacho Universal del Estado, Oct. 11, 1856, AGEO, G, GD, Ejutla.

70. Francisco Santiago, Alcalde of San Agustín Yataruni, Oct. 8, 1856, AGEO, G, GD, Centro.

71. "San Pedro el Alto. Se declara nula la venta de un terreno de dicho pueblo por el Subprefecto de Zimatlán a favor de Gregorio Valencia," Laureano Gómez, Alcalde of San Pedro el Alto; Manuel Gaspar, Pascual Sánchez, and Antonio Marcos, Regidores; and Juan López, Scribe, Nov. 4, 1856; Tomás, Narciso, and José Gaspar and José María Luis, Oct. 29, 1856; Juan Escobar, Subprefect of Zimatlan, Nov. 2, 1856, AGEO, G, GD, Centro.

72. Juan Escobar, Subprefect of Zimatlán, Jan. 20, 1857, AGEO, G, GD, Zimatlán.

73. Ramón Cajiga, *Memoria que el C. Ramón Cajiga, Gobernador Constitucional del Estado, presenta al segundo congreso de Oaxaca en el primer periódo de sus sesiones ordinarias, el 16 de septiembre de 1861* (Oaxaca, Mexico: Imprenta de Ignacio Rincón, 1861), SMGE, Biblioteca Benito Juárez.

74. For an excellent discussion of this process, see Jennie Purnell, "Citizens and Sons of the *Pueblo*."

NOTES TO CHAPTER 6

1. On the regional beginnings of the rebellion, see Terry Rugeley's careful reconstruction of the years leading up to the outbreak of war in the communities where it began, in Rugeley, *Yucatán's Maya Peasantry*, 149–162. For numbers of participants, see Dumond, *The Machete and the Cross*, 131. For the numbers of those killed, see Wells and Joseph, *Summer of Discontent*, 27.

2. This debate was carried out publicly in Mexico City's newspapers, including *El Siglo XIX, El Monitor Republicano*, and *El Universal*, especially between 1848 and 1850. For a summary, see Hale, *Mexican Liberalism*, 236–244.

3. For an overview of literature on economic change in Yucatán in the nineteenth century, see Joseph, *Rediscovering the Past*, 27–36. Of particular importance are Remmers, "Henequén, the Caste War and Economy of Yucatán"; Patch, "Decolonization, the Agrarian Problem, and the Origins of the Caste War"; Pedro Bracamonte y Sosa, *Amos y sirvientes. Las haciendas de Yucatán, 1789–1860* (Mérida, Mexico: Universidad Autónoma de Yucatán, 1993); and Víctor M. Suárez Molina, *Evolución económica de Yucatán á través del siglo XIX: Apuntes Históricos*, 2 vols. (Mérida, Mexico: Ediciones de la Universidad de Yucatán, 1977).

4. See Allen Wells: "The boom required constraints on the *indio*'s freedom of movement, on his ability to provide for himself and his family, and on his perception of his own role in society. The planter's success in altering past labor patterns demanded a geographic and demographic change in regional distribution patterns, which forced a contraction in the size of villages and induced a migration from the marginal southeast to the henequen zone in the northwest. In short, the rise of the henequen plantation effected a revolution, transforming local labor arrangements and upsetting the regional economic framework" (Allen Wells, *Yucatán's Gilded Age: Haciendas, Henequen, and International Harvester, 1860–1915* [Albuquerque: University of New Mexico Press, 1985], 153). At the same time, Wells has probably come closest to documenting the actual process of change, especially in his "From Hacienda to Plantation: The Transformation of Santo Domingo Xcuyum," in *Land, Labor, & Capital in Modern Yucatán*, ed. Brannon and Joseph, 112–142.

5. Renán Irigoyen, writing in 1947, was an early proponent of the view that the war was vital to the expansion of the henequen industry, arguing that the war destroyed all other industries and forced the government to put its energies into the only one still available to it. Moisés González Navarro, writing in 1970, agreed that the Caste War was vital to the henequen boom, adding that the flow of refugees to the northwest solved the initial labor problem faced by landowners. The

contrary view is represented by Remmers and Wells, who argue that the industry had made notable progress before the war broke out, dominating the economy of the northeast, and that the boom was a result of technological improvement and rapidly increasing demand in the United States (Renan Irigoyen, "¿Fué el auge del henequén producto de la guerra de castas?" [1947], in *Ensayos Henequeneros* [Mérida: Ediciones de Cordemex, 1975], 7–44; Moisés González Navarro, *Raza y tierra: La Guerra de Castas y el Henequén*, 2nd edition [Mexico City: El Colegio de México, 1979], 179–190; Remmers, "Henequén, the Caste War and Economy of Yucatan," 386–387; Wells, *Yucatán's Gilded Age*, 26–28).

6. Pedro Regil y Estrada to Ministro de Relaciones Exteriores, July 6, 1848, AGN, G s/s, Box 256, Exp. 5; *La Revista Yucateca*, no date, 1847, CAIHY, CCCA, D, Box VI, No. 11. For an account of the massacre at Tepich, see Rugeley, *Yucatán's Maya Peasantry*, 179, and Dumond, *The Machete and the Cross*, 95.

7. "Restableciendo y reglamentando las antiguas leyes para el régimen de los indios," Aug. 27, 1847, *Colección de leyes . . . de Yucatán*, III:146–151.

8. Specifically, the decree ruled that alcaldes or jueces de paz, named by the state government for each town, would have the same relationship with the indígenas exercised in the late colonial period by the "jueces españoles," meaning that they would serve as the intermediaries through which the indígenas had to deal with the state on all matters. Jueces españoles, along with subdelegados, were an innovation in Yucatán with the Bourbon reforms in the late eighteenth century. Patch suggests that they were intended to replace the capitanes a guerra, whose presence among the Maya had been both infrequent and ineffective. The new appointed local officials usually resided in the cabeceras and were thus the government officials presiding most closely over the state's Maya villages (Patch, *Maya and Spaniard*, 45–46, 164; Farriss, *Maya Society*, 357–358).

9. "Restableciendo y reglamentando las antiguas leyes . . . "

10. Secretaría de Guerra y Marina, Aug. 31, 1847, AGEY, PE, Box 66, G, Congreso de Yucatán, Decretos; Ancona, *Historia de Yucatán*, IV:32. For more accounts of such persecution, see Baqueiro, *Ensayo histórico sobre las revoluciones de Yucatán*, I:264–276. See also Dumond, *The Machete and the Cross*, 99; Reed, *The Caste War of Yucatán*, 63.

11. Ygnacio Quijano Escudero to Jefe Político Superior de Mérida, Aug. 22, 1847, AGEY, PE, Box 65, J, Juicios a indígenas sublevados.

12. Dec. 7, 1847, AGEY, PE, Box 64, G, Consejo de Estado; Secretario de Gobierno, Dec. 24, 1847, AGEY, PE, Box 64, G, Decretos. In a letter to the Mexican Minister of Relations, Governor Barbachano referred to the Maya's "extraordinary frugality that makes them see . . . as superfluous what is necessary for other men in bearing the fatigues of war" (Miguel Barbachano to Ministro de Relaciones de la República, Apr. 17, 1848, AGN, G s/s, Box 256, Exp. 5).

13. Dec. 13, 1847, AGEY, PE, Box 64, G, Consejo de Estado.

14. One national government minister wrote to the congress that "His Excellency the President can never permit that Mexican citizens, whatever their condition, be subjected to slavery, the abolition of which is proclaimed in the most solemn manner in the legislation of the Republic." Yucatán's indígenas, he insisted, "although rebels, do not because of this cease to be Mexicans" (L. G. Cuevas

to Sres. Srios. de la Cámara de Diputados, Apr. 15, 1849, ASRE, 41-23-29). For Barbachano's response, see Miguel Barbachano to Minister Cuevas, Apr. 19 and May 25, 1849, ASRE, 41-23-29, "Sobre contrata que se ha hecho. . . ." For the national government's acquiescence to the Yucatecan activities, see Lacunza, July 13, 1849, ASRE, 41-23-29, "Sobre contrata que se ha hecho. . . ." For examples of the contracts that the Yucatecan government issued for the deported prisoners, see Apr. 5, 1849, AGEY, PE, Box 71, G, Lista de Pasaportes; and ASRE, 41-23-29, "Sobre contrata que se ha hecho. . . ."

15. Javier Rodríguez Piña, *Guerra de castas. La venta de indios mayas a Cuba, 1848–1861* (Mexico City: Consejo Nacional para la Cultura y las Artes, 1990), 178. This "incident," which in fact lasted through much of the war, has been written about in great detail. In 1923, Carlos R. Menéndez offered a scathing indictment of the government's actions in his *Historia del infame y vergonzoso comercio de indios vendidos a los esclavistas de Cuba por los políticos yucatecos desde 1848 hasta 1861. Justificación de la revolución indígena de 1847. Documentos irrefutables que los comprueban* (Mérida, Mexico: La Revista de Yucatán, 1923). More recently, González Navarro presented the results of his investigations in *Raza y tierra*, 108–139. See also Dumond, *The Machete and the Cross*, 168–170, 230–232. On Yucatecan indígenas in Cuba, see Paul Estrade, "Los colonos yucatecos como sustitutos de los esclavos negros," in *Cuba, la perla de las Antillas*, ed. Consuelo Naranjo Orovio and Tomás Mallo Gutíerrez (Aránjuez, Mexico: Doce Calles, 1994), 93–107.

16. The first argument was made by Justo Sierra O'Reilly in *El Fénix: Periódico Noticioso, Político, Literario y Mercantil*, Nov. 15, 1848. For an example of the argument for renewed military effort, see *La Armonía: Periódico y Literario*, Dec. 20, 1850.

17. Secretaría de Gobierno, Dec. 13, 1847, AGEY, PE, Box 64, G, Consejo de Estado; Comisión de Justicia, Sept. 14, 1847, AGEY, Box 66, PE, G, Congreso de Yucatán, Decretos.

18. "De Miguel Barbachano y Gregorio Cantón a los indios sublevados del sur y oriente de esta Península," Letter 4 in Fidelio Quintal Martín, *Correspondencia de la guerra de castas: Epistolario documental, 1843–1866* (Mérida, Mexico: Universidad Autónoma de Yucatán, 1992), 17–18; "De Miguel Barbachano y Gregorio Cantón a Jacinto Pat," Letter 7 in Quintal Martín, *Correspondencia*, 23–25; Dumond, *The Machete and the Cross*, 118–119.

19. Dumond, *The Machete and the Cross*, 119.

20. "De Miguel Barbachano y Gregorio Cantón a los indios sublevados del sur y oriente de esta Península," 18; "Miguel Barbachano y Gregorio Cantón a Jacinto Pat," 24. The emphasis in the quote is mine.

21. Indeed, increasingly, the leadership itself reflected the rank and file; the early leaders of the rebellion had all come from the indigenous elite, but after their deaths they were often replaced by commoners (Rugeley, "The Maya Elites of Nineteenth-Century Yucatán," *Ethnohistory* 42:3 [Summer, 1995]: 186).

22. Santiago Méndez, Mar. 1, 1848, AGEY, PE, Box 68, G, Decretos; Secretario de Gobierno, Dec. 24, 1847, AGEY, PE, Box 64, G, Decretos; Comisión de Puntos Constitucionales, Dec. 28, 1847, AGEY, PE, Box 68, G, Consejo de Estado.

23. "Amnistia y penas de los sublevados que no se acojan a ella," Feb. 6, 1848, Áznar Pérez, ed., *Colección de leyes*, III:186–187. For other tax-related decrees, see "Extinguiendo la contribución religiosa," Jan. 26, 1848; "Se extingue la contribución personal," Dec. 7, 1849; "Estableciendo una contribución religiosa para sostenimiento del culto y sus ministros," Jan. 12, 1850, Aznar Pérez, ed., *Colección de leyes*, III:182, 302, 312–313. The government was constantly tinkering with this strategy to provide the necessary incentive while also ensuring that it would have an income, alternating between the abolition of religious and civil taxes.

24. "Amnistía y penas de los sublevados que no se acojan a ella"; "Indulto a los sublevados indígenas," Sept. 27, 1847; "Amnistía," Aug. 18, 1848; "Amnistía a los sublevados que vuelvan a la obediencia del gobierno," Sept. 24, 1849; "Indulto a todos los sublevados que sometan a la obediencia del gobierno," Feb. 2, 1850, Áznar Pérez, ed., *Colección de leyes*, III:156, 221–222, 266, 315; "Se indulta a los indios sublevados que se someten a la obediencia del gobierno y se faculta á éste para nombrar comisiones que procuren su reducción," Apr. 1, 1851; "Concede una amnistía a los indios sublevados que se presentan en el término que expresa," Dec. 18, 1858, Eligio Ancona, ed., *Colección de leyes, decretos, órdenes y demás disposiciones de tendencia general, expedidas por el poder legislativo del estado de Yucatán* (Mérida, Mexico: Imprenta de "El Eco del Comercio", 1882–1883), I:54–55; II:15–17.

25. Secretaría de Gobierno, Dec. 13, 1847, AGEY, PE, Box 64, G, Consejo de Estado.

26. *La Revista Yucateca*, no date, 1847, CAIHY, CCCA, D, Box VI, No. 3.

27. Dec. 13, 1847, AGEY, PE, Box 64, G, Consejo de Estado; "Amnistía y penas de los sublevados que no se acojan a ella."

28. Rugeley, *Yucatán's Maya Peasantry*, 27; 92–93.

29. "Se declara hidalgo y exento de la contribución personal a Felipe Cauich," Jan. 1, 1848, Áznar Pérez, ed., *Colección de leyes*, III:17; Miguel Barbachano, Apr. 3, 1848, AGEY, PE, Box 68, G, Decretos; Miguel Barbachano, Apr. 27, 1848, AGEY, PE, Box 68, G, Decretos. For an example of the printed form used to name hidalgos, see CAIHY, CCCA, M, Box XLIII, Doc. 037. This particular form was for Pablo Sebastián Chable, from the town of Tepakan.

30. "Condiciones bajo las que se emplean á los hidalgos en el servicio de la campaña, obrando las secciones segun las destine el Sr. general en jefe," May 26, 1848; "Aprobando la organización de hidalgos para el servicio de campaña," May 27, 1848; Áznar Pérez, ed., *Colección de leyes*, III:208–209.

31. For an example of a request for the title, see Jefe Político Superior of Mérida, May 23, 1848, AGEY, PE, Box 68, G, Secretaría General de Gobierno. For Barbachano's assertion, see [Miguel Barbachano], Aug. 5, 1848, AGN, G s/s, Box 256, Exp. 5. There is disagreement about how many hidalgos there were. Gabbert, basing his estimation on later nineteenth-century sources, puts the number at "no less than 10,000 . . . men fighting the rebels" in 1848. Remmers, on the other hand, estimates that in 1849, there were 2,000 hidalgos serving in the field, in addition to "public security forces who guarded the towns outside the war zone" (Gabbert, *Becoming Maya*, 178n.35; Remmers, "Henequén, the Caste War and Economy of Yucatán," 330).

32. "Constitución política del estado libre de Yucatán" (1825); "Constitución política del estado" (1850), in *Yucatán a través de sus constituciones*, 56; Oct. 26, 1850, AGEY, PE, Box 76, G, Congreso del Estado.

33. "Se indulta a los indios sublevados que se someten a la obediencia del gobierno y se faculta á éste para nombrar comisiones que procuren su reducción."

34. Nelson Reed estimates that between September of 1849 and April of 1850, 4,400 refugees were brought in by armed patrols (Nelson Reed, *The Caste War of Yucatán* [Stanford, CA: Stanford University Press, 1964], 125; Barbara A. Angel, "The Reconstruction of Rural Society in the Aftermath of the Mayan Rebellion of 1847," *Journal of the Canadian Historical Association*, New Series 4 [1993]: 46).

35. *El Fénix: Periódico Noticioso, Político, Literario y Mercantil*, Jan. 10, 1850.

36. Vásquez Mantecon, *Santa Anna*, 167–168.

37. Baltasar Cob and Luciano Canul to Comandante General, May 20, 1853, AGEY, PE, Box 95, G, Jefatura Política de Mérida.

38. Pinelo, May 31, 1853, AGEY, PE, Box 95, G, Jefatura Política de Mérida.

39. Miguel Barbachano, Aug. 17 and Sept. 28, 1848, AGEY, PE, Box 68, G, Decretos; "Requisitos para ser juez de paz," Jan. 14, 1848, Áznar Pérez, ed., *Colección de leyes*, III:174.

40. "Se suspende la elección de juntas municipales, mandando conservar interinamente a los jueces de paz," Nov. 2, 1849, Áznar Pérez, ed., *Colección de leyes*, 281; Nov. 2, 1849, AGEY, PE, Box 75, G, Consejo de Estado; *Ley constitucional para el gobierno interior de los pueblos* (Mérida, Mexico: Nazario Novelo, 1850), 11, CAIHY, Documentos, Caja VII, No. 7. In November of 1849, the governor called for elections in the *cabeceras* other than those "in which because of the events of the war it is not convenient according to the judgment of the Government" (Nov. 7, 1849, AGEY, PE, Box 74, G, Consejo de Estado).

41. Caciques of Campeche to Jefe Político of Campeche, Aug. 30, 1851, AGEY, PE, Box 85, G, Secretaría General de Gobierno; Subdelegado of Campeche to Secretary of the Treasury, Aug. 31, 1849, and Juez de paz of Chiná in Subdelegado of Campeche to Secretary of the Treasury, Aug. 13, 1849, AGEY, PE, Box 72, G, Secretaría General de Gobierno; Párroco of Tixmeuac, Jan. 4, 1852, AGEY, PE, Box 89, G, Secretaría General de Gobierno.

42. Andres Pat, Pedro Chilum, Pedro José Tec, Juan Dzul, Esteban Cauich, and José Ynocente Chulim to Governor of Yucatán, Dec. 18, 1854, AGEY, PE, Box 98, G, Prefectura del Distrito de Valladolid.

43. Juan José Mex, Felipe Ek, Anastacio Xool, and Vicente Canul, Oct. 18, 1852, and Sept. 20, 1852, AGEY, PE, Box 87, G, Secretaría General de Gobierno.

44. Pedro Vicab, Aug. 10, 1848, AGEY, PE, Box 67, G, Correspondencia; Sept. 6, 1852, AGEY, PE, Box 90, G, Consejo de Estado.

45. *El Regenerador: Periódico Oficial*, Mar. 11, 1853.

46. Dumond, *The Machete and the Cross*, 143–168.

47. *Boletín Oficial del Estado de Yucatán*, Feb. 16, 1850.

48. For a detailed discussion of population changes effected by the war, see Remmers, "The Caste War, Henequén and Economy of Yucatán," 310–327. In 1853, the political chief of Izamal reported that the town of San José had only

twenty-eight families remaining and that Ticum had only five (Jefe Político de Izamal, Aug. 16, 1853, AGEY, PE, Box 93, G, Secretaría General de Gobierno).

49. Jefe Político of Peto, Nov. 22, 1847, AGEY, PE, Box 66, G, Programa de Indios Sublevados; Juez de Paz of Dzan, May 4, 1848, AGEY, PE, Box 67, G, Secretaría General de Gobierno; Feb. 5, 1848, AGEY, PE, Box 69, G, Consejo de Estado. For an example of nonindigenous authorities fleeing, see Jefe Político of Peto, Nov. 22, 1847, AGEY, PE, Box 66, G, Programa de Indios Sublevados.

50. Dec. 24, 1847, AGEY, PE, Box 64, G, Consejo de Estado; Jefe Político of Motul, Dec. 22, 1852, AGEY, PE, Box 87, G, Secretaría General de Gobierno.

51. Jefe Político of Valladolid, Dec. 27, 1851, AGEY, PE, Box 85, G, Secretaría General de Gobierno; Crescencio José Pinelo, CAIHY, CCCA, M, Box XXXVIII, Document 018, Apr. 29, 1853; Jefe Político of Motul to Governor, Mar. 5 and 14, 1857, AGEY, PE, Box 109, G, Jefatura Politica del partido de Motul.

52. Governor Santiago Méndez, Feb. 6, 1848, AGEY, PE, Box 68, G, Decretos; Miguel Barbachano to Ministro de Relaciones de la República, May 24, 1848, AGN, G s/s, Box 256, Exp. 5; "Mandando que á los que emigren por temor á los bárbaros, se les obligue á volver á sus respectivas vecindades," Oct. 14, 1852, Ancona, ed., Colección de leyes, I:148–149; El Regenerador: Periódico Oficial, Mar. 11, 1850; Santiago Méndez to Consejo de Estado, AGEY, PE, Box 106, G, Consejo de Estado.

53. Letter cited in El Fénix: Periódico Notiocioso, Político, Literario, y Mercantil, Mar. 1, 1850.

54. J. A. García to J. Sierra O'Reilly, cited in Dumond, The Machete and the Cross, 163.

55. Subdelegado of Izamal, May 25, 1848, AGEY, PE, Box 67, G, Secretaría General de Gobierno; Subdelegado of Campeche to Secretary of the Treasury, Aug. 31, 1849, AGEY, PE, Box 72, G, Secretaría General de Gobierno; Boletín Oficial del Estado de Yucatán, Apr. 6, 1850.

56. "Restableciendo y reglamentando las antiguas leyes para el régimen de los indios"; "Que solo sean considerados prisioneros de guerra los indígenas aprehendidos con las armas en la mano," Nov. 7, 1849, Áznar Pérez, ed., Colección de leyes, III:343; Ley constitucional para el gobierno interior de los pueblos, 1850; "Que se impida la formación de nuevas poblaciones de indios presentados," April 5, 1850, Áznar Pérez, ed., Colección de leyes, III:343; Julián Asueta, Marcelino Santos, José Eulalio Asueta, José Encarnación Ek, and José María Dzul to Governor; Jefe Político of Mérida, Feb. 25, 1857, AGEY, PE, Box 109, G, Jefatura de Mérida.

57. El Fénix: Periódico Noticioso, Político, Literario y Mercantil, Feb. 1, 1849, and Dec. 10, 1850.

58. Consejo de Estado, Feb. 26, 1848, AGEY, PE, Box 67, G, Secretaría General de Gobierno; Miguel Barbachano, Nov. 16, 1848, AGEY, PE, Box 68, G, Decretos; Dec. 5, 1849, AGEY, PE, Box 74, G, Congreso del Estado.

59. For one of the lists compiled at the request of the government, see April 3, 1848, AGEY, PE, Box 69, G. In this list from Mérida, 119 people were said to owe a total of 1,884 pesos and 7 reales. Lists such as this are scattered throughout the archival documents for 1848 and beyond. For a detailed list showing the

small numbers of those who owed taxes, see May 1, 1850, AGEY, PE, Box 78, G, Padron. The actual numbers of taxpayers in this census for the Izamal region are as follows: thirty (Izamal), thirty-six (Temax), fourteen (Tekantó), thirteen (Seyé), eleven (Hoctún), ten (Hocabá), nine (Homún), six (Huhí), five (Tunkás), five (Xocchel), five (Dzuncauich), four (Buctzotz), four (Cuzamá), three (Kantunil), three (Kimbilá), three (Tahmek), two (Citilcum), two (Sanahcat), and one (Tekal). Of all these individuals, only seven had Maya surnames.

60. Juez de paz of Dzidzantún to Comandante General, May 19, 1849, AGEY, PE, Box 75, J.

61. Juez de paz of Tekit to Jefe Político of Ticul, Mar. 20–21, 1848, AGEY, PE, Box 67, G, Secretaría General de Gobierno.

62. María Dolores Correa, Jan. 16, 1850, AGEY, PE, Box 76, G, Jefatura Política de Motul; Domingo Tenreiro, July 12, 1851, AGEY, PE, Box 82, G, Milicia; Juez de Paz of Dzidzantún to Comandante General, May 19, 1849, AGEY, PE, Box 75, Justicia.

63. Propietarios of Seybaplaya, Apr. 30. 1848, AGEY, PE, Box 67, G, Secretaría General de Gobierno.

64. Subdelegado of Campeche to Secretary of the Treasury, Aug. 13, 1849, AGEY, PE, Box 72, G, Secretaría General de Gobierno; Hacendados to Govenor, June 29, 1852, AGEY, PE, Box 91, G, Suspensión de la contribución a la guardia nacional; Jefe Político of Hecelchakán to Governor, AGEY, PE, Box 109, 6, Jefatura Política del partido de Hecelchakán.

65. Jefe Político of Tizimín, July 29, 1849, AGEY, PE, Box 71, G, Secretaría General de Gobierno; "Que los jefes políticos envien hidalgos para cosechar las milpas de los sublevados," April 12, 1850, Áznar Pérez, ed., *Colección de leyes*, III:344; *Boletín Oficial del Estado de Yucatán*, Apr. 13, 1850; Jefe Político of Maxcanú, July 15, 1851, AGEY, PE, Box 83, G, Jefatura Política de Campeche.

66. "Se indulta a los indios sublevados que se someten a la obediencia del gobierno y se faculta á éste para nombrar comisiones que procuren su reducción." A previous law had allowed for former employers to claim their servants, but this was the first to extend that privilege to anyone who needed workers. See "Que se impida la formación de nuevas poblaciones de indios presentados," April 5, 1850, Áznar Pérez, ed., *Colección de leyes*, III:343.

67. Juez de paz of Hopelchen, Feb. 24, 1851, AGEY, PE, Box 83, G, Autoridad Primera de Hopelchen. For lists of presentados, see July 12, 14, and 18, 1850, AGEY, PE, Box 82, G, Milicia. These are lists of individuals who arrived in Tizimín (eleven) and Chemax (twenty-eight). There are many such lists among the documents for these years in the state archive.

68. July 1, 1851, AGEY, PE, Box 85, G, Secretaría General de Gobierno; Jefe Político of Espita to Governor, July 2, 1851, AGEY, PE, Box 85, G, Secretaría General de Gobierno; Juez de paz of Hopelchen, Feb. 24, 1851, AGEY, PE, Box 83, G, Autoridad Primera de Hopelchen.

69. Angel, "The Reconstruction of Rural Society," 46.

70. Jefe Político de Carmen, Apr. 30, 1852, AGEY, PE, Box 87, G, Secretaría General de Gobierno; Juez de Primera Instancia of Izamal to Governor, May 5, 1852, AGEY, PE, Box 92, J, Juzgado de Primera Instancia de Izamal.

71. "Renueva la prohibición de que se emplee a los indios en los trabajos agrícolas contra su voluntad," Dec. 31, 1856, Ancona, ed., *Colección de leyes*, I:263. This decree cites in particular the complaints of two indígenas from Nunkiní who claimed that their jueces de paz had forced them to labor in the milpas of private individuals.

72. "Declara lo que es permitido hacer á cada vecino en los ejidos de sus pueblos," Sept. 26, 1857, Ancona, ed., *Colección de leyes*, I:364.

73. Santiago Méndez, *Discurso pronunciado por el Excmo. Sr. Gobernador D. Santiago Méndez, en la solemne apertura de las sesiones del H. Congreso constituyente del Estado, verificado el 5 de julio de 1857* (Mérida, Mexico: Mariano Guzman, 1857), CAIHY, CCCA, F, Box XXII, No. 6.

74. Jefe Político of Ticul, Feb. 18, 1851, AGEY, PE, Box 85, G, Secretaría General de Gobierno; Juez de Paz of Dzitbalché, Nov. 19, 1853, AGEY, PE, Box 93, G, Secretaría General de Gobierno; Jefe Político of Hopelchen to Consejo de Estado, June 20, 1856, AGEY, PE, Box 104, G, Jefatura Política del partido de Hopelchen; Paulino Gonzalez, Ygnacio Vado, and Jose Cruz, May 29, 1853, AGEY, PE, Box 95, G, Jefatura Política de Mérida.

75. José Tomás Kolloc, Pedro Kuk, and Simon Uc to Governor of Yucatán, May 26, 1852; 2nd Juez de Paz of Kopomá, June 3, 1852; Miguel Barbachano, June 7, 1852, AGEY, PE, Box 92, J, Juzgado de Paz de Kopomá; Indígenas of Yaxkukul, Apr. 6, 1853, AGEY, PE, Box 96, J, Juzgado de Paz de Yaxkukul; República of Tekantó, Jan. 10, 1856, AGEY, PE, Box 109, J, Juez de Primera Instancia.

76. Juan Esteban Pech, Isidro Dzul, Felipe Tut, Alejandro Lima, and Nabón Chan, Mar. 29, 1853, AGEY, PE, Box 96, J, Juzgado de Paz de Chocholá; Aug. 24, 1853, AGEY, PE, Box 96, J, Juzgado de Paz de Yaxkukul; Baltasar Cob and Luciano Canul to Comandante General, May 20, 1853, AGEY, PE, Box 95, Jefatura Política de Mérida.

77. *Las Garantías Sociales: Periódico Oficial*, May 20, 1856.

78. Turner, *Barbarous Mexico*.

79. Sept. 23, 1857, AGEY, PE, Box 93, G, Secretaría General de Gobierno.

80. Manuel José Peón, Eusebio Escalante, Manuel Medina, and Antonio [Medis] to Governor of Yucatán, Feb. 12, 1859, AGEY, PE, Box 119, G, Junta Patriótica sobre la guerra de castas.

81. Miguel Barbachano, *Discurso pronunciado por el Excmo. Sr. Gobernador D. Miguel Barbachano, el 1.o de enero en 1853 en el seno del H. Congreso del Estado, al abrir éste con la solemnidad acostumbrada sus sesiones ordinarias del primer periódo constitucional* (Mérida, Mexico: Tipografía de Rafael Pedrera, 1853), CAIHY, CCCA, D, Box IX, No. 13.

82. Indígenas of Yaxkukul, Apr. 6, 1853, AGEY, PE, Box 96, J, Juzgado de Paz de Yaxkukul.

83. Eusebio Mex, Feb. 25, 1857, AGEY, PE, Box 109, G, Jefatura Politica de Mérida; José Antonio Castilla, Feb. 25, 1857, AGEY, PE, Box 109, G, Jefatura Política de Mérida.

84. In 1901, the army finally took the last stronghold of the Maya at Chan Santa Cruz. The following year, the national congress excised the eastern part of

the Yucatecan peninsula from Yucatán, creating the federal Territory of Quintana Roo (Marvin Aliskey, "The Relations of the State of Yucatán and the Federal Government of Mexico, 1823–1978," in *Yucatán: A World Apart*, ed. Moseley and Terry (Tuscaloosa: University of Alabama Press, 1980), 250.

85. "Constitución política del estado," (1862) in *Yucatán a través de sus constituciones*, 71–88.

86. Philip C. Thompson, "The Structure of Civil Hierarchy in Tekantó, Yucatán," *Estudios de Cultura Maya* XVI (1986): 183.

NOTES TO CONCLUSION

1. Chassen-López, *From Liberal to Revolutionary Oaxaca*, 133–286; Wells, *Yucatán's Gilded Age*.

2. In 1878, 77 percent of the population was indigenous; 18 percent were registered as "mestizo," 3 percent as "black," and only 2 percent as "white." The average town size was only 2,247, and there were 463 municipalities. Only 3.75 percent of the population lived on haciendas; more that 70 percent lived in autonomous pueblos (Paul Garner, *La revolución en provincia. Soberanía estatal y caudillismo en las montañas de Oaxaca [1910–1920]* [Mexico City: Fondo de Cultura Económica, 1988], 25–39). On the slow and limited growth of haciendas in Oaxaca, see Thomas J. Cassidy, "Las haciendas oaxaqueñas en el siglo XIX," in *Lecturas históricas del estado de Oaxaca*, ed. Romero Frizzi, 292–323. One early account claimed that, as late as 1910, 99.8 percent of Oaxacan heads of family lacked individual private property, a fact that could be attributed to the continued prevalence of communal village landholding (George McCutchen McBride, *The Land Systems of Mexico* [New York: American Geographical Society, 1923], 146). He writes: "Conditions in Oaxaca are rendered less serious than in other states by the fact that many of the pueblos have retained their communal holdings." Such early findings are supported by more recent research, including Purnell, "Citizens and Sons of the Pueblo," and Chassen-López, *From Liberal to Revolutionary Oaxaca*, 88–105.

3. Paul Garner, "Federalism and Caudillismo in the Mexican Revolution: The Genesis of the Oaxaca Sovereignty Movement (1915–1920)," *Journal of Latin American Studies* 17 (1985): 117–122; Chassen-López, *From Liberal to Revolutionary Oaxaca*, 133–186.

4. Wells and Joseph, *Summer of Discontent*, 27; Joseph, *Revolution from Without*, 82–89; Piedad Peniche Rivero, "Gender, Bridewealth, and Marriage: Peonage and Social Reproduction in the Henequen Hacienda of Yucatán, Mexico, 1870–1901," in *Women of the Mexican Countryside, 1850–1980: Creating Spaces, Shaping Transitions*, ed. Heather Fowler-Salamini and Mary Kay Vaughan (Tucson: University of Arizona Press, 1994), 74–89.

5. McNamara, *Sons of the Sierra*, 31–95.

6. Mcnamara, 118–137; Wells and Joseph, *Summer of Discontent*. See also Chassen-López, *From Liberal to Revolutionary Oaxaca*, especially her discussion of Oaxaca's "War of the Pants" in 1896, 370–377.

10–11, 30–33, 38–39, 41; and military
service, 81–88; nonindígenas in relation
to, 30–32, 39, 188; in Oaxaca, 15–26,
30, 32, 34, 36, 63–101, 145–80; political role of, 3, 16–17, 31, 109–10, 192;
poverty of, 77–78, 81; and the Reform,
150–52; removal of, 202; and taxation,
74–81; terminology related to, 227n2;
in Yucatán, 15–20, 26–30, 32, 35–37,
56–57, 102–47, 181–215, 243n34
Institutions: hybrid, 6; liberal foundation
of, 5, 6, 12–14, 33–34, 45–61
Intendentes, 24
Irigoyen, Renán, 275n5
Isthmian rebellions, 63
Iturbide, Agustín, 40

Jacobsen, Nils, 4
Jefes de policía, 94
Juárez, Benito, 36, 147, 149–54, 157,
164–65, 172, 175, 219, 252n57, 268n4
Jueces de paz (justices of the peace):
appointment of, 90–91, 117–18,
167–68, 194–95; authority of, 91–92;
case examples concerning, 95–96;
establishment of, 89, 117, 129, 166;
hostility toward, 118–20, 193–94; and
indigenous labor, 118–19, 209–10;
removal of, 92; responsibilities of,
89–90; and taxation, 118–19; villagers'
embrace of, 93–94
Juntas municipales. *See* Municipal juntas

Knight, Alan, 230n19

Labor, indigenous, 22, 26, 28–29, 52, 105,
118–19, 145, 182–83, 198–99, 203–11
Land: communal holding of, 10, 16, 36,
139, 171–78, 272n53, 283n2; disputes
over, 71–72, 172; in Oaxaca, 36, 71–72,
170–79; in Yucatán, 36–37, 120–26,
138–44, 208–9. *See also* Ley Lerdo;
Private property
Language, 84–85
León, Antonio de, 66
Ley Lerdo, 10, 36, 149–50, 172–80, 273n61
Ley Orgánica, 67
Liberalism: colonialism and, 9–10, 41–42;
concept of, 4–9; economic, 37, 150–51,
174, 183, 213, 215, 217–18; education
and, 157, 160–61; failures of, 1, 9–11,

220–21, 229n17; government officials
and, 7, 32; indígenas and, 7, 10–11,
30–33, 38–39, 41; institutions grounded
in, 5, 6, 12–14, 33–34, 45–61; interpretations of, 9–12, 15, 42; local, 3–4, 7–9,
13–15, 18, 146–47, 149–50, 179–80,
214–22; Mexico and, 4–15, 216–22; as
movement/ideology, 6, 8, 11–12;
national, 3–4, 7–9, 146–47, 149, 179–80,
217, 219–22; nonindígenas and, 51;
in Oaxaca, 64, 66, 148–52, 214–15,
220–21; political culture of, 6–7; popular, 11–12; rebellions in response to,
63–64; the Reform and, 8; in Spain,
38–40; transition to, 1–3; in Yucatán,
128, 183, 213–15, 220–21. *See also*
Reform (La Reforma)
Liberal party, 219
Literacy, 68, 109, 129–31, 191
Local liberalisms, 3–4, 7–9, 13–15, 18,
146–47, 149–50, 179–80, 214–22

Mallon, Florencia, 11–12
Maya. *See* Yucatán: indígenas of
McNamara, Patrick J., 218, 219
Meléndez, José Gregorio, 63, 164
Méndez, Santiago, 187, 189, 201, 208–9,
264n74
Mendistas, 132, 264n74
Mexica empire, 20
Mexican Revolution, 10, 221, 230n19
Mexico: independence of, 1–2, 40; and lib-
eralism, 4–15, 216–22; Oaxaca's relation
to, 64–65, 67; revolution in, 10, 221,
230n19; Yucatán's relation to, 105, 116,
127. *See also* New Spain
Military, composition of, 82, 262n56
Military service: exemption claims against,
86; money offered in lieu of, 85–86;
in Oaxaca, 73–74, 81–88, 166; process
of, 83–84; vagrancy laws and, 86–88; in
Yucatán, 127, 135–37
Militias. *See* Civic militias
Milpas, 121
Mixtecos, 20–23, 155–56
El Monitor Républicano (newspaper), 210–11
Mora, José María Luis, 254n83
Morelos, José María, 40, 45
Municipal commissaries, 168
Municipal juntas, 107–9, 111–12, 114–15,
195